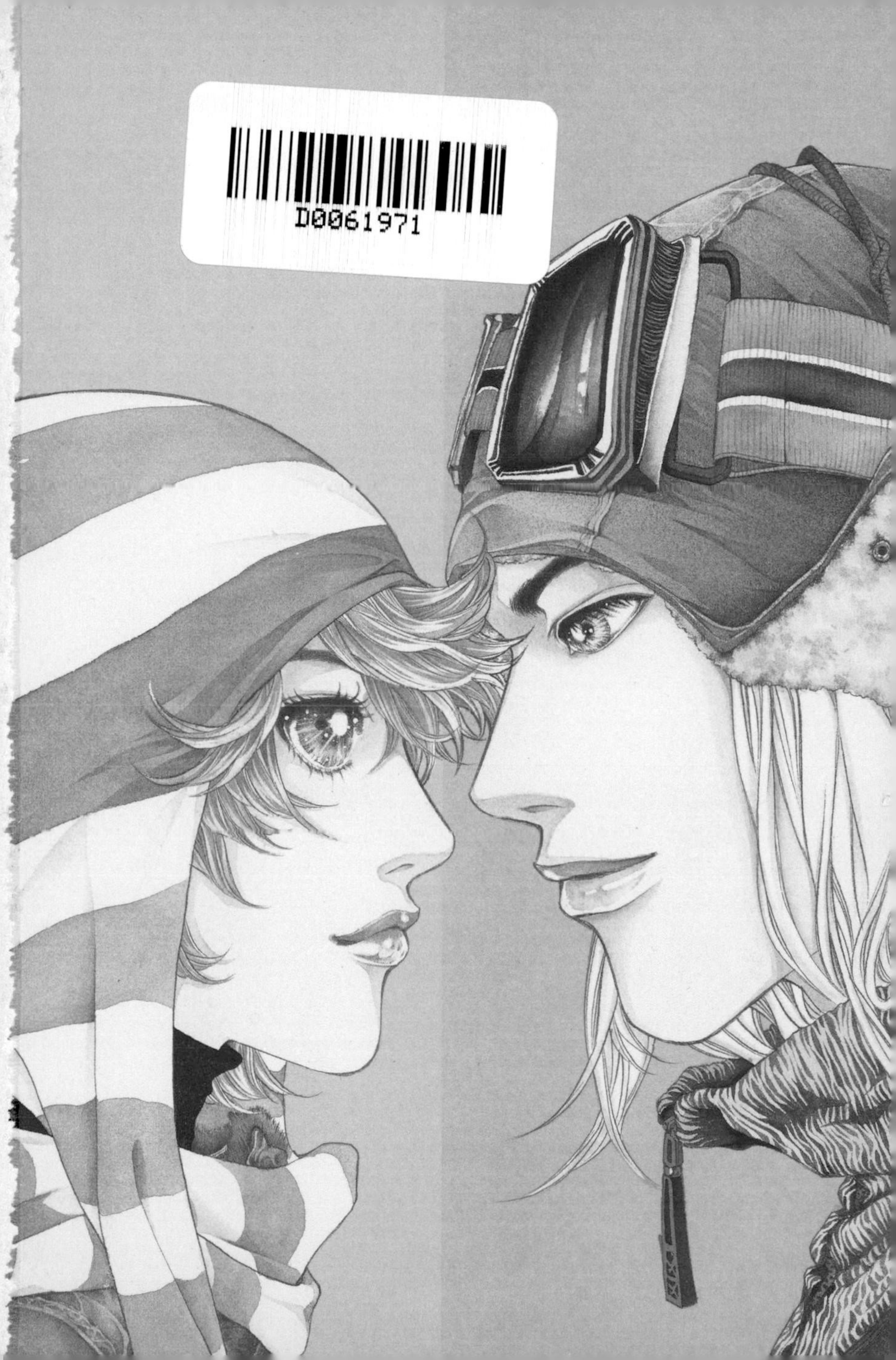

**_Fever Volume 1_**

Created by Hee Jung Park


Translation - Hye Young Im
English Adaptation - Ailen Lujo
Copy Editor - Shannon Watters
Retouch and Lettering - Star Print Brokers
Production Artist - Lauren O'Connell
Graphic Designer - Chelsea Windlinger

Editor - Lillian Diaz-Przybyl
Digital Imaging Manager - Chris Buford
Pre-Production Supervisor - Erika Terriquez
Production Manager - Elisabeth Brizzi
Managing Editor - Vy Nguyen
Creative Director - Anne Marie Horne
Editor-in-Chief - Rob Tokar
Publisher - Mike Kiley
President and C.O.O. - John Parker
C.E.O. and Chief Creative Officer - Stuart Levy

A TOKYOPOP® Manga



TOKYOPOP and are trademarks or registered trademarks of TOKYOPOP Inc.



TOKYOPOP Inc.
5900 Wilshire Blvd. Suite 2000
Los Angeles, CA 90036

E-mail: info@TOKYOPOP.com
Come visit us online at www.TOKYOPOP.com



FEVER 1 © 2003 by Park, Hee Jung All rights reserved. Original Korean Edition published by Seoul Cultural Publishers, Inc. through Shinwon Agency Co. in Korea. English edition Volume 1 © 2008 by TOKYOPOP Inc.

All rights reserved. No portion of this book may be reproduced or transmitted in any form or by any means without written permission from the copyright holders. This manga is a work of fiction. Any resemblance to actual events or locales or persons, living or dead, is entirely coincidental.



ISBN: 978-1-4278-0532-4

First TOKYOPOP printing: March 2008

10 9 8 7 6 5 4 3 2 1

Printed in the USA

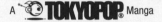

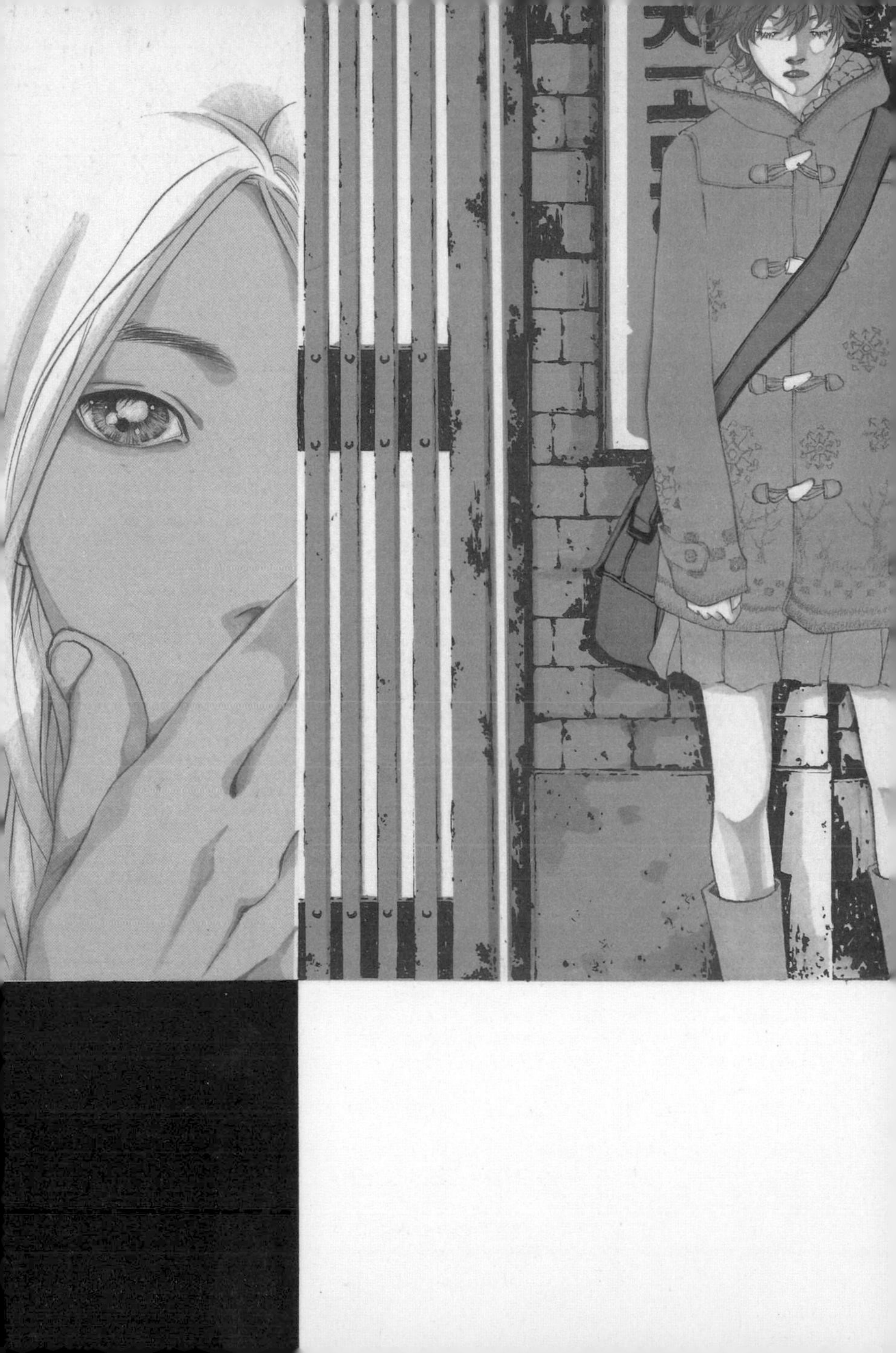

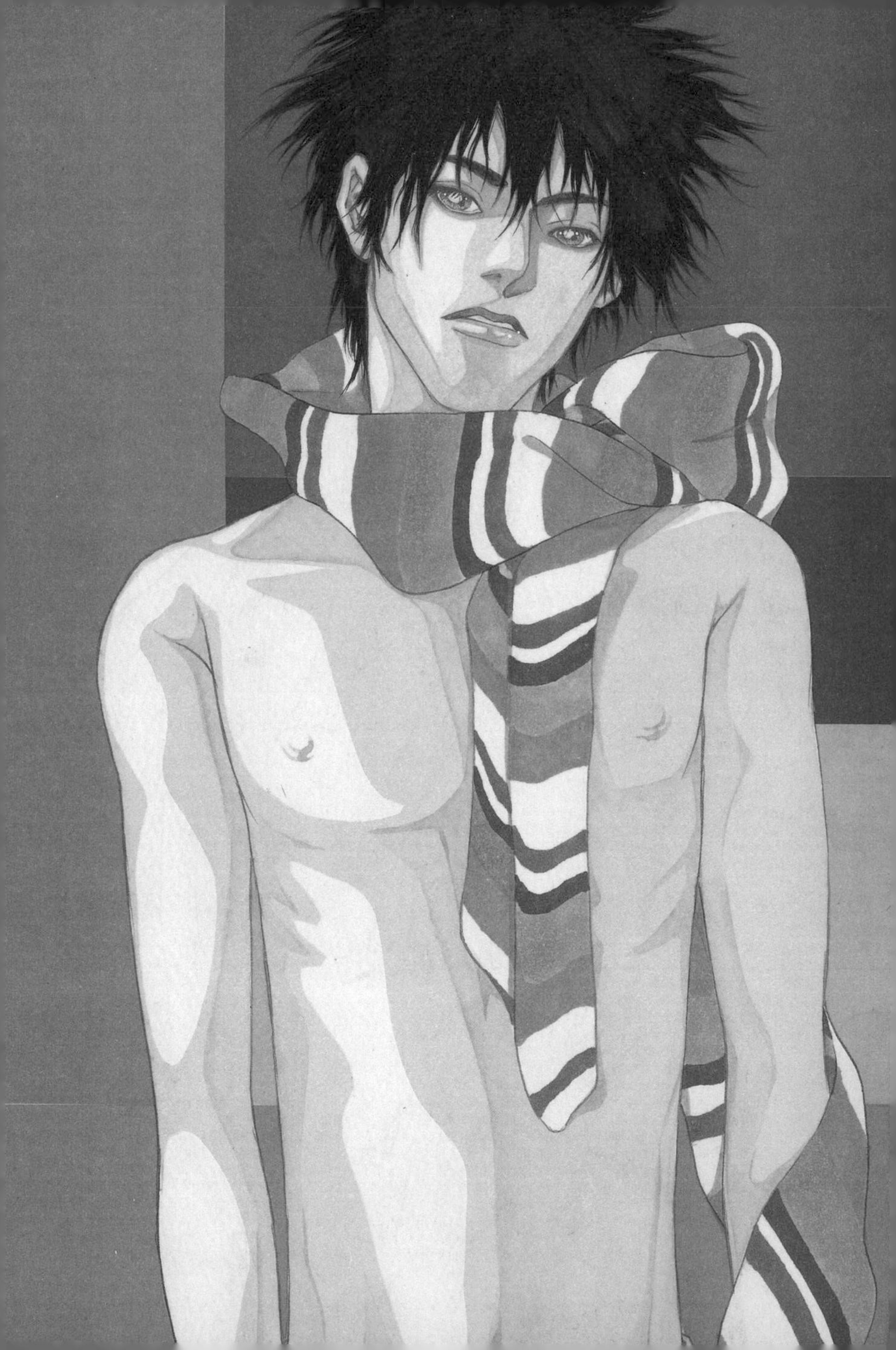

# -fever-

## VOL 1

### CREATED BY
### HEE JUNG PARK

HAMBURG // LONDON // LOS ANGELES // TOKYO

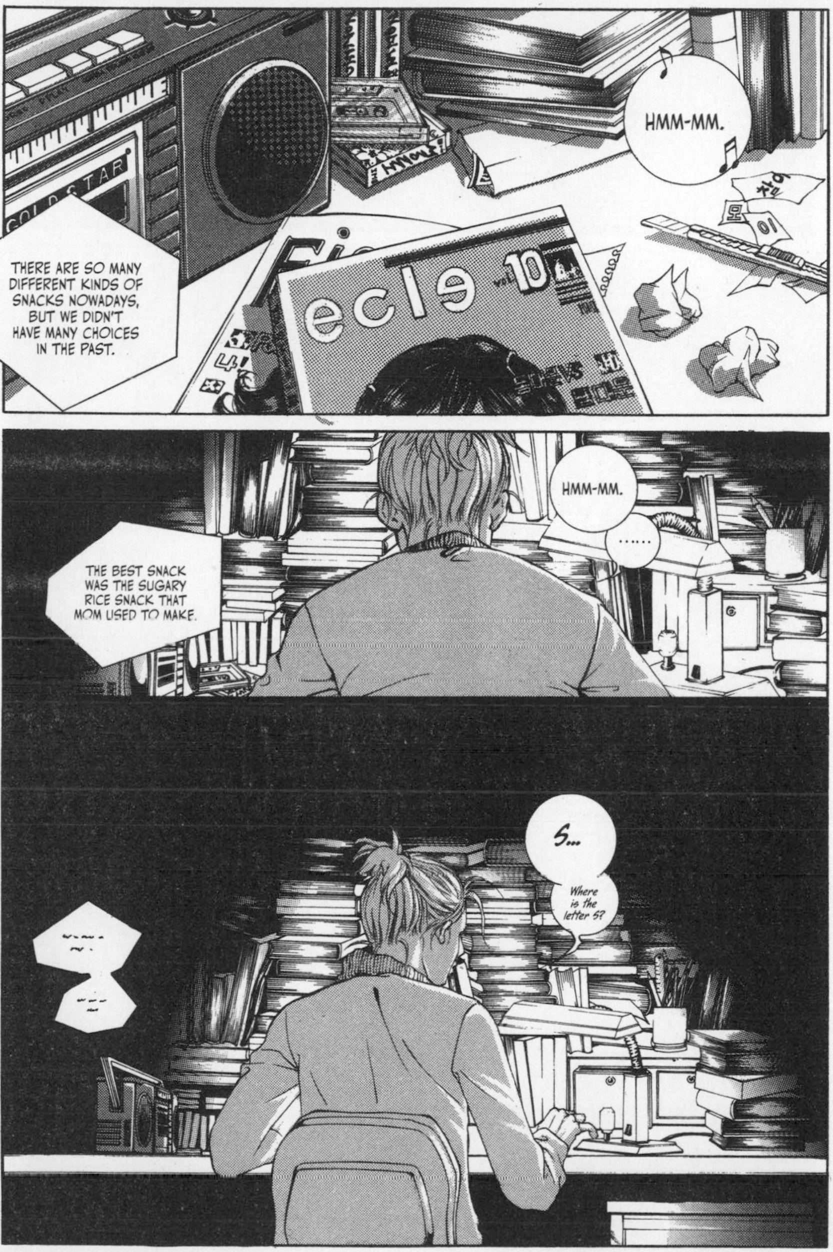
THERE ARE SO MANY DIFFERENT KINDS OF SNACKS NOWADAYS, BUT WE DIDN'T HAVE MANY CHOICES IN THE PAST.
HMM-MM.
GOLDSTAR
THE BEST SNACK WAS THE SUGARY RICE SNACK THAT MOM USED TO MAKE.
HMM-MM.
......
S...
Where is the letter S?

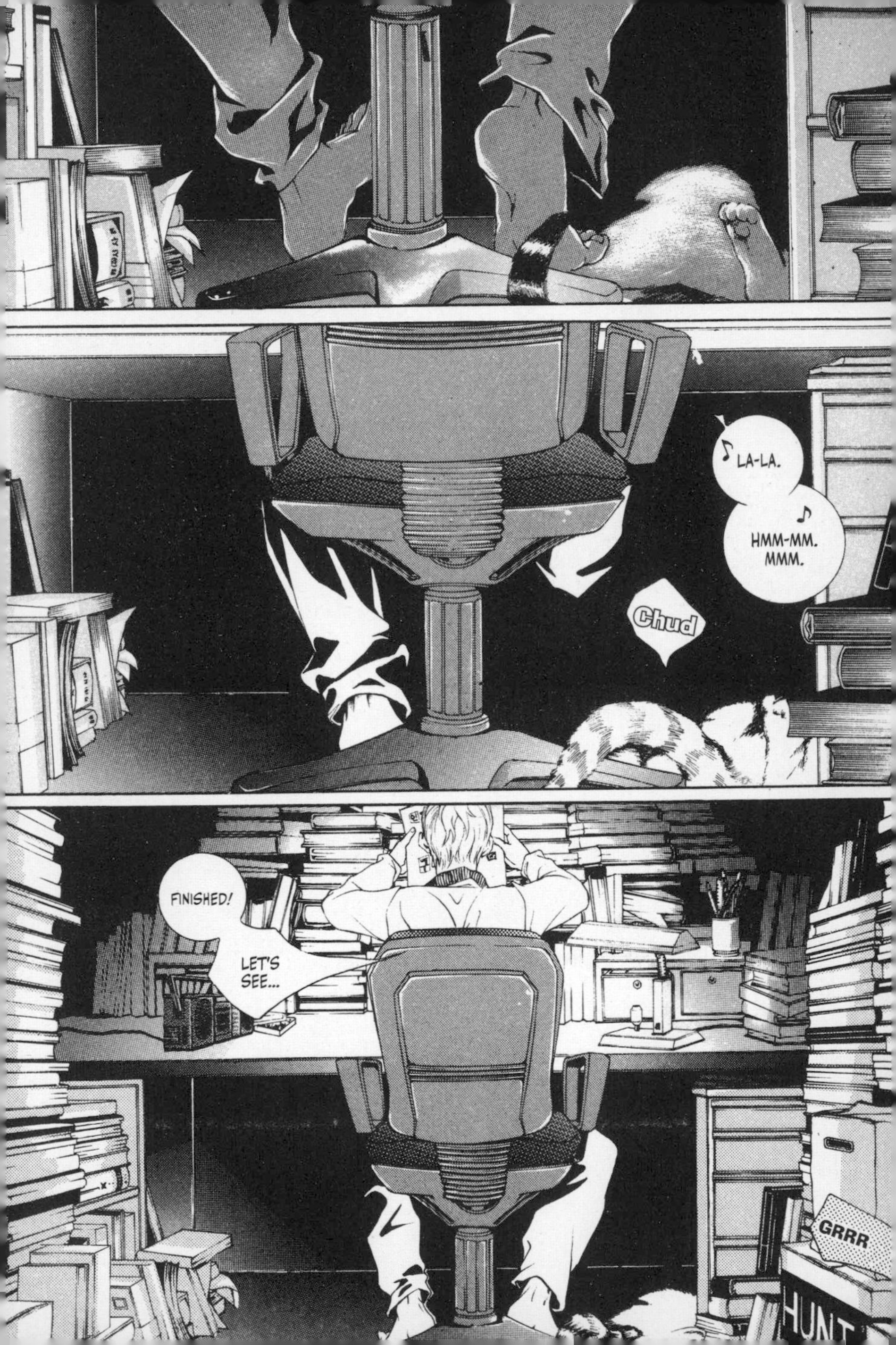
♪ LA-LA.
♪ HMM-MM. MMM.
Chud
FINISHED!
LET'S SEE...
GRRR
HUNT

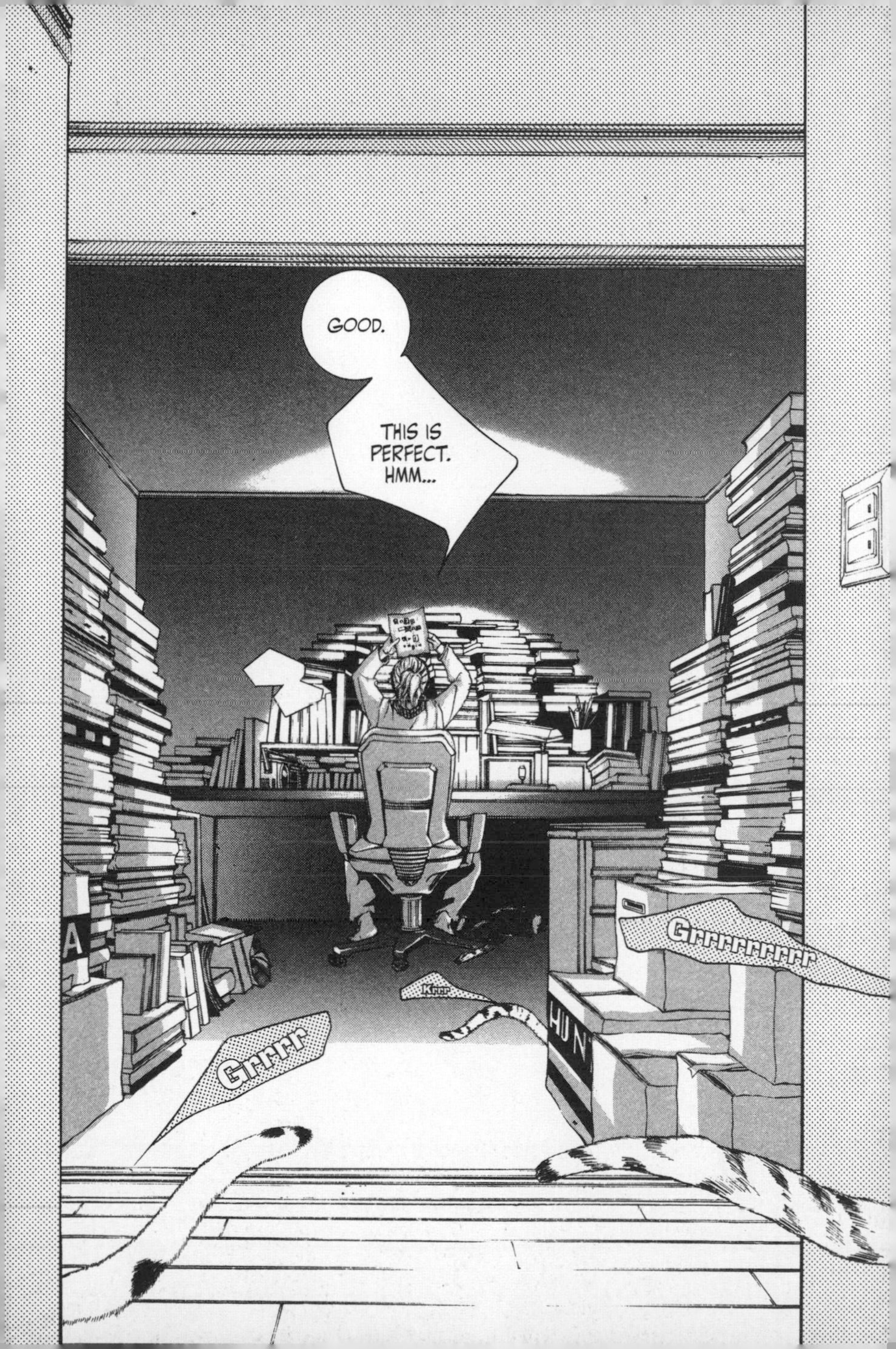
GOOD.
THIS IS PERFECT. HMM...
Grrrrrrrrrr
Krrr
Grrrr

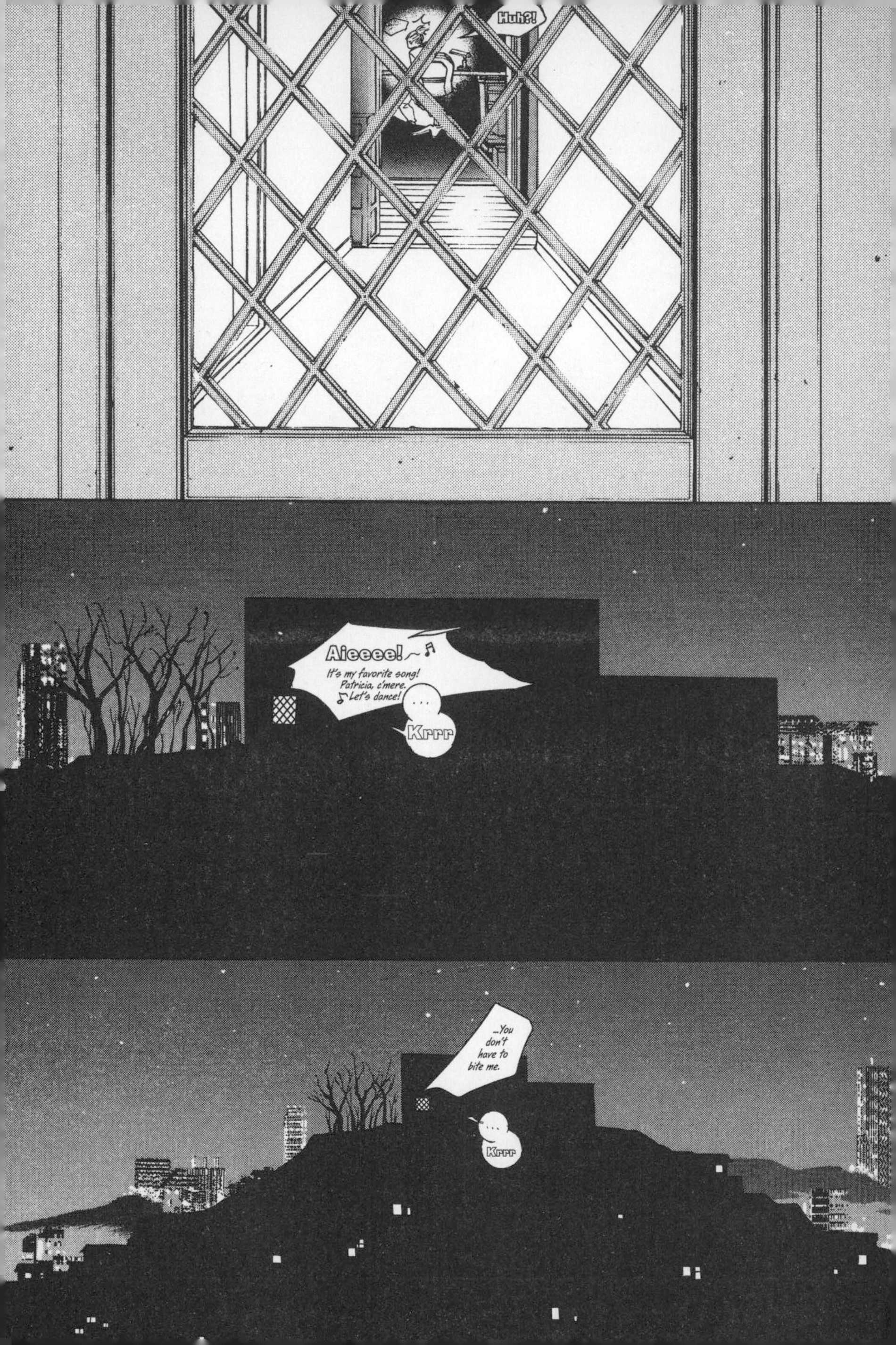
Huh?!
Aieeee! ~♪
It's my favorite song! Patricia, c'mere. ♪ Let's dance!
...
Krrr
...You don't have to bite me.
...
Krrr

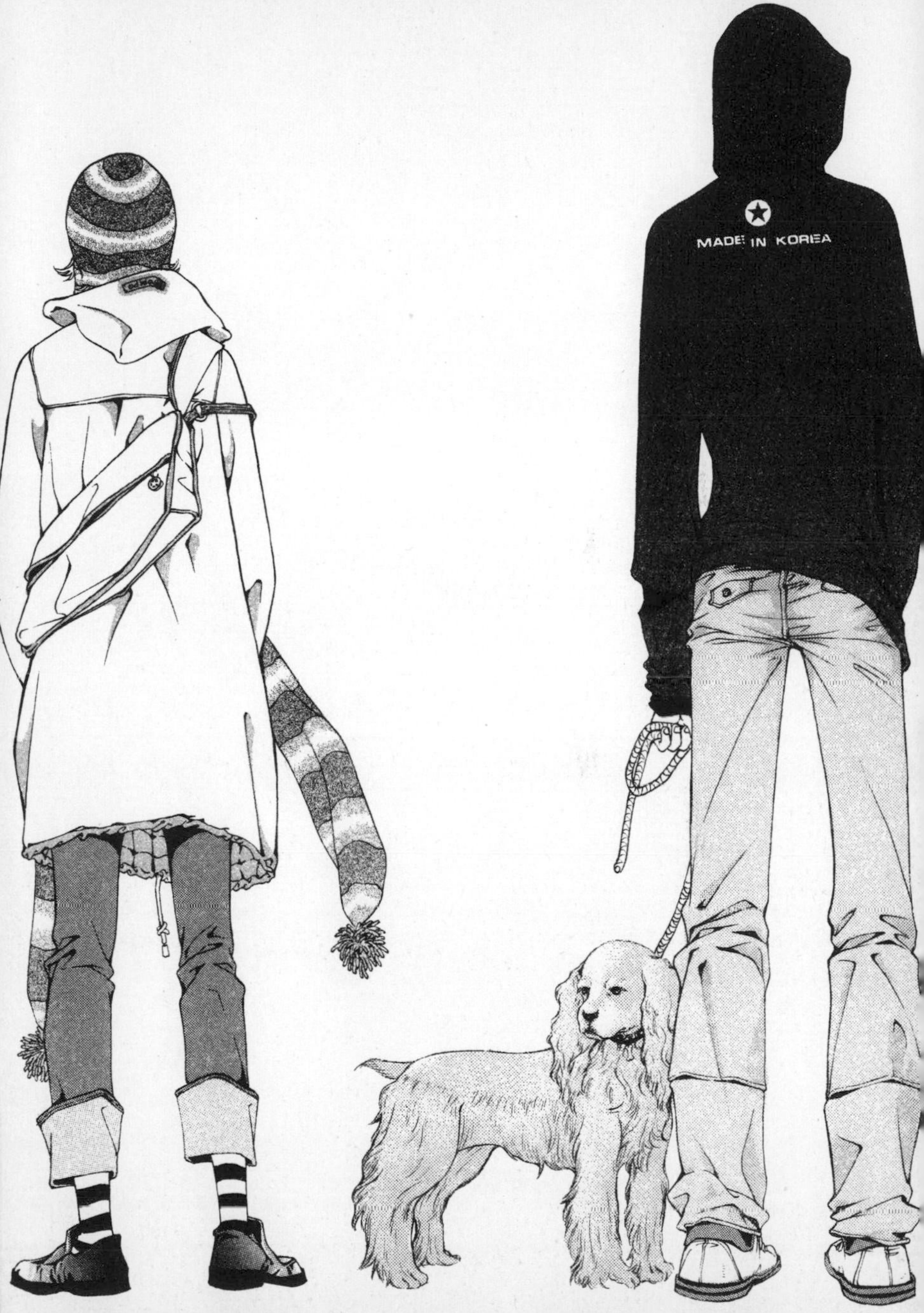
MADE IN KOREA

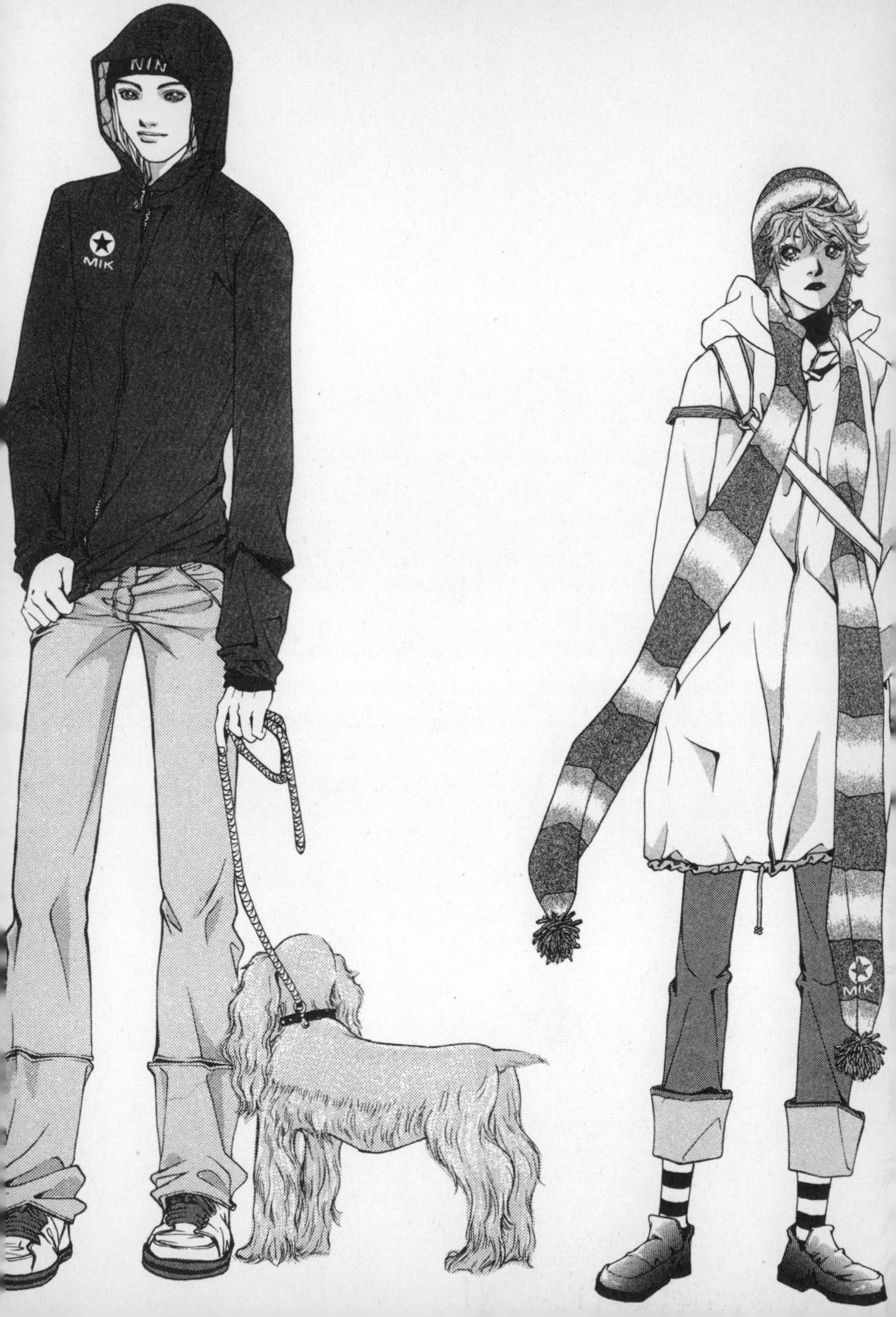
NIN
MIK
MIK

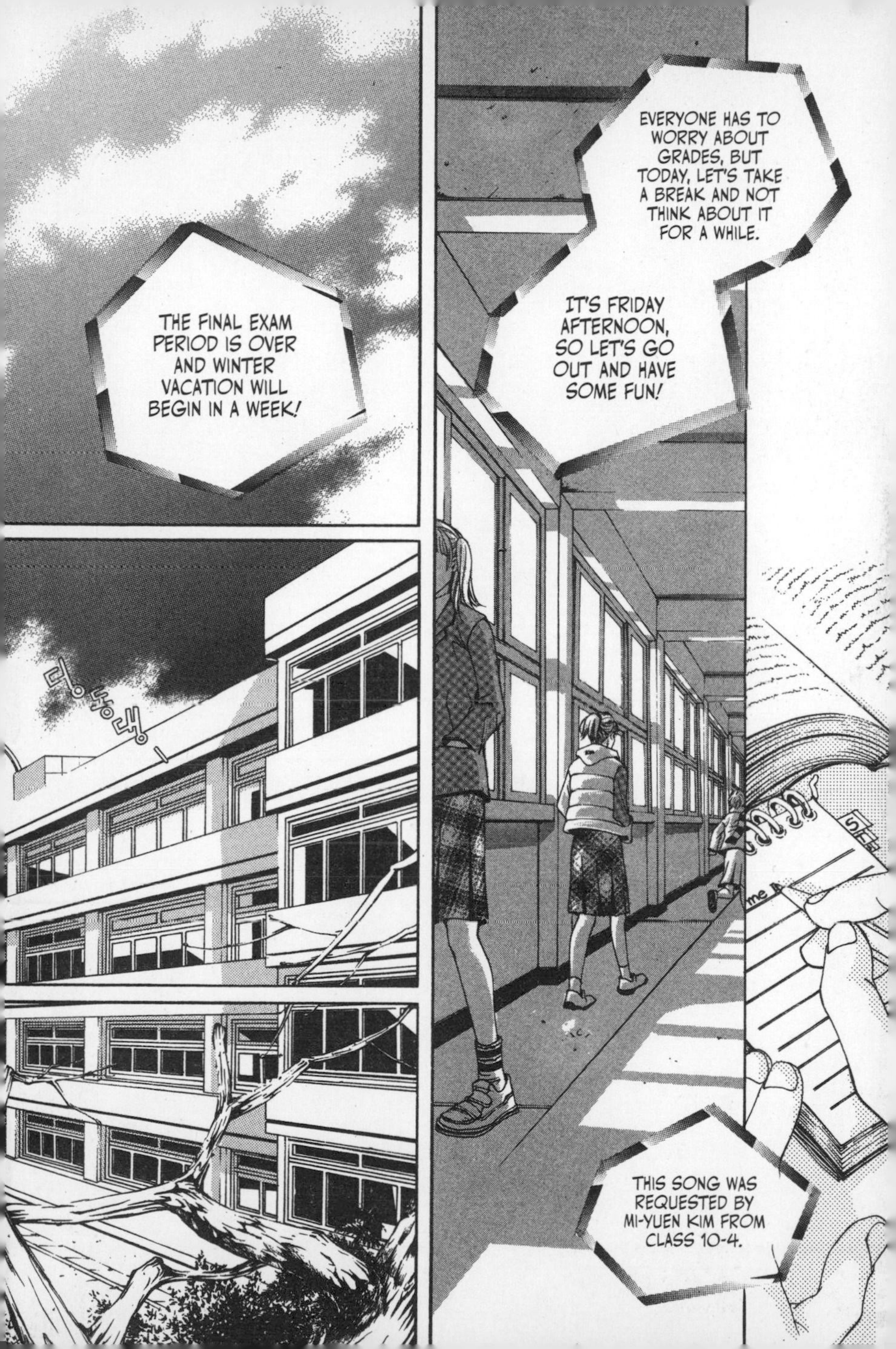

THE FINAL EXAM PERIOD IS OVER AND WINTER VACATION WILL BEGIN IN A WEEK!
딩동댕
EVERYONE HAS TO WORRY ABOUT GRADES, BUT TODAY, LET'S TAKE A BREAK AND NOT THINK ABOUT IT FOR A WHILE.
IT'S FRIDAY AFTERNOON, SO LET'S GO OUT AND HAVE SOME FUN!
THIS SONG WAS REQUESTED BY MI-YUEN KIM FROM CLASS 10-4.

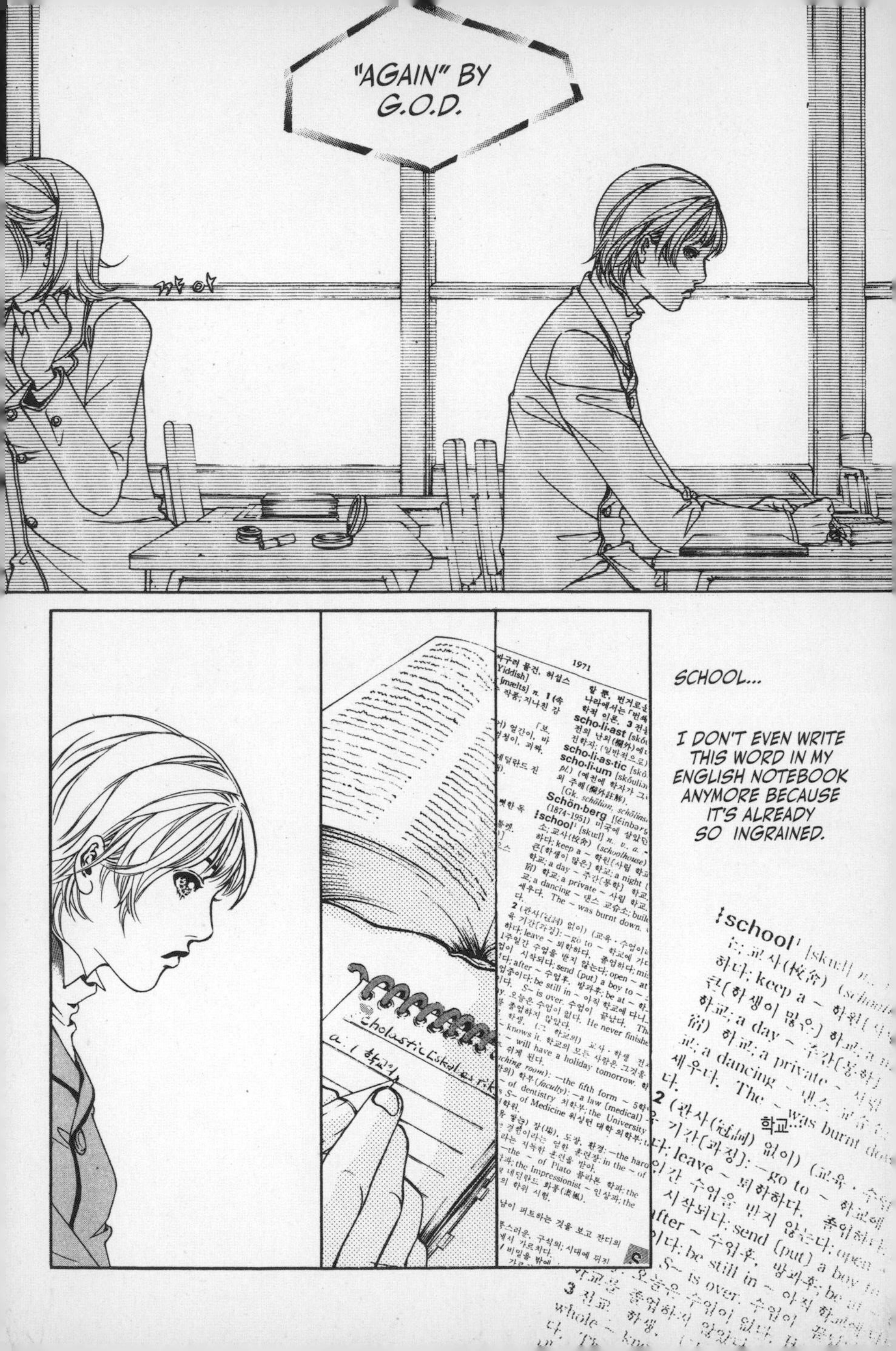
"AGAIN" BY G.O.D.
SCHOOL...
I DON'T EVEN WRITE THIS WORD IN MY ENGLISH NOTEBOOK ANYMORE BECAUSE IT'S ALREADY SO INGRAINED.
학교...

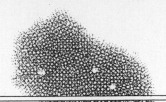

SCHOOL IS THE PLACE I GO TO EVERY DAY. I GET UP AT 6 O'CLOCK IN THE MORNING AND TAKE THE 63 BUS FOR AN HOUR.

MY NAME AT SCHOOL IS...

...NUMBER 37...

# Step 1:
# Number 37, Hyung-In Kim

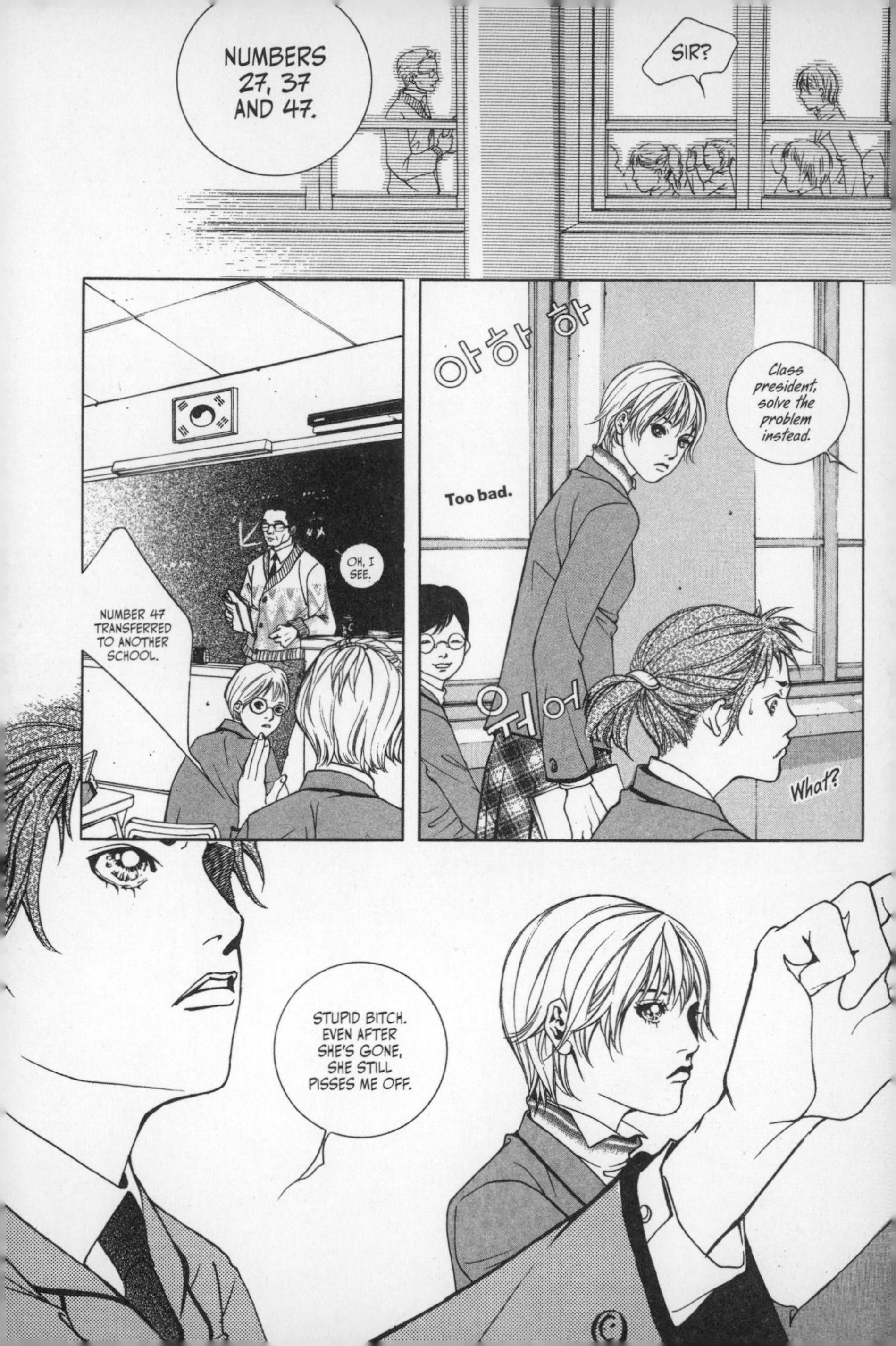
NUMBERS 27, 37 AND 47.
SIR?
NUMBER 47 TRANSFERRED TO ANOTHER SCHOOL.
OH, I SEE.
아하하
Class president, solve the problem instead.
Too bad.
워어
What?
STUPID BITCH. EVEN AFTER SHE'S GONE, SHE STILL PISSES ME OFF.

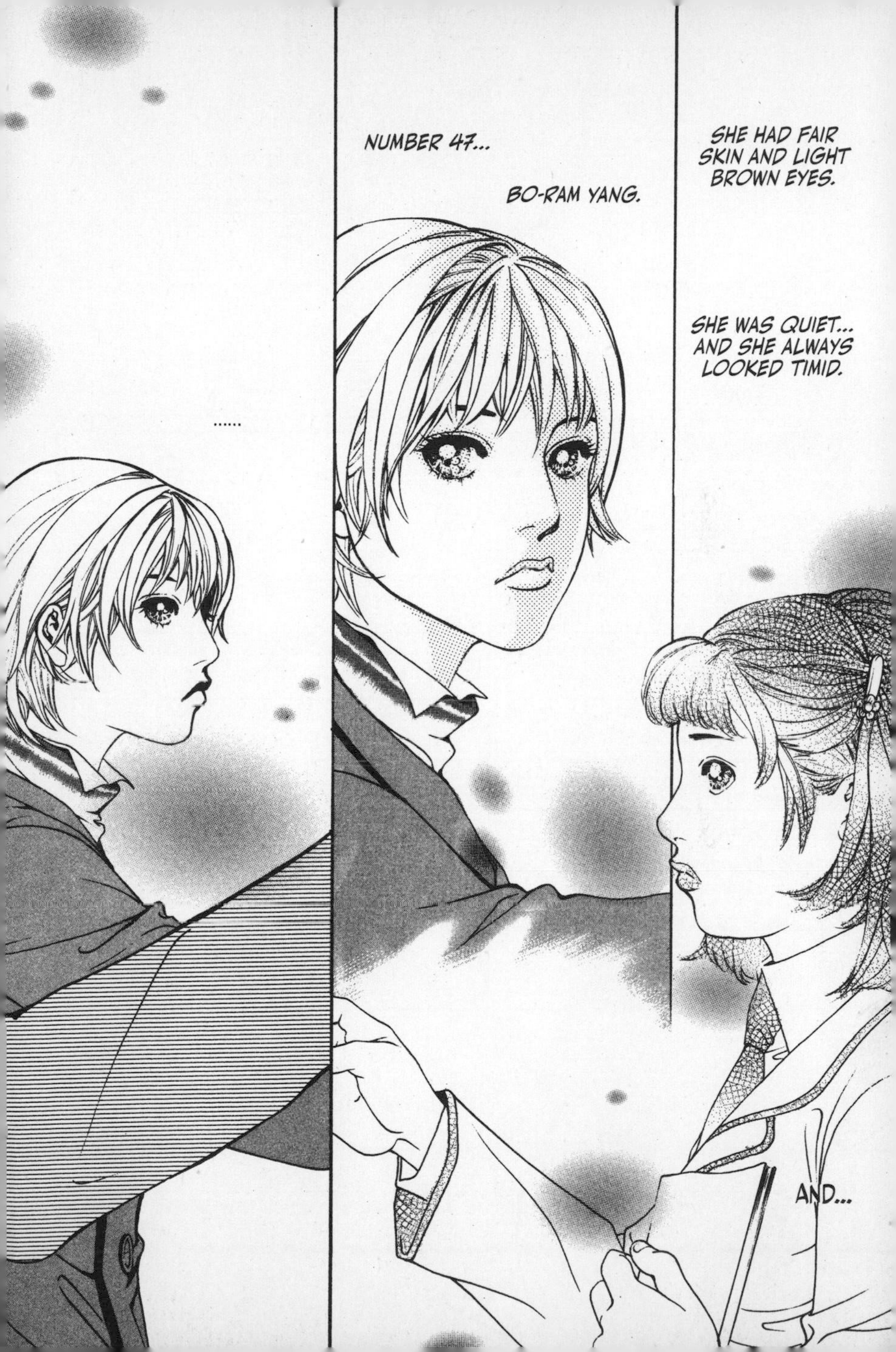
......
NUMBER 47...
BO-RAM YANG.
SHE HAD FAIR SKIN AND LIGHT BROWN EYES.
SHE WAS QUIET... AND SHE ALWAYS LOOKED TIMID.
AND...

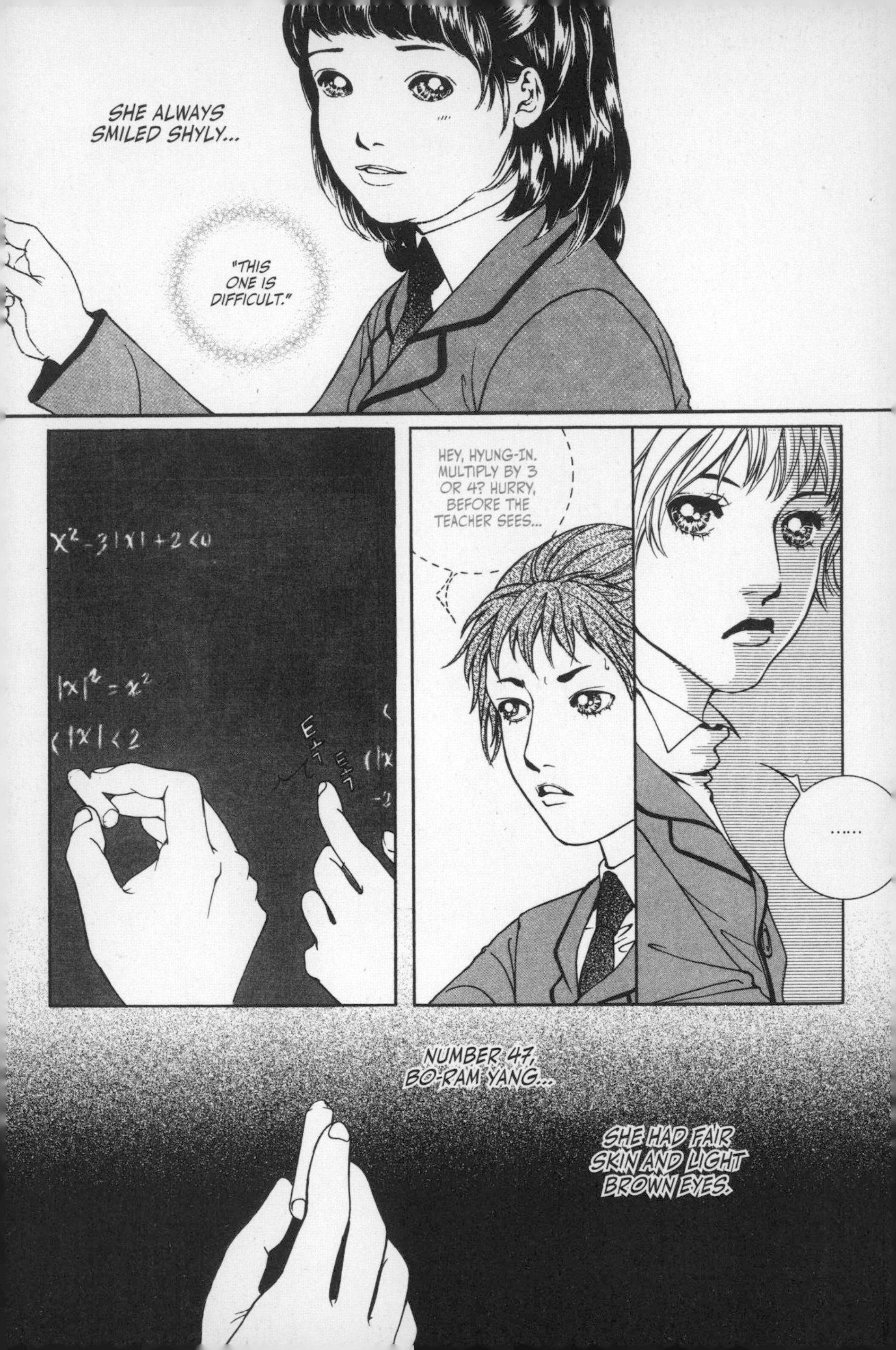
SHE ALWAYS SMILED SHYLY...
"THIS ONE IS DIFFICULT."
$x^2-3|x|+2<0$
$|x|^2=x^2$
HEY, HYUNG-IN. MULTIPLY BY 3 OR 4? HURRY, BEFORE THE TEACHER SEES...
......
NUMBER 47, BO-RAM YANG...
SHE HAD FAIR SKIN AND LIGHT BROWN EYES.

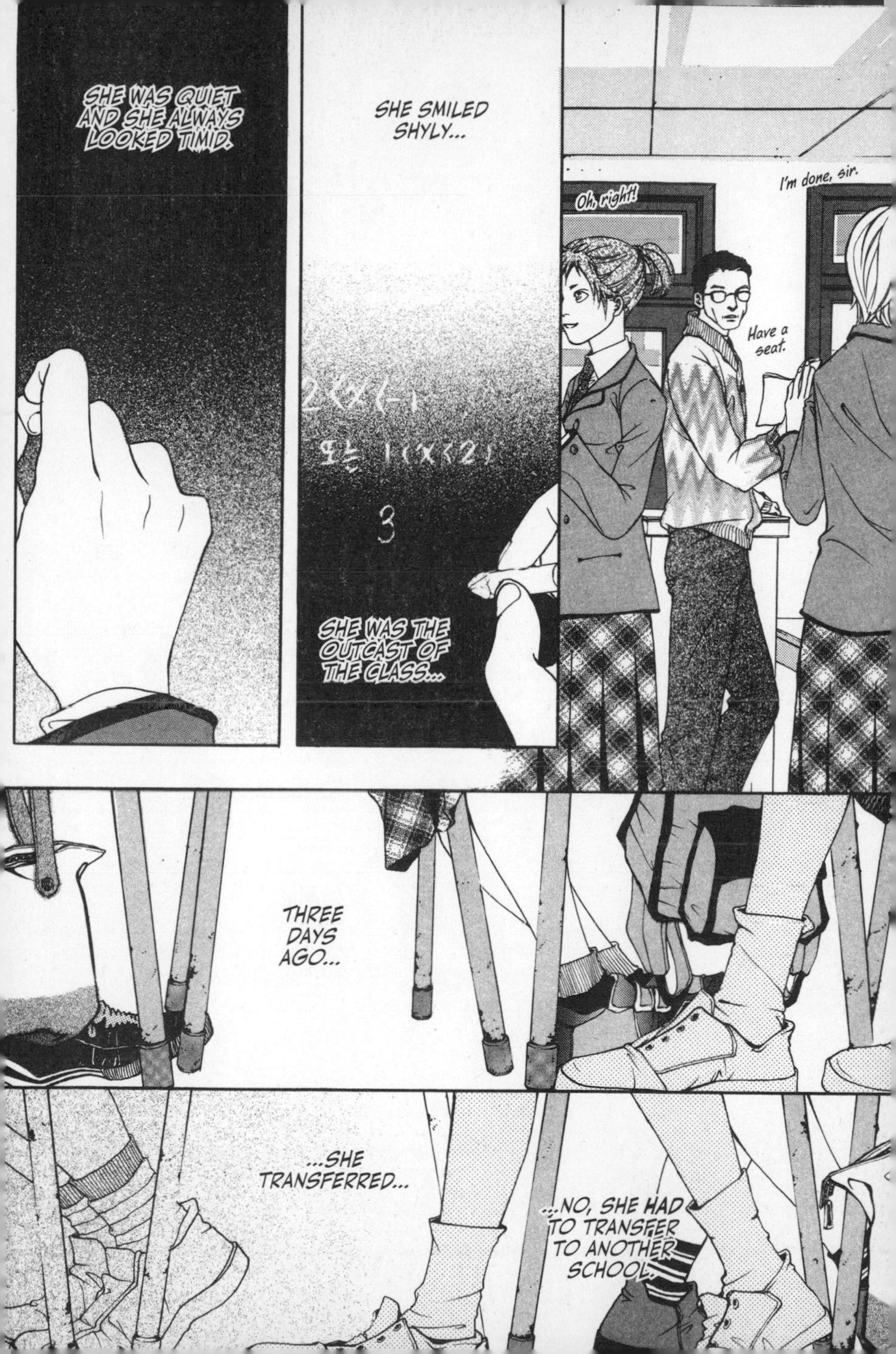
SHE WAS QUIET AND SHE ALWAYS LOOKED TIMID.
SHE SMILED SHYLY...
SHE WAS THE OUTCAST OF THE CLASS...
Oh, right!
I'm done, sir.
Have a seat.
THREE DAYS AGO...
...SHE TRANSFERRED...
...NO, SHE HAD TO TRANSFER TO ANOTHER SCHOOL.

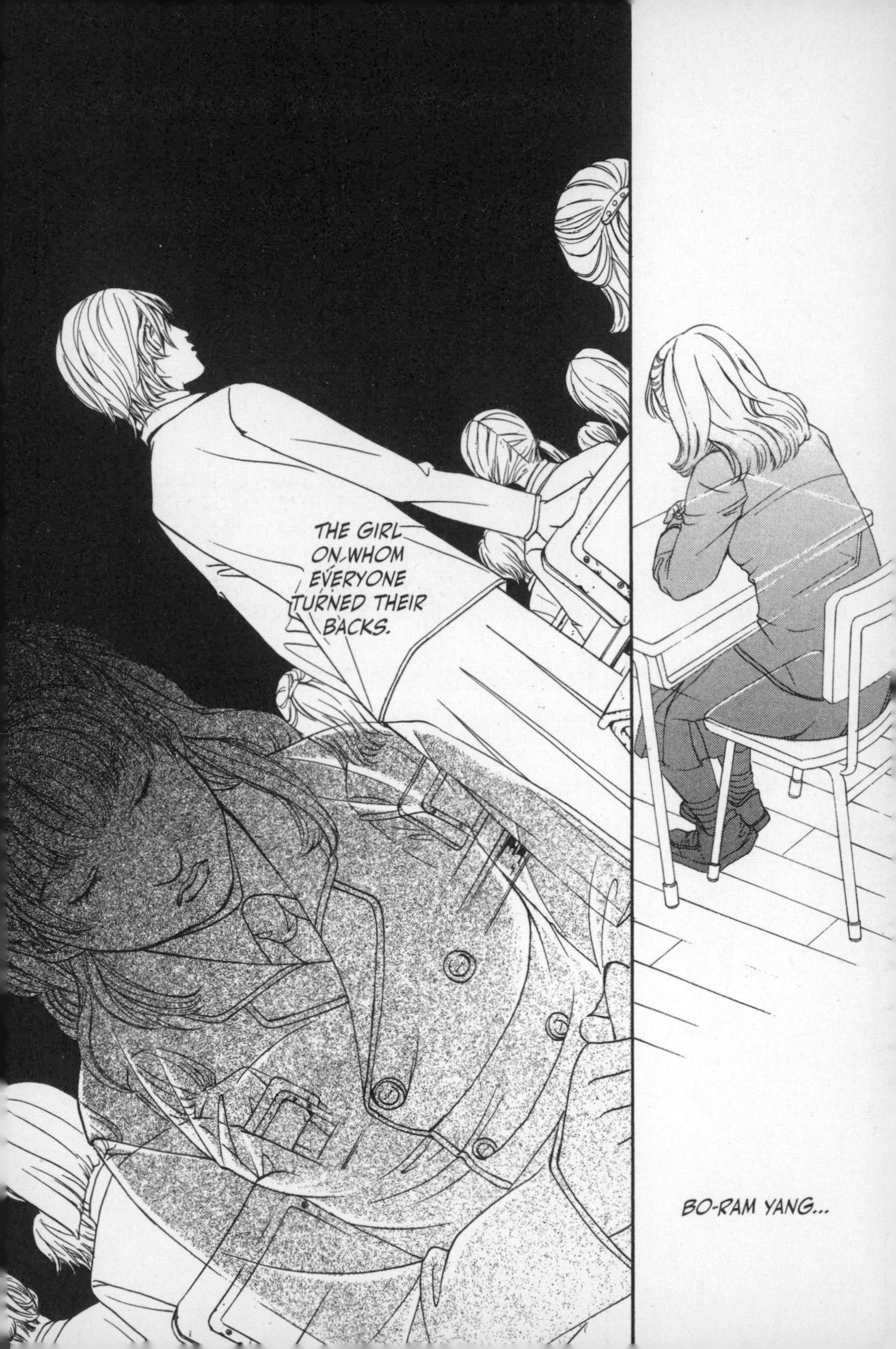
THE GIRL ON WHOM EVERYONE TURNED THEIR BACKS.
BO-RAM YANG...

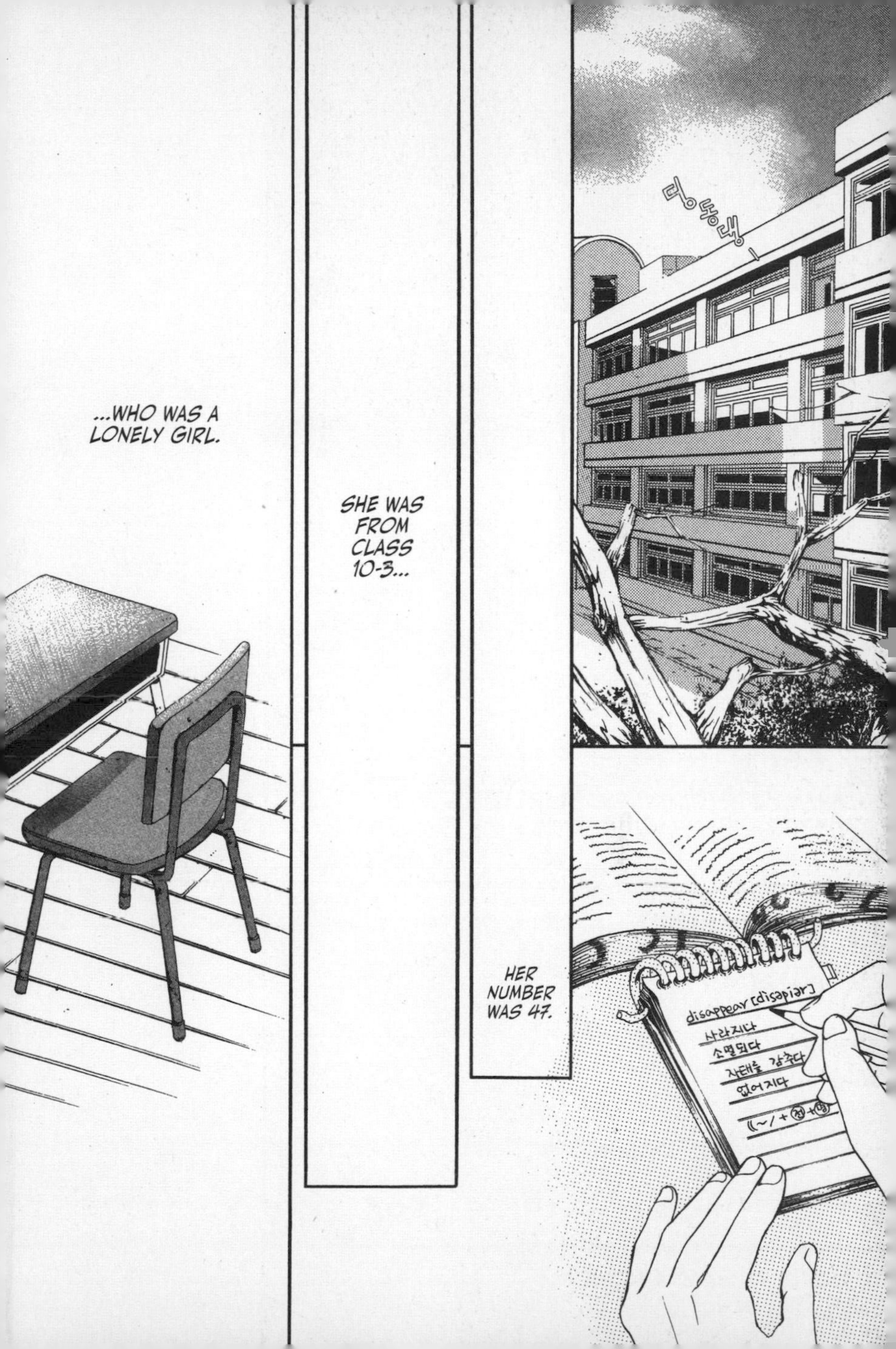
...WHO WAS A LONELY GIRL.
SHE WAS FROM CLASS 10-3...
딩동댕~
HER NUMBER WAS 47.
disappear
사라지다
소멸되다
자태를 감추다
없어지다

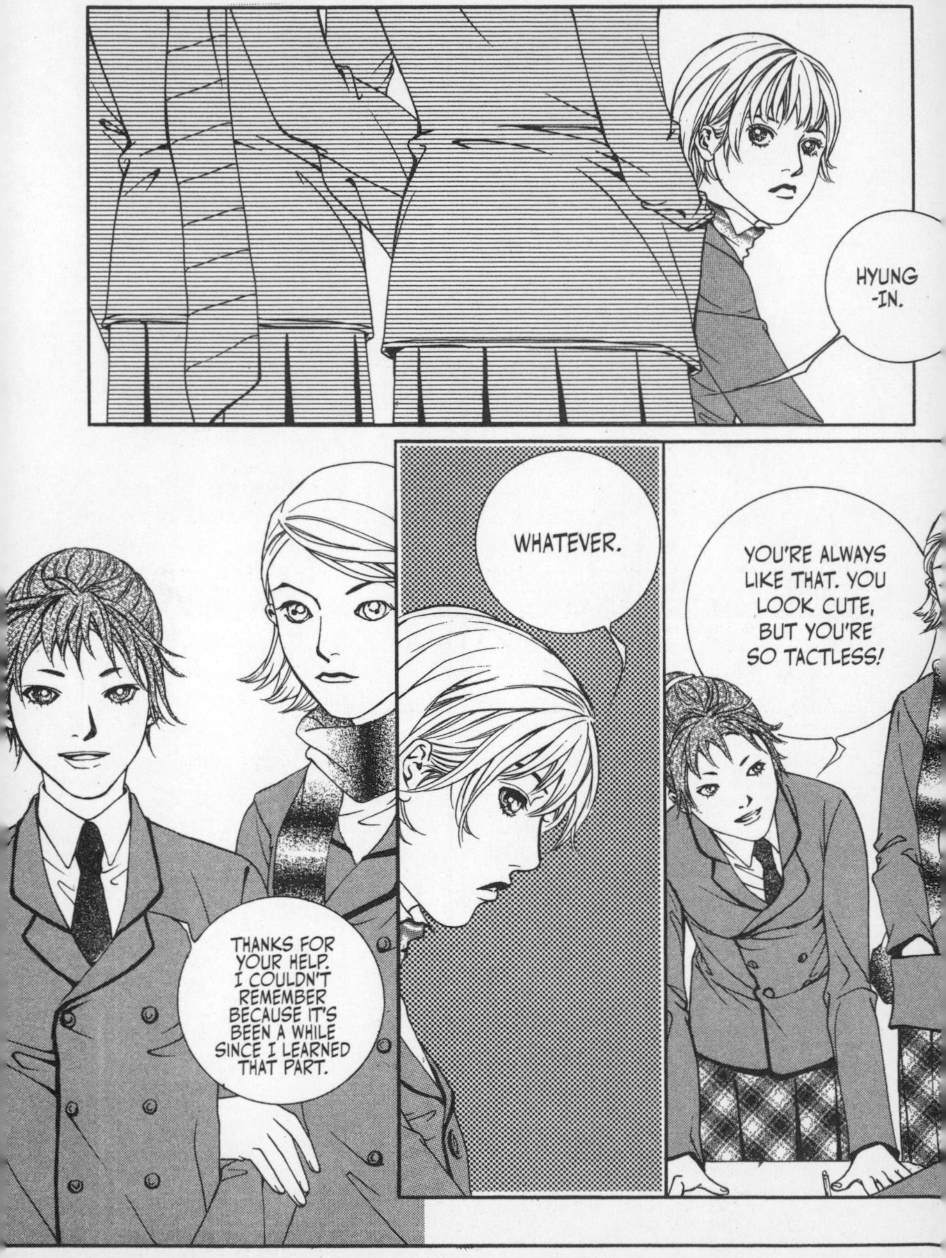
HYUNG-IN.
THANKS FOR YOUR HELP. I COULDN'T REMEMBER BECAUSE IT'S BEEN A WHILE SINCE I LEARNED THAT PART.
WHATEVER.
YOU'RE ALWAYS LIKE THAT. YOU LOOK CUTE, BUT YOU'RE SO TACTLESS!

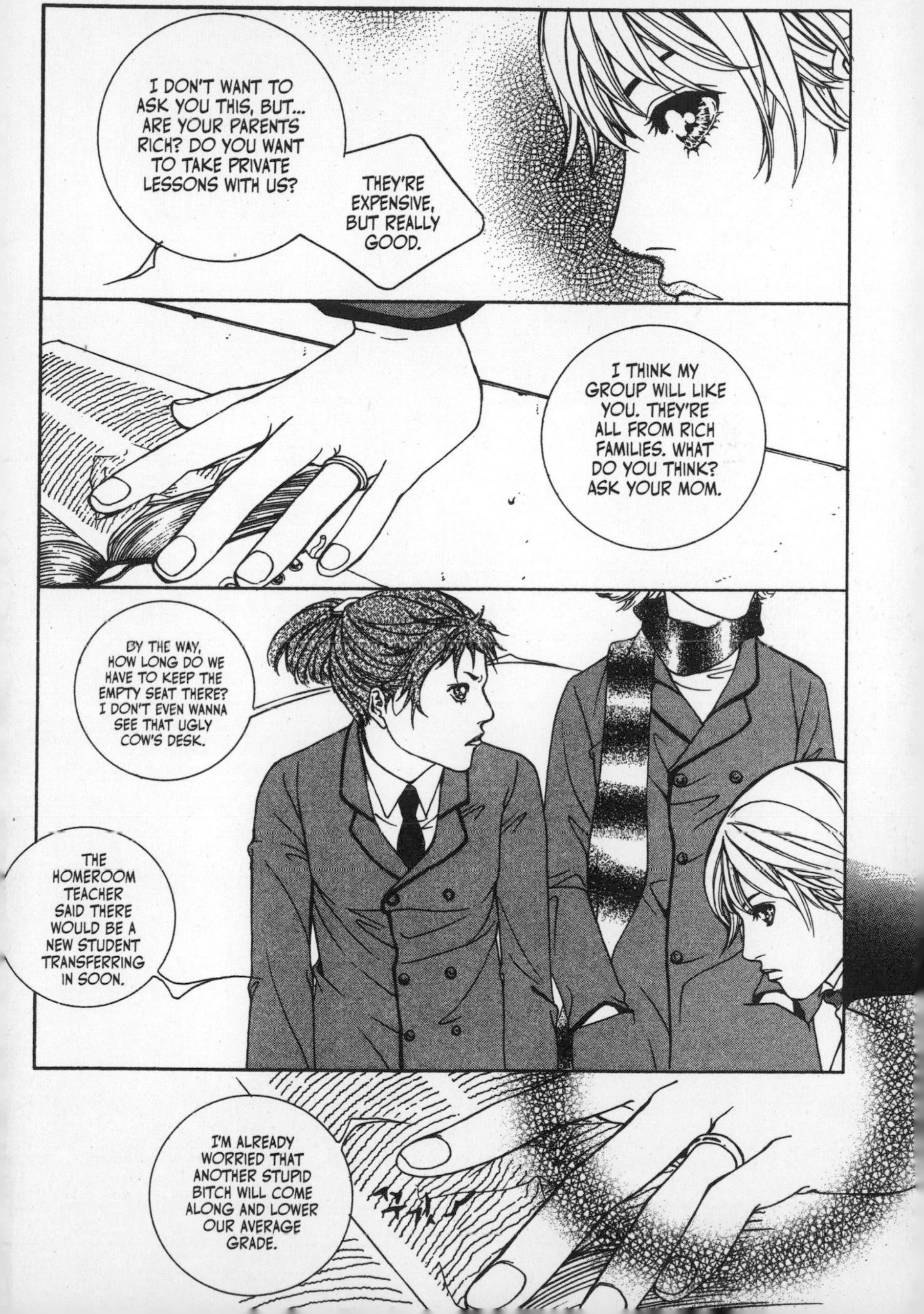
I DON'T WANT TO ASK YOU THIS, BUT... ARE YOUR PARENTS RICH? DO YOU WANT TO TAKE PRIVATE LESSONS WITH US?
THEY'RE EXPENSIVE, BUT REALLY GOOD.
I THINK MY GROUP WILL LIKE YOU. THEY'RE ALL FROM RICH FAMILIES. WHAT DO YOU THINK? ASK YOUR MOM.
BY THE WAY, HOW LONG DO WE HAVE TO KEEP THE EMPTY SEAT THERE? I DON'T EVEN WANNA SEE THAT UGLY COW'S DESK.
THE HOMEROOM TEACHER SAID THERE WOULD BE A NEW STUDENT TRANSFERRING IN SOON.
I'M ALREADY WORRIED THAT ANOTHER STUPID BITCH WILL COME ALONG AND LOWER OUR AVERAGE GRADE.

DO YOU THINK WE'RE GONNA GET SOMEONE WORSE THAN BO-RAM?
Heh...
NO WAY. IT CAN'T GET ANY WORSE THAN BO-RAM.
WELL, I GUESS YOU'RE RIGHT.
BOOK...
HUH? WHAT?
MY BOOK...

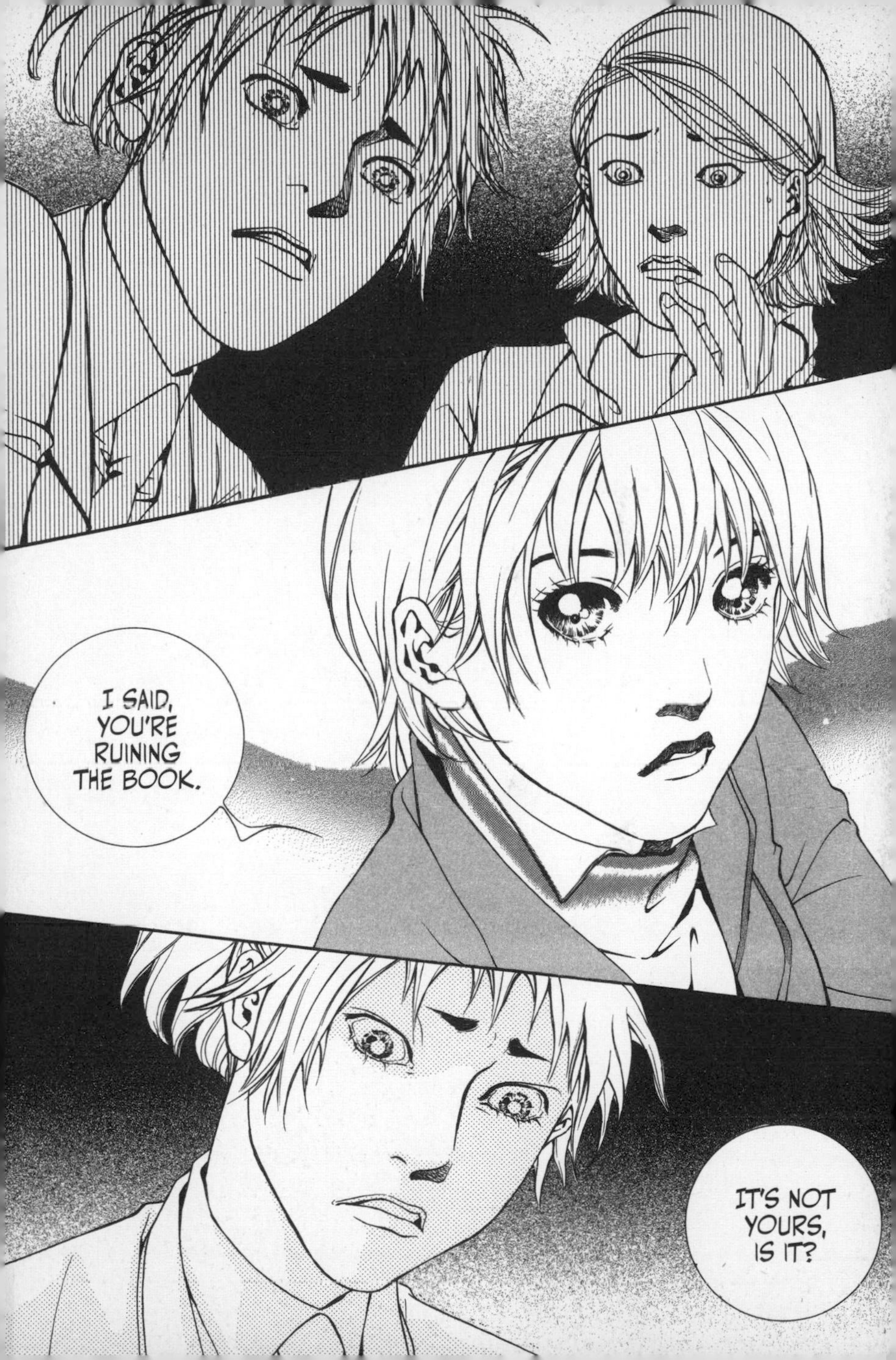
I SAID, YOU'RE RUINING THE BOOK.
IT'S NOT YOURS, IS IT?

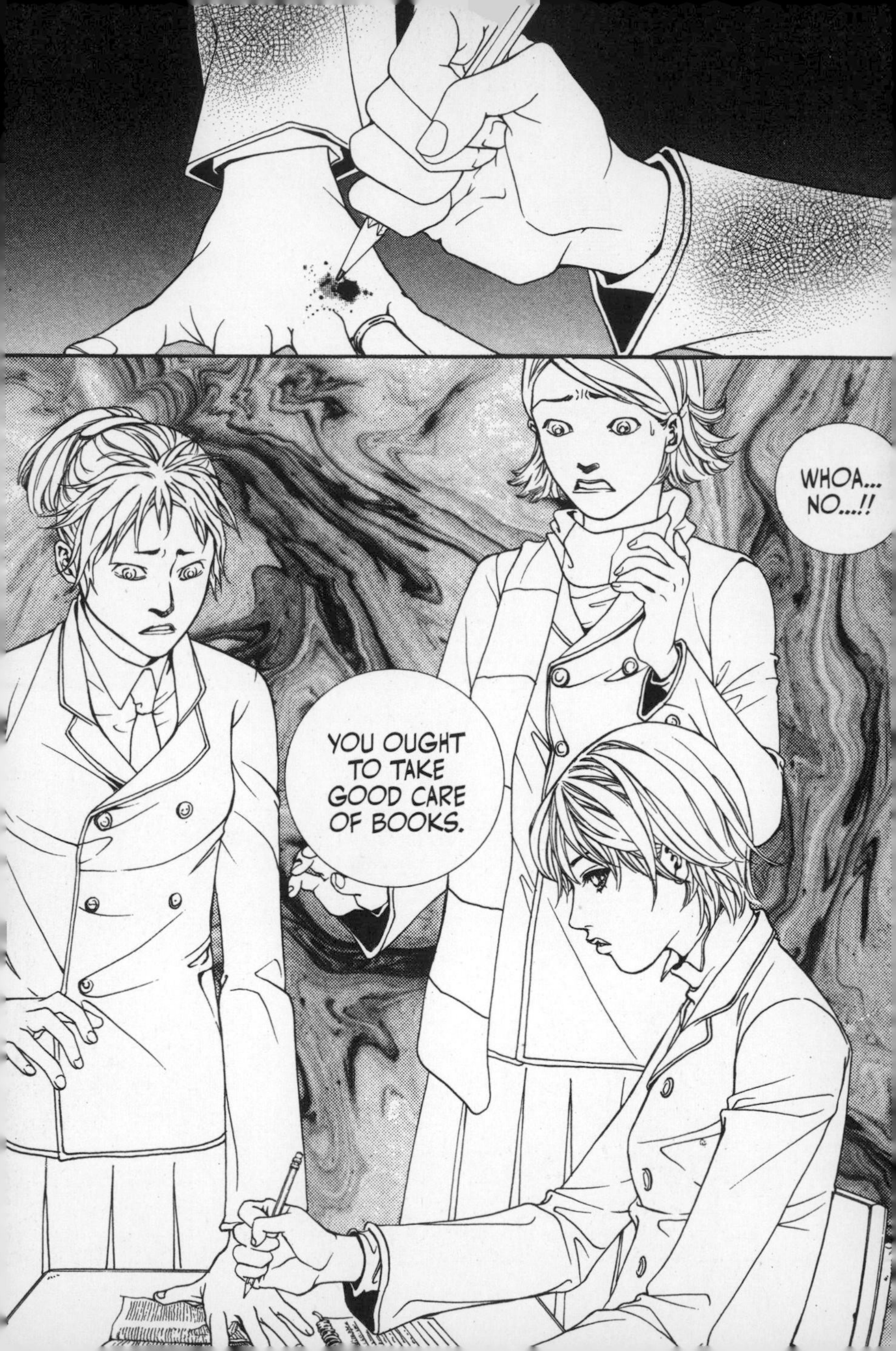
WHOA... NO...!!
YOU OUGHT TO TAKE GOOD CARE OF BOOKS.

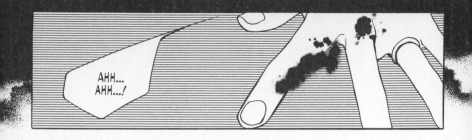

AHH...
AHH....!

Gyaaah!

OH MY
GOD! OH
MY GOD!

ARE YOU OKAY?
WANNA GO TO
THE NURSE?

WHAT
HAPPENED?

HUH?

SOMEONE, GET
THE TEACHER!

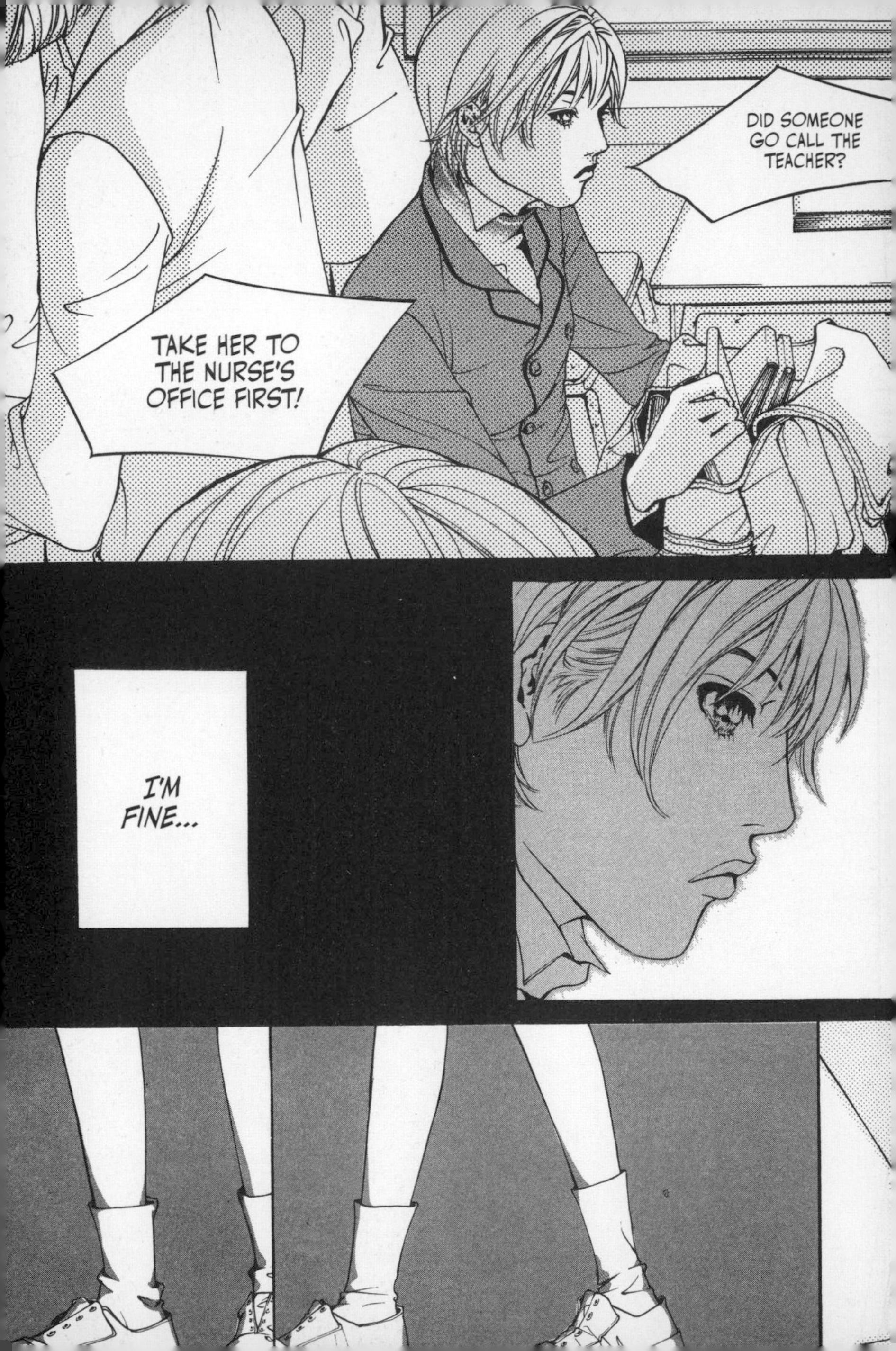
DID SOMEONE GO CALL THE TEACHER?
TAKE HER TO THE NURSE'S OFFICE FIRST!
I'M FINE...

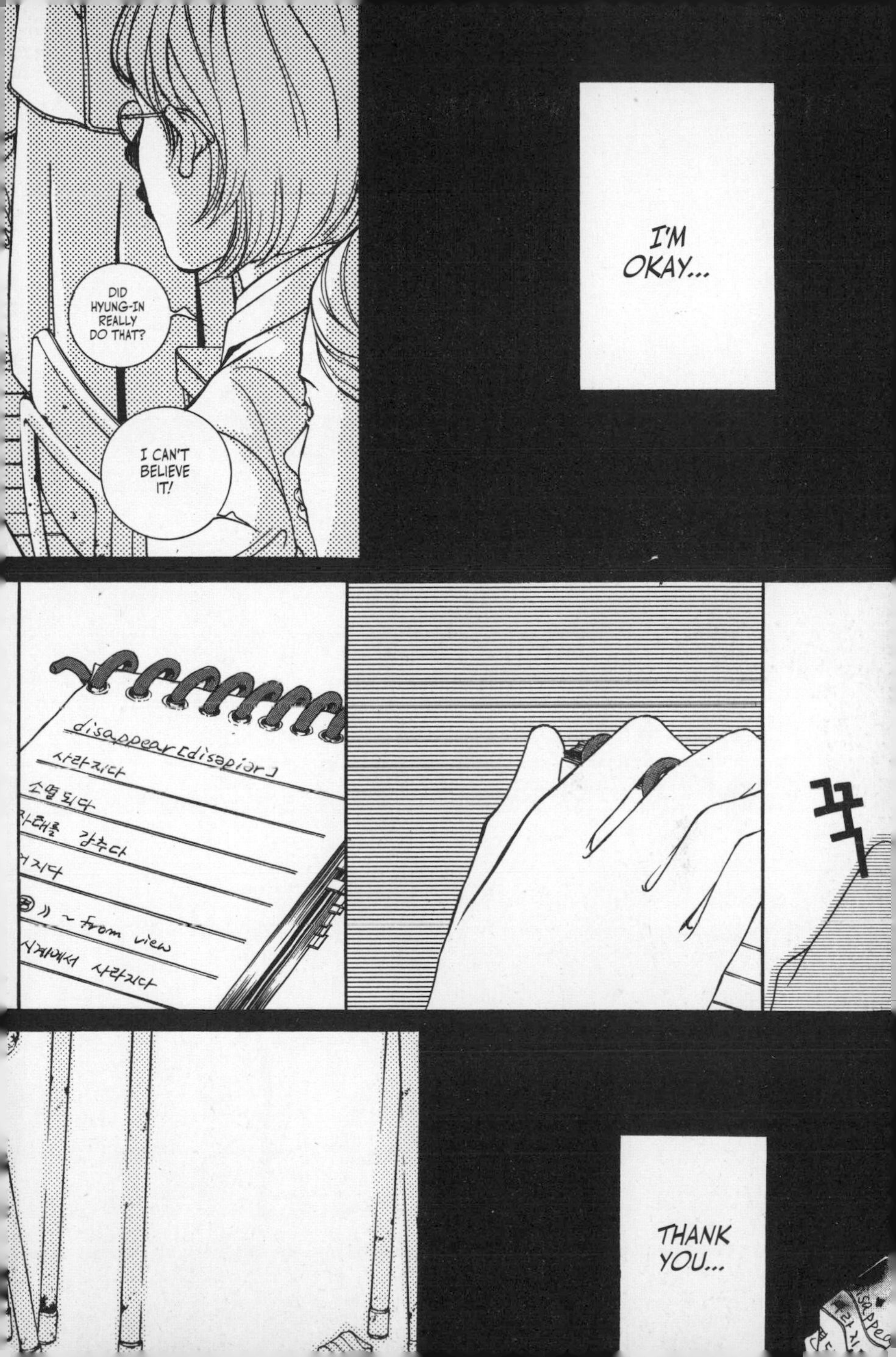
DID HYUNG-IN REALLY DO THAT?
I CAN'T BELIEVE IT!
I'M OKAY...
disappear [disəpiər]
사라지다
소멸되다
~ from view
꾹
THANK YOU...

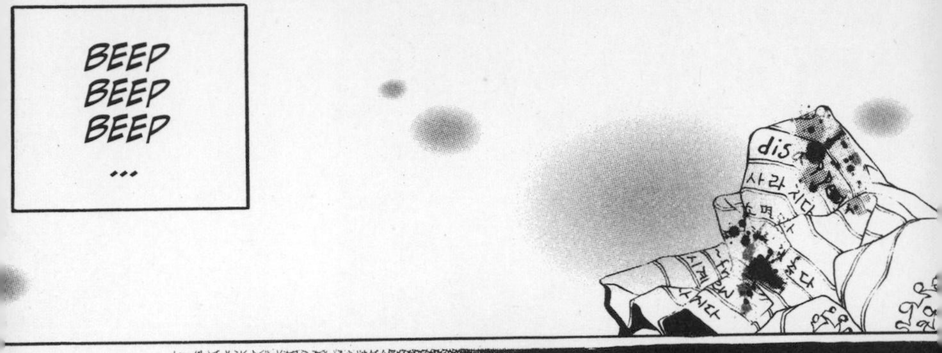
BEEP
BEEP
BEEP
...
dis
사라 지다

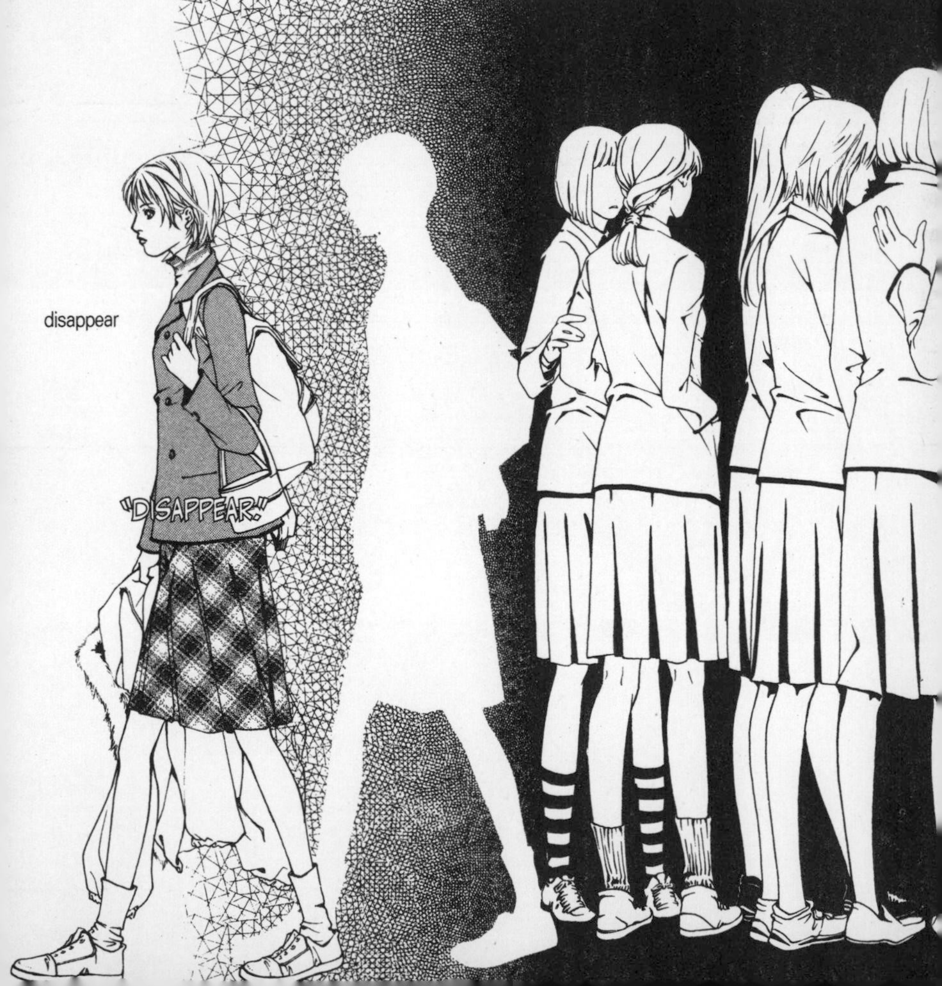
disappear
"DISAPPEAR."

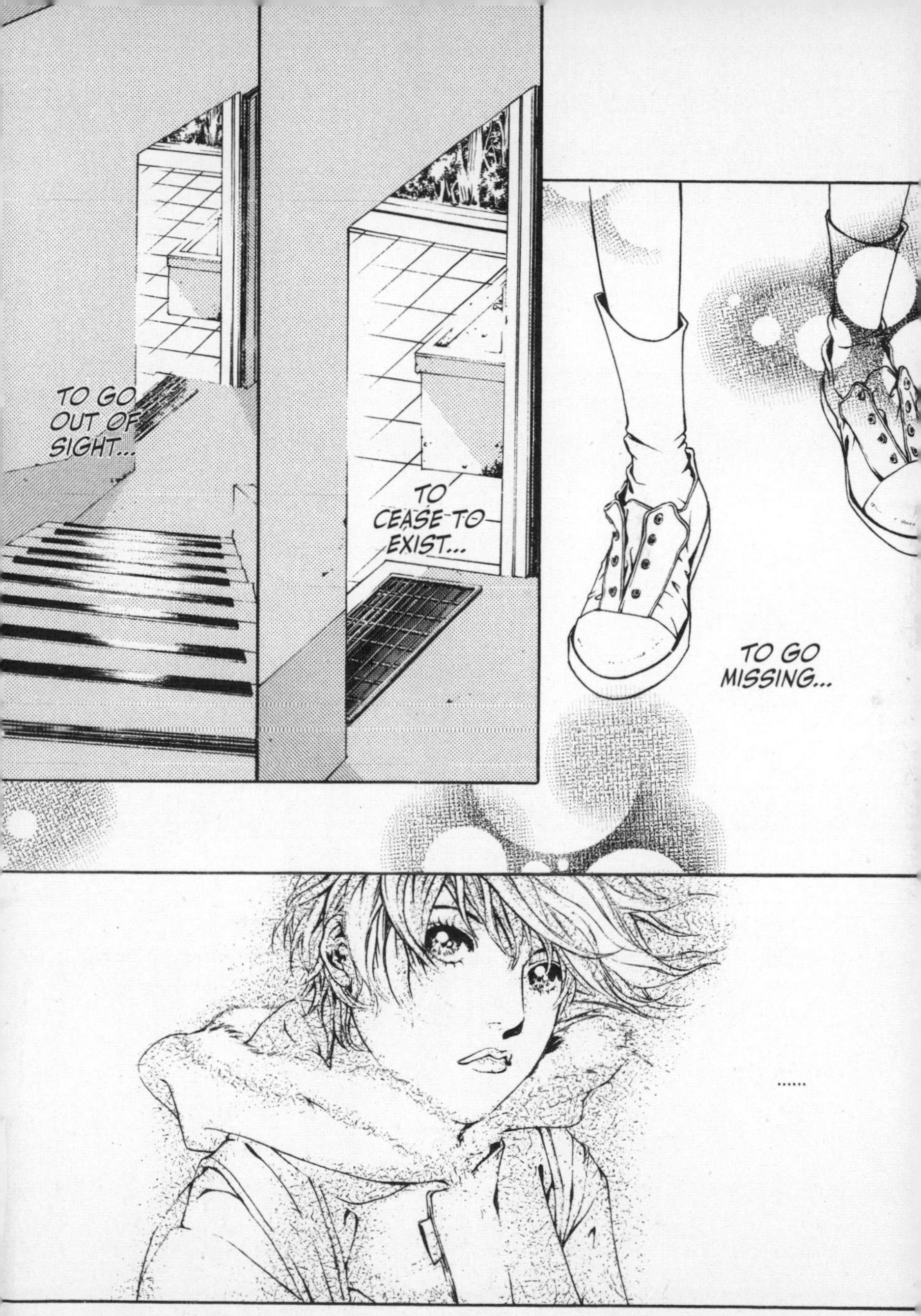
TO GO OUT OF SIGHT...
TO CEASE TO EXIST...
TO GO MISSING...
......

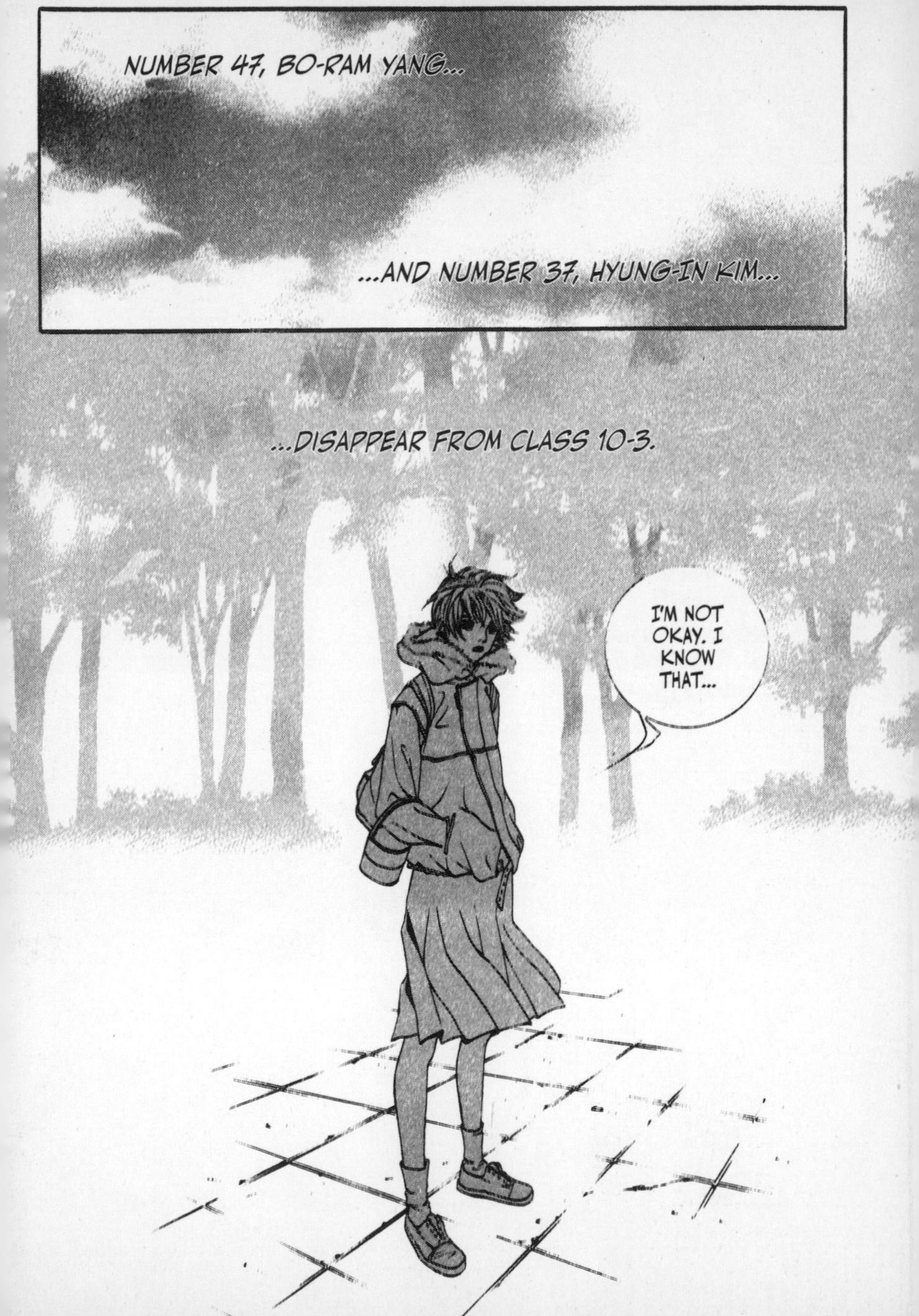
NUMBER 47, BO-RAM YANG...
...AND NUMBER 37, HYUNG-IN KIM...
...DISAPPEAR FROM CLASS 10-3.
I'M NOT OKAY. I KNOW THAT...

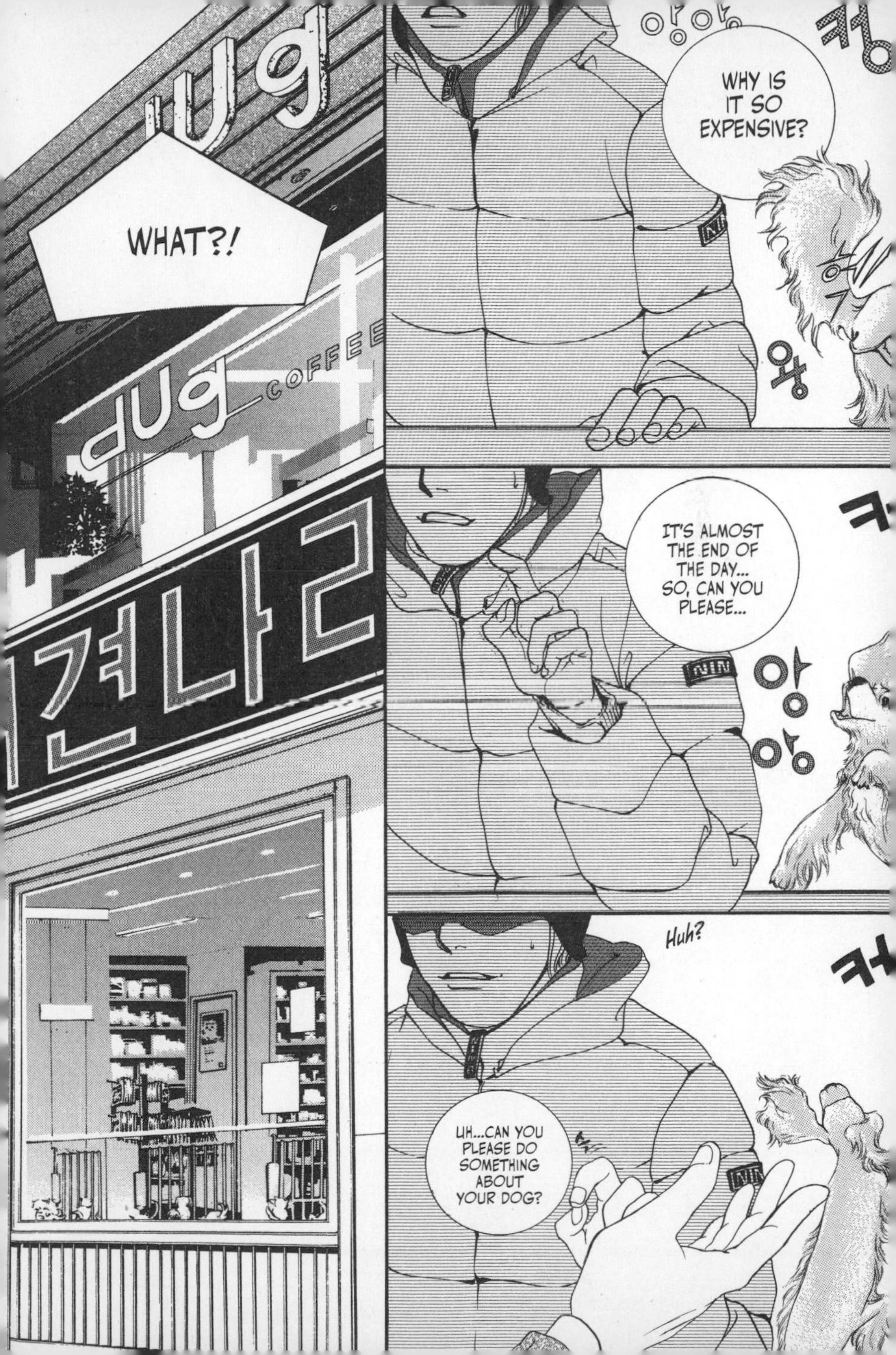

WHAT?!
dug COFFEE
앙앙
WHY IS IT SO EXPENSIVE?
왕
IT'S ALMOST THE END OF THE DAY... SO, CAN YOU PLEASE...
앙
앙
Huh?
UH...CAN YOU PLEASE DO SOMETHING ABOUT YOUR DOG?

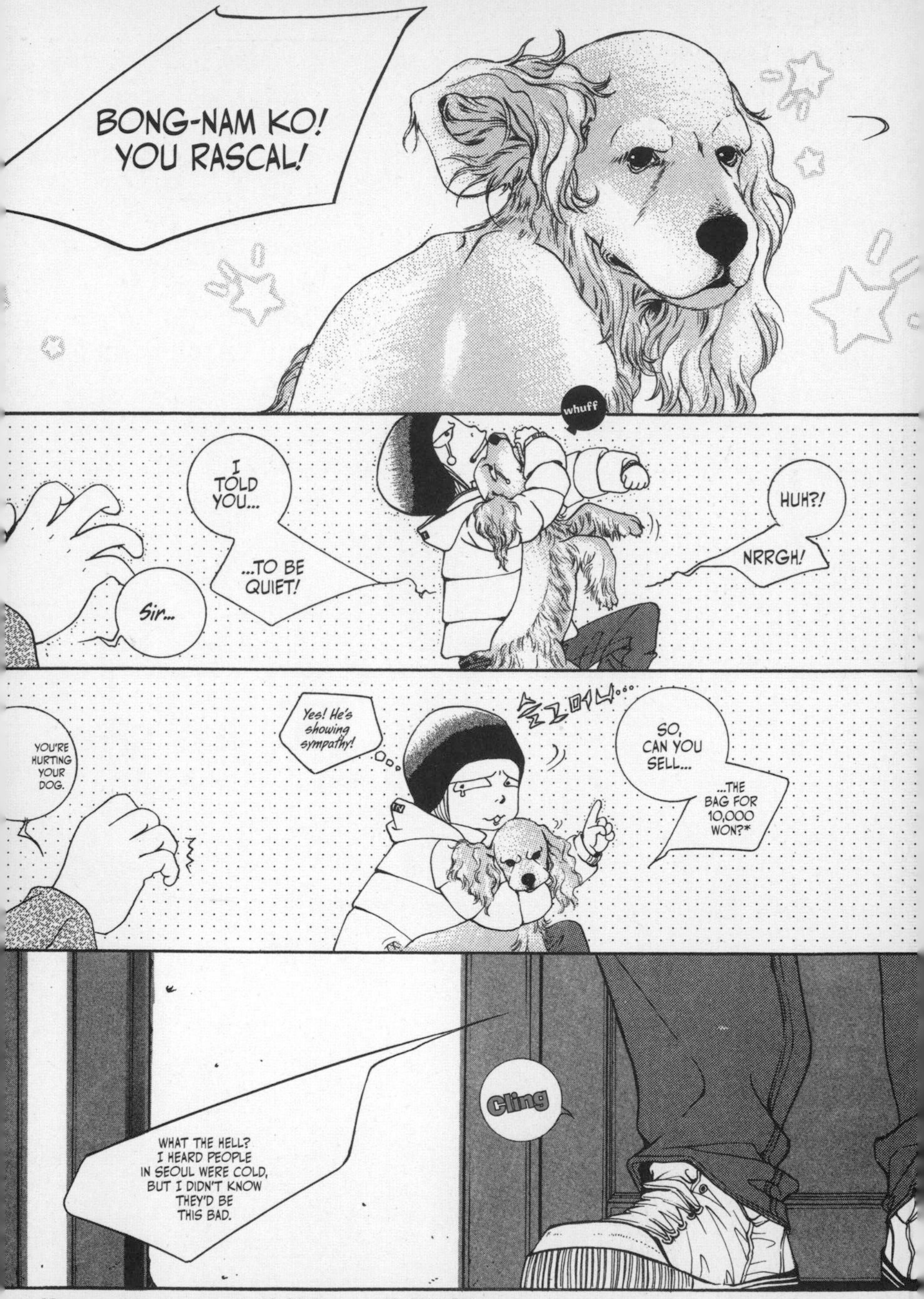
BONG-NAM KO! YOU RASCAL!
whuff
I TOLD YOU...
...TO BE QUIET!
Sir...
HUH?!
NRRGH!
YOU'RE HURTING YOUR DOG.
Yes! He's showing sympathy!
SO, CAN YOU SELL...
...THE BAG FOR 10,000 WON?*
WHAT THE HELL? I HEARD PEOPLE IN SEOUL WERE COLD, BUT I DIDN'T KNOW THEY'D BE THIS BAD.
Cling

**Korean monetary unit. 10,000 won = 10.65 USD**

# Step 2: Kang-Dae Gets Lost with Bong-Nam

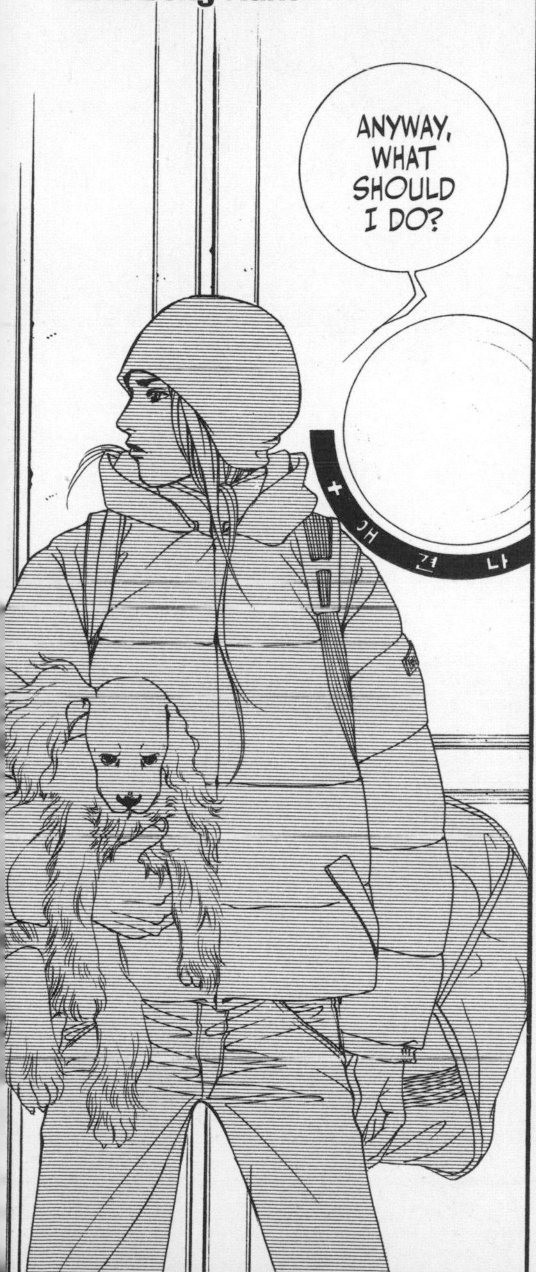
ANYWAY, WHAT SHOULD I DO?

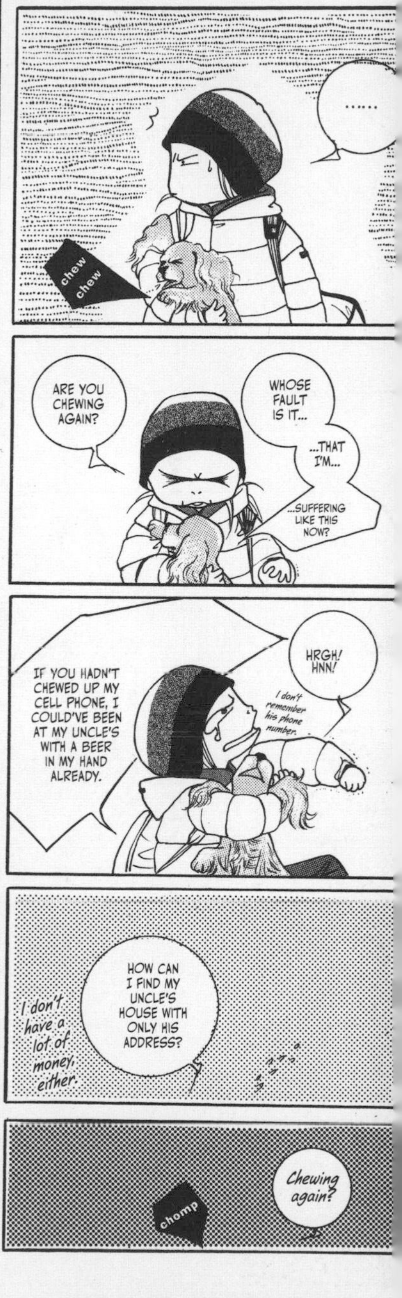
chew chew
......
ARE YOU CHEWING AGAIN?
WHOSE FAULT IS IT...
...THAT I'M...
...SUFFERING LIKE THIS NOW?
IF YOU HADN'T CHEWED UP MY CELL PHONE, I COULD'VE BEEN AT MY UNCLE'S WITH A BEER IN MY HAND ALREADY.
HRGH! HNN!
I don't remember his phone number.
I don't have a lot of money, either.
HOW CAN I FIND MY UNCLE'S HOUSE WITH ONLY HIS ADDRESS?
chomp
Chewing again?

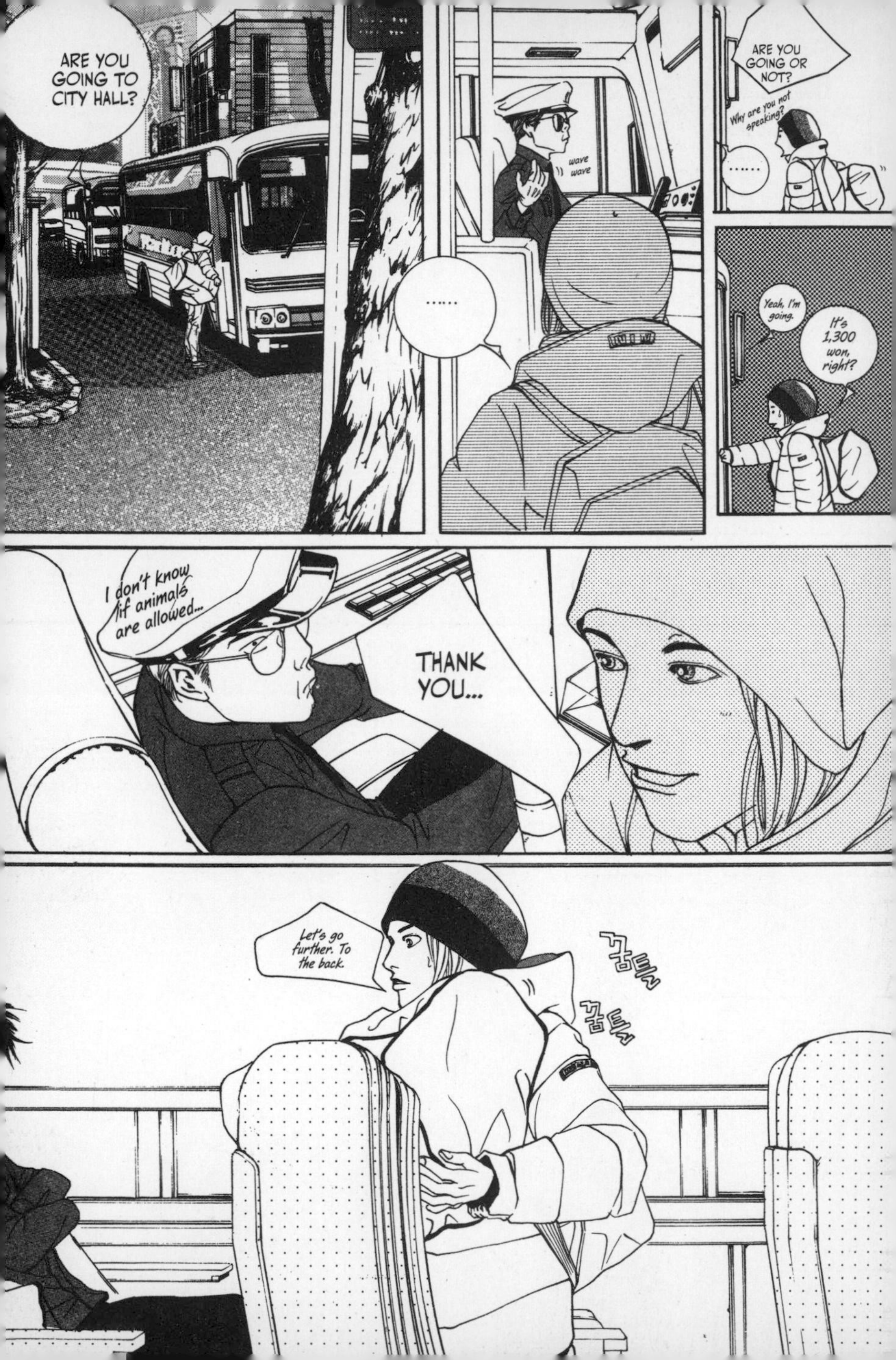

ARE YOU GOING TO CITY HALL?
wave wave
......
ARE YOU GOING OR NOT?
Why are you not speaking?
......
Yeah, I'm going.
It's 1,300 won, right?
I don't know if animals are allowed...
THANK YOU...
Let's go further. To the back.
꿈틀
꿈틀

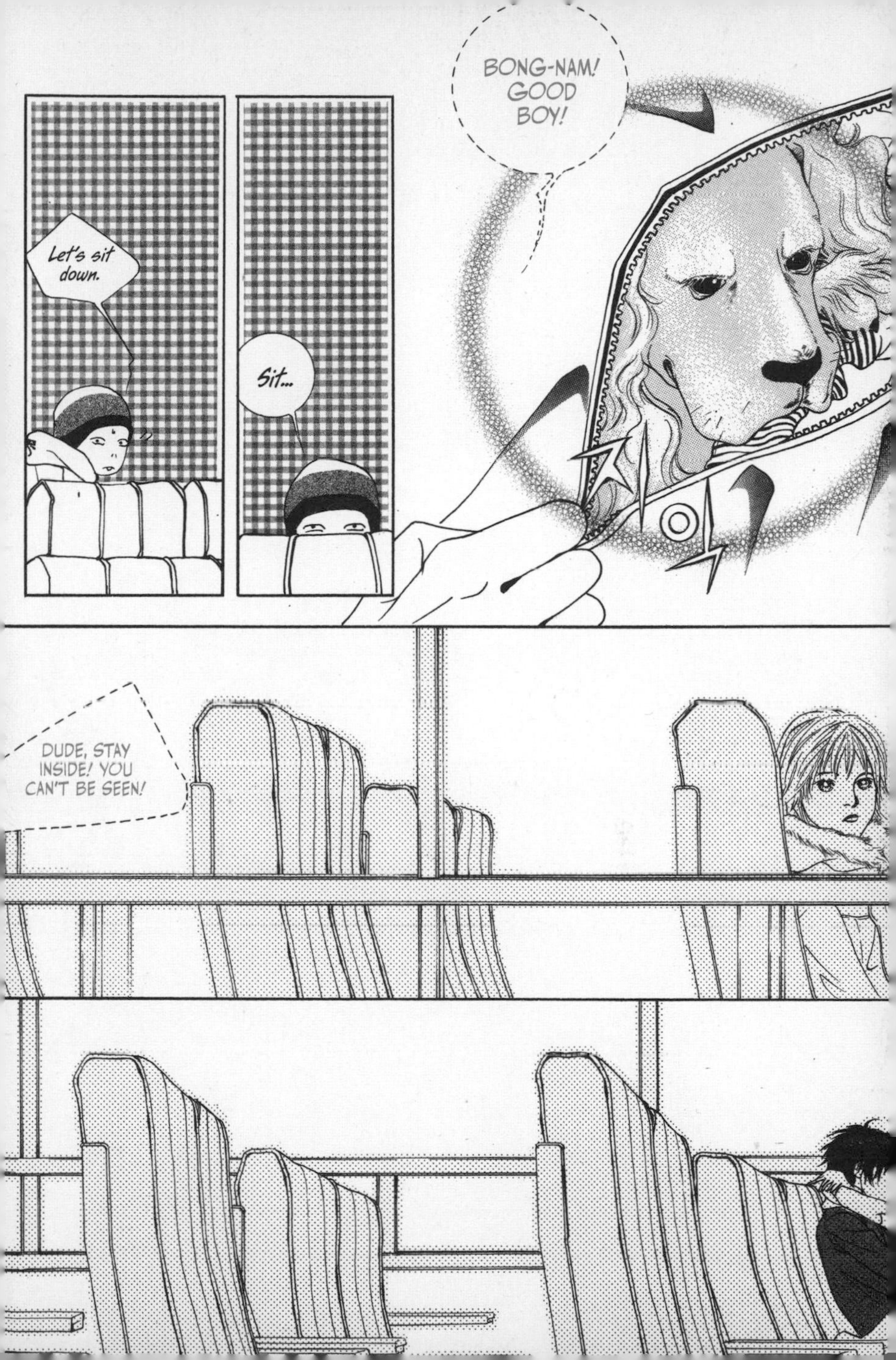
Let's sit down.
Sit...
BONG-NAM! GOOD BOY!
DUDE, STAY INSIDE! YOU CAN'T BE SEEN!

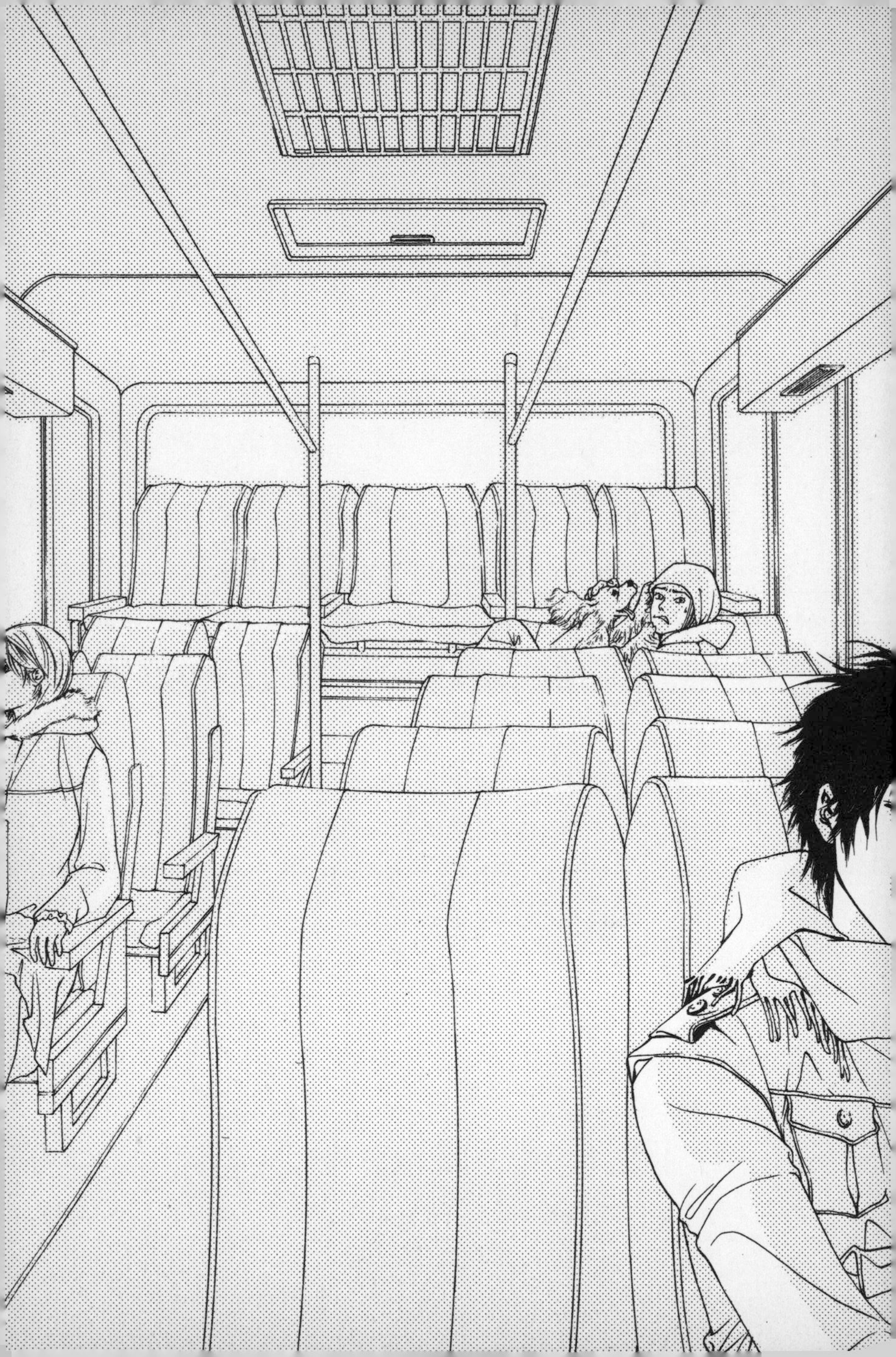

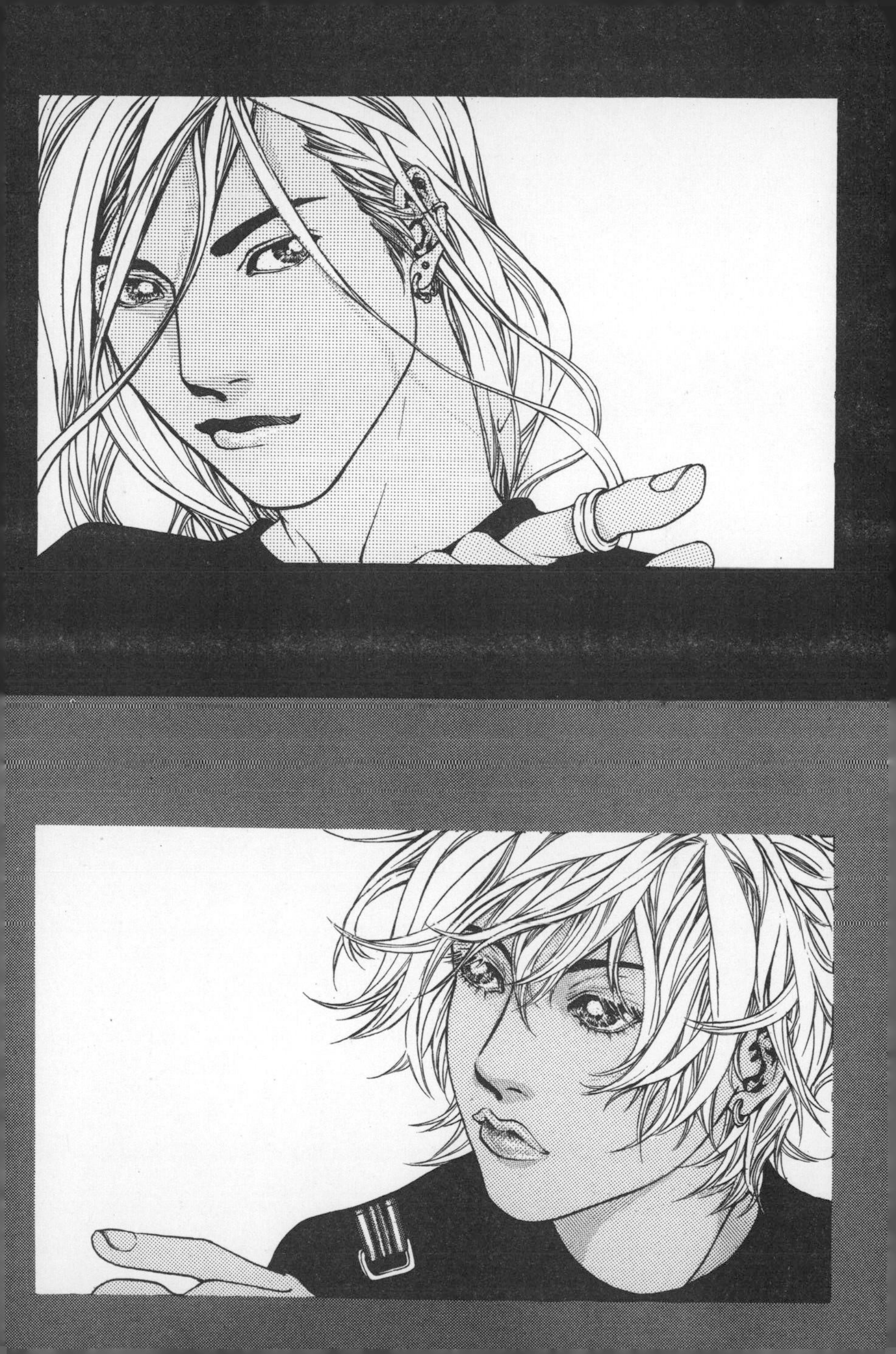

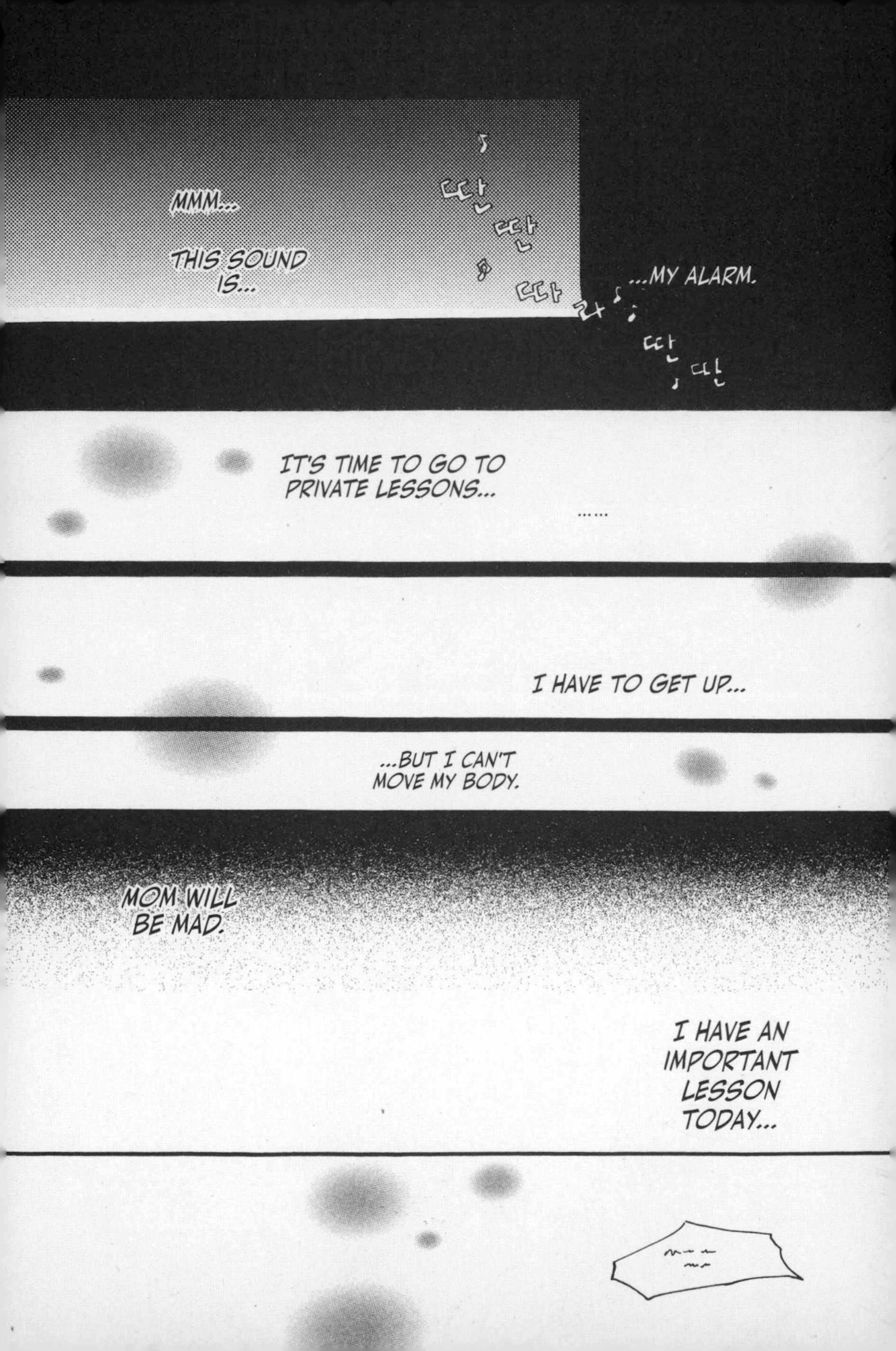
MMM...
THIS SOUND IS...
딴 딴 따라
...MY ALARM.
딴 띤
IT'S TIME TO GO TO PRIVATE LESSONS...
......
I HAVE TO GET UP...
...BUT I CAN'T MOVE MY BODY.
MOM WILL BE MAD.
I HAVE AN IMPORTANT LESSON TODAY...

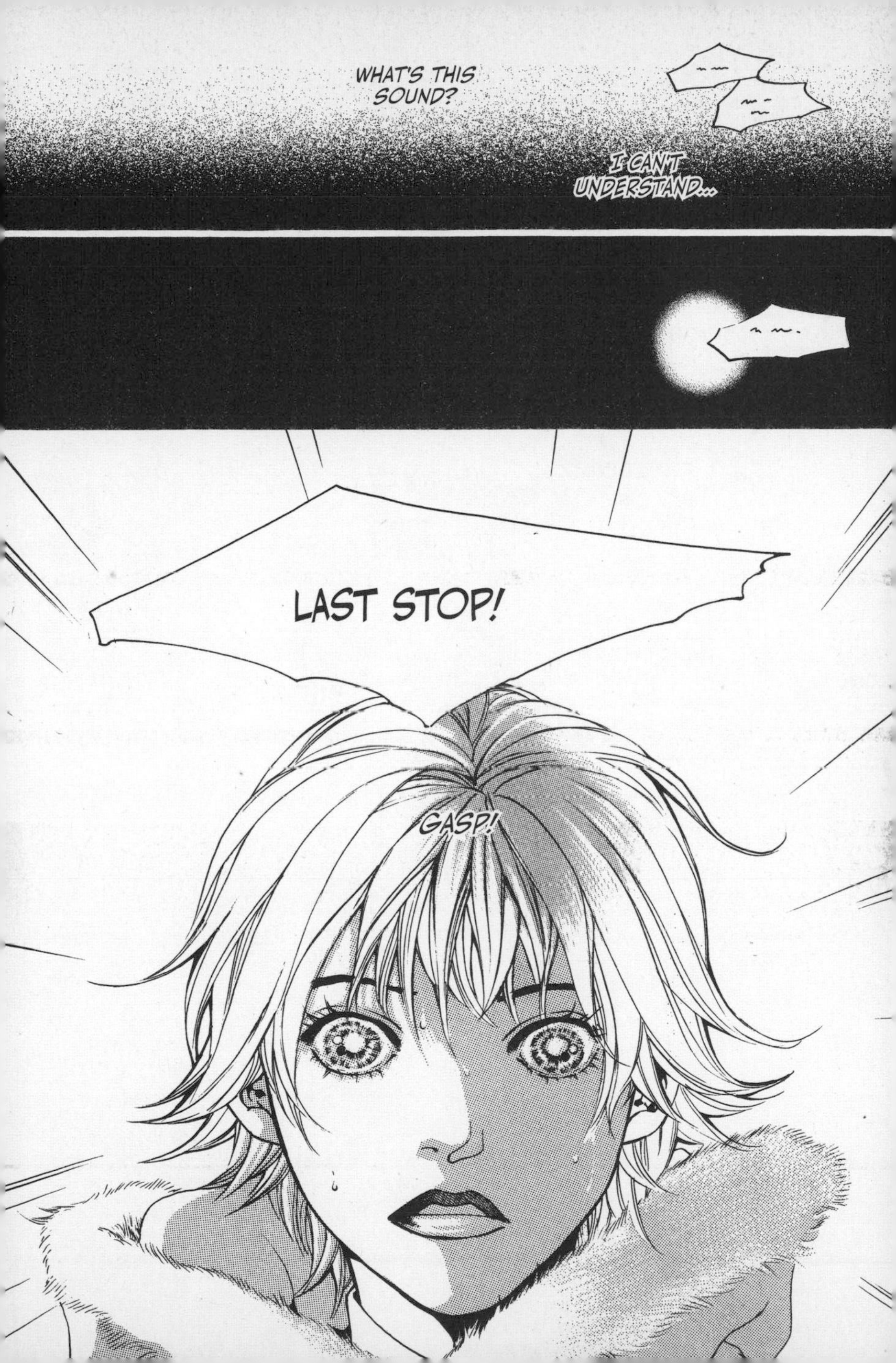
WHAT'S THIS SOUND?
I CAN'T UNDERSTAND...
LAST STOP!
GASP!

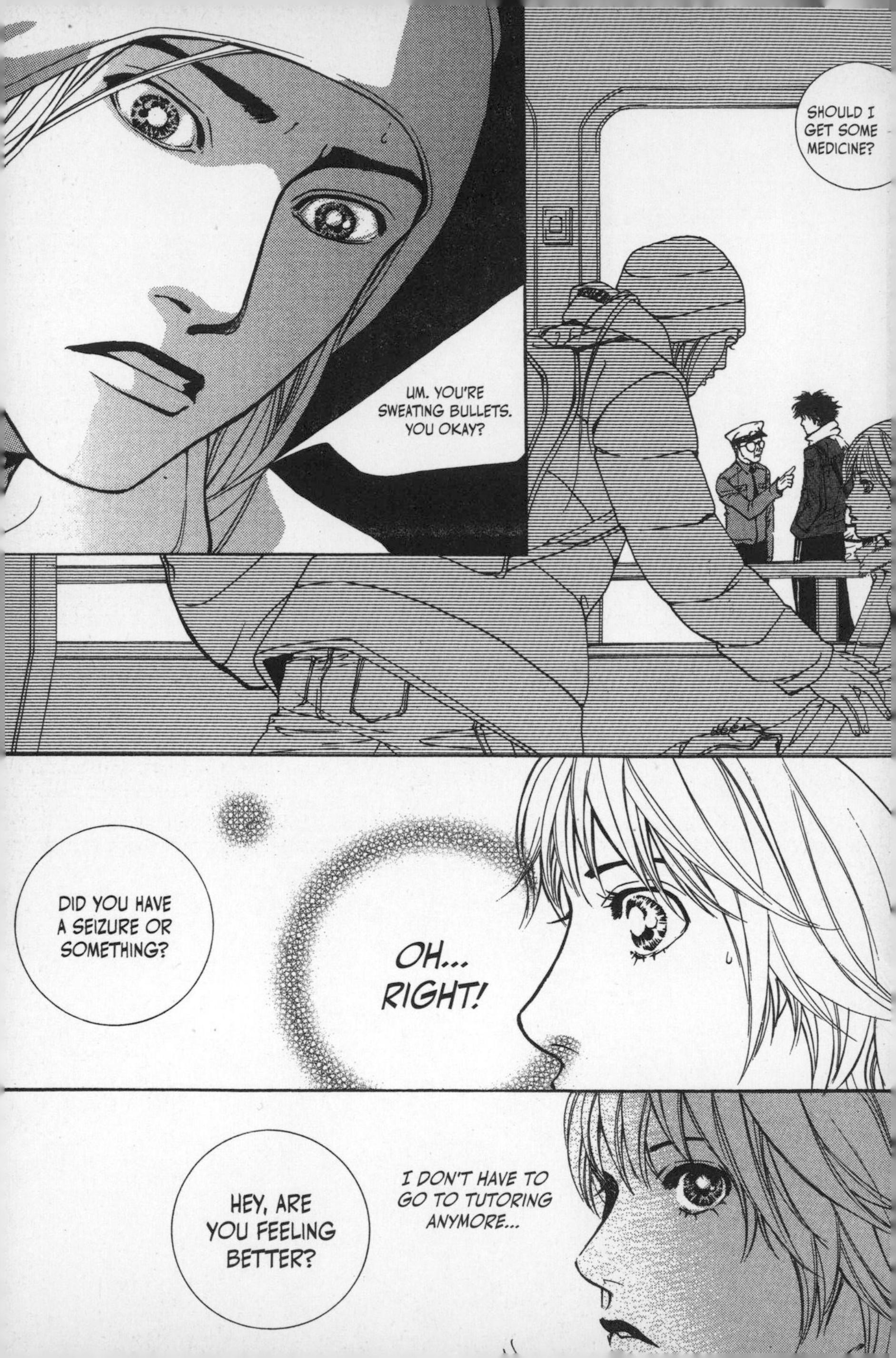
UM. YOU'RE SWEATING BULLETS. YOU OKAY?
SHOULD I GET SOME MEDICINE?
DID YOU HAVE A SEIZURE OR SOMETHING?
OH... RIGHT!
HEY, ARE YOU FEELING BETTER?
I DON'T HAVE TO GO TO TUTORING ANYMORE...

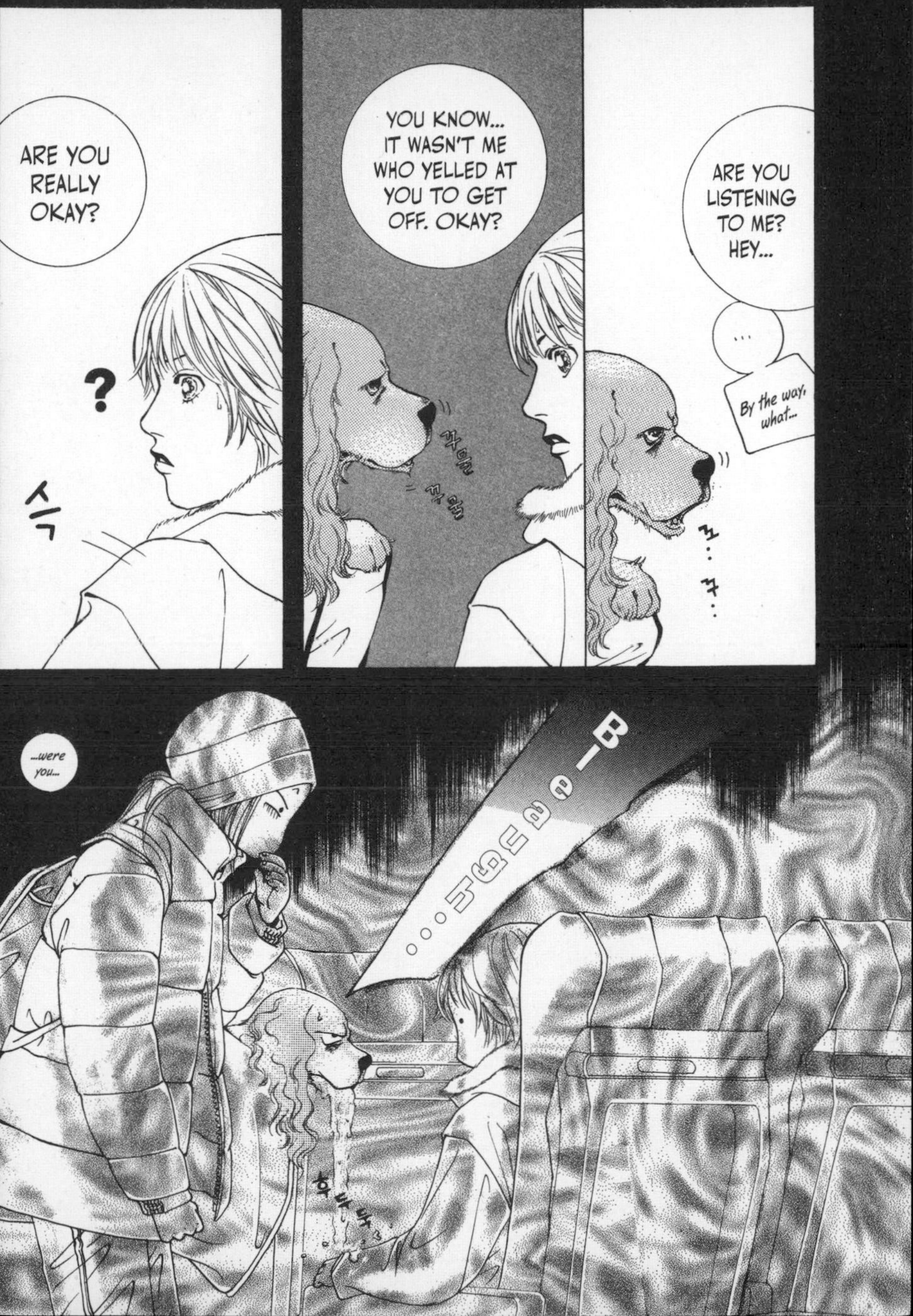
ARE YOU REALLY OKAY?
?
YOU KNOW... IT WASN'T ME WHO YELLED AT YOU TO GET OFF. OKAY?
ARE YOU LISTENING TO ME? HEY...
...
By the way, what...
...were you...
B—eagle...

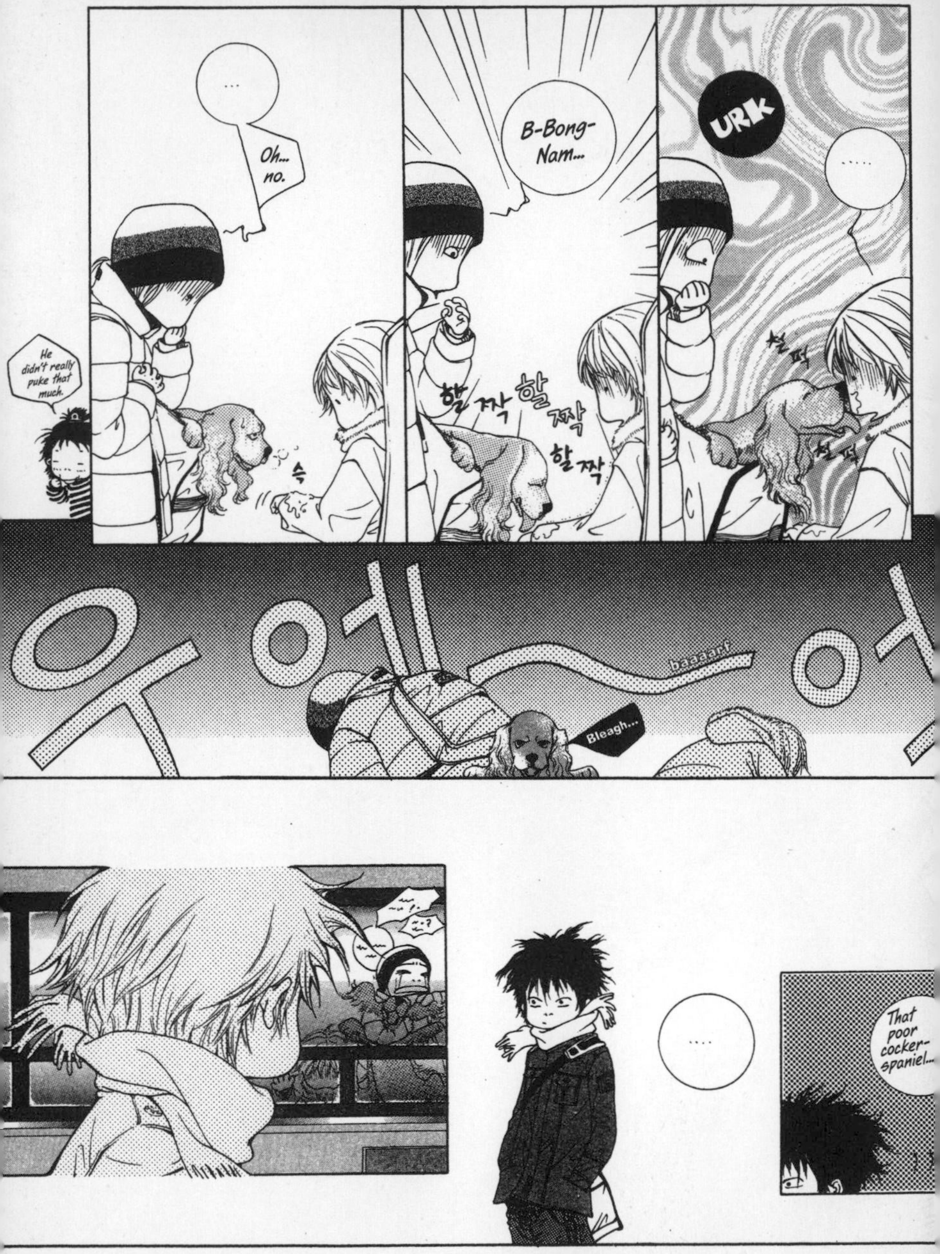
He didn't really puke that much.
...
Oh... no.
슥
B-Bong-Nam...
할짝 할짝
할짝
URK
.....
baaaarf
Bleagh...
...
That poor cocker-spaniel...

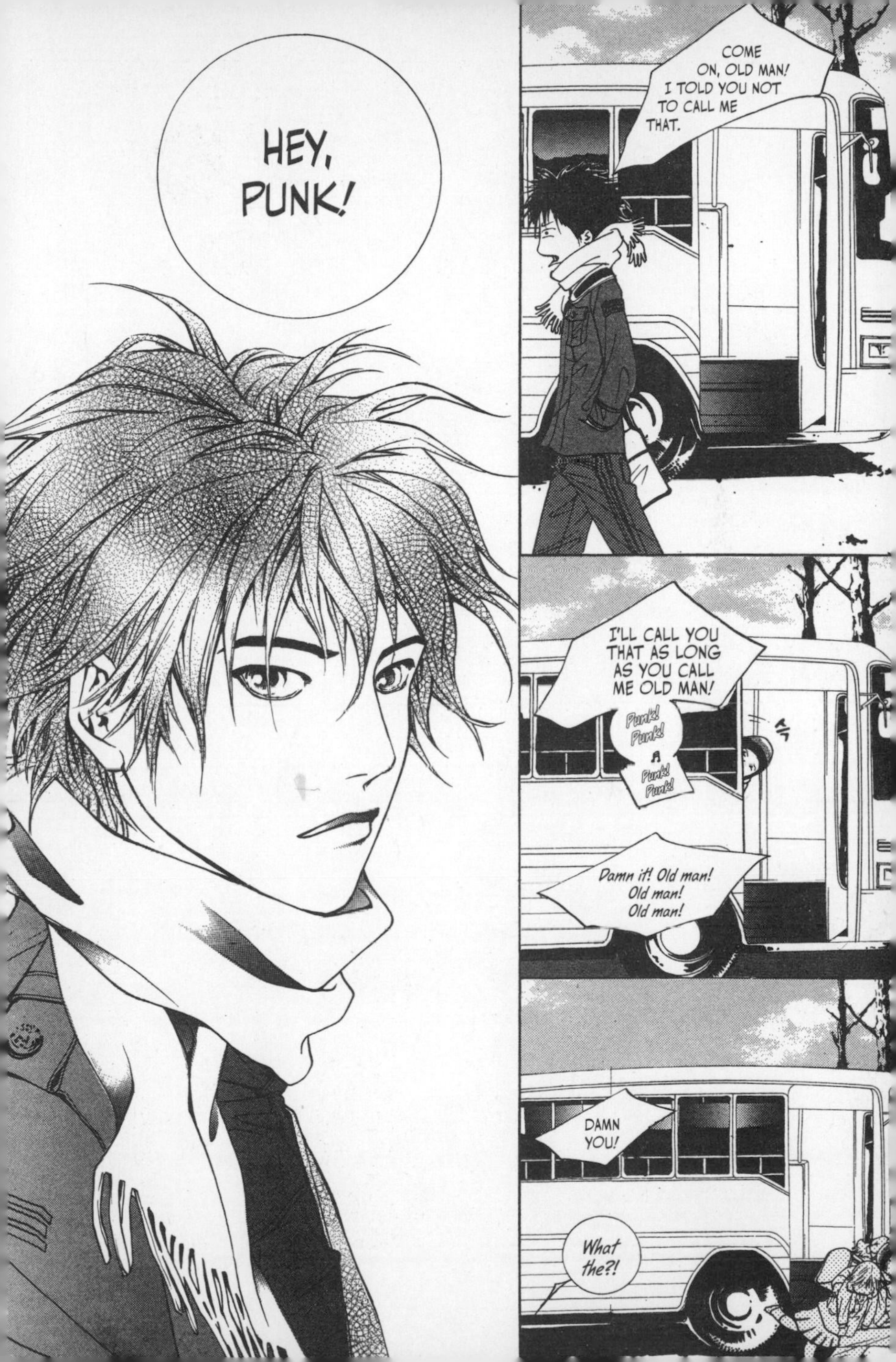
HEY, PUNK!
COME ON, OLD MAN! I TOLD YOU NOT TO CALL ME THAT.
I'LL CALL YOU THAT AS LONG AS YOU CALL ME OLD MAN!
Punk! Punk!
Punk! Punk!
Damn it! Old man! Old man! Old man!
DAMN YOU!
What the?!

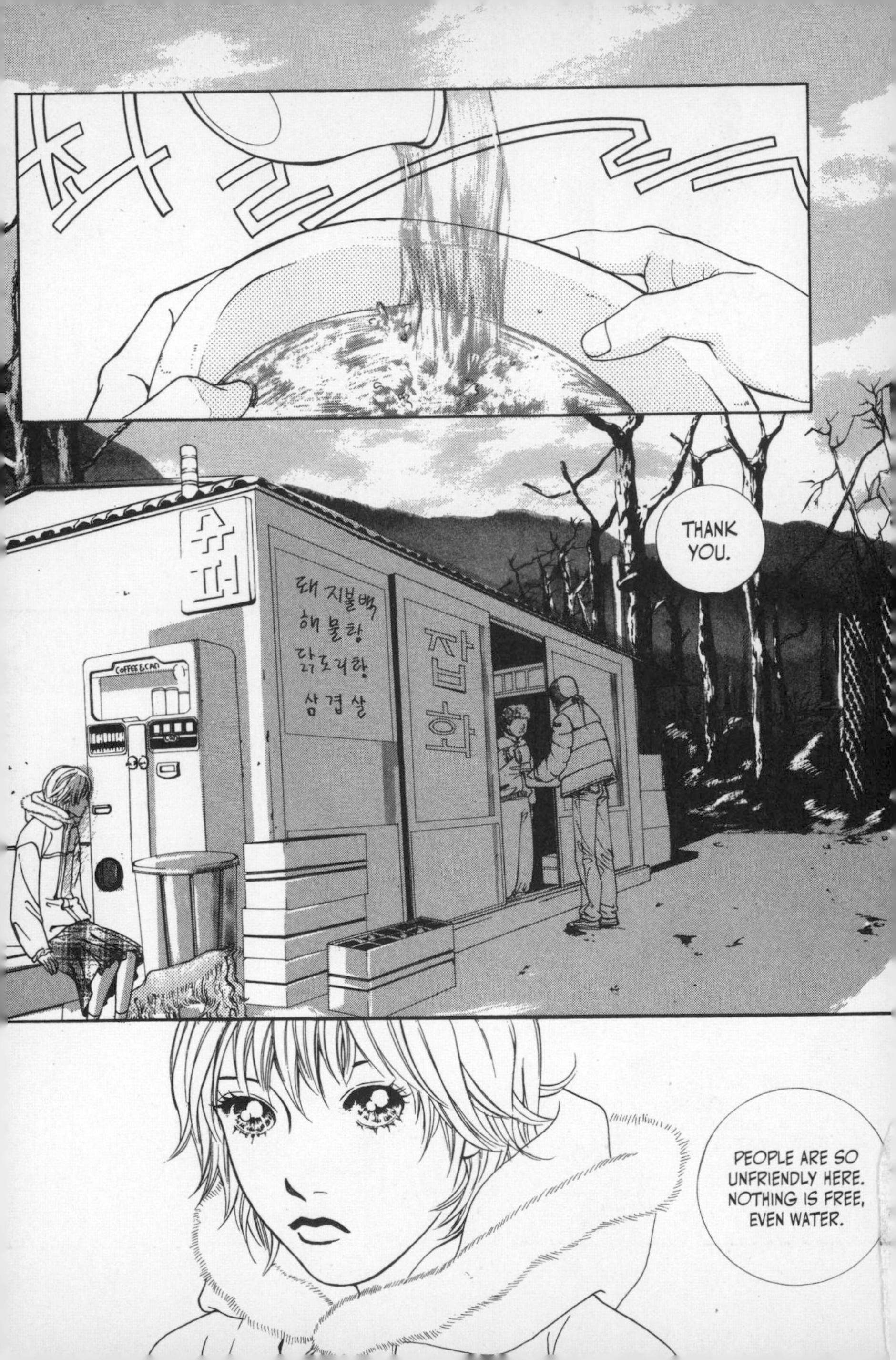
수퍼
돼지불백
해물탕
닭도리탕
삼겹살
잡화
COFFEE & CAN
THANK YOU.
PEOPLE ARE SO UNFRIENDLY HERE. NOTHING IS FREE, EVEN WATER.

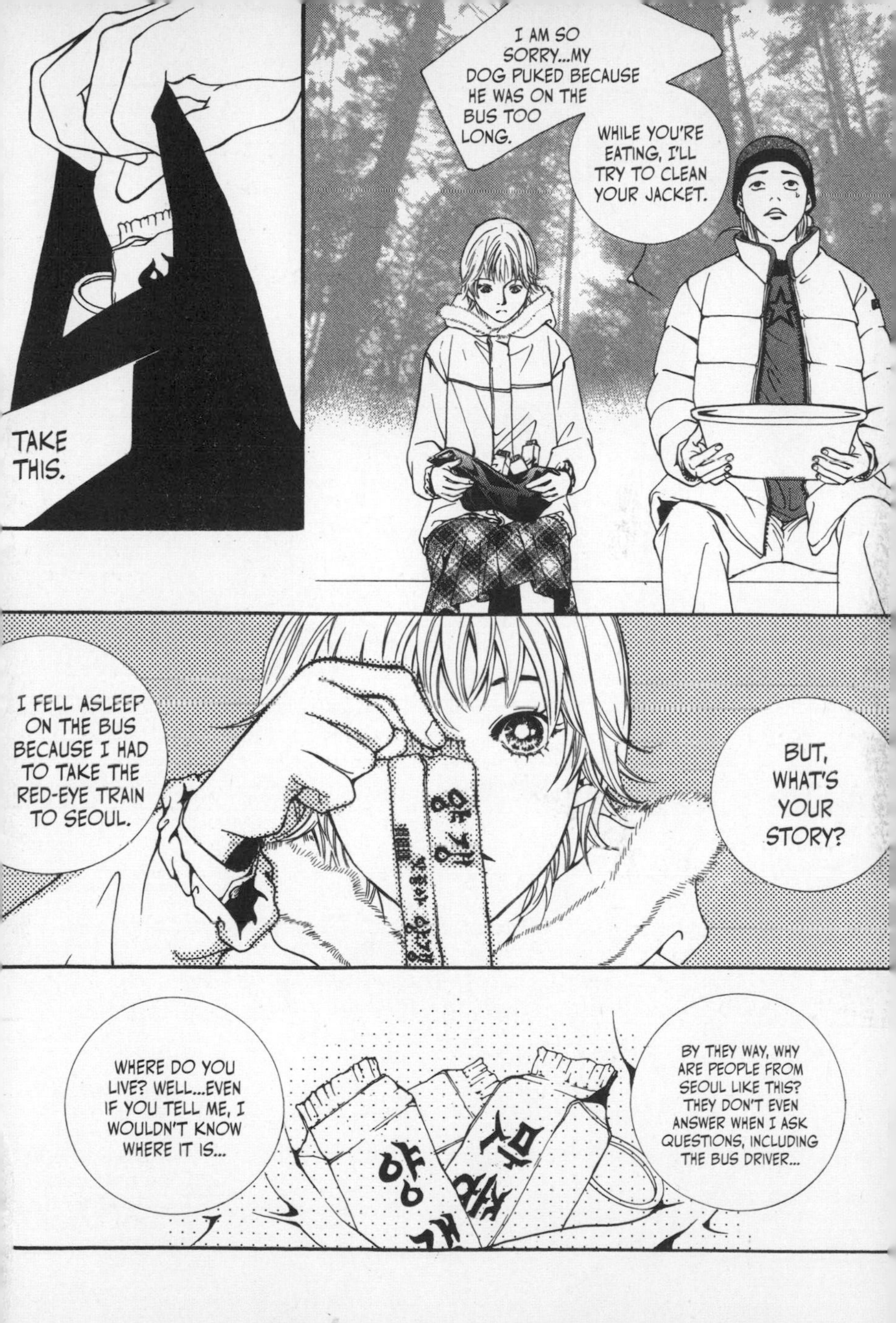
TAKE THIS.
I AM SO SORRY...MY DOG PUKED BECAUSE HE WAS ON THE BUS TOO LONG.
WHILE YOU'RE EATING, I'LL TRY TO CLEAN YOUR JACKET.
I FELL ASLEEP ON THE BUS BECAUSE I HAD TO TAKE THE RED-EYE TRAIN TO SEOUL.
BUT, WHAT'S YOUR STORY?
WHERE DO YOU LIVE? WELL...EVEN IF YOU TELL ME, I WOULDN'T KNOW WHERE IT IS...
BY THEY WAY, WHY ARE PEOPLE FROM SEOUL LIKE THIS? THEY DON'T EVEN ANSWER WHEN I ASK QUESTIONS, INCLUDING THE BUS DRIVER...

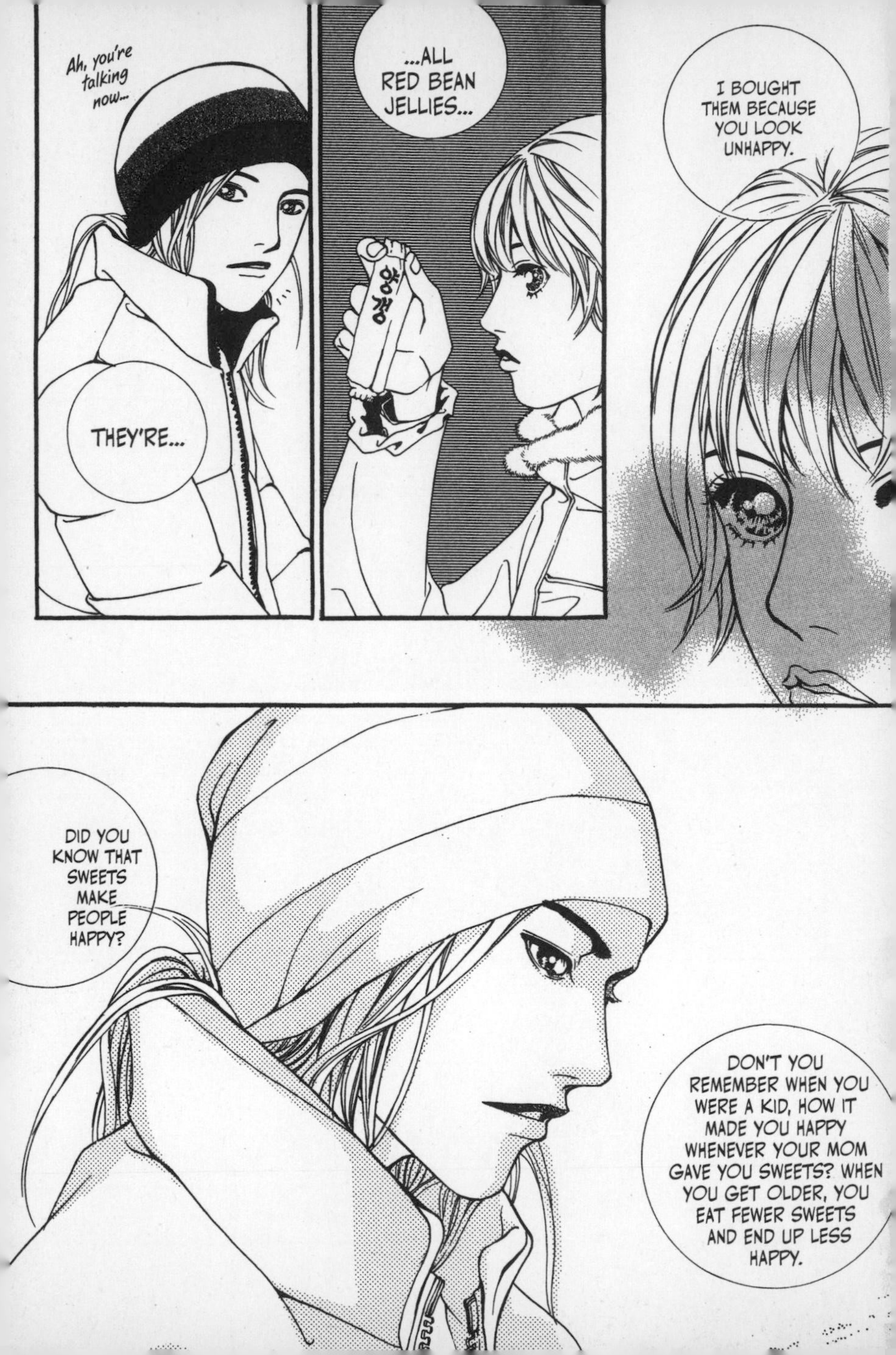
Ah, you're talking now...
THEY'RE...
...ALL RED BEAN JELLIES...
양갱
I BOUGHT THEM BECAUSE YOU LOOK UNHAPPY.
DID YOU KNOW THAT SWEETS MAKE PEOPLE HAPPY?
DON'T YOU REMEMBER WHEN YOU WERE A KID, HOW IT MADE YOU HAPPY WHENEVER YOUR MOM GAVE YOU SWEETS? WHEN YOU GET OLDER, YOU EAT FEWER SWEETS AND END UP LESS HAPPY.

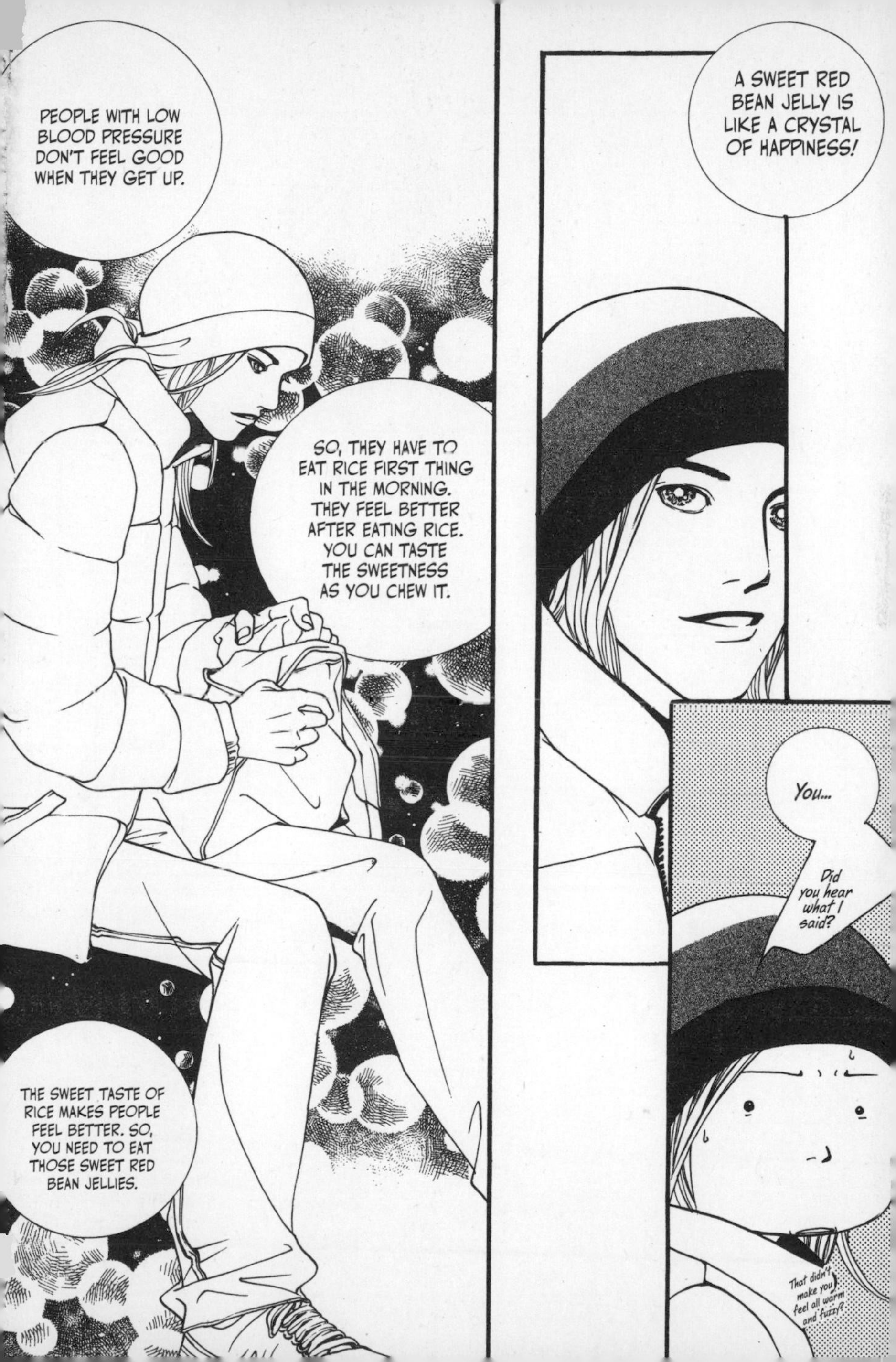
PEOPLE WITH LOW BLOOD PRESSURE DON'T FEEL GOOD WHEN THEY GET UP.
SO, THEY HAVE TO EAT RICE FIRST THING IN THE MORNING. THEY FEEL BETTER AFTER EATING RICE. YOU CAN TASTE THE SWEETNESS AS YOU CHEW IT.
THE SWEET TASTE OF RICE MAKES PEOPLE FEEL BETTER. SO, YOU NEED TO EAT THOSE SWEET RED BEAN JELLIES.
A SWEET RED BEAN JELLY IS LIKE A CRYSTAL OF HAPPINESS!
You...
Did you hear what I said?
That didn't make you feel all warm and fuzzy?

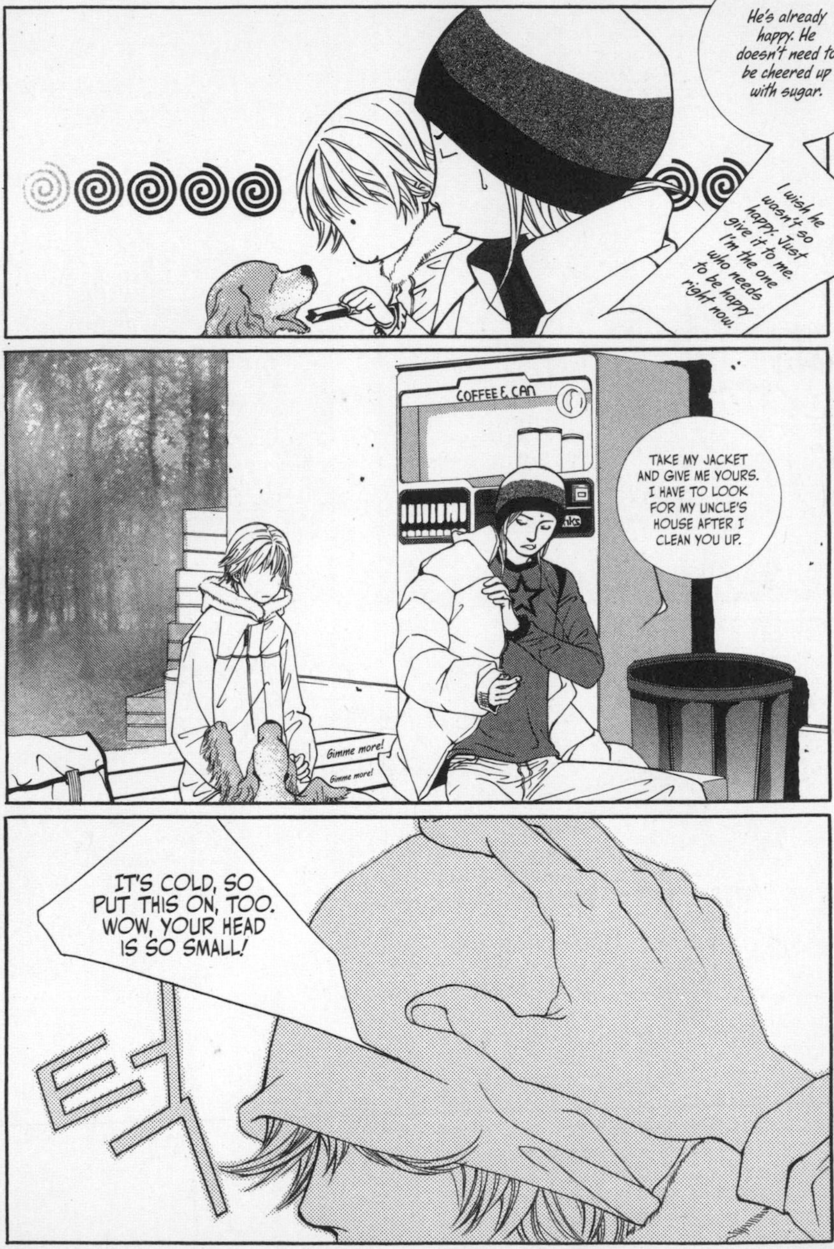
He's already happy. He doesn't need to be cheered up with sugar.
I wish he wasn't so happy. Just give it to me. I'm the one who needs to be happy right now.
COFFEE & CAN
TAKE MY JACKET AND GIVE ME YOURS. I HAVE TO LOOK FOR MY UNCLE'S HOUSE AFTER I CLEAN YOU UP.
Gimme more!
Gimme more!
IT'S COLD, SO PUT THIS ON, TOO. WOW, YOUR HEAD IS SO SMALL!

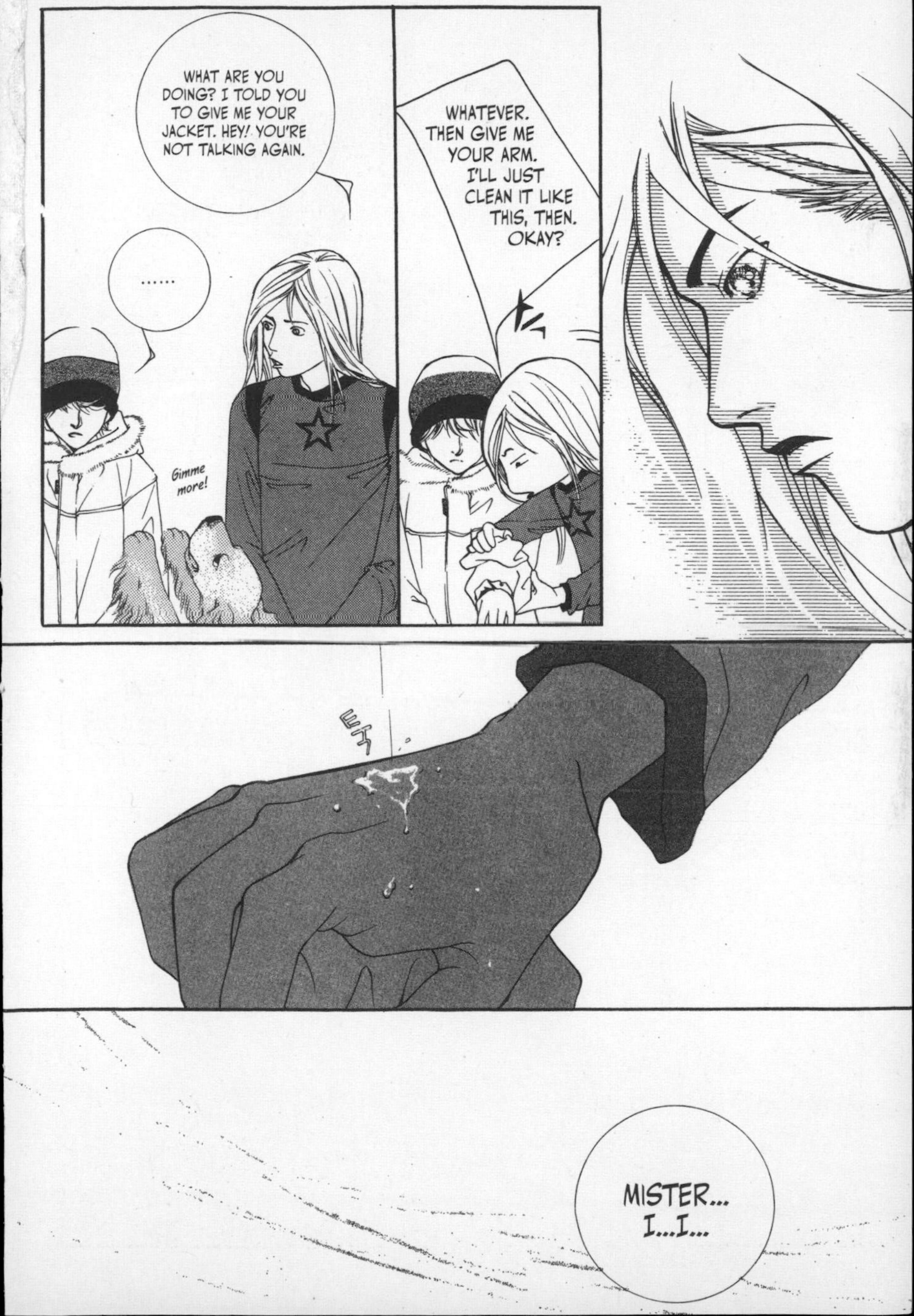
WHAT ARE YOU DOING? I TOLD YOU TO GIVE ME YOUR JACKET. HEY! YOU'RE NOT TALKING AGAIN.
......
Gimme more!
WHATEVER. THEN GIVE ME YOUR ARM. I'LL JUST CLEAN IT LIKE THIS, THEN. OKAY?
MISTER... I...I...

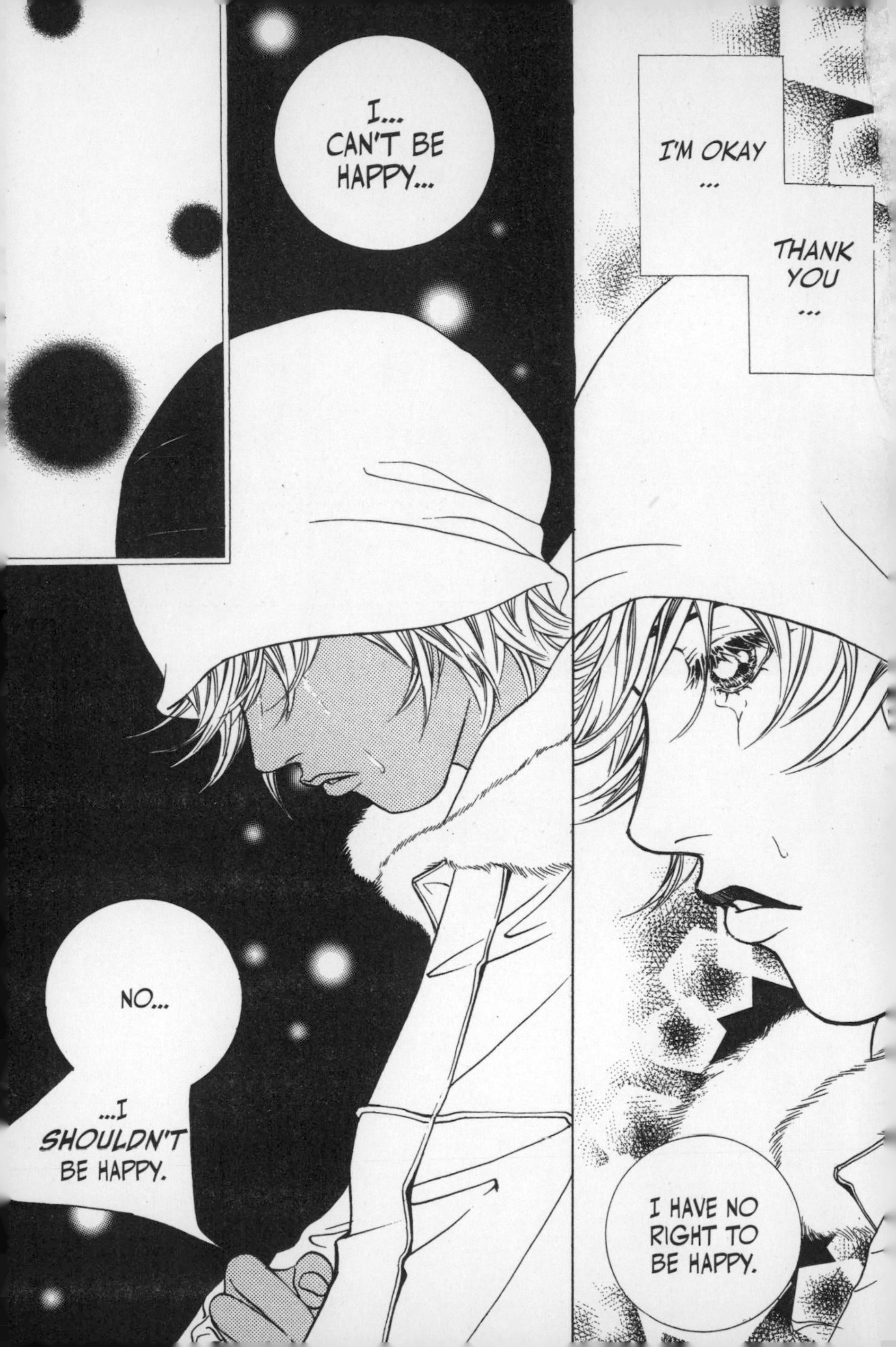
I... CAN'T BE HAPPY...
NO...
...I *SHOULDN'T* BE HAPPY.
I'M OKAY ...
THANK YOU ...
I HAVE NO RIGHT TO BE HAPPY.

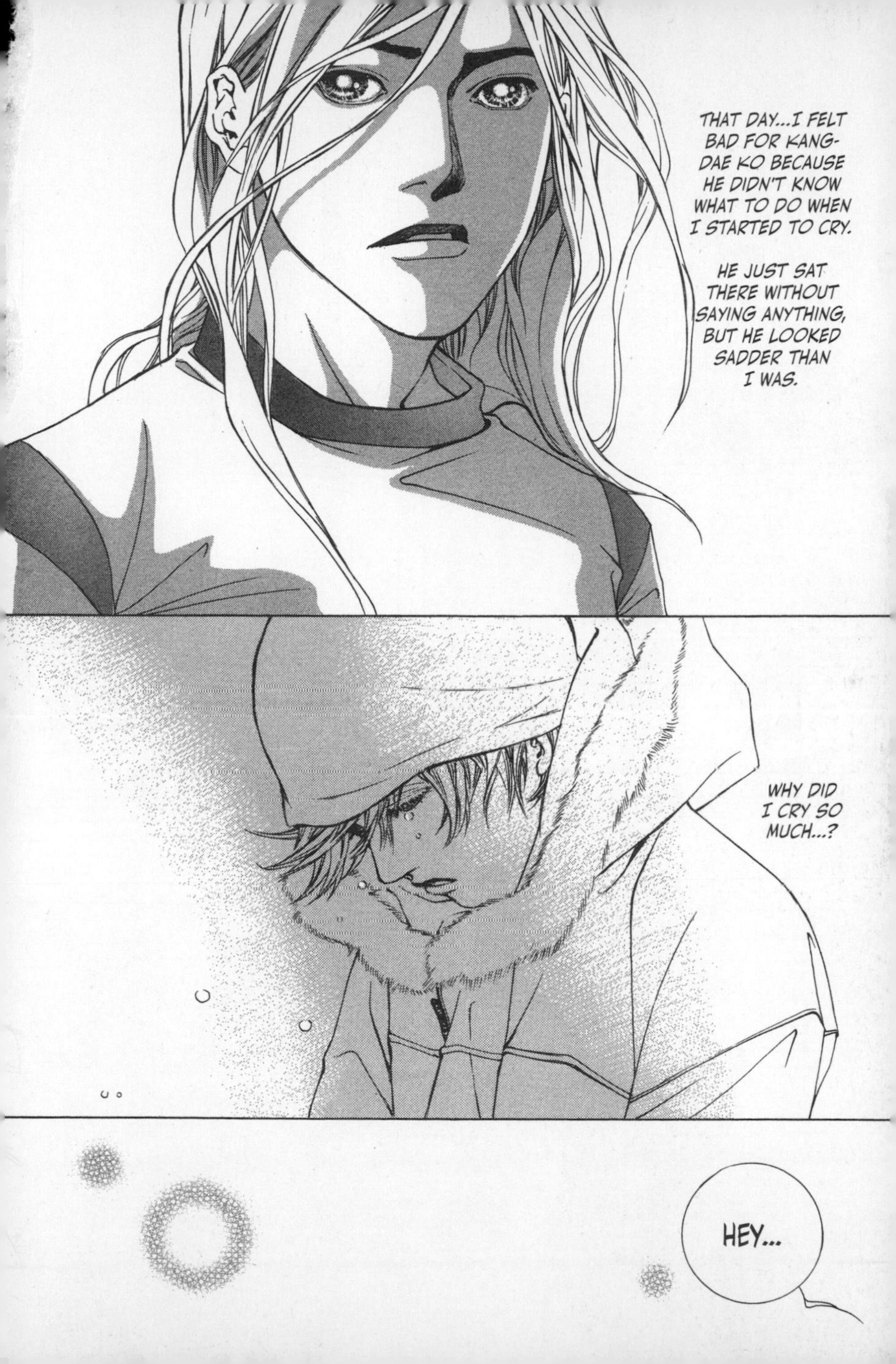
THAT DAY...I FELT BAD FOR KANG-DAE KO BECAUSE HE DIDN'T KNOW WHAT TO DO WHEN I STARTED TO CRY.
HE JUST SAT THERE WITHOUT SAYING ANYTHING, BUT HE LOOKED SADDER THAN I WAS.
WHY DID I CRY SO MUCH...?
HEY...

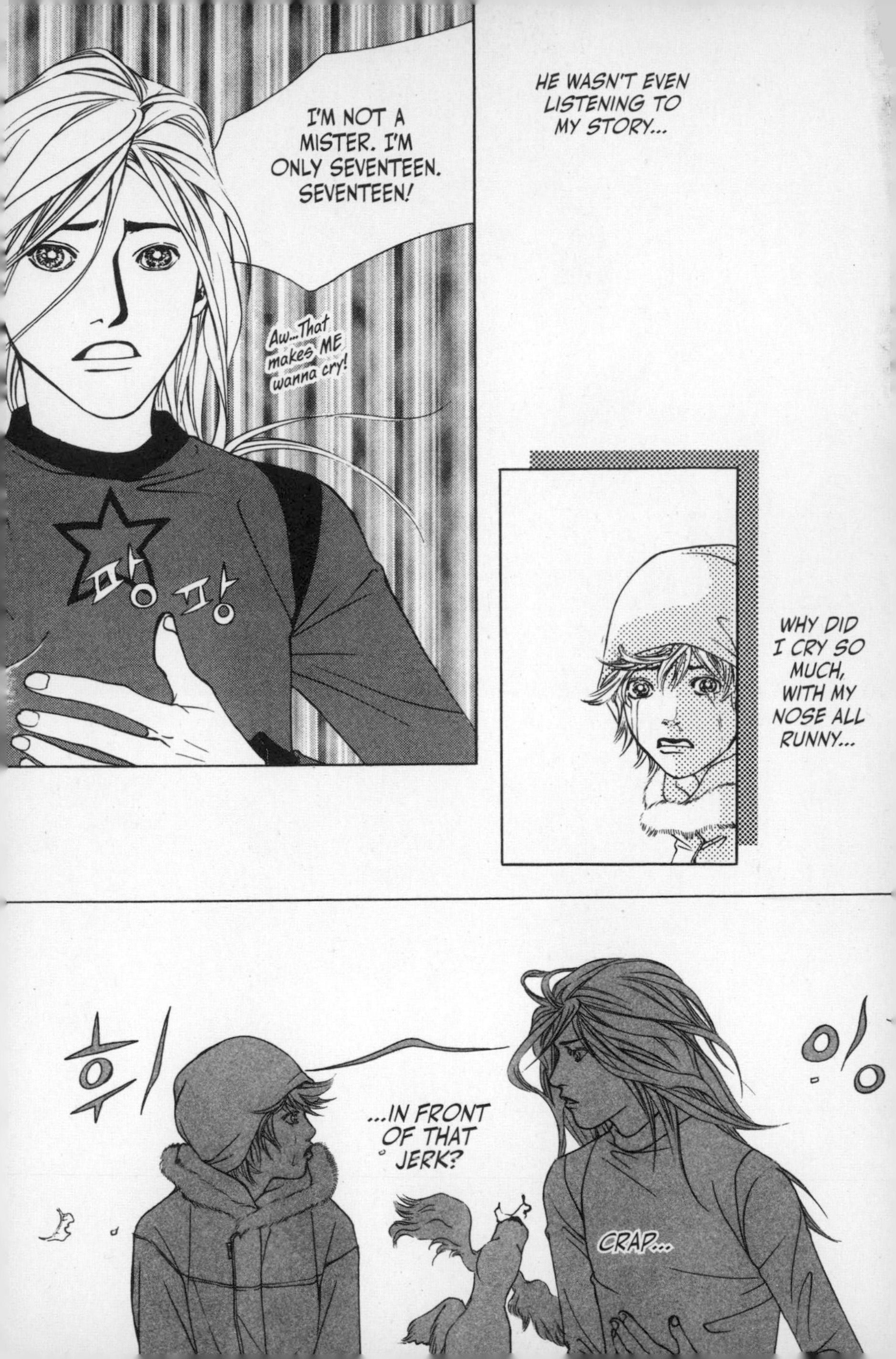
I'M NOT A MISTER. I'M ONLY SEVENTEEN. SEVENTEEN!
Aw...That makes ME wanna cry!
HE WASN'T EVEN LISTENING TO MY STORY...
WHY DID I CRY SO MUCH, WITH MY NOSE ALL RUNNY...
...IN FRONT OF THAT JERK?
CRAP...

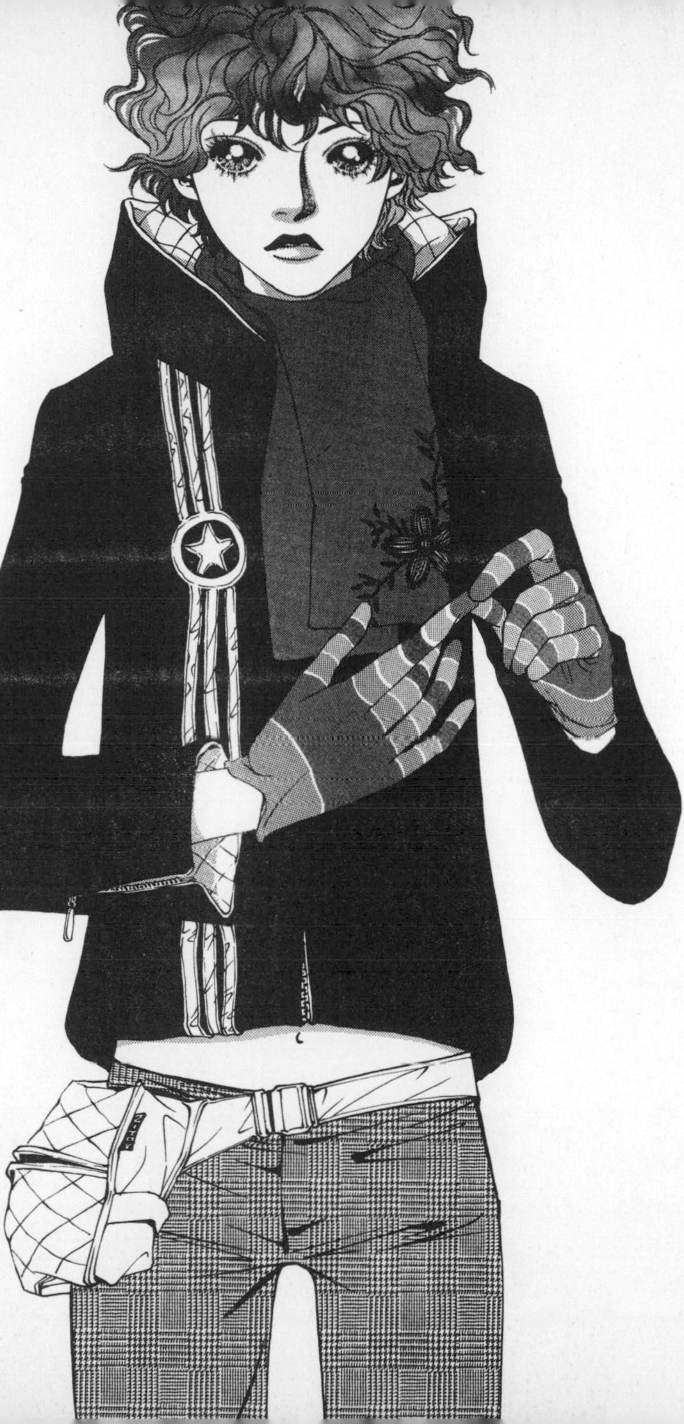

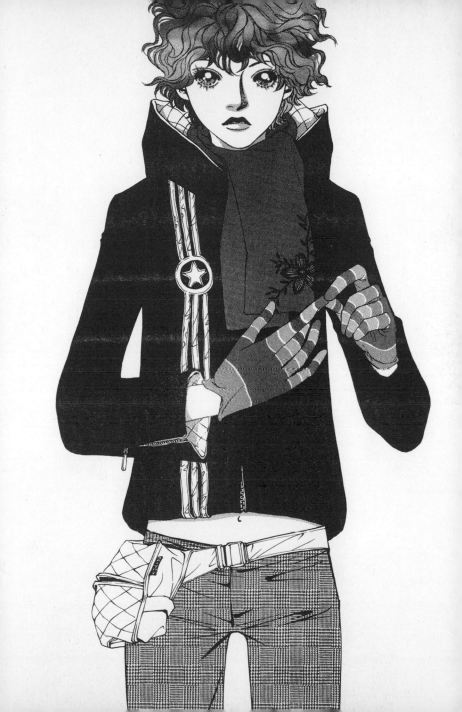

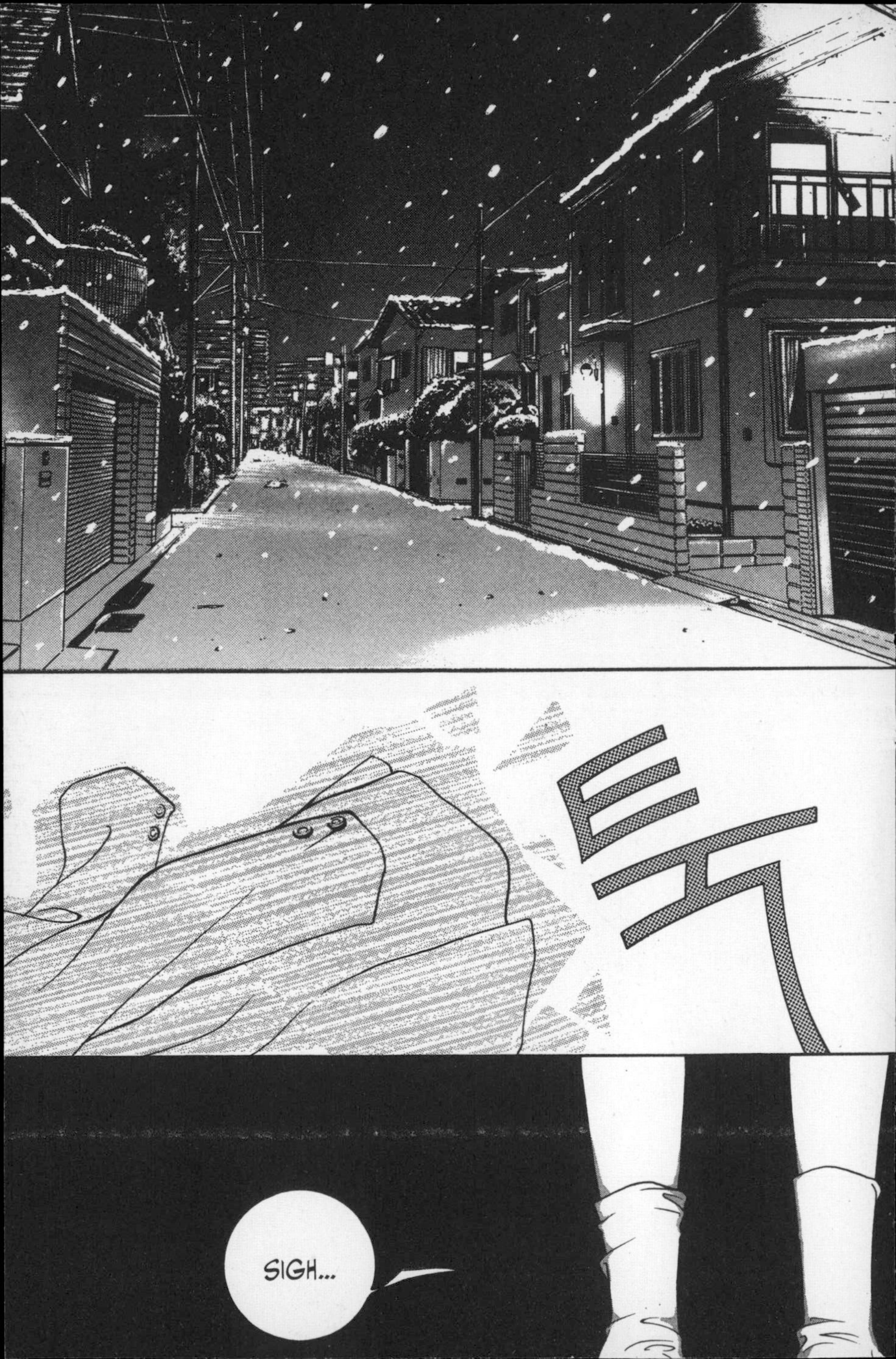
SIGH...

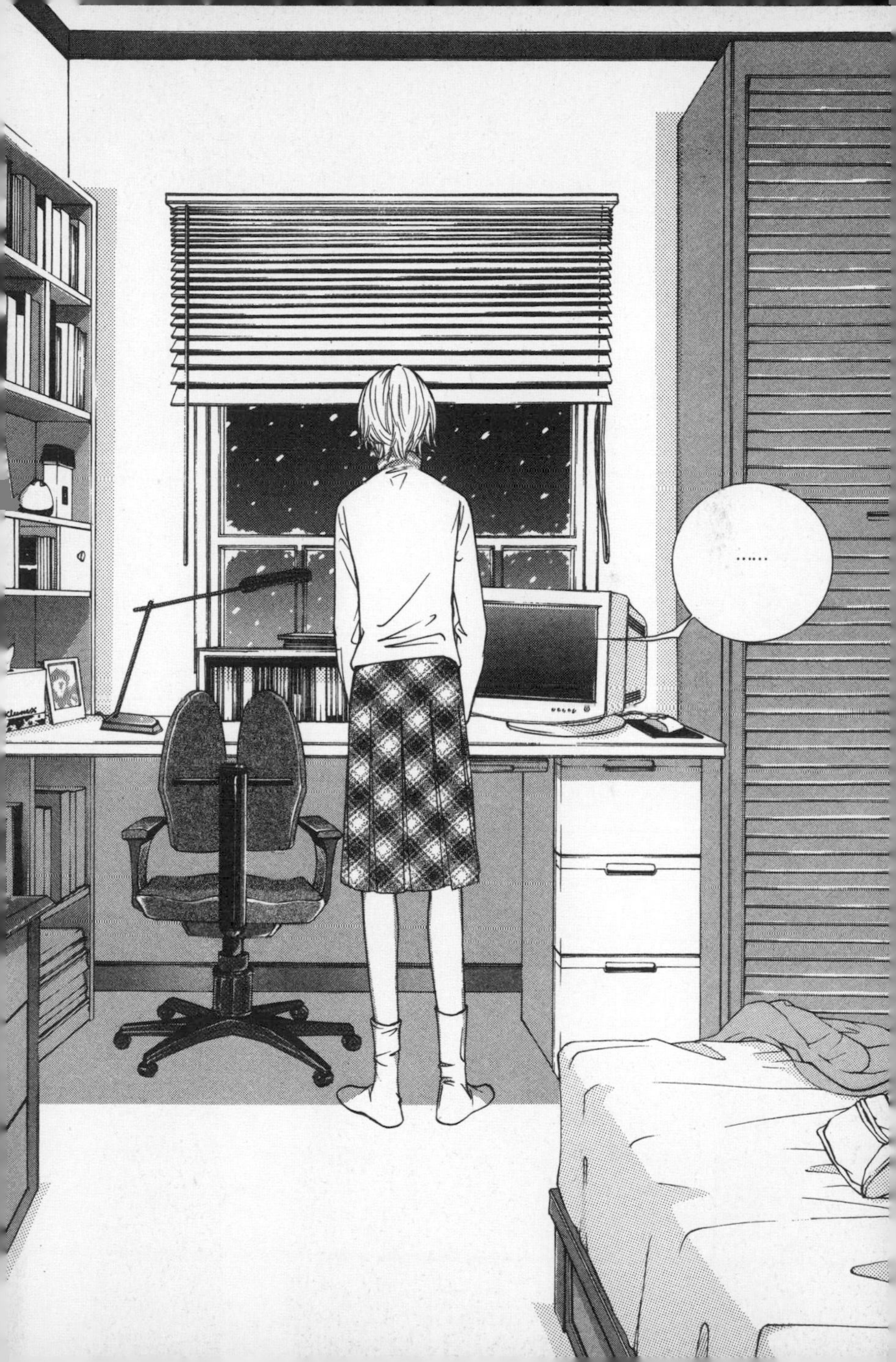
……

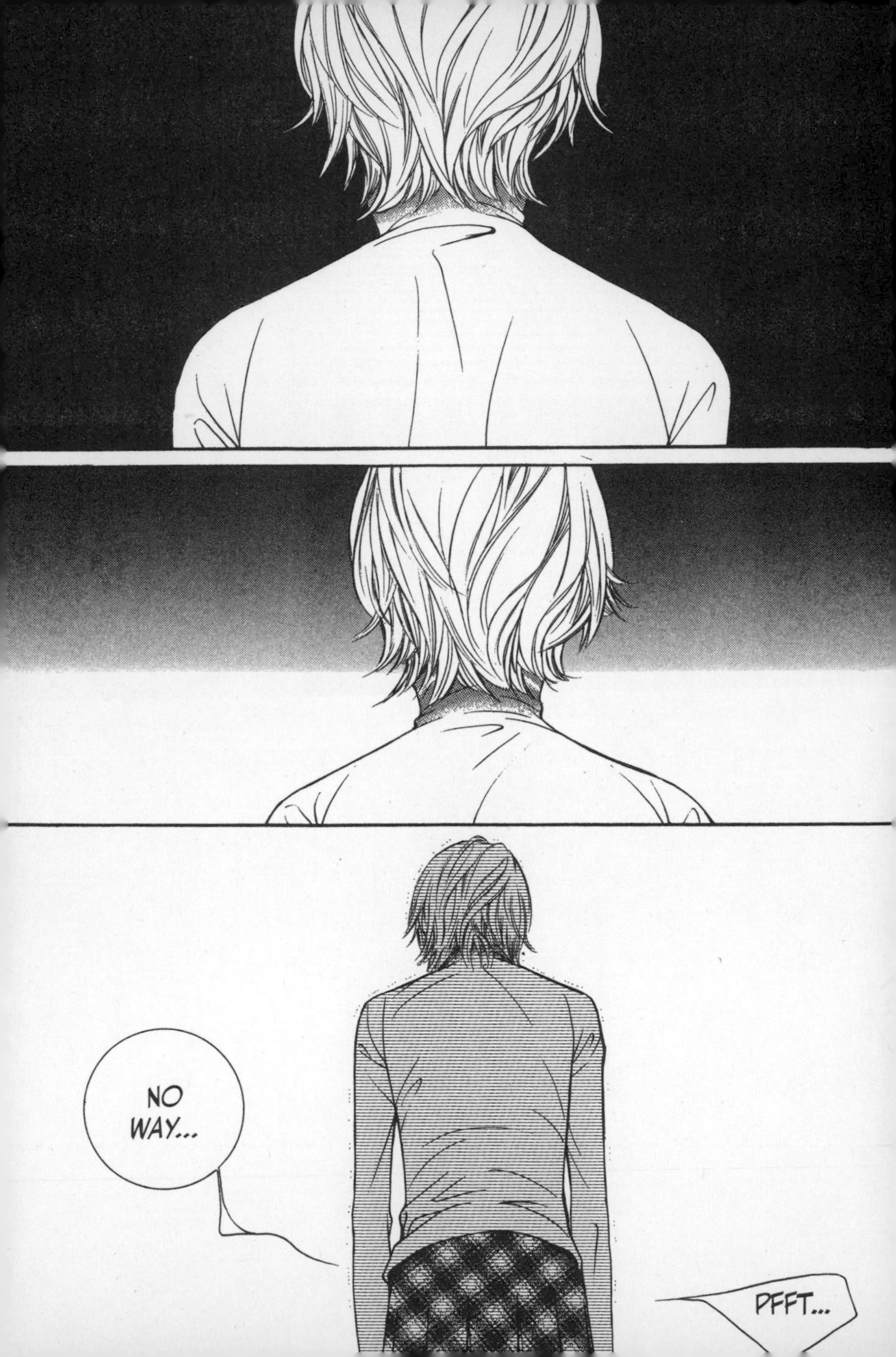
NO WAY...
PFFT...

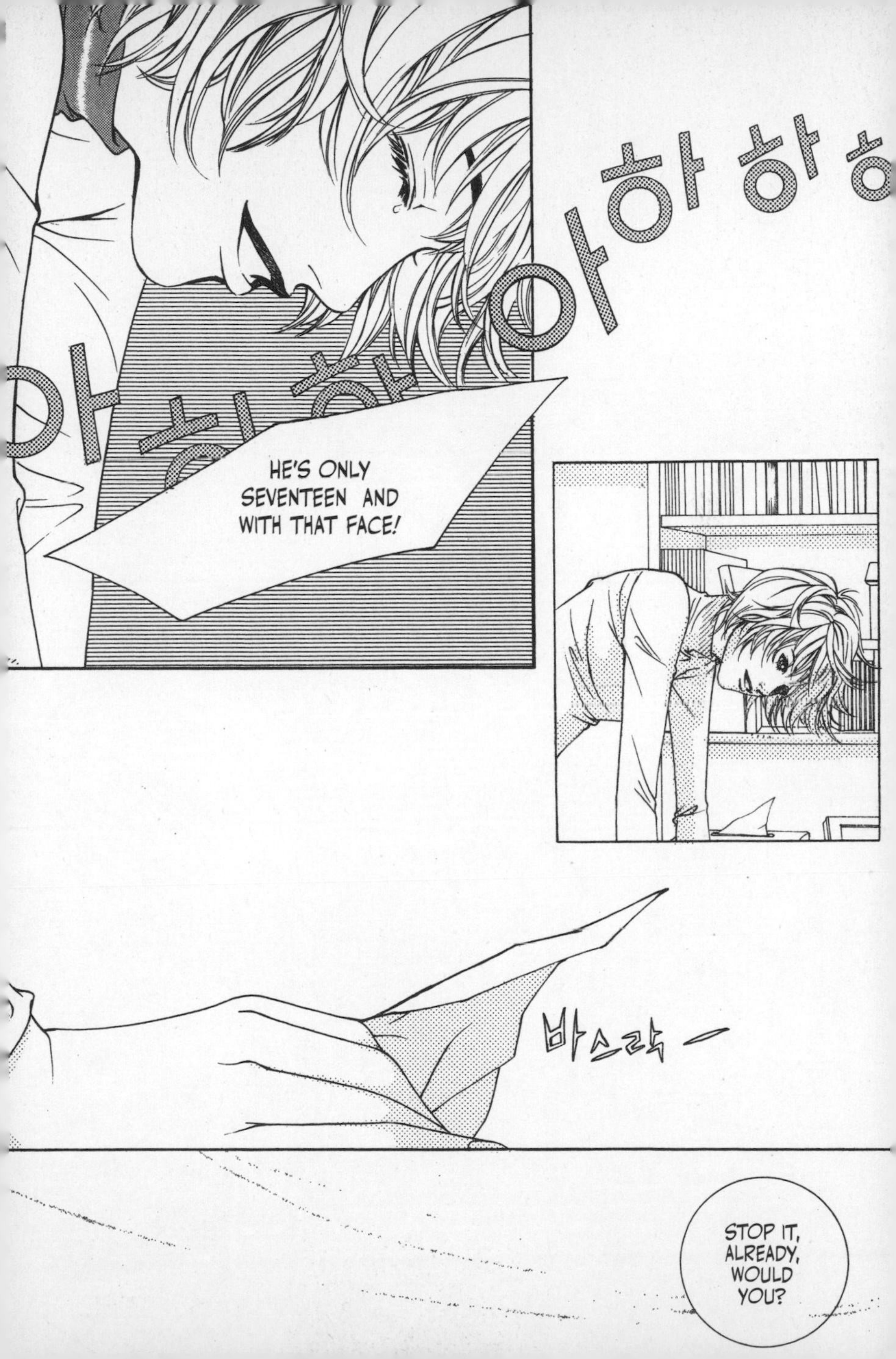
아하하아하하
HE'S ONLY SEVENTEEN AND WITH THAT FACE!
바스락 —
STOP IT, ALREADY, WOULD YOU?

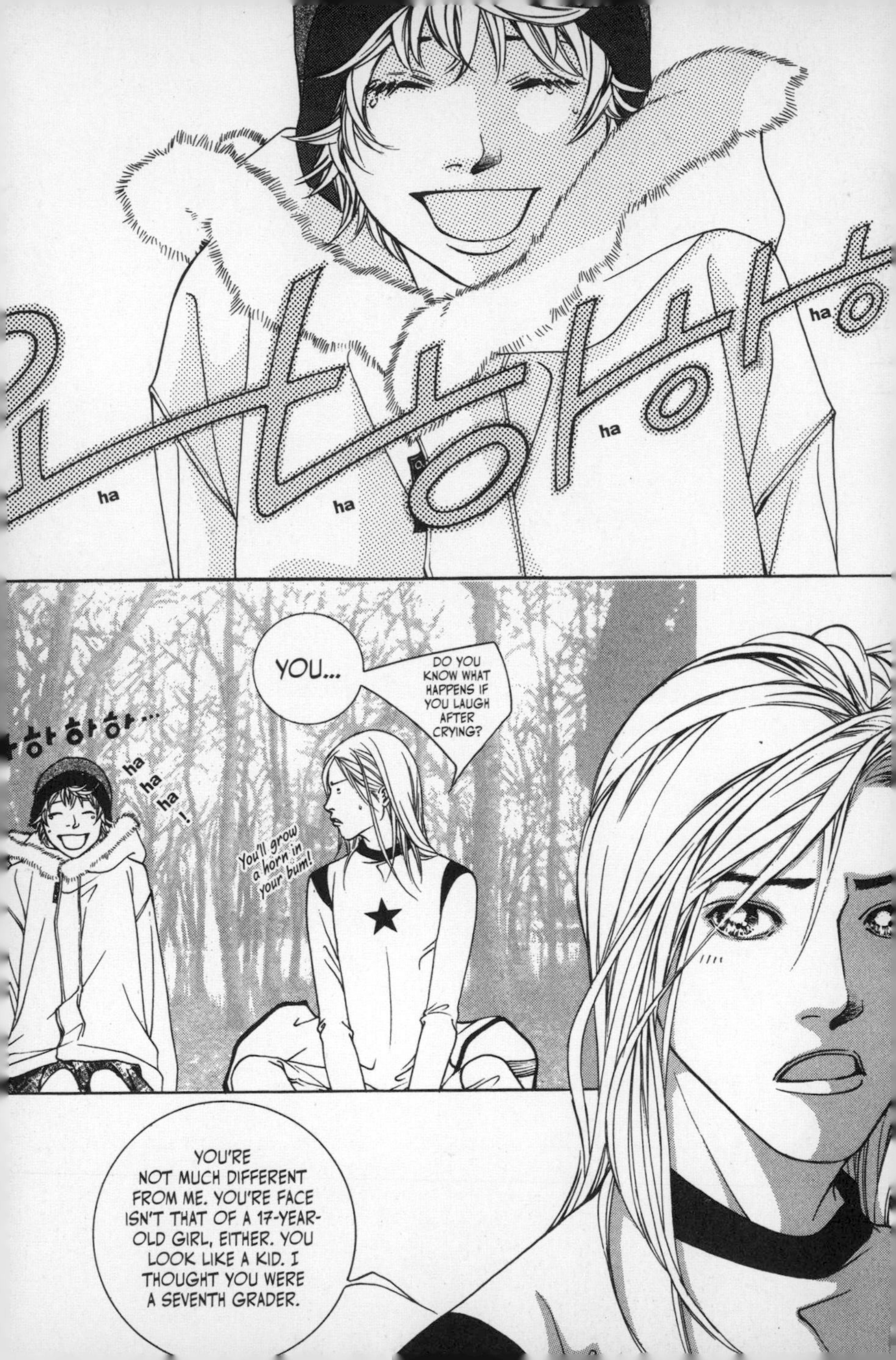
ha
ha
ha
ha
하하하…
ha ha ha !
YOU...
DO YOU KNOW WHAT HAPPENS IF YOU LAUGH AFTER CRYING?
You'll grow a horn in your bum!
YOU'RE NOT MUCH DIFFERENT FROM ME. YOU'RE FACE ISN'T THAT OF A 17-YEAR-OLD GIRL, EITHER. YOU LOOK LIKE A KID. I THOUGHT YOU WERE A SEVENTH GRADER.

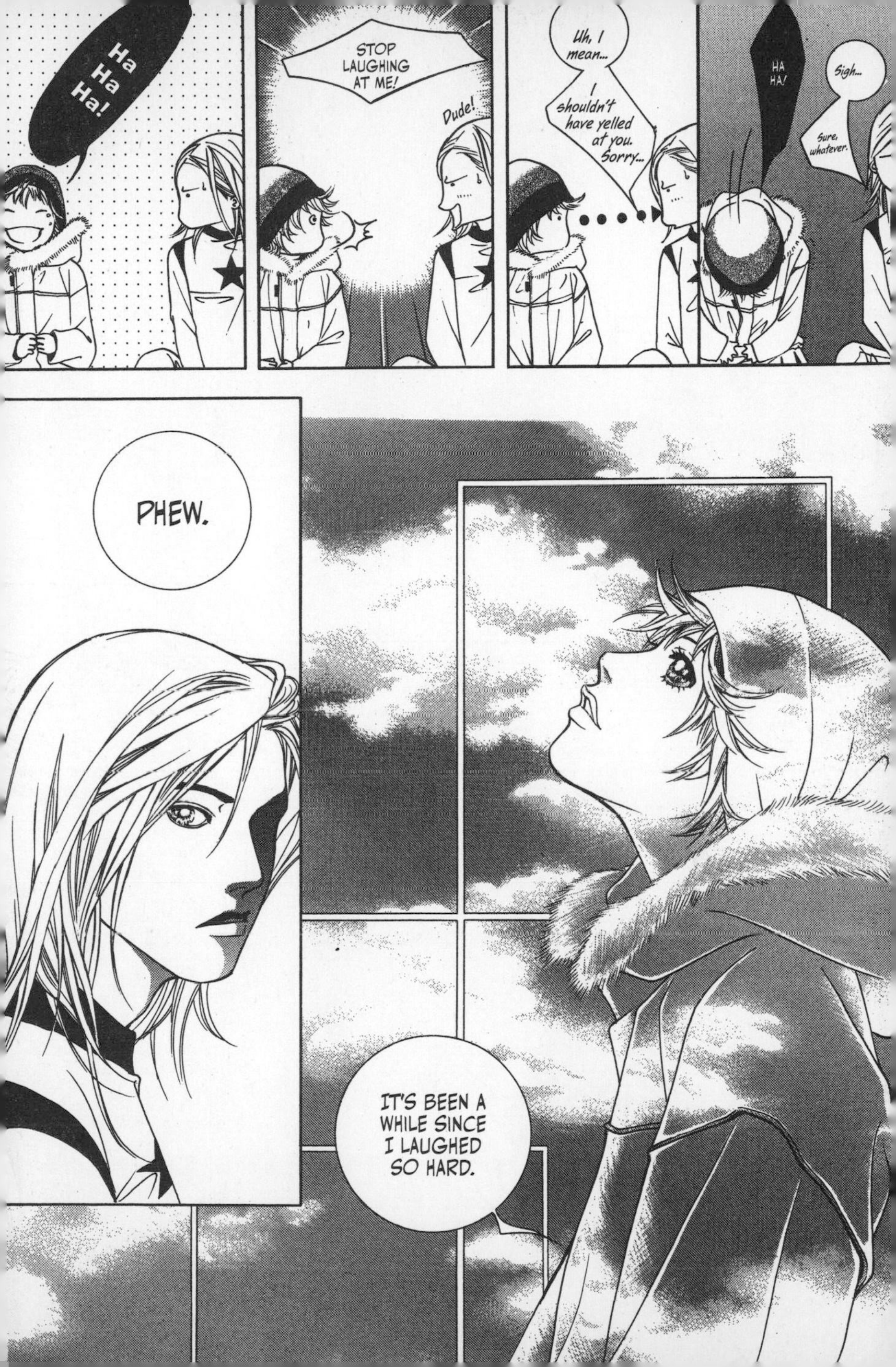

Ha Ha Ha!
STOP LAUGHING AT ME!
Dude!
Uh, I mean...
I shouldn't have yelled at you. Sorry...
HA HA!
Sigh...
Sure, whatever.
PHEW.
IT'S BEEN A WHILE SINCE I LAUGHED SO HARD.

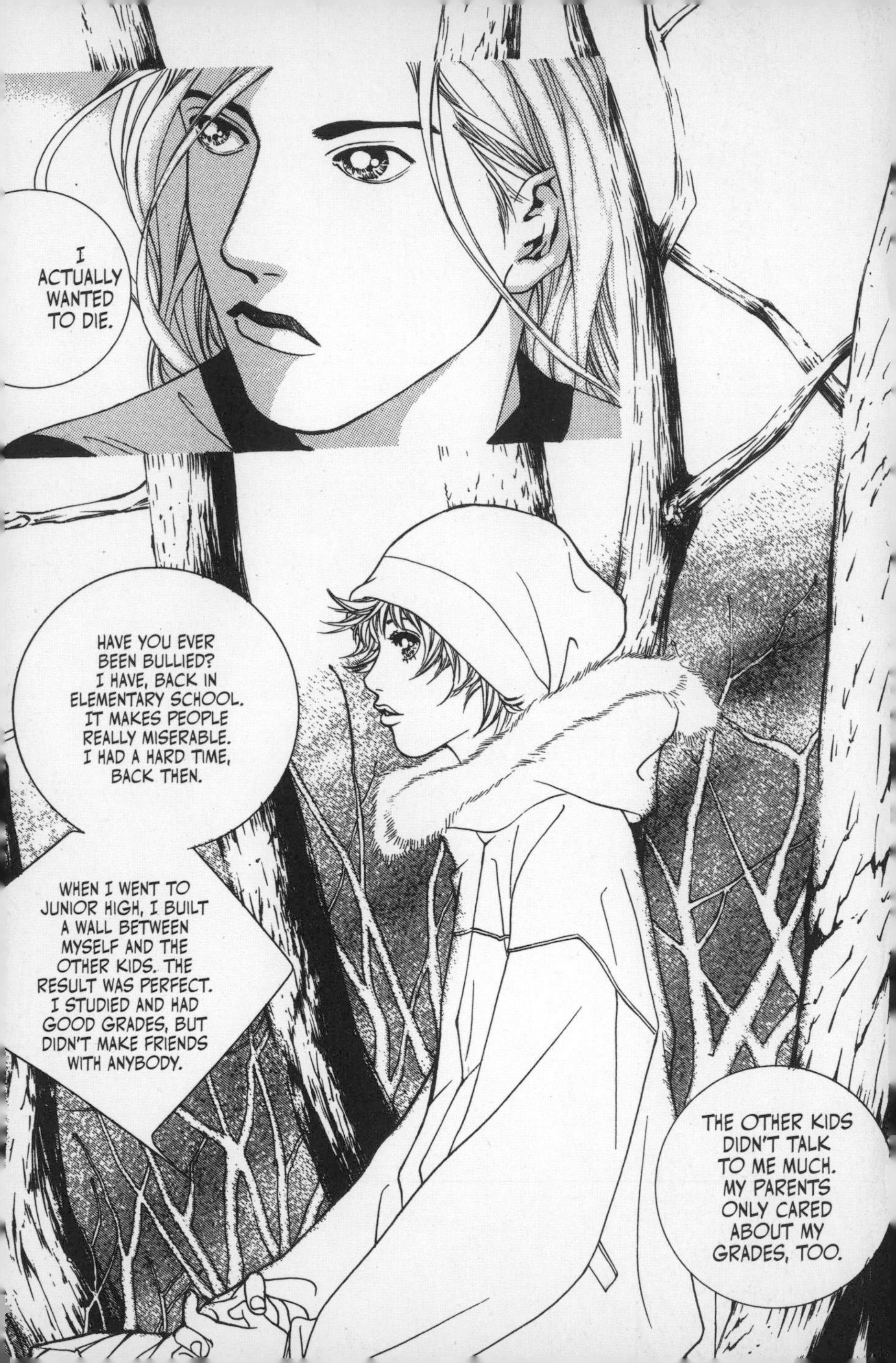
I ACTUALLY WANTED TO DIE.
HAVE YOU EVER BEEN BULLIED? I HAVE, BACK IN ELEMENTARY SCHOOL. IT MAKES PEOPLE REALLY MISERABLE. I HAD A HARD TIME, BACK THEN.
WHEN I WENT TO JUNIOR HIGH, I BUILT A WALL BETWEEN MYSELF AND THE OTHER KIDS. THE RESULT WAS PERFECT. I STUDIED AND HAD GOOD GRADES, BUT DIDN'T MAKE FRIENDS WITH ANYBODY.
THE OTHER KIDS DIDN'T TALK TO ME MUCH. MY PARENTS ONLY CARED ABOUT MY GRADES, TOO.

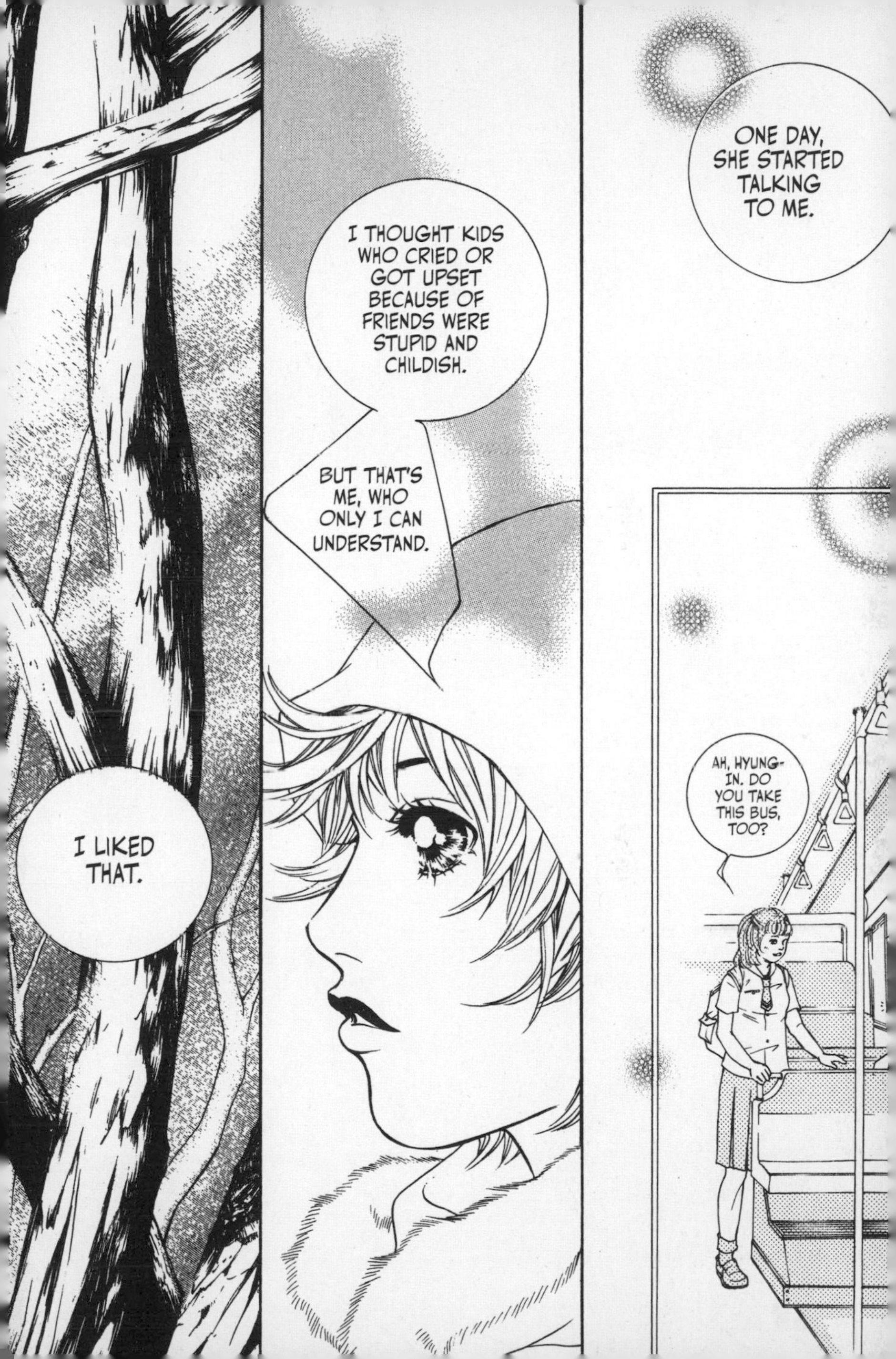
I LIKED THAT.
I THOUGHT KIDS WHO CRIED OR GOT UPSET BECAUSE OF FRIENDS WERE STUPID AND CHILDISH.
BUT THAT'S ME, WHO ONLY I CAN UNDERSTAND.
ONE DAY, SHE STARTED TALKING TO ME.
AH, HYUNG-IN. DO YOU TAKE THIS BUS, TOO?

BO-RAM WAS DIFFE-RENT OUT-SIDE OF SCHOOL.

SHE WAS SHY, BUT SHE LAUGHED A LOT AND WAS FUNNY. SHE ALSO HAD MANY DREAMS.

AT FIRST...I DIDN'T KNOW WHAT TO DO WITH THAT DIFFERENT SIDE TO HER, BUT...

...I FOUND MYSELF LAUGHING WITH HER. PEOPLE PROBABLY THOUGHT WE WERE BEST FRIENDS.

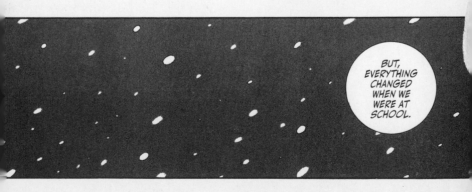

BUT, EVERYTHING CHANGED WHEN WE WERE AT SCHOOL.

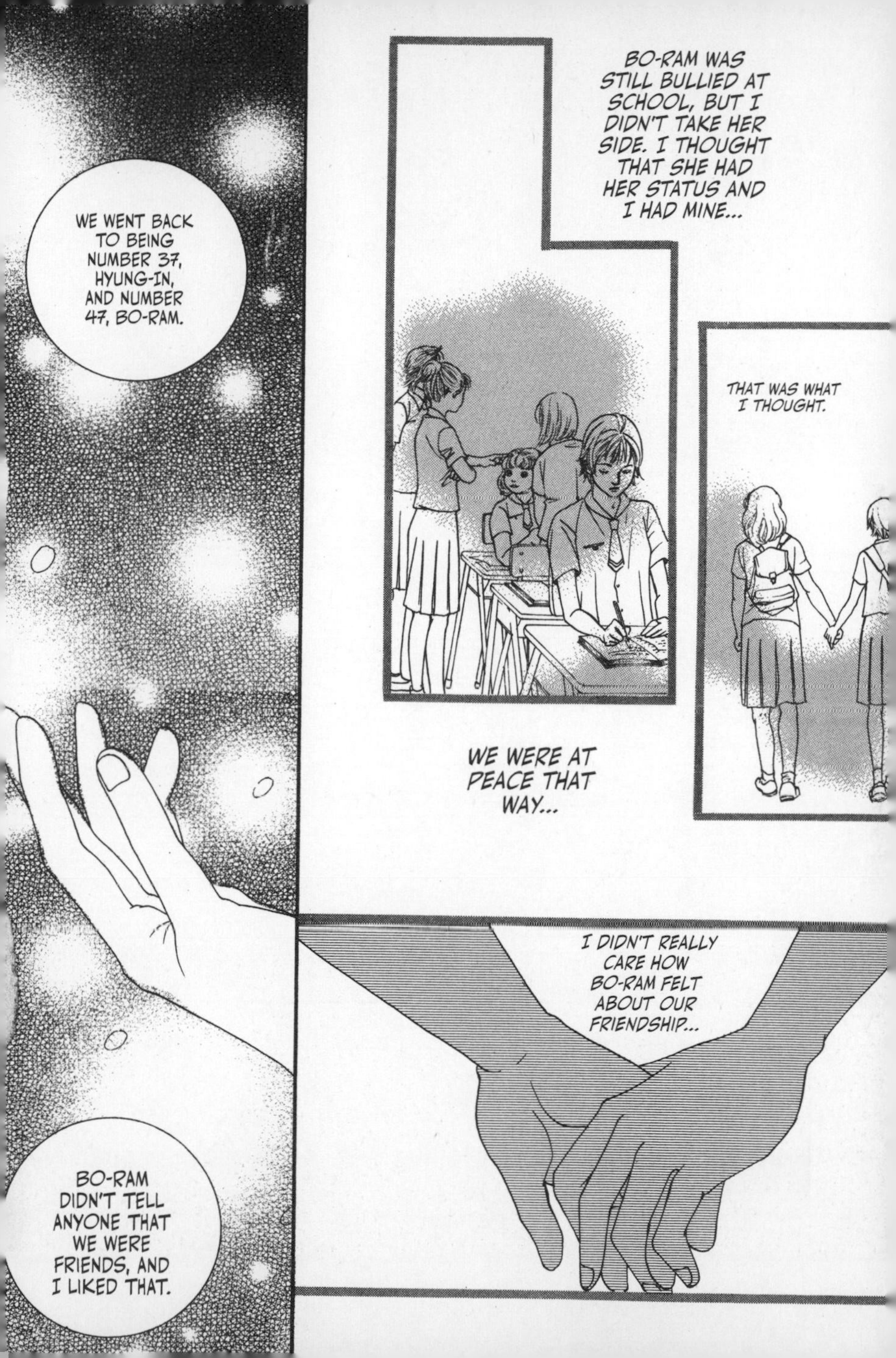
WE WENT BACK TO BEING NUMBER 37, HYUNG-IN, AND NUMBER 47, BO-RAM.
BO-RAM DIDN'T TELL ANYONE THAT WE WERE FRIENDS, AND I LIKED THAT.
BO-RAM WAS STILL BULLIED AT SCHOOL, BUT I DIDN'T TAKE HER SIDE. I THOUGHT THAT SHE HAD HER STATUS AND I HAD MINE...
THAT WAS WHAT I THOUGHT.
WE WERE AT PEACE THAT WAY...
I DIDN'T REALLY CARE HOW BO-RAM FELT ABOUT OUR FRIENDSHIP...

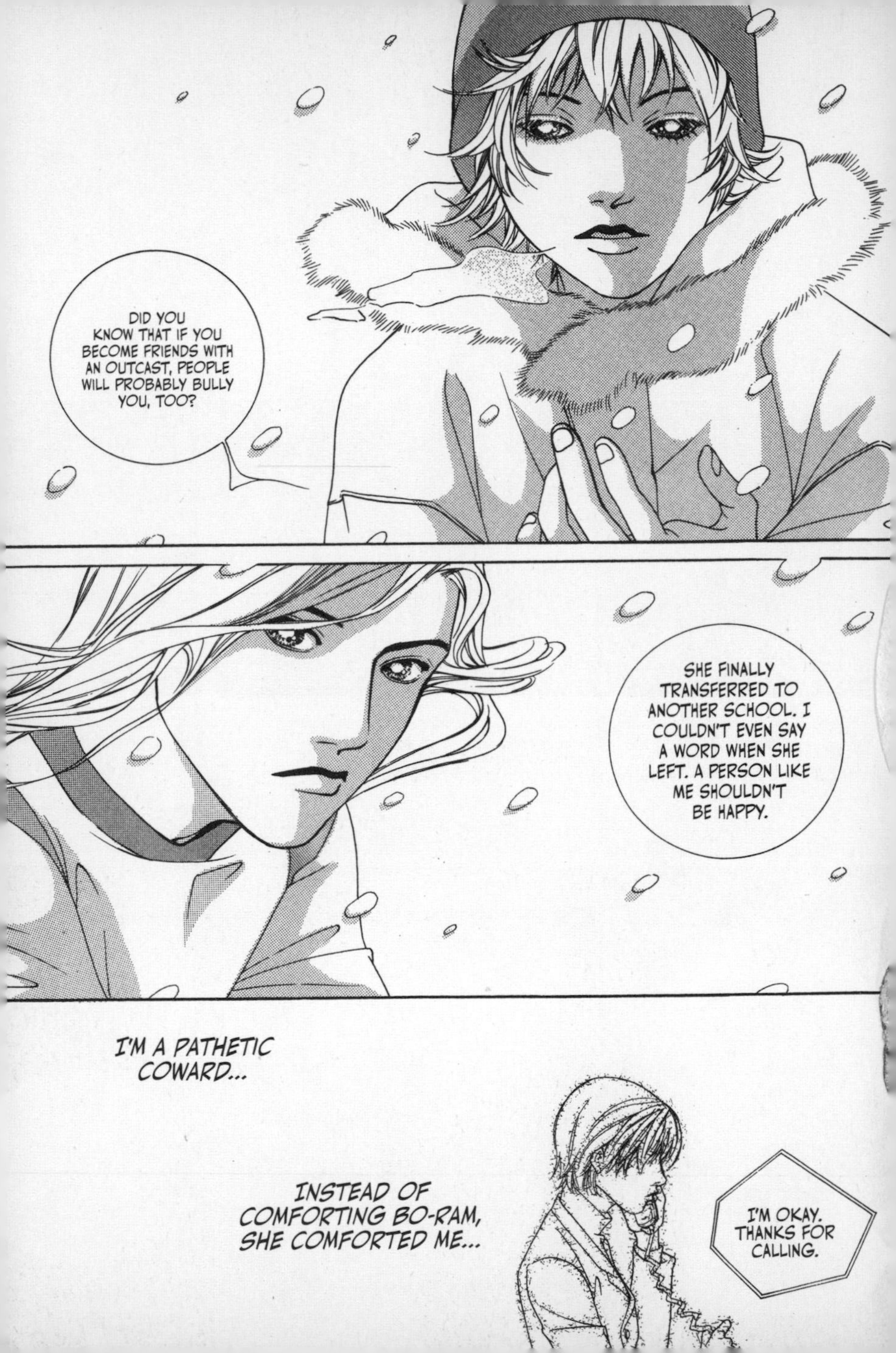
DID YOU KNOW THAT IF YOU BECOME FRIENDS WITH AN OUTCAST, PEOPLE WILL PROBABLY BULLY YOU, TOO?
SHE FINALLY TRANSFERRED TO ANOTHER SCHOOL. I COULDN'T EVEN SAY A WORD WHEN SHE LEFT. A PERSON LIKE ME SHOULDN'T BE HAPPY.
I'M A PATHETIC COWARD...
INSTEAD OF COMFORTING BO-RAM, SHE COMFORTED ME...
I'M OKAY. THANKS FOR CALLING.

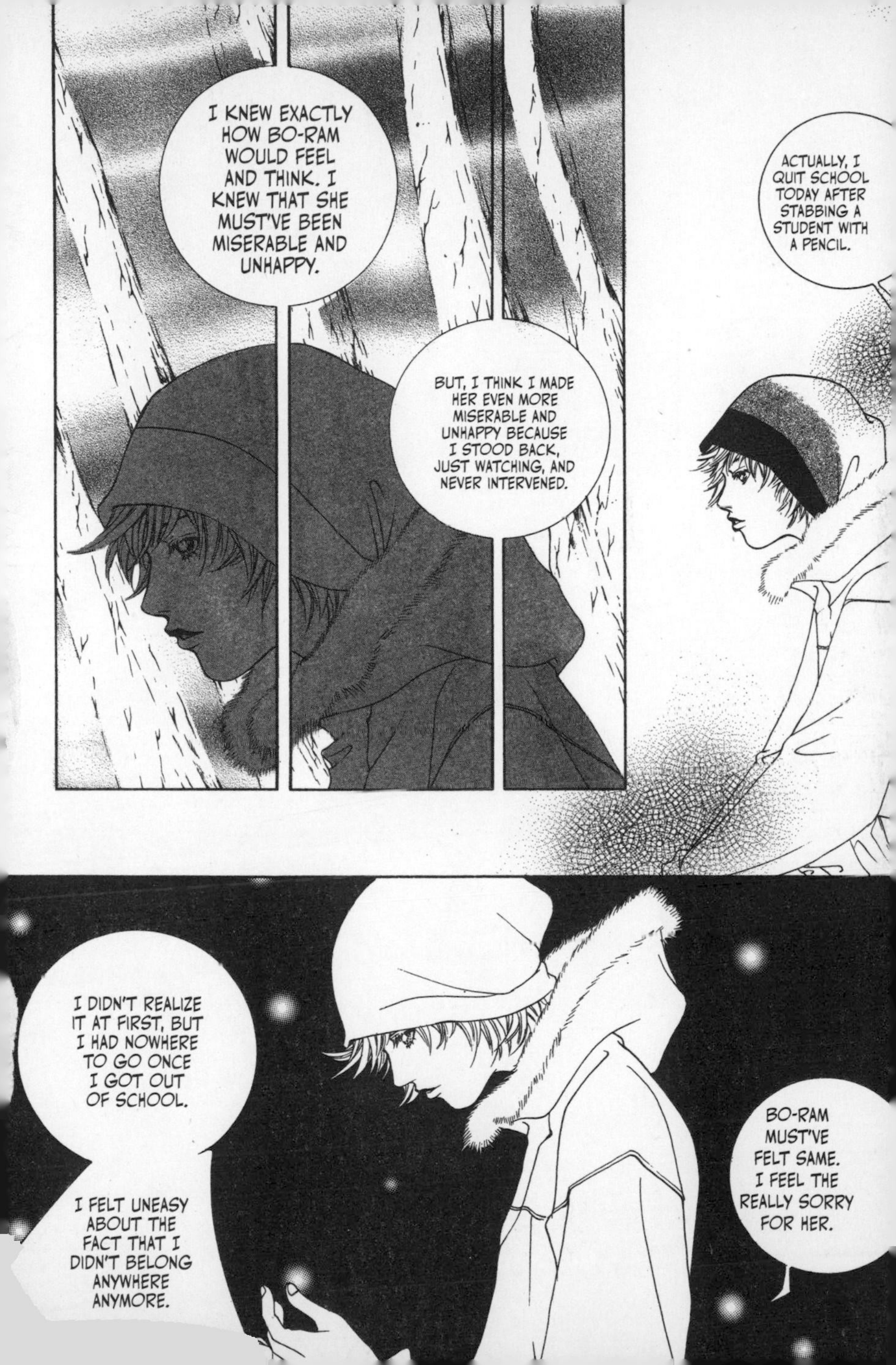

I KNEW EXACTLY HOW BO-RAM WOULD FEEL AND THINK. I KNEW THAT SHE MUST'VE BEEN MISERABLE AND UNHAPPY.
BUT, I THINK I MADE HER EVEN MORE MISERABLE AND UNHAPPY BECAUSE I STOOD BACK, JUST WATCHING, AND NEVER INTERVENED.
ACTUALLY, I QUIT SCHOOL TODAY AFTER STABBING A STUDENT WITH A PENCIL.
I DIDN'T REALIZE IT AT FIRST, BUT I HAD NOWHERE TO GO ONCE I GOT OUT OF SCHOOL.
I FELT UNEASY ABOUT THE FACT THAT I DIDN'T BELONG ANYWHERE ANYMORE.
BO-RAM MUST'VE FELT SAME. I FEEL THE REALLY SORRY FOR HER.

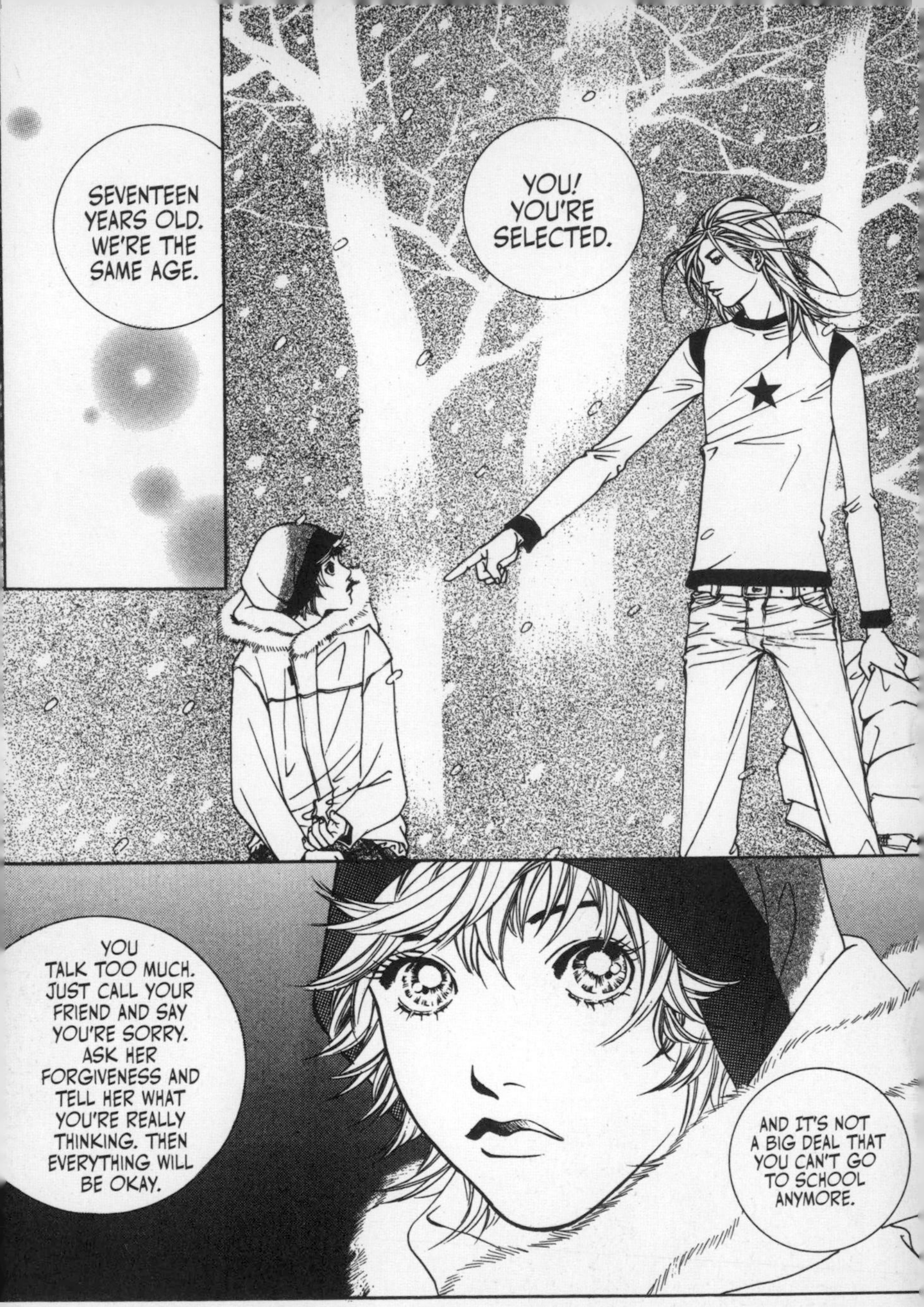
SEVENTEEN YEARS OLD. WE'RE THE SAME AGE.
YOU! YOU'RE SELECTED.
YOU TALK TOO MUCH. JUST CALL YOUR FRIEND AND SAY YOU'RE SORRY. ASK HER FORGIVENESS AND TELL HER WHAT YOU'RE REALLY THINKING. THEN EVERYTHING WILL BE OKAY.
AND IT'S NOT A BIG DEAL THAT YOU CAN'T GO TO SCHOOL ANYMORE.

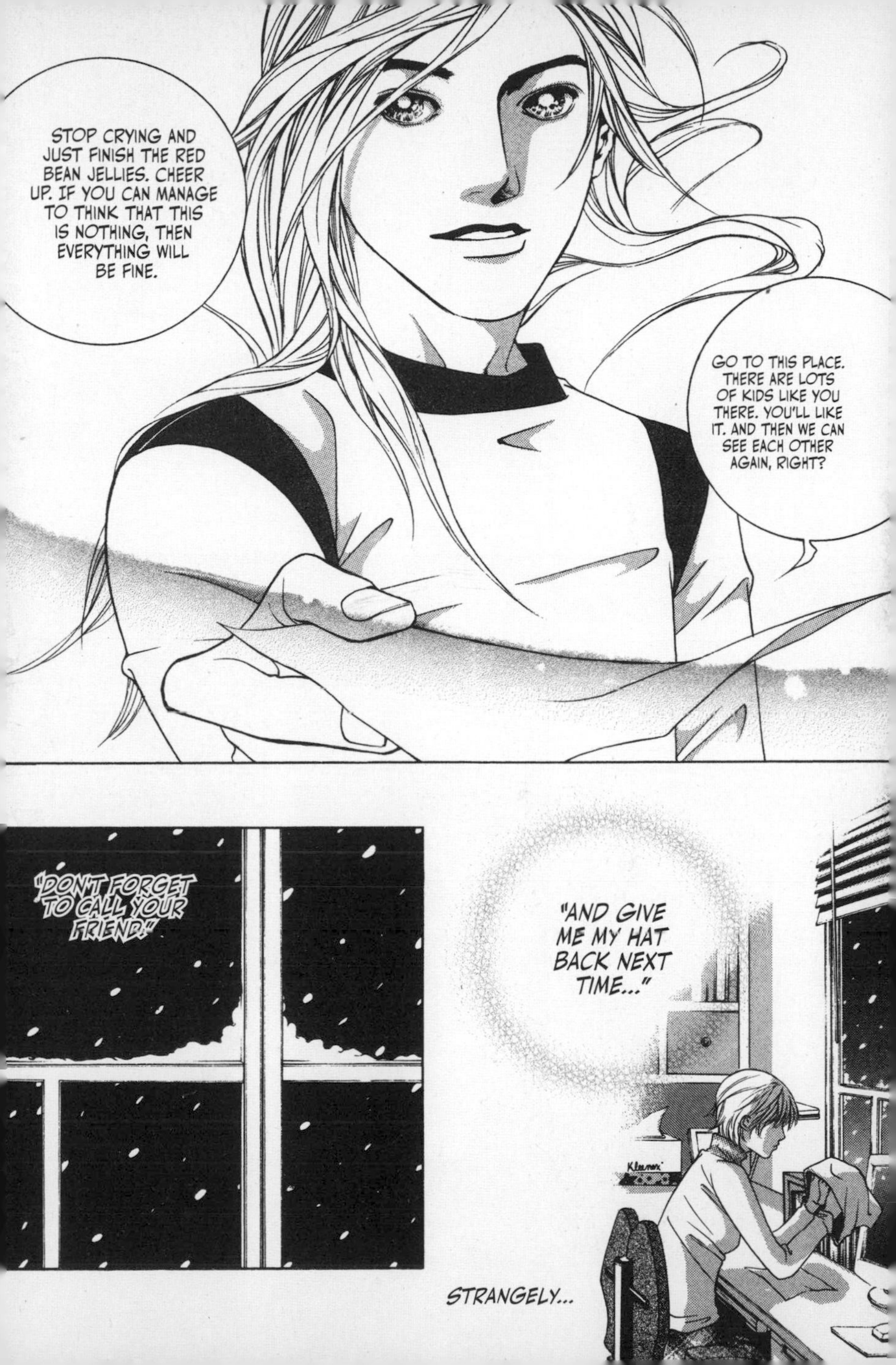
STOP CRYING AND JUST FINISH THE RED BEAN JELLIES. CHEER UP. IF YOU CAN MANAGE TO THINK THAT THIS IS NOTHING, THEN EVERYTHING WILL BE FINE.
GO TO THIS PLACE. THERE ARE LOTS OF KIDS LIKE YOU THERE. YOU'LL LIKE IT. AND THEN WE CAN SEE EACH OTHER AGAIN, RIGHT?
"DON'T FORGET TO CALL YOUR FRIEND."
"AND GIVE ME MY HAT BACK NEXT TIME..."
Kleenex
STRANGELY...

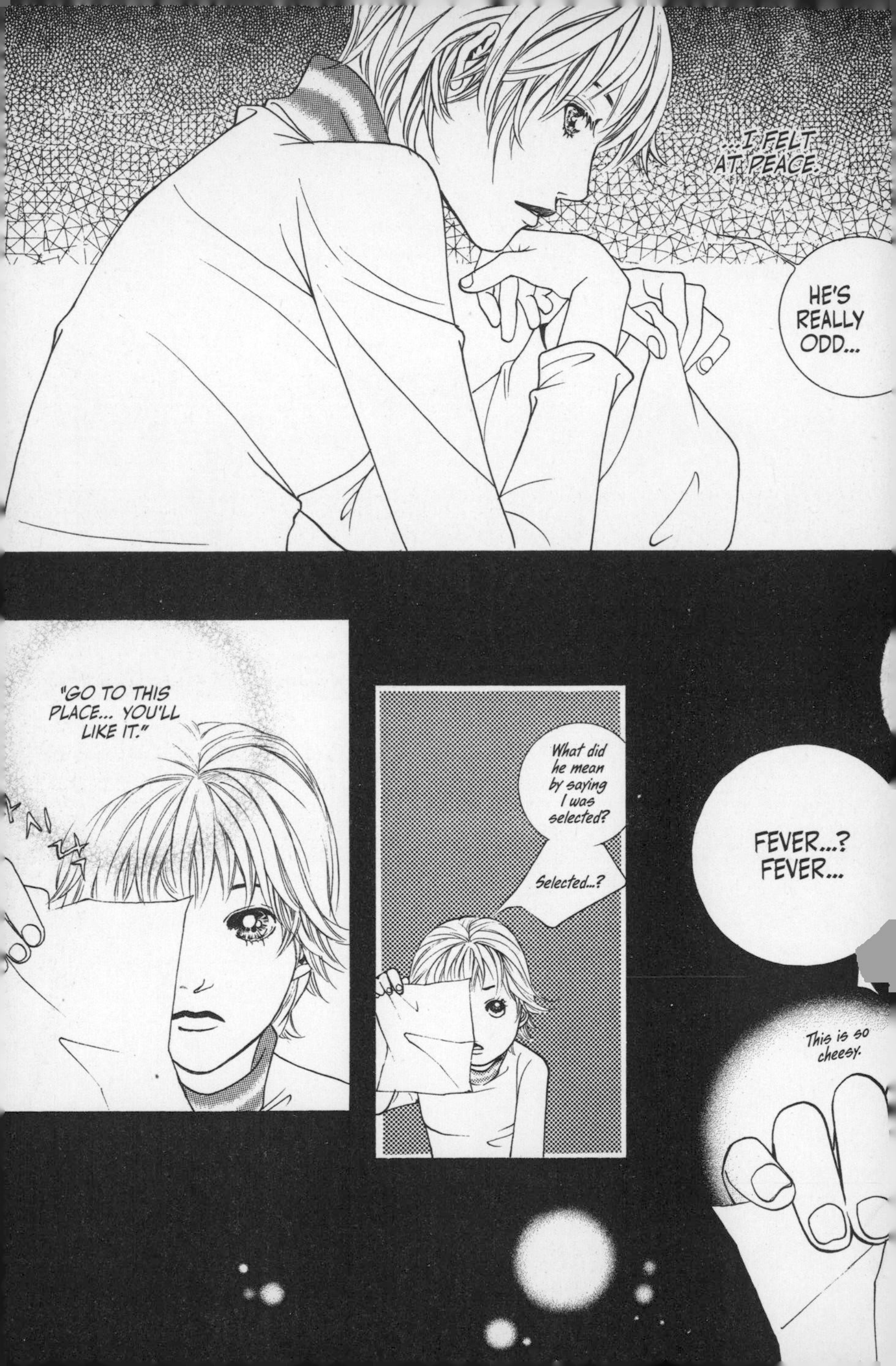
...I FELT AT PEACE.
HE'S REALLY ODD...
"GO TO THIS PLACE... YOU'LL LIKE IT."
What did he mean by saying I was selected?
Selected...?
FEVER...? FEVER...
This is so cheesy.

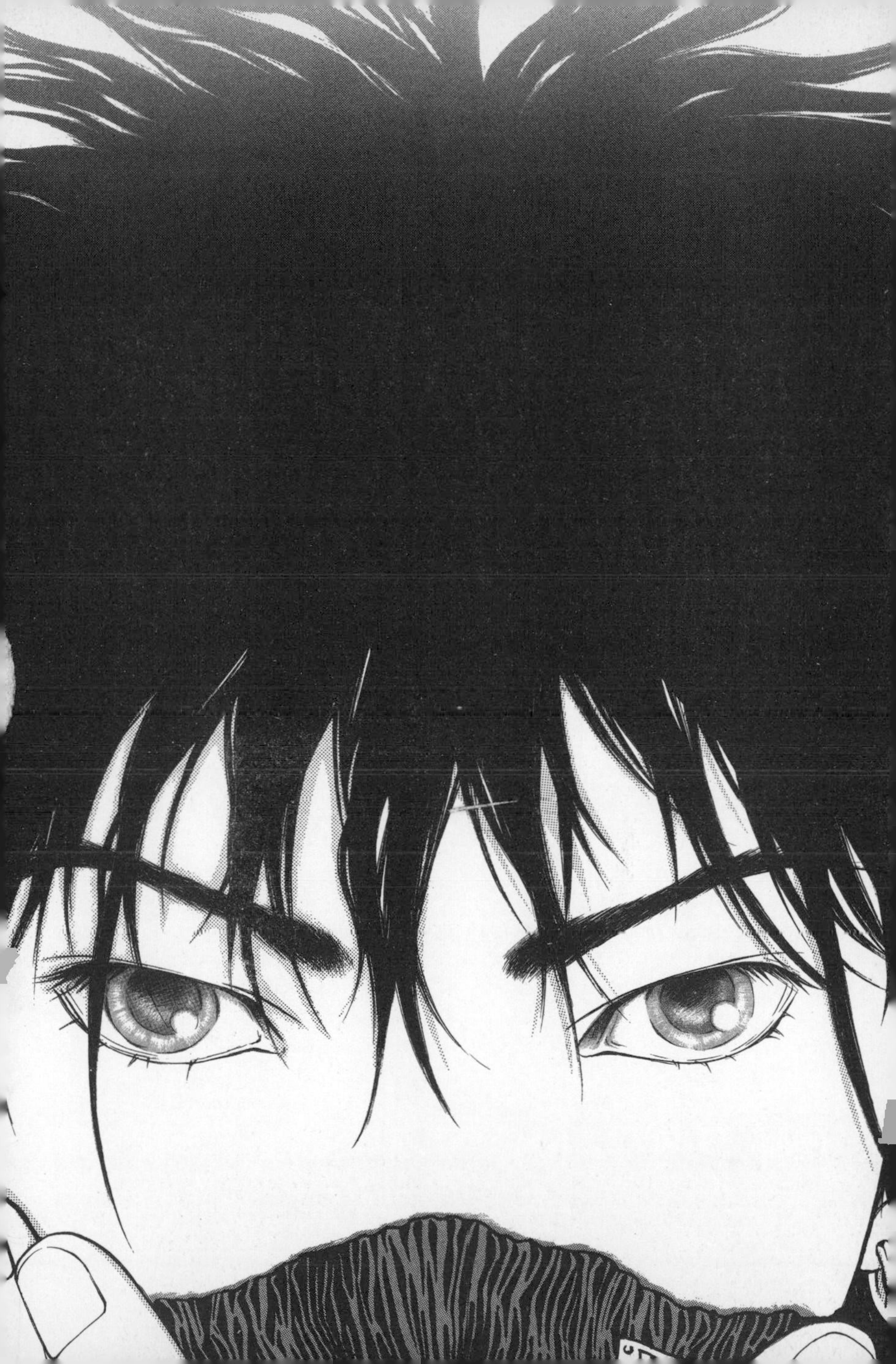

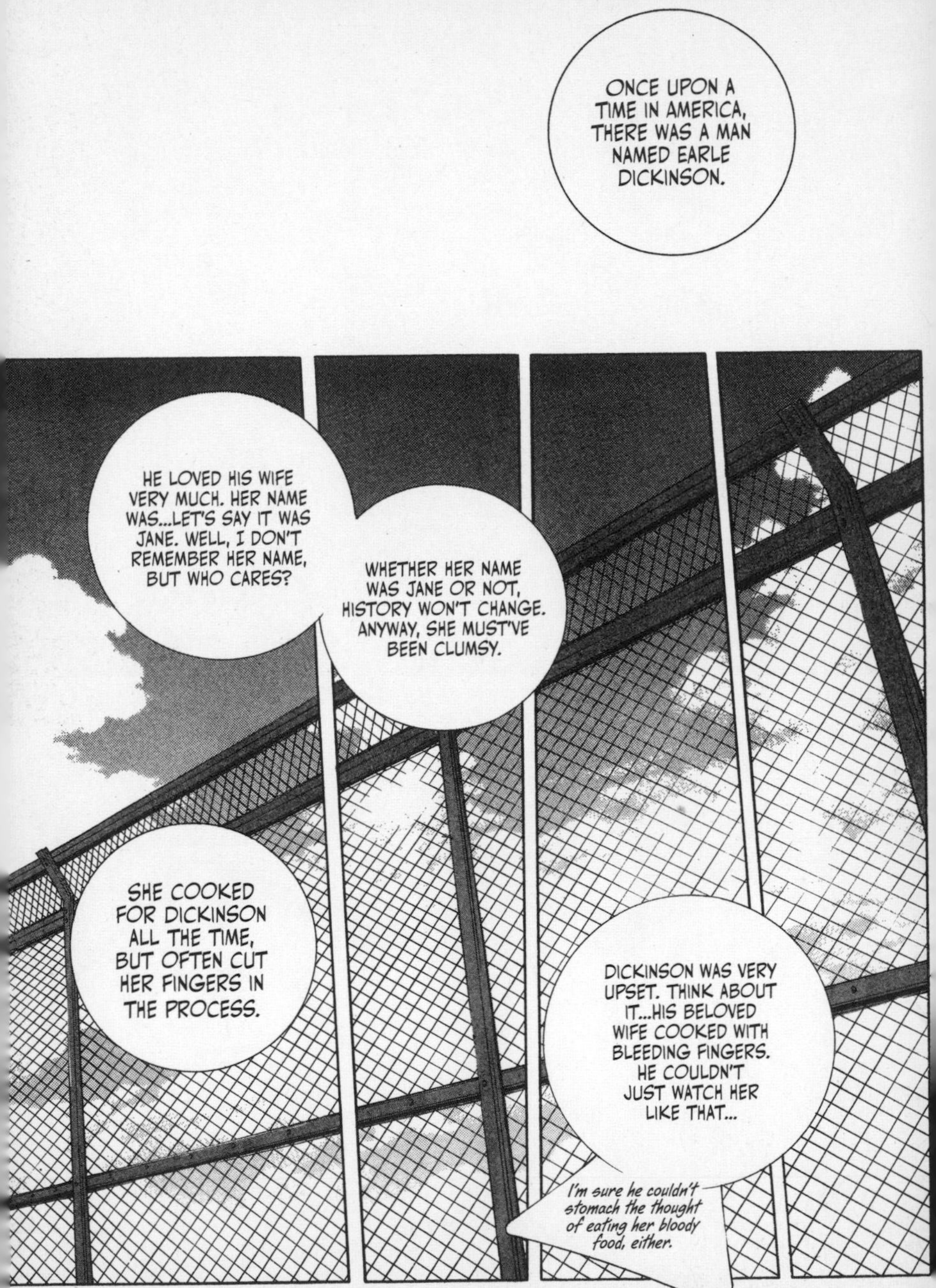
ONCE UPON A TIME IN AMERICA, THERE WAS A MAN NAMED EARLE DICKINSON.
HE LOVED HIS WIFE VERY MUCH. HER NAME WAS...LET'S SAY IT WAS JANE. WELL, I DON'T REMEMBER HER NAME, BUT WHO CARES?
WHETHER HER NAME WAS JANE OR NOT, HISTORY WON'T CHANGE. ANYWAY, SHE MUST'VE BEEN CLUMSY.
SHE COOKED FOR DICKINSON ALL THE TIME, BUT OFTEN CUT HER FINGERS IN THE PROCESS.
DICKINSON WAS VERY UPSET. THINK ABOUT IT...HIS BELOVED WIFE COOKED WITH BLEEDING FINGERS. HE COULDN'T JUST WATCH HER LIKE THAT...
I'm sure he couldn't stomach the thought of eating her bloody food, either.

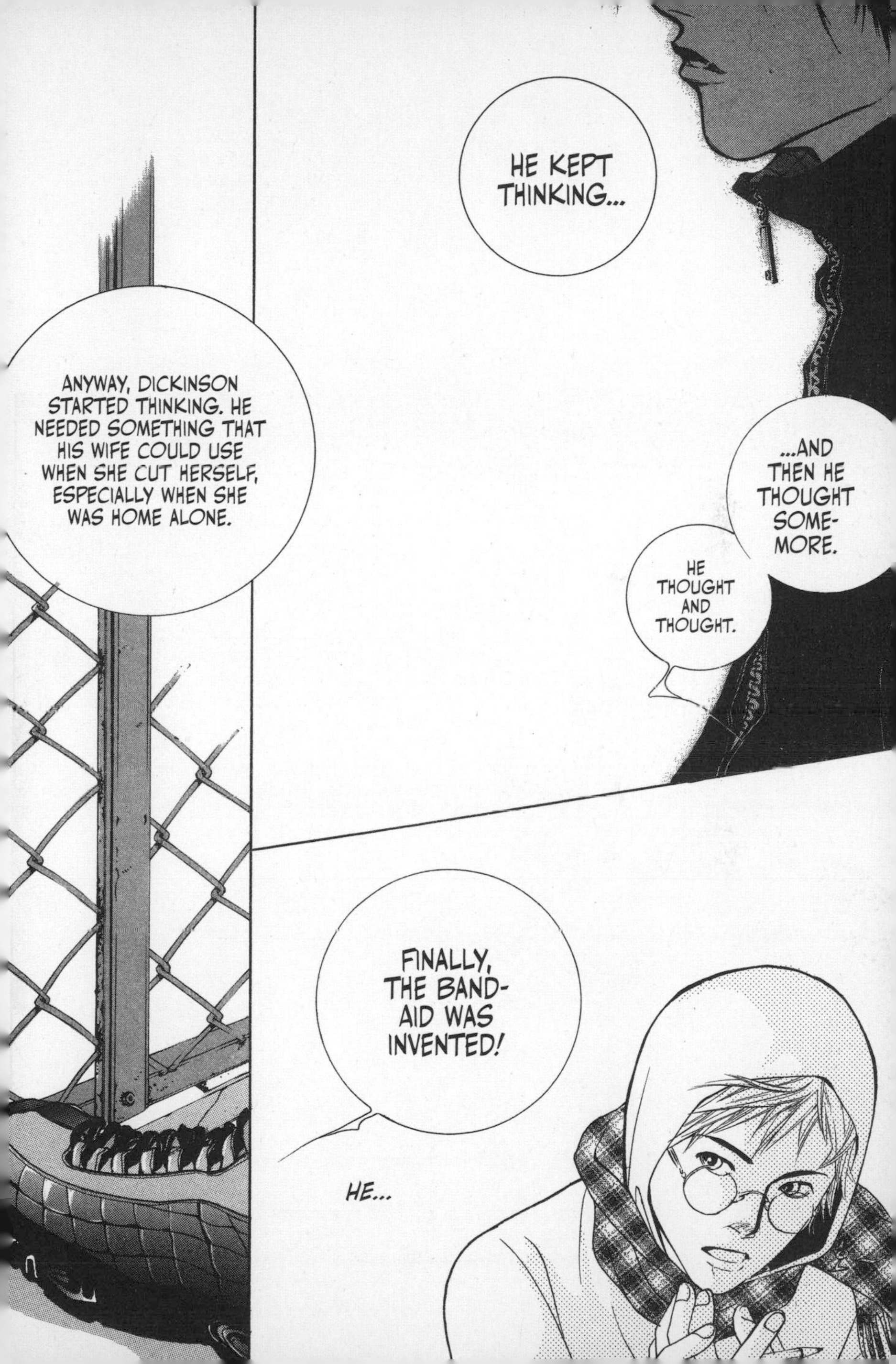
ANYWAY, DICKINSON STARTED THINKING. HE NEEDED SOMETHING THAT HIS WIFE COULD USE WHEN SHE CUT HERSELF, ESPECIALLY WHEN SHE WAS HOME ALONE.
HE KEPT THINKING...
HE THOUGHT AND THOUGHT.
...AND THEN HE THOUGHT SOME-MORE.
FINALLY, THE BAND-AID WAS INVENTED!
HE...

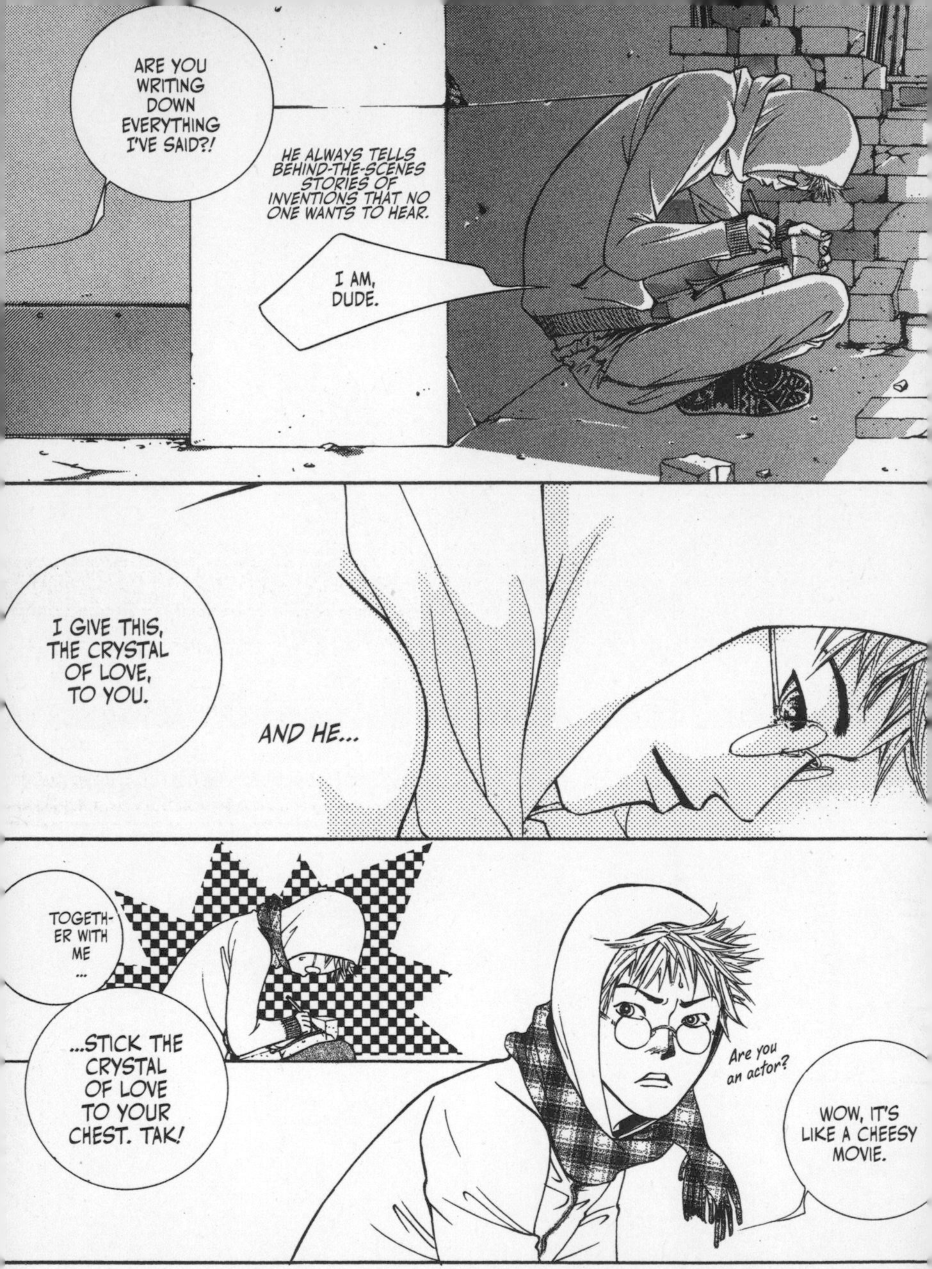
ARE YOU WRITING DOWN EVERYTHING I'VE SAID?!
HE ALWAYS TELLS BEHIND-THE-SCENES STORIES OF INVENTIONS THAT NO ONE WANTS TO HEAR.
I AM, DUDE.
I GIVE THIS, THE CRYSTAL OF LOVE, TO YOU.
AND HE...
TOGETH-ER WITH ME ...
...STICK THE CRYSTAL OF LOVE TO YOUR CHEST. TAK!
Are you an actor?
WOW, IT'S LIKE A CHEESY MOVIE.

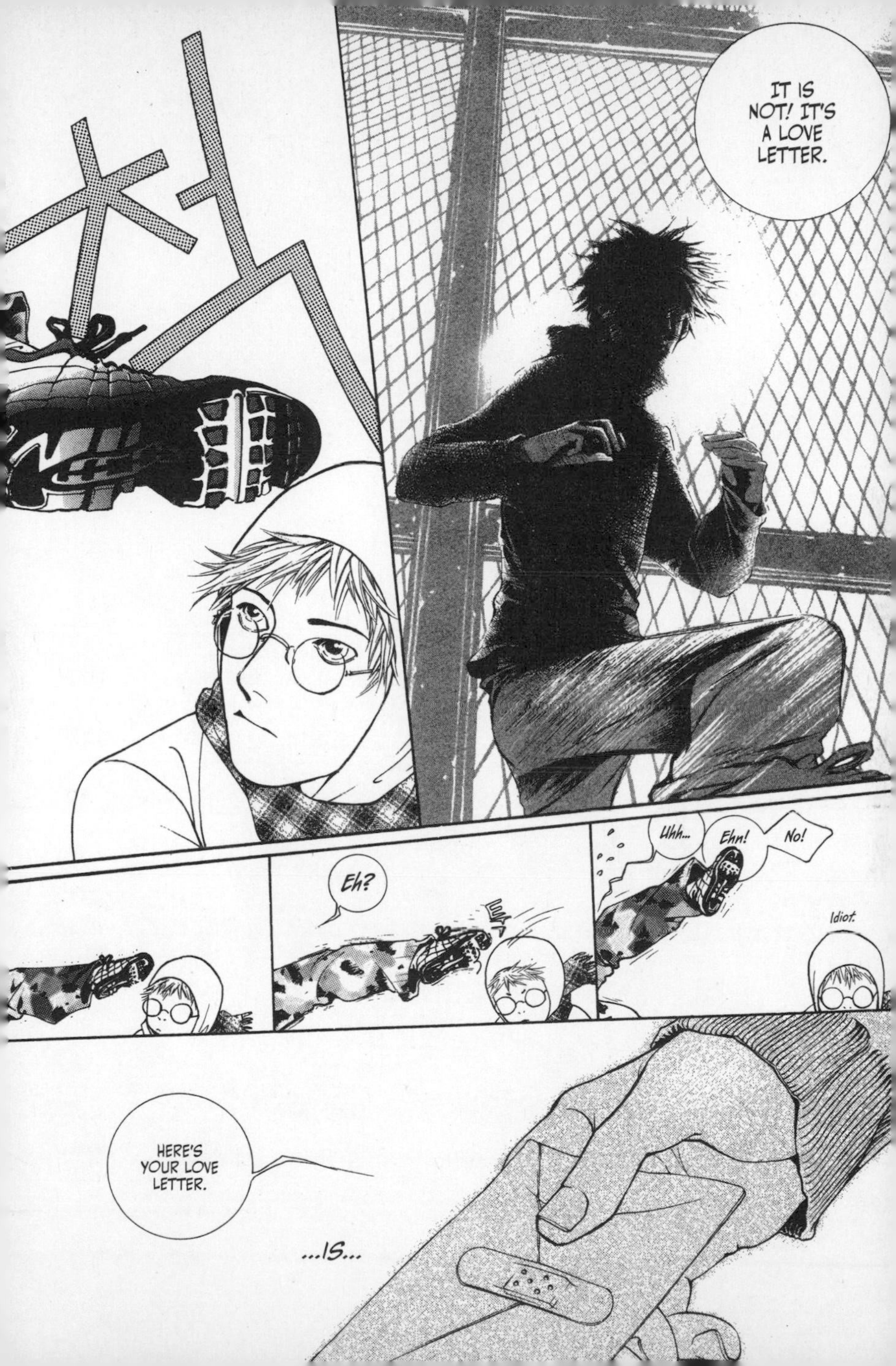
IT IS NOT! IT'S A LOVE LETTER.
Eh?
Uhh...
Ehn!
No!
Idiot.
HERE'S YOUR LOVE LETTER.
...IS...

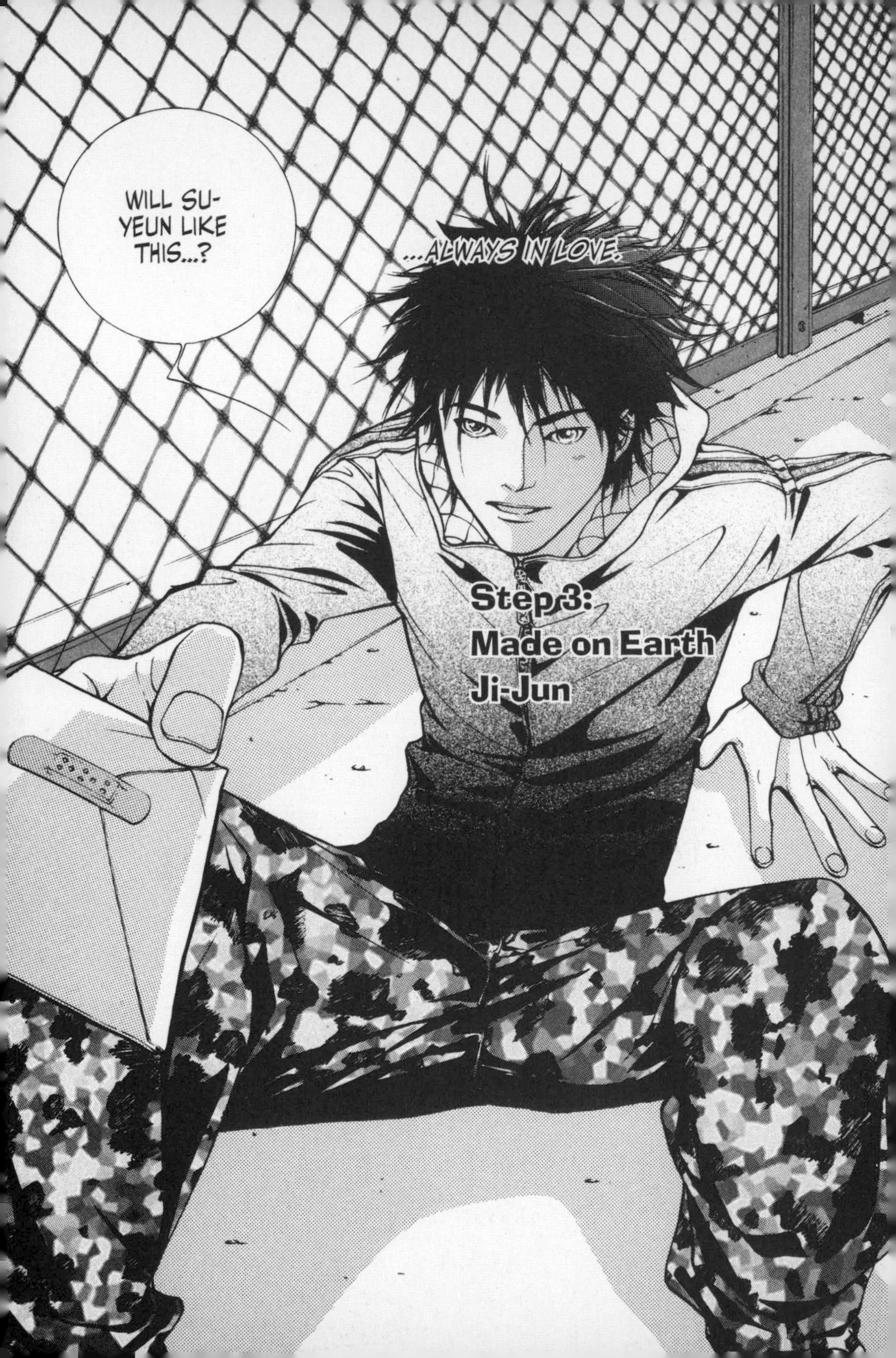
WILL SU-YEUN LIKE THIS...?
...ALWAYS IN LOVE.
Step 3:
Made on Earth
Ji-Jun

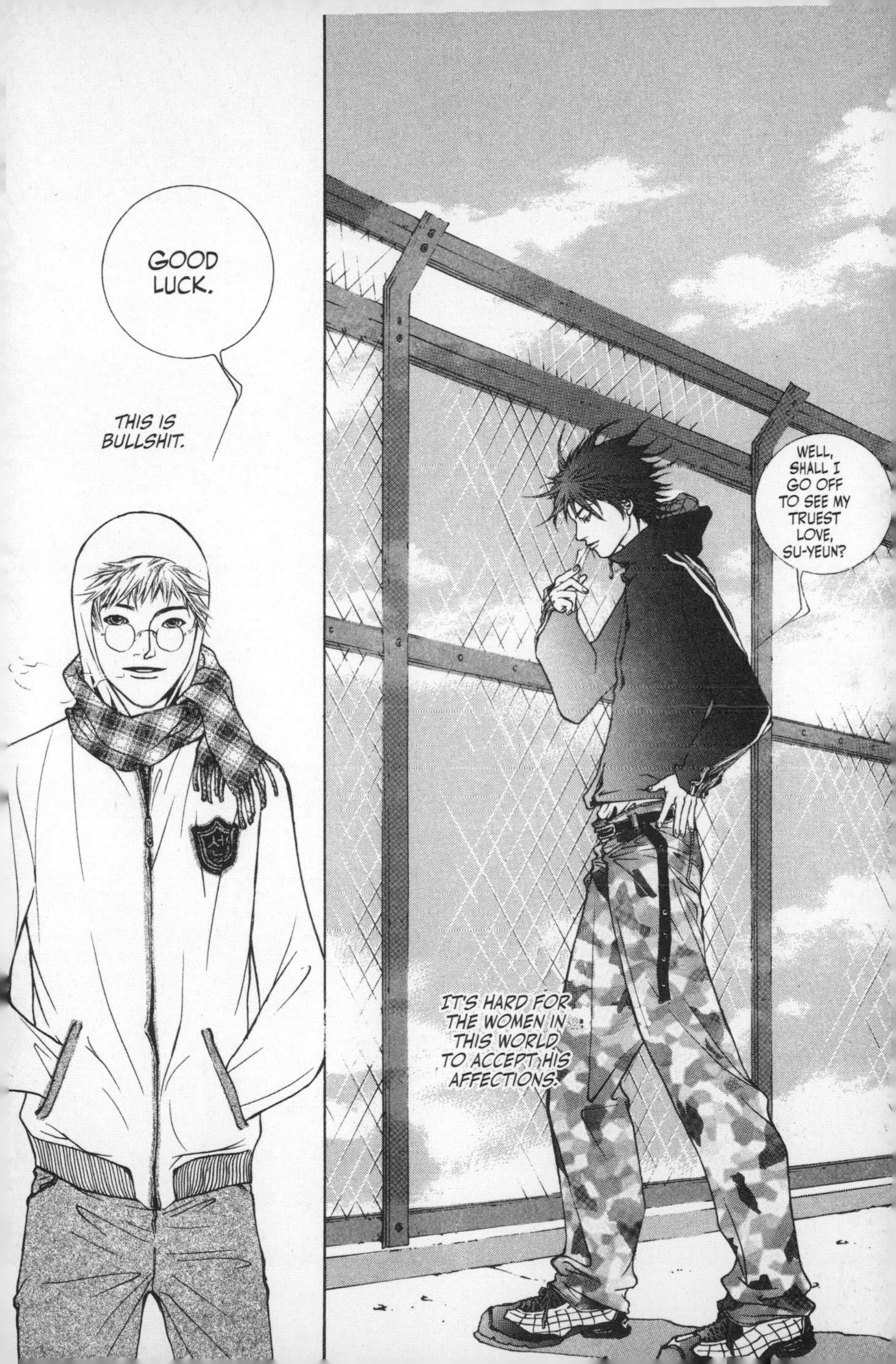
GOOD LUCK.
THIS IS BULLSHIT.
WELL, SHALL I GO OFF TO SEE MY TRUEST LOVE, SU-YEUN?
IT'S HARD FOR THE WOMEN IN THIS WORLD TO ACCEPT HIS AFFECTIONS.

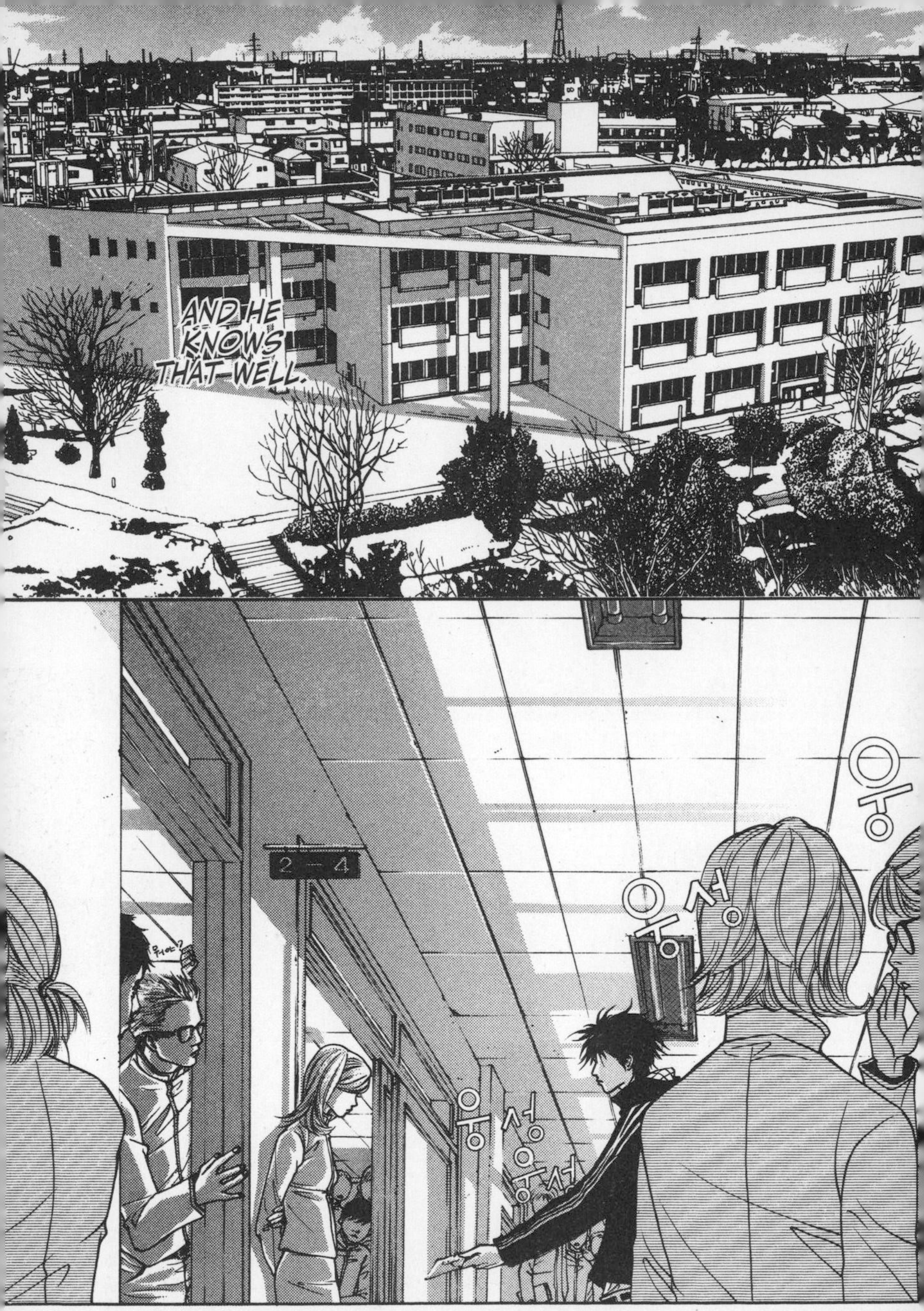
AND HE KNOWS THAT WELL.
2 — 4

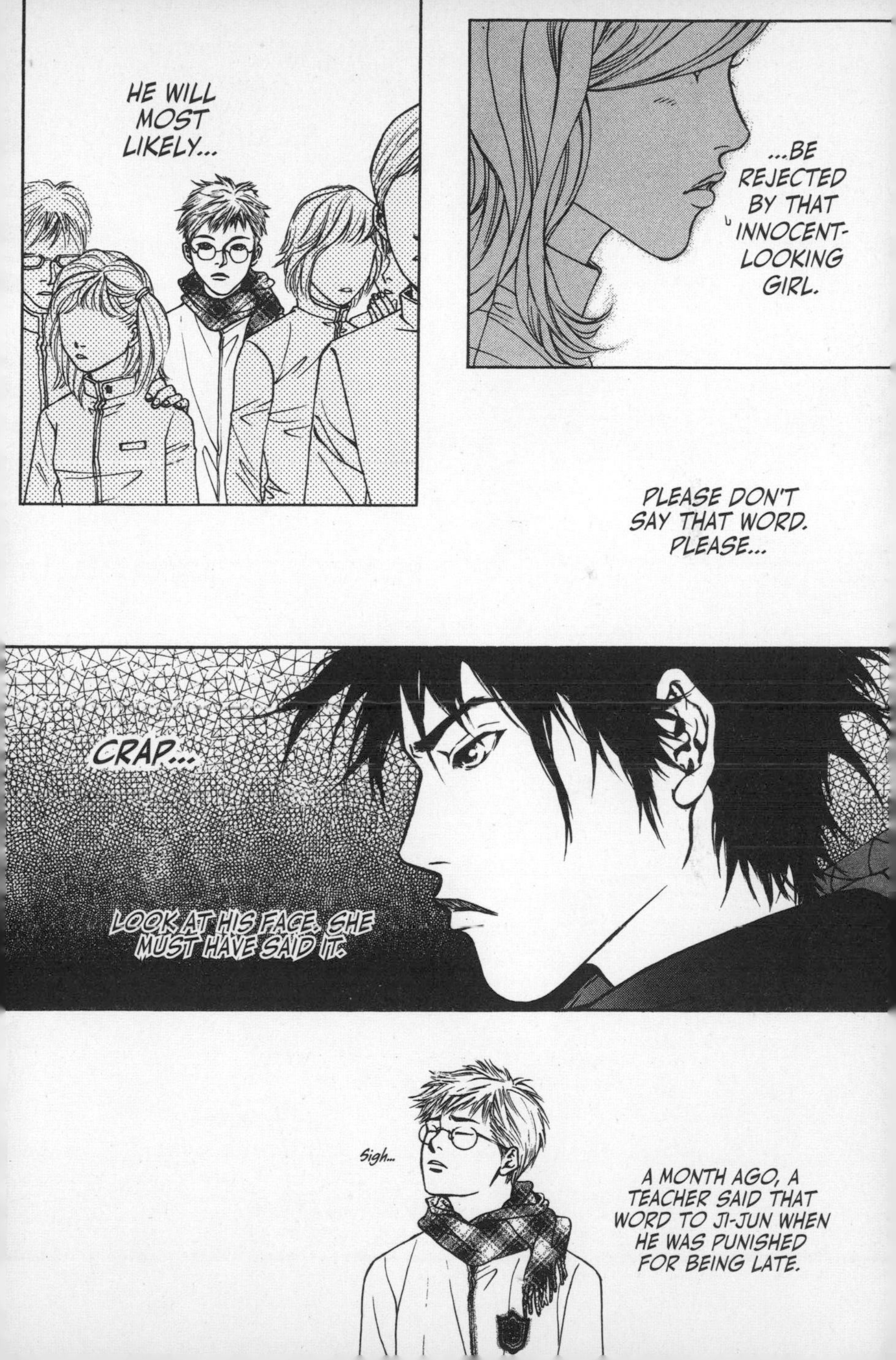
HE WILL MOST LIKELY...
...BE REJECTED BY THAT INNOCENT-LOOKING GIRL.
PLEASE DON'T SAY THAT WORD. PLEASE...
CRAP...
LOOK AT HIS FACE. SHE MUST HAVE SAID IT.
Sigh...
A MONTH AGO, A TEACHER SAID THAT WORD TO JI-JUN WHEN HE WAS PUNISHED FOR BEING LATE.

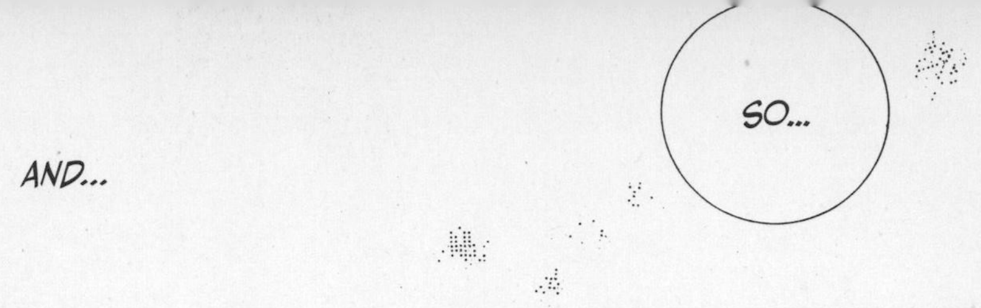
AND...
SO...
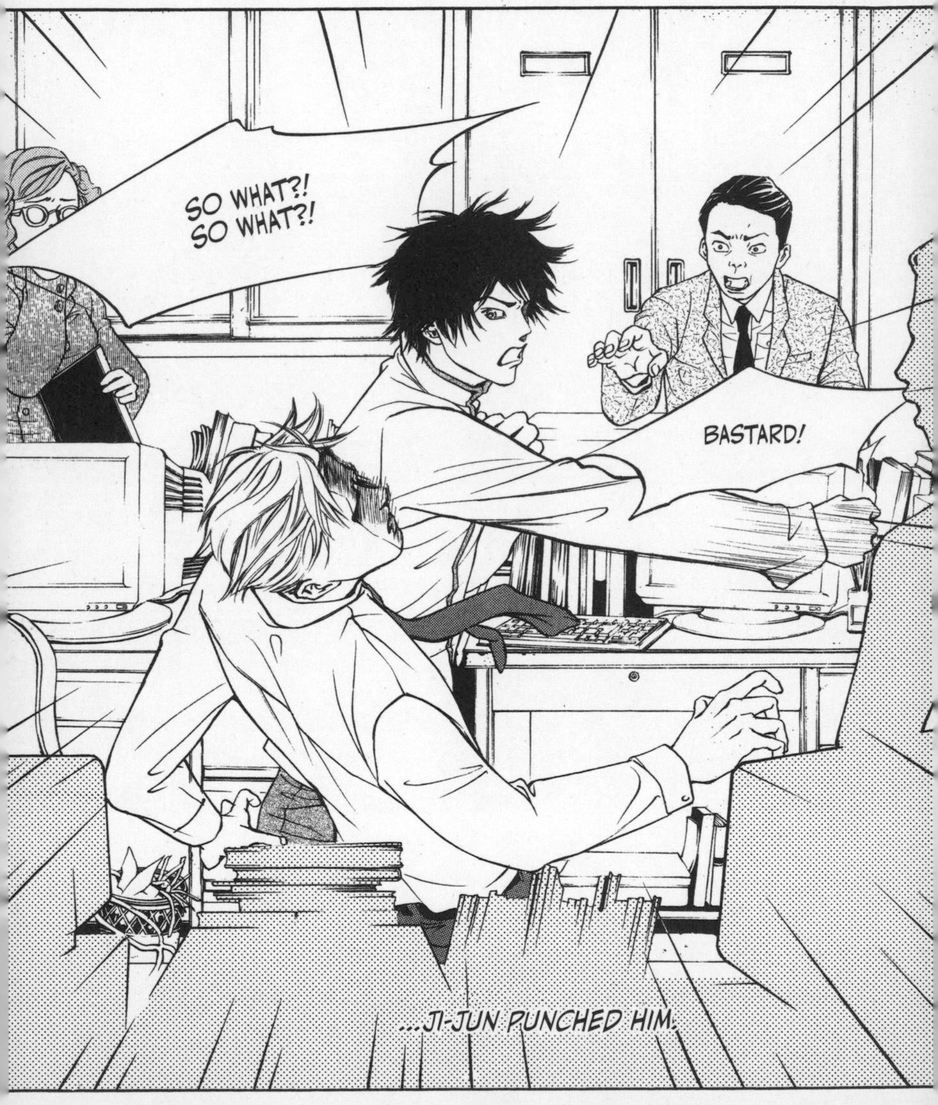
SO WHAT?! SO WHAT?!
BASTARD!
...JI-JUN PUNCHED HIM.

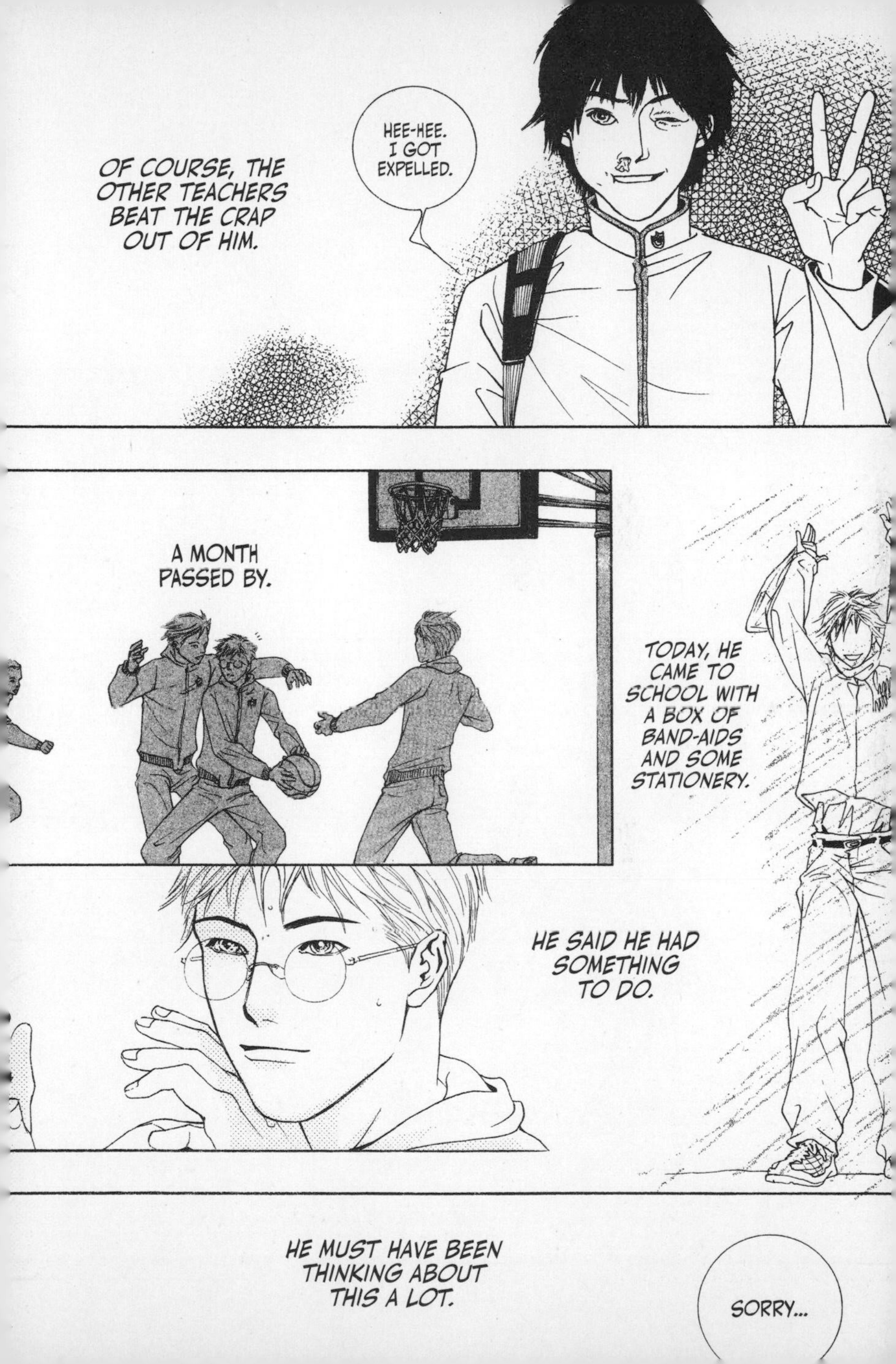
OF COURSE, THE OTHER TEACHERS BEAT THE CRAP OUT OF HIM.
HEE-HEE. I GOT EXPELLED.
A MONTH PASSED BY.
TODAY, HE CAME TO SCHOOL WITH A BOX OF BAND-AIDS AND SOME STATIONERY.
HE SAID HE HAD SOMETHING TO DO.
HE MUST HAVE BEEN THINKING ABOUT THIS A LOT.
SORRY...

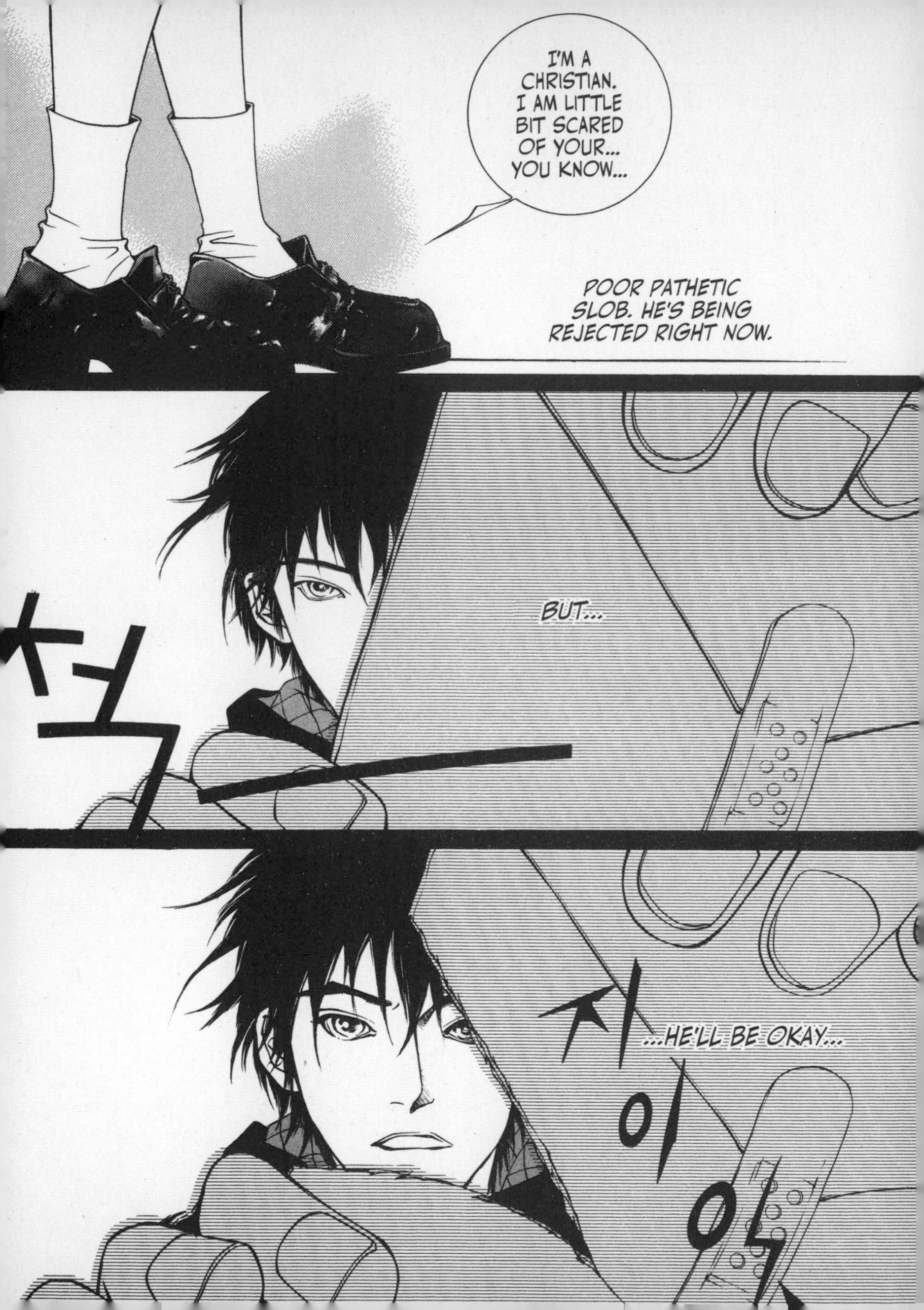
I'M A CHRISTIAN. I AM LITTLE BIT SCARED OF YOUR... YOU KNOW...
POOR PATHETIC SLOB. HE'S BEING REJECTED RIGHT NOW.
척
BUT...
...HE'LL BE OKAY...

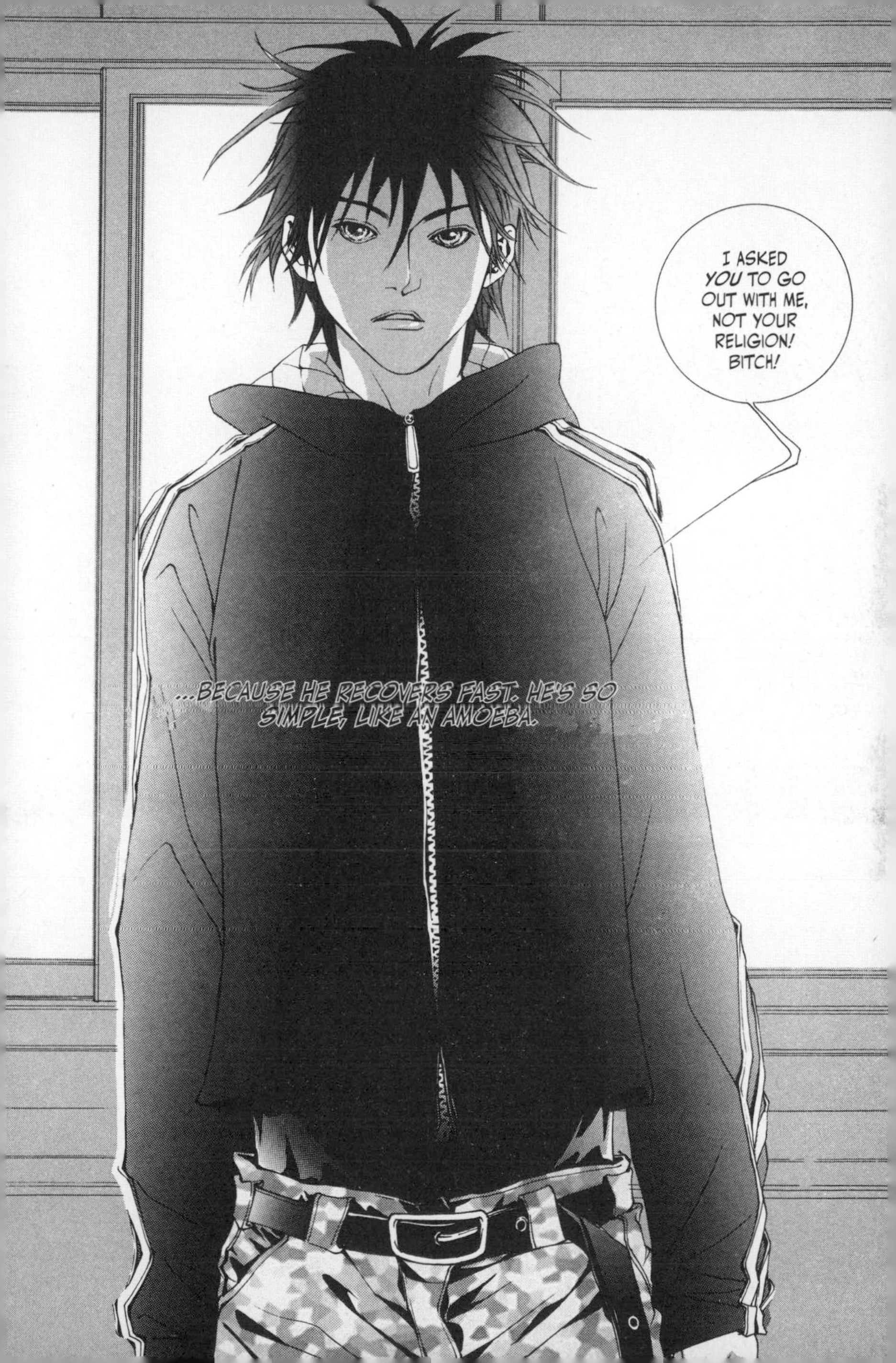
I ASKED YOU TO GO OUT WITH ME, NOT YOUR RELIGION! BITCH!
...BECAUSE HE RECOVERS FAST. HE'S SO SIMPLE, LIKE AN AMOEBA.

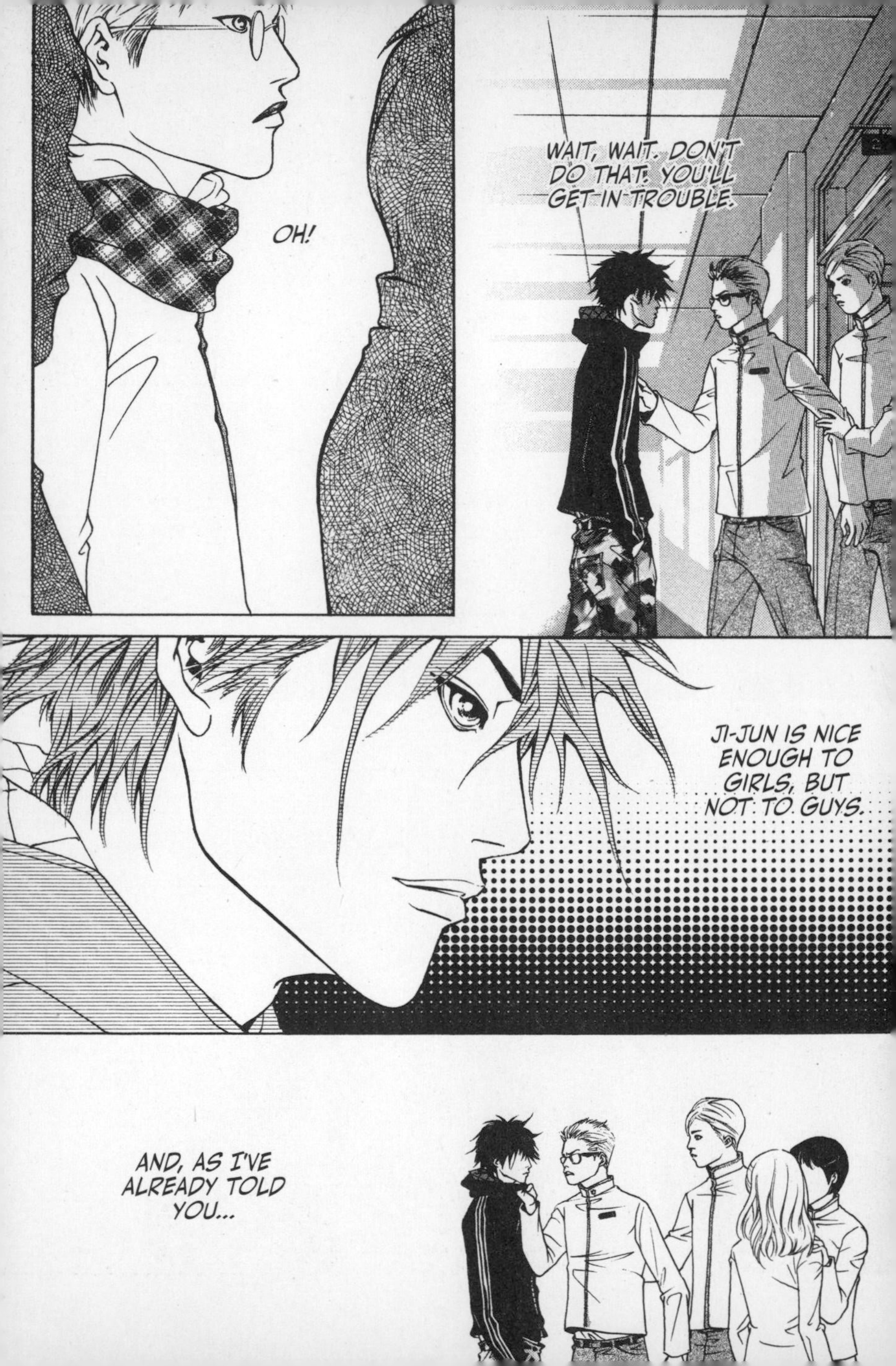
OH!
WAIT, WAIT. DON'T DO THAT. YOU'LL GET IN TROUBLE.
JI-JUN IS NICE ENOUGH TO GIRLS, BUT NOT TO GUYS.
AND, AS I'VE ALREADY TOLD YOU...

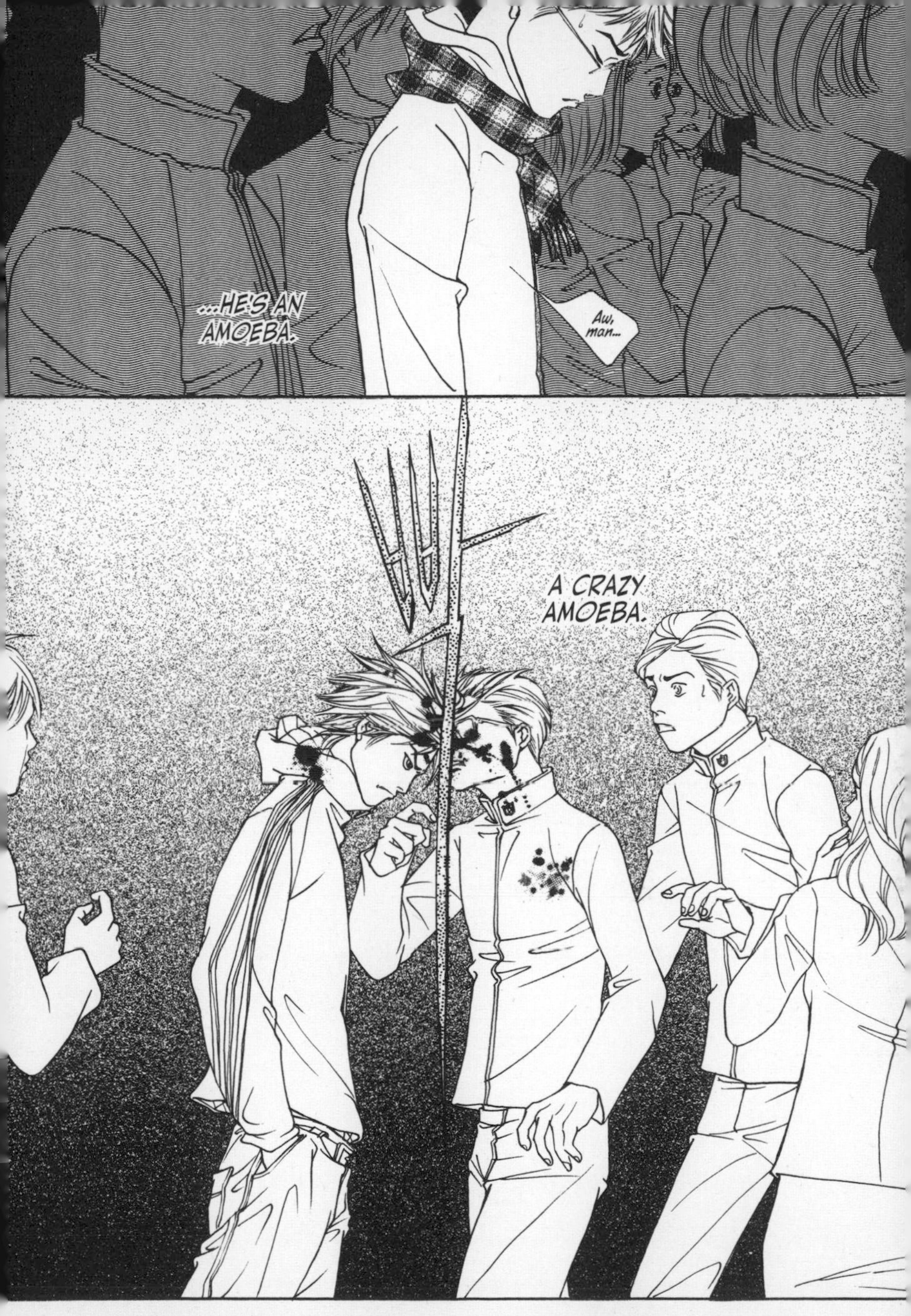
...HE'S AN AMOEBA.
Aw, man...
A CRAZY AMOEBA.

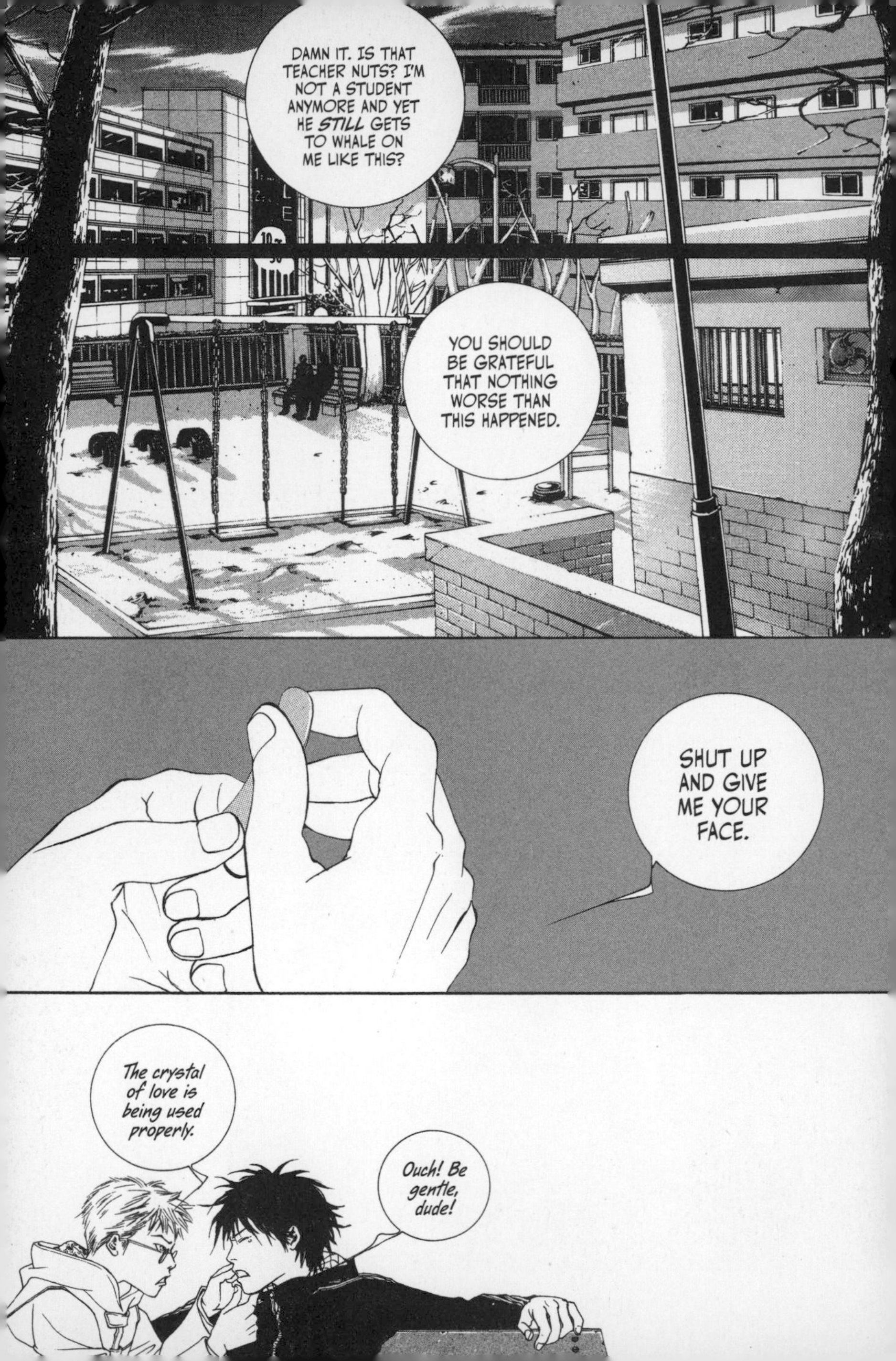
DAMN IT. IS THAT TEACHER NUTS? I'M NOT A STUDENT ANYMORE AND YET HE *STILL* GETS TO WHALE ON ME LIKE THIS?
YOU SHOULD BE GRATEFUL THAT NOTHING WORSE THAN THIS HAPPENED.
SHUT UP AND GIVE ME YOUR FACE.
The crystal of love is being used properly.
Ouch! Be gentle, dude!

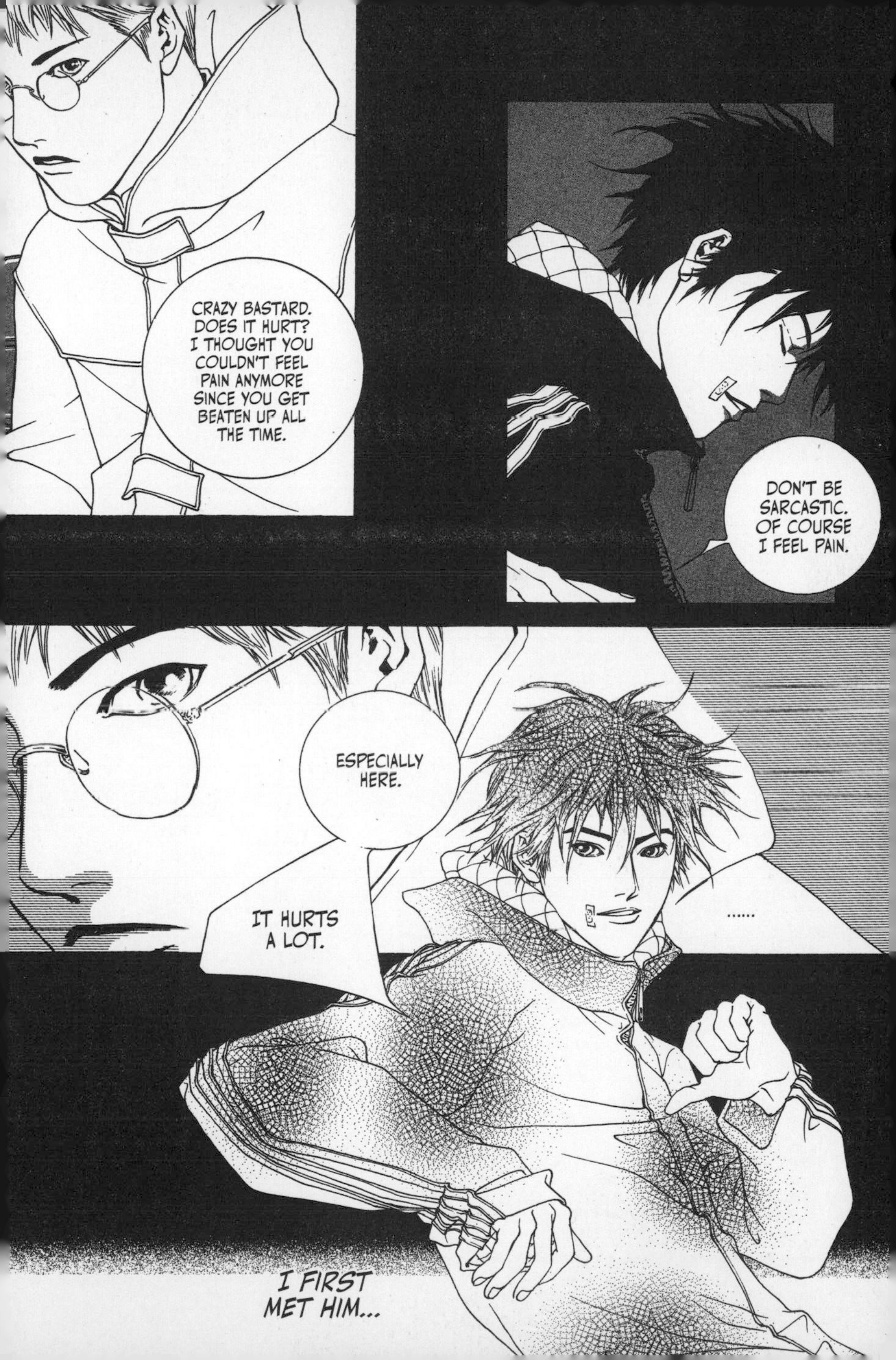
CRAZY BASTARD. DOES IT HURT? I THOUGHT YOU COULDN'T FEEL PAIN ANYMORE SINCE YOU GET BEATEN UP ALL THE TIME.
DON'T BE SARCASTIC. OF COURSE I FEEL PAIN.
ESPECIALLY HERE.
IT HURTS A LOT.
......
I FIRST MET HIM...

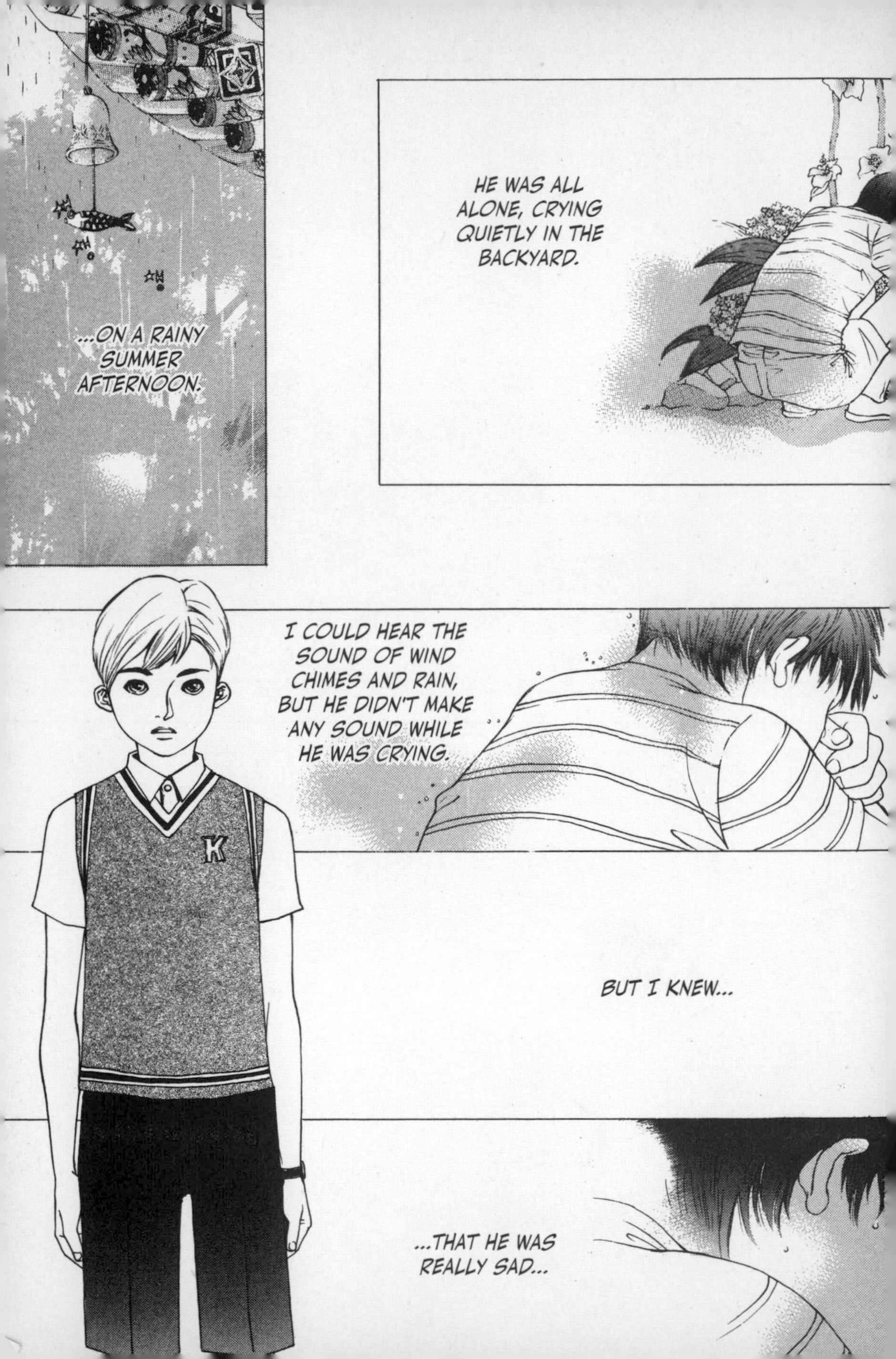
...ON A RAINY SUMMER AFTERNOON.
HE WAS ALL ALONE, CRYING QUIETLY IN THE BACKYARD.
I COULD HEAR THE SOUND OF WIND CHIMES AND RAIN, BUT HE DIDN'T MAKE ANY SOUND WHILE HE WAS CRYING.
BUT I KNEW...
...THAT HE WAS REALLY SAD...

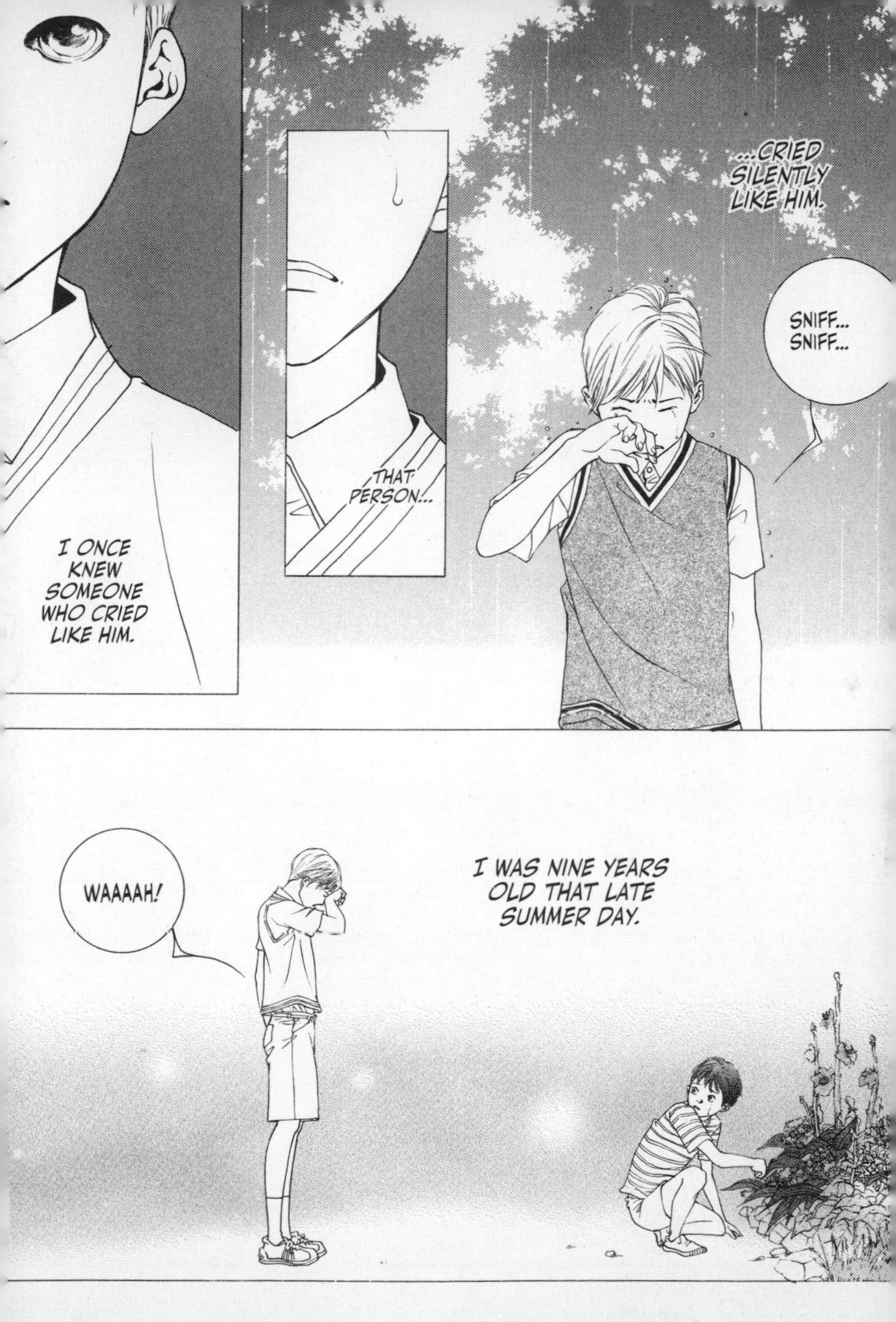
I ONCE KNEW SOMEONE WHO CRIED LIKE HIM.
THAT PERSON...
...CRIED SILENTLY LIKE HIM.
SNIFF... SNIFF...
WAAAAH!
I WAS NINE YEARS OLD THAT LATE SUMMER DAY.

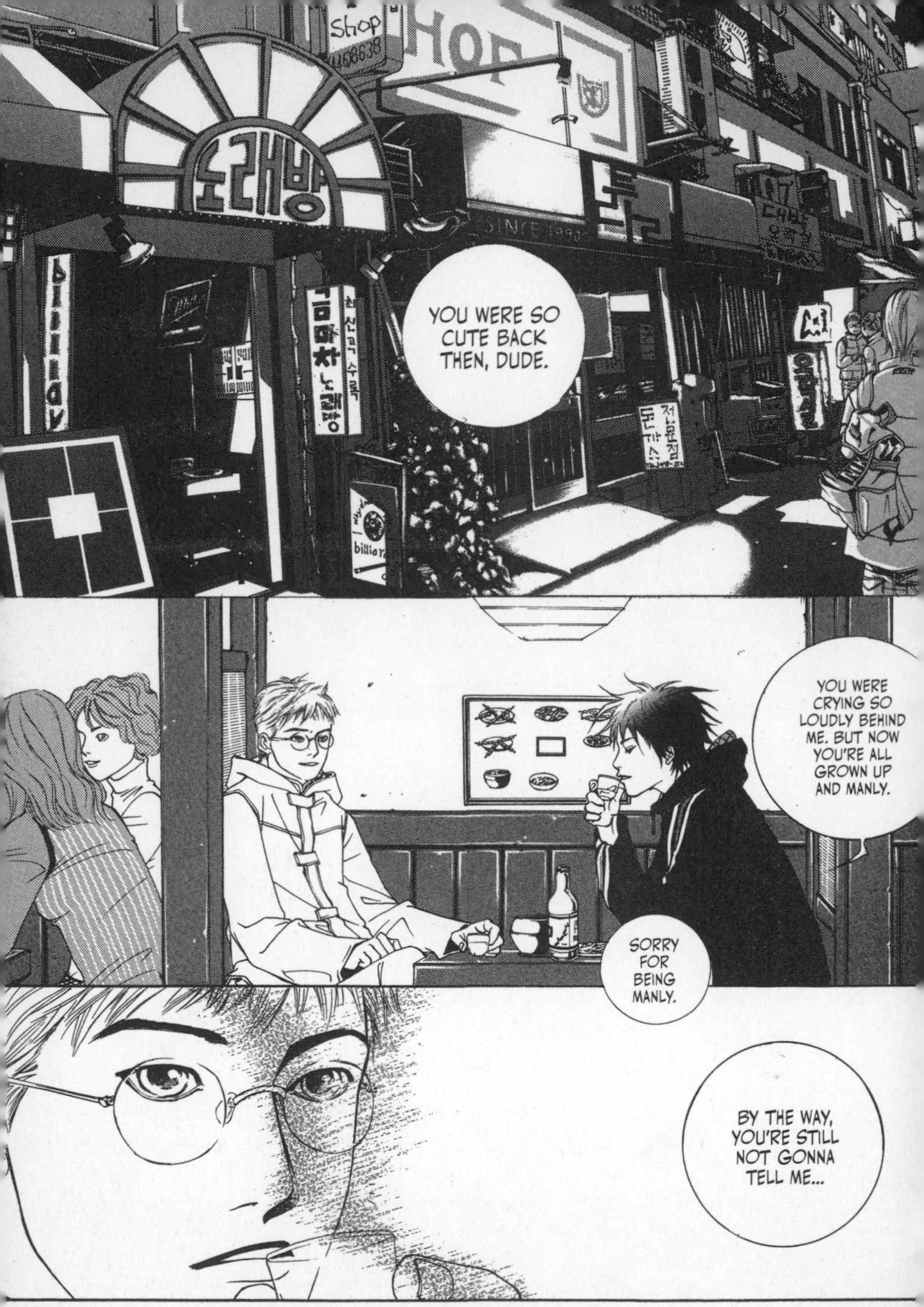
Shop
HOF
YOU WERE SO CUTE BACK THEN, DUDE.
YOU WERE CRYING SO LOUDLY BEHIND ME. BUT NOW YOU'RE ALL GROWN UP AND MANLY.
SORRY FOR BEING MANLY.
BY THE WAY, YOU'RE STILL NOT GONNA TELL ME...

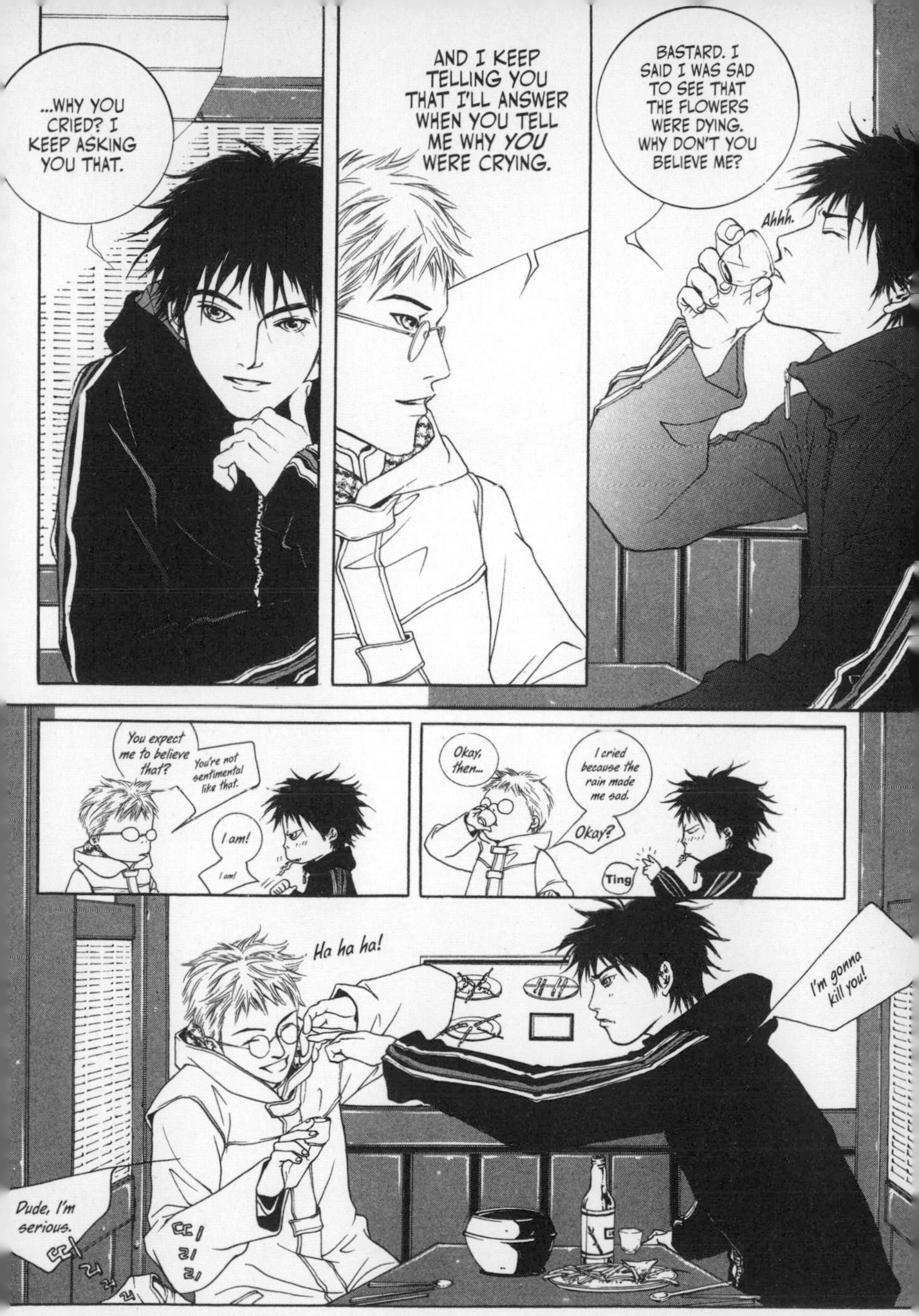
...WHY YOU CRIED? I KEEP ASKING YOU THAT.
AND I KEEP TELLING YOU THAT I'LL ANSWER WHEN YOU TELL ME WHY *YOU* WERE CRYING.
BASTARD. I SAID I WAS SAD TO SEE THAT THE FLOWERS WERE DYING. WHY DON'T YOU BELIEVE ME?
Ahhh.
You expect me to believe that?
You're not sentimental like that.
I am!
I am!
Okay, then...
I cried because the rain made me sad.
Okay?
Ting
Ha ha ha!
I'm gonna kill you!
Dude, I'm serious.

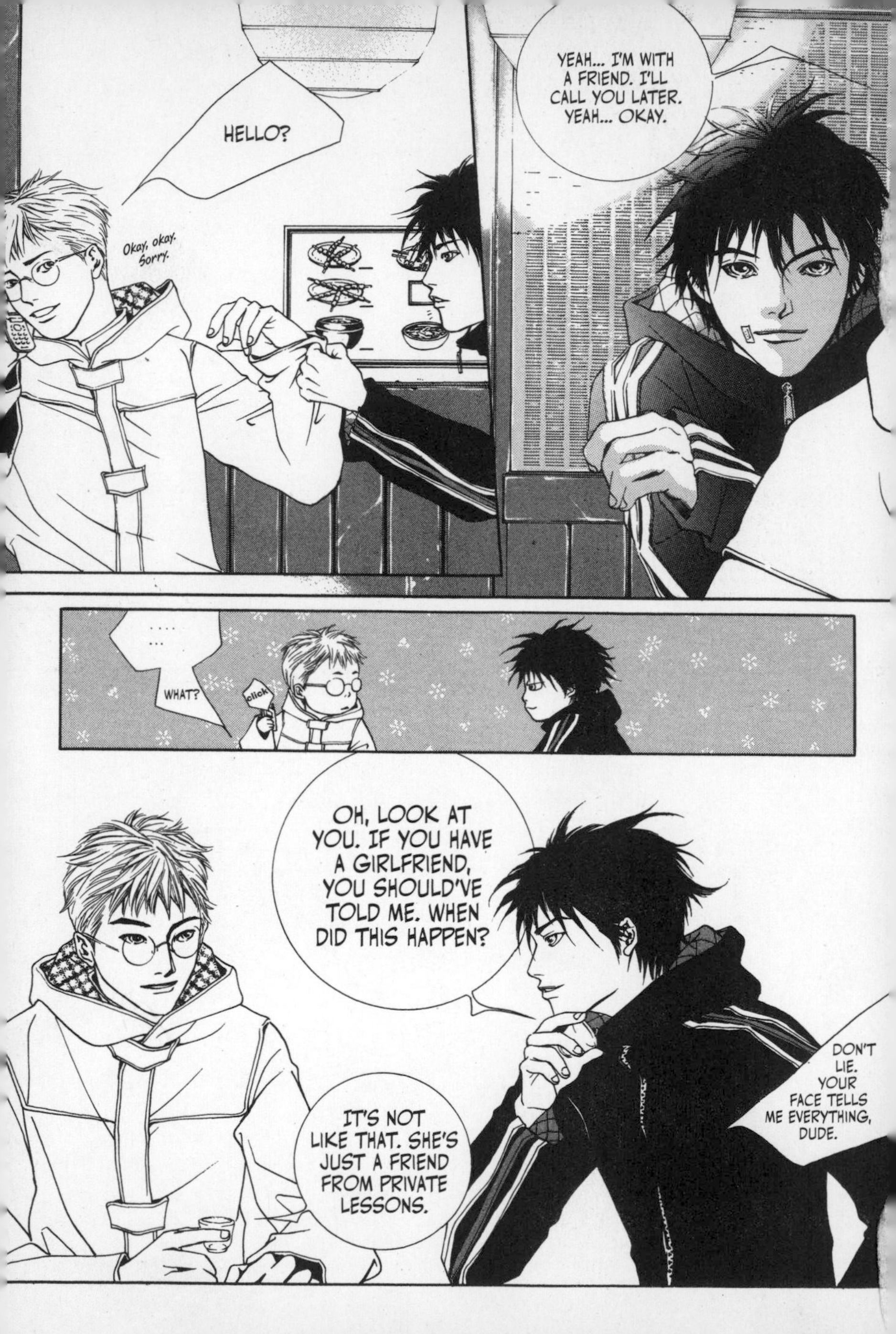
HELLO?
Okay, okay. Sorry.
YEAH... I'M WITH A FRIEND. I'LL CALL YOU LATER. YEAH... OKAY.
....
...
WHAT?
click
OH, LOOK AT YOU. IF YOU HAVE A GIRLFRIEND, YOU SHOULD'VE TOLD ME. WHEN DID THIS HAPPEN?
IT'S NOT LIKE THAT. SHE'S JUST A FRIEND FROM PRIVATE LESSONS.
DON'T LIE. YOUR FACE TELLS ME EVERYTHING, DUDE.

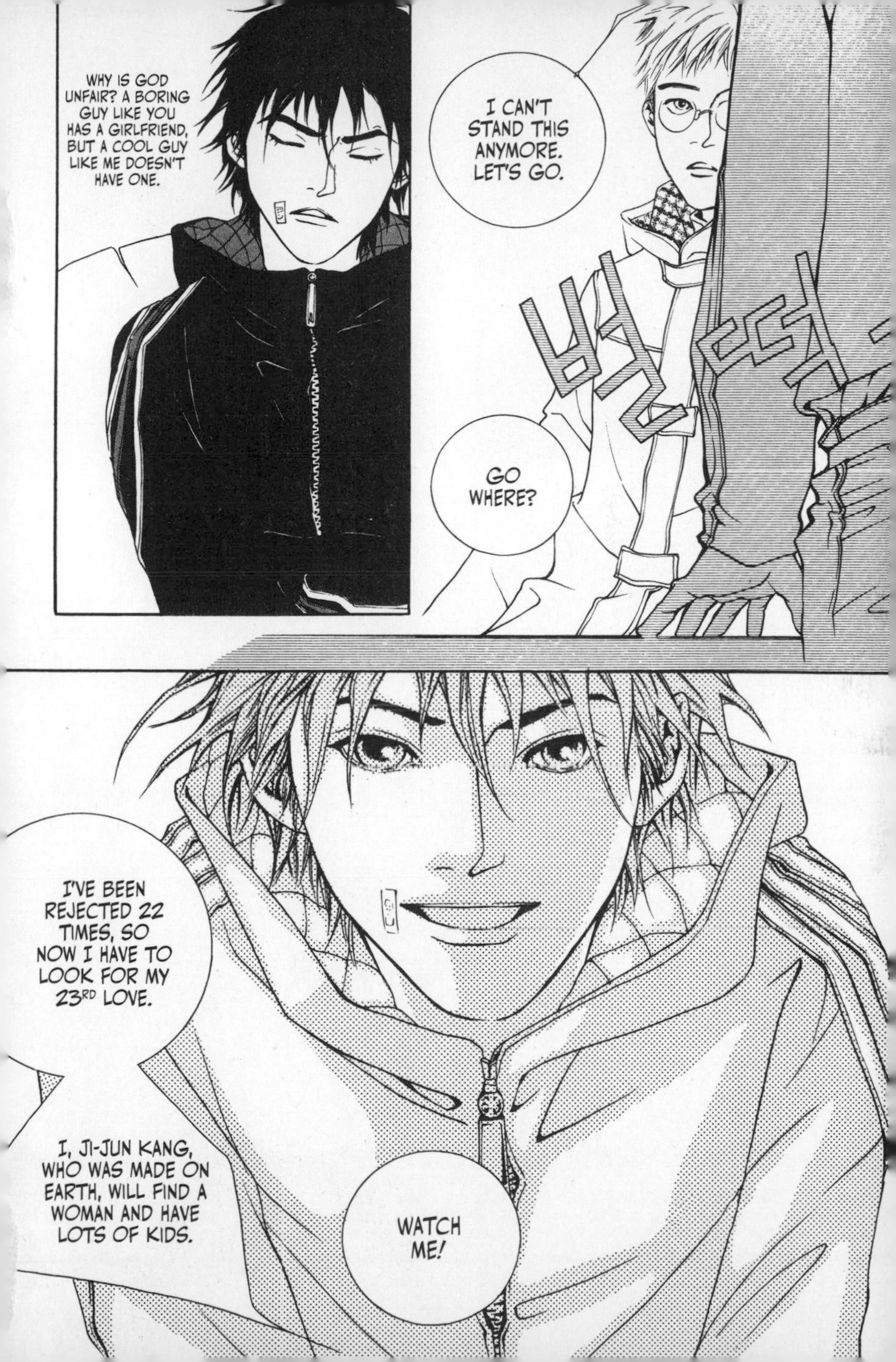
WHY IS GOD UNFAIR? A BORING GUY LIKE YOU HAS A GIRLFRIEND, BUT A COOL GUY LIKE ME DOESN'T HAVE ONE.
I CAN'T STAND THIS ANYMORE. LET'S GO.
GO WHERE?
I'VE BEEN REJECTED 22 TIMES, SO NOW I HAVE TO LOOK FOR MY 23RD LOVE.
I, JI-JUN KANG, WHO WAS MADE ON EARTH, WILL FIND A WOMAN AND HAVE LOTS OF KIDS.
WATCH ME!

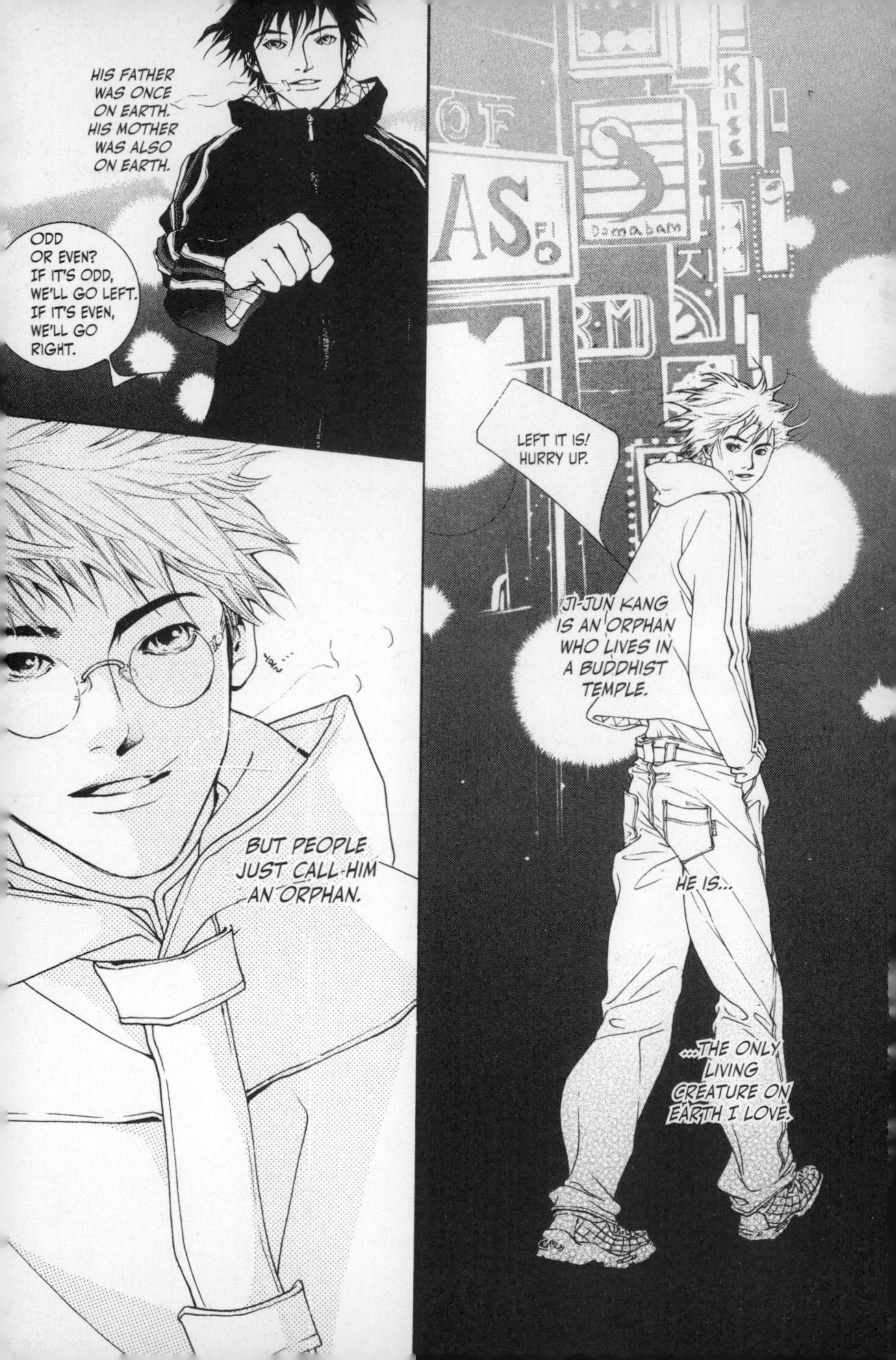
HIS FATHER WAS ONCE ON EARTH. HIS MOTHER WAS ALSO ON EARTH.
ODD OR EVEN? IF IT'S ODD, WE'LL GO LEFT. IF IT'S EVEN, WE'LL GO RIGHT.
BUT PEOPLE JUST CALL HIM AN ORPHAN.
LEFT IT IS! HURRY UP.
JI-JUN KANG IS AN ORPHAN WHO LIVES IN A BUDDHIST TEMPLE.
HE IS...
...THE ONLY LIVING CREATURE ON EARTH I LOVE.

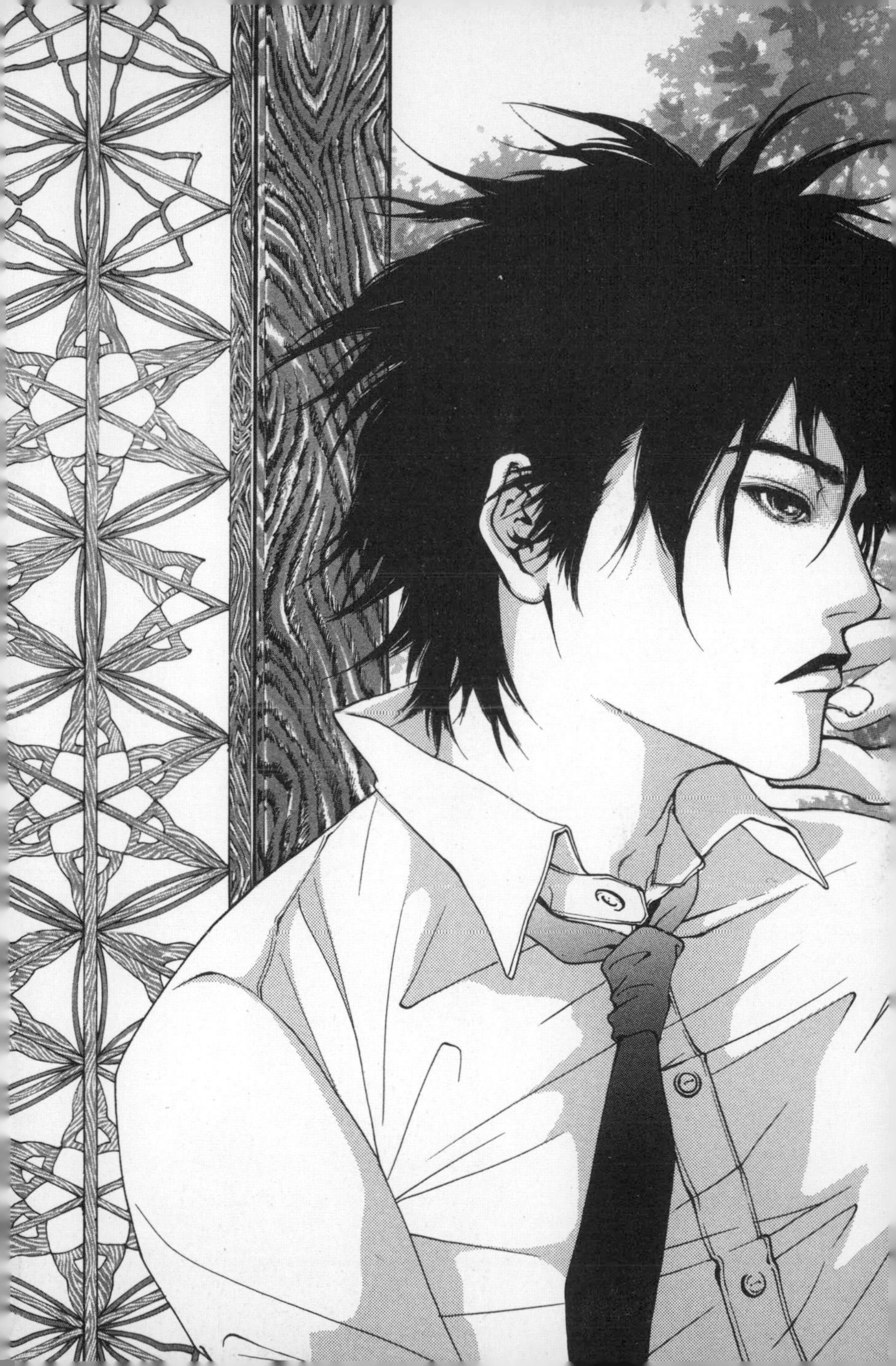

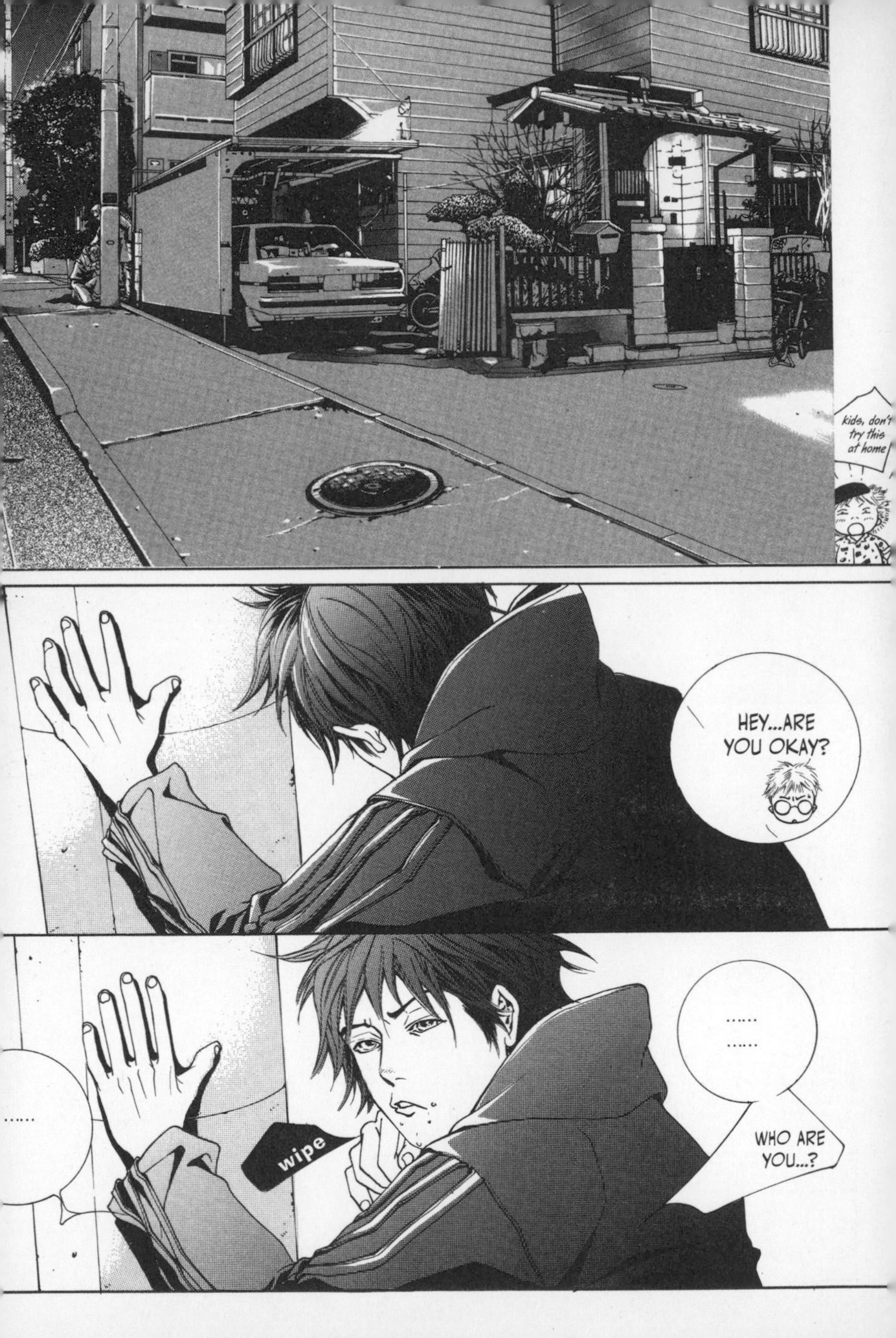
kids, don't try this at home
HEY...ARE YOU OKAY?
......
wipe
......
......
WHO ARE YOU...?

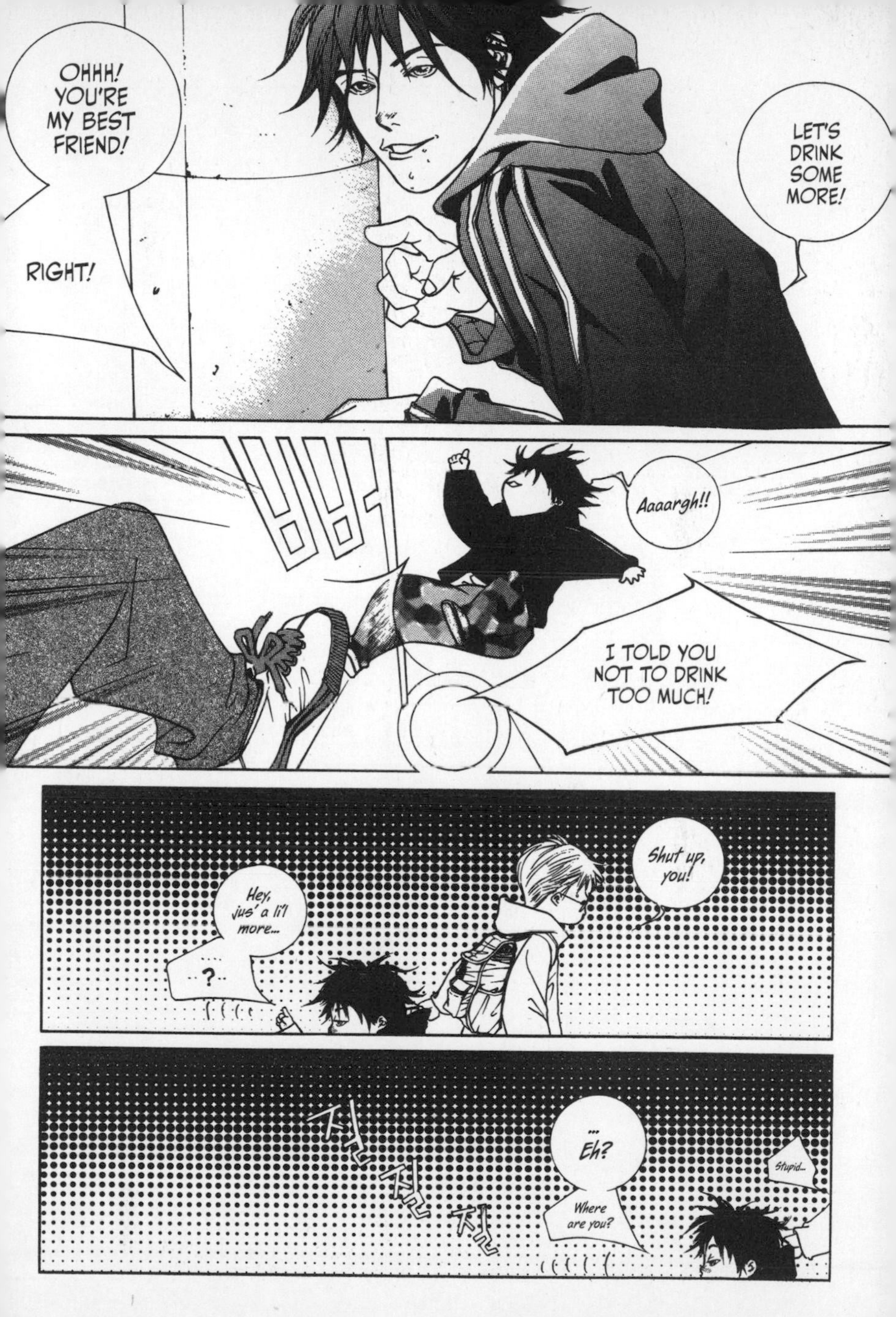
OHHH! YOU'RE MY BEST FRIEND!
RIGHT!
LET'S DRINK SOME MORE!
Aaaargh!!
I TOLD YOU NOT TO DRINK TOO MUCH!
Hey, jus' a li'l more...
....
?
Shut up, you!
...
Eh?
Where are you?
Stupid...

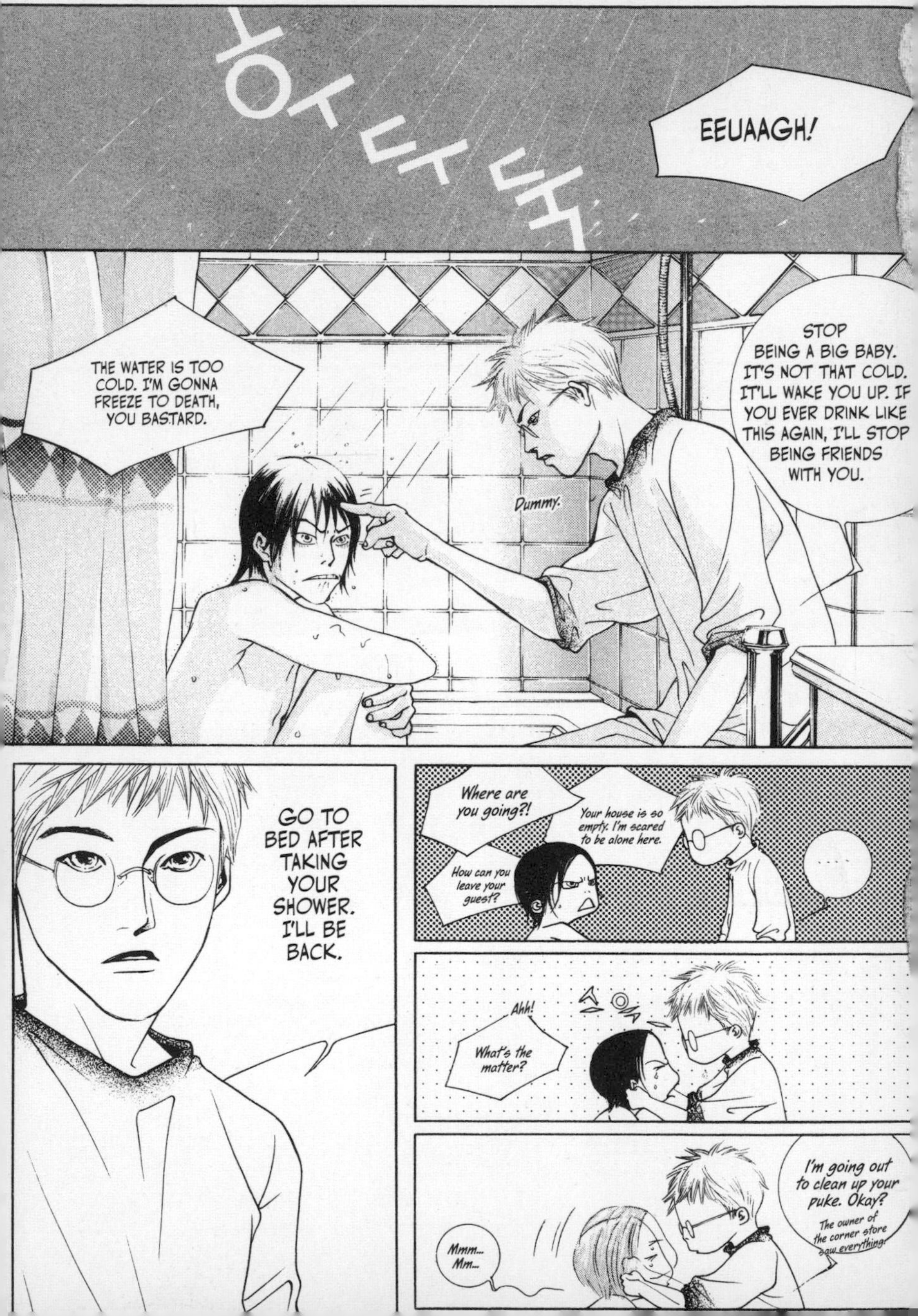
EEUAAGH!
THE WATER IS TOO COLD. I'M GONNA FREEZE TO DEATH, YOU BASTARD.
Dummy.
STOP BEING A BIG BABY. IT'S NOT THAT COLD. IT'LL WAKE YOU UP. IF YOU EVER DRINK LIKE THIS AGAIN, I'LL STOP BEING FRIENDS WITH YOU.
GO TO BED AFTER TAKING YOUR SHOWER. I'LL BE BACK.
Where are you going?!
Your house is so empty. I'm scared to be alone here.
How can you leave your guest?
....
Ahh!
What's the matter?
Mmm... Mm...
I'm going out to clean up your puke. Okay?
The owner of the corner store saw everything!

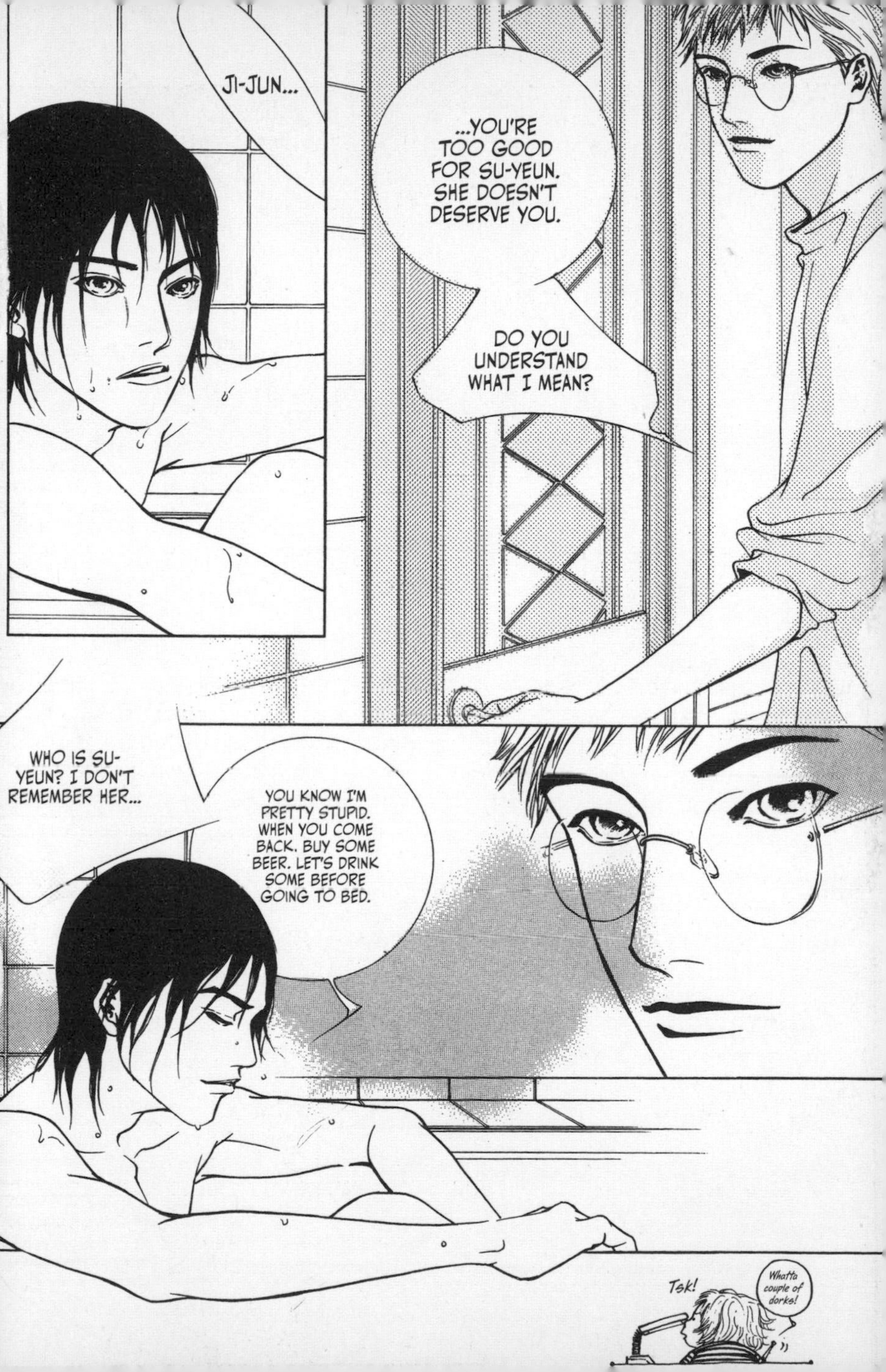
JI-JUN...
...YOU'RE TOO GOOD FOR SU-YEUN. SHE DOESN'T DESERVE YOU.
DO YOU UNDERSTAND WHAT I MEAN?
WHO IS SU-YEUN? I DON'T REMEMBER HER...
YOU KNOW I'M PRETTY STUPID. WHEN YOU COME BACK. BUY SOME BEER. LET'S DRINK SOME BEFORE GOING TO BED.
Tsk!
Whatta couple of dorks!

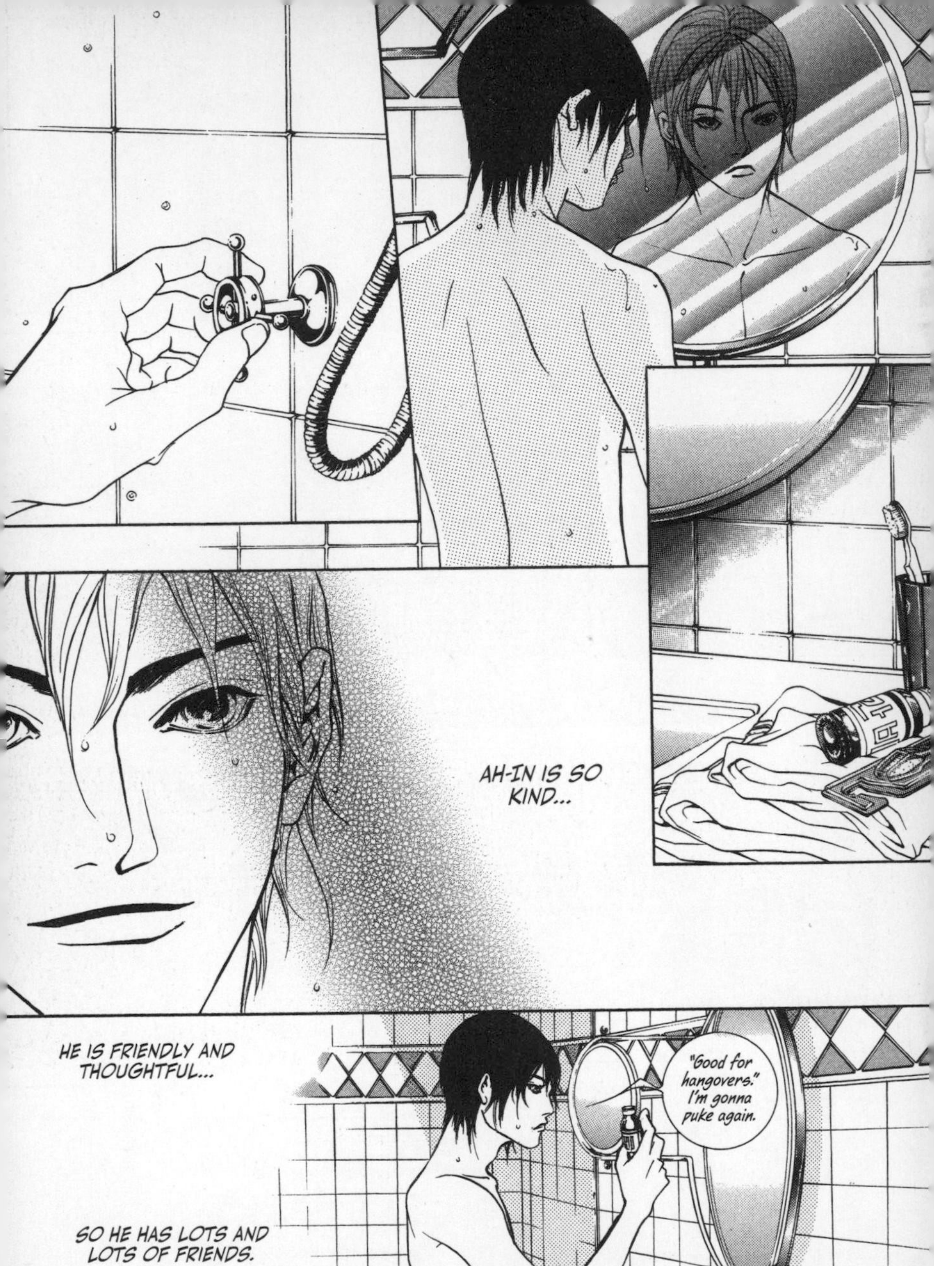
AH-IN IS SO KIND...
HE IS FRIENDLY AND THOUGHTFUL...
"Good for hangovers." I'm gonna puke again.
SO HE HAS LOTS AND LOTS OF FRIENDS.

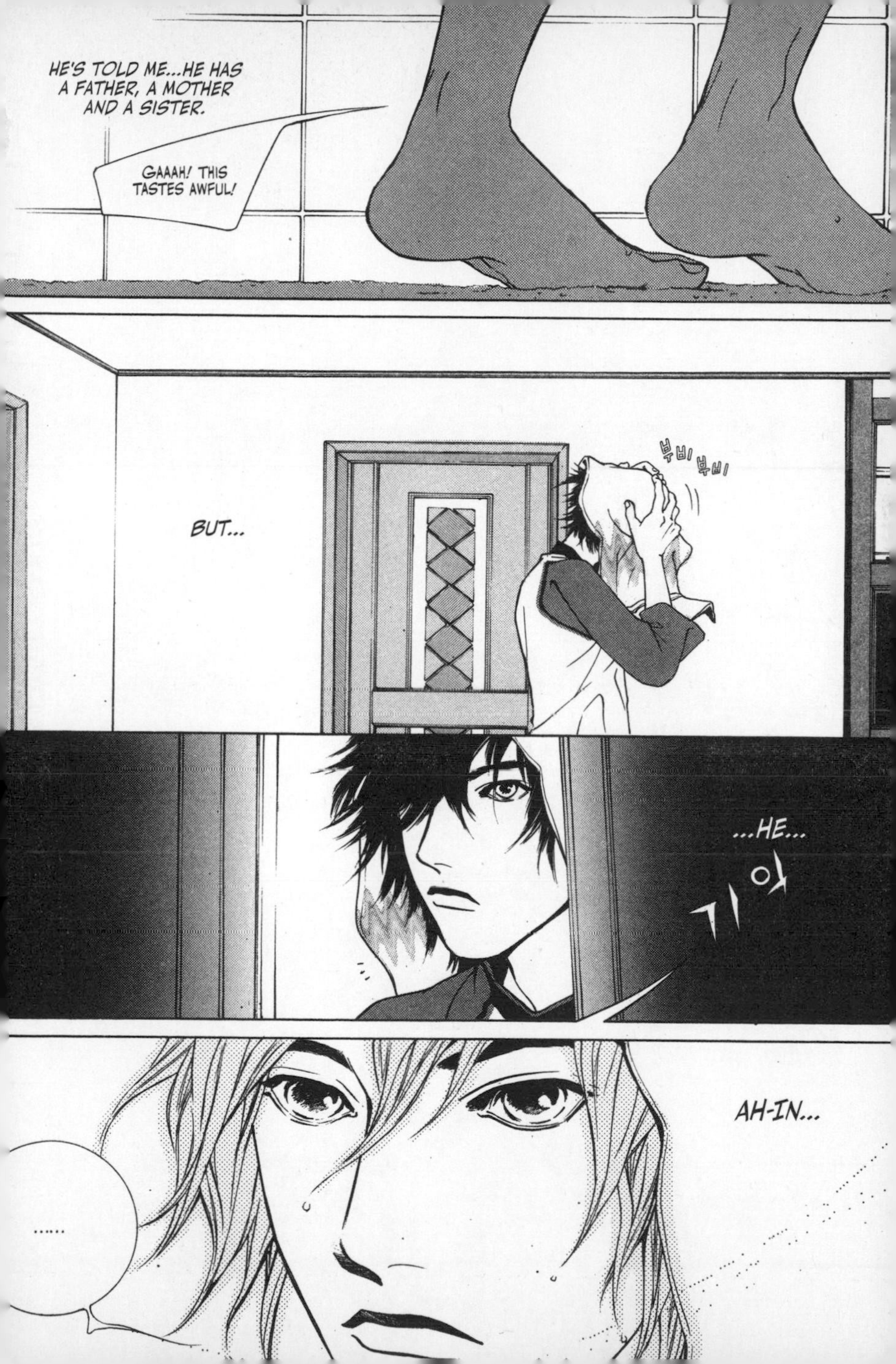
HE'S TOLD ME...HE HAS A FATHER, A MOTHER AND A SISTER.
GAAAH! THIS TASTES AWFUL!
BUT...
부비 부비
...HE...
기억
AH-IN...
......

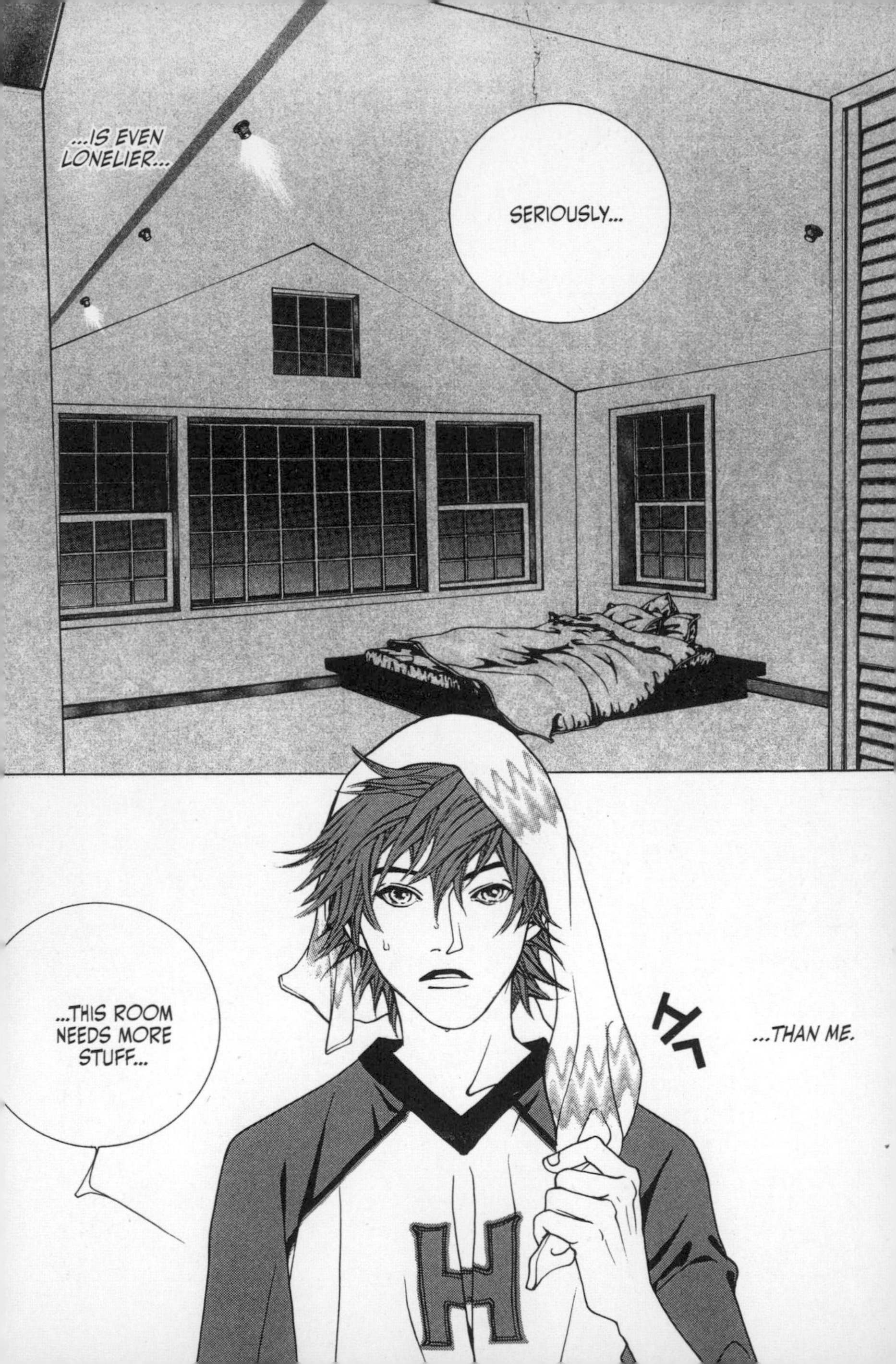
...IS EVEN LONELIER...
SERIOUSLY...
...THIS ROOM NEEDS MORE STUFF...
...THAN ME.

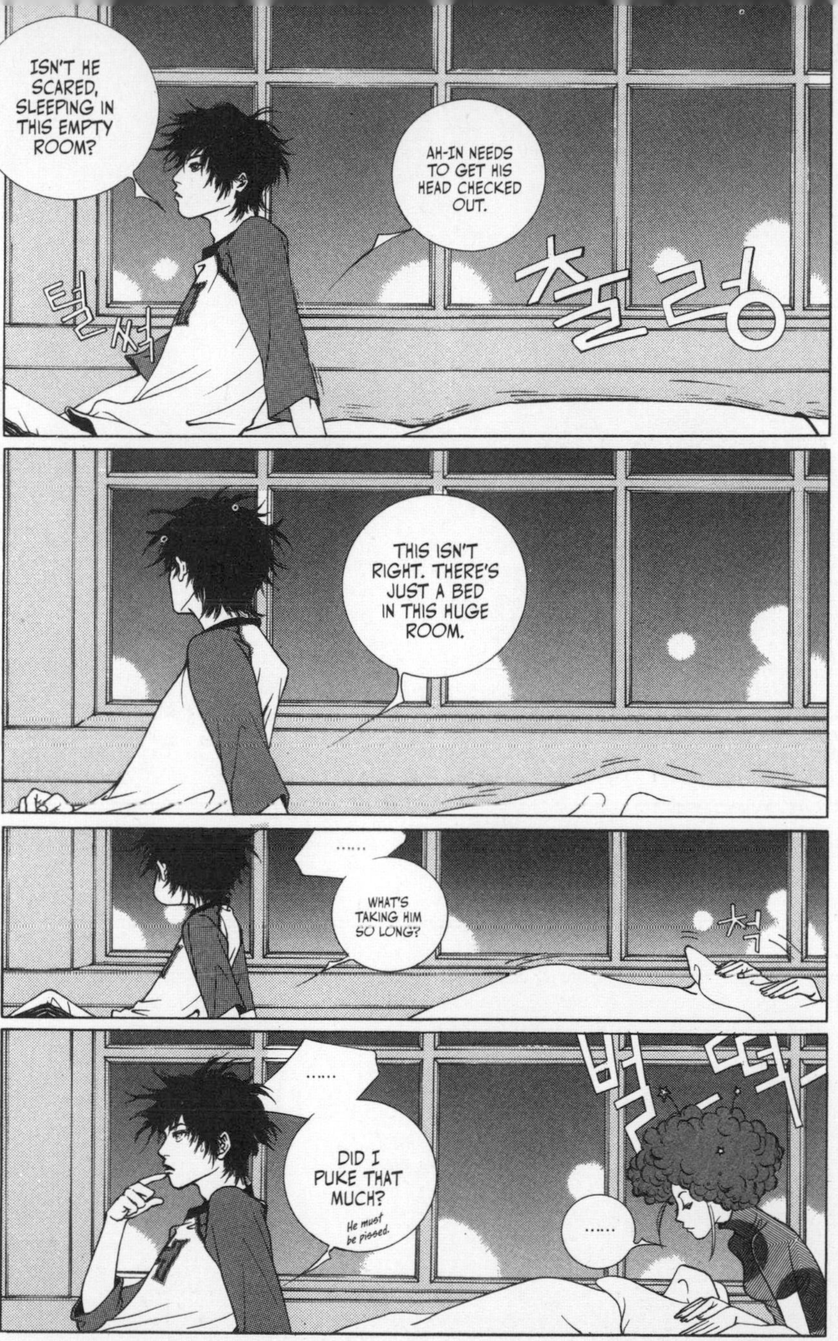
ISN'T HE SCARED, SLEEPING IN THIS EMPTY ROOM?
AH-IN NEEDS TO GET HIS HEAD CHECKED OUT.
THIS ISN'T RIGHT. THERE'S JUST A BED IN THIS HUGE ROOM.
......
WHAT'S TAKING HIM SO LONG?
척
......
DID I PUKE THAT MUCH?
He must be pissed.
벌떡
......

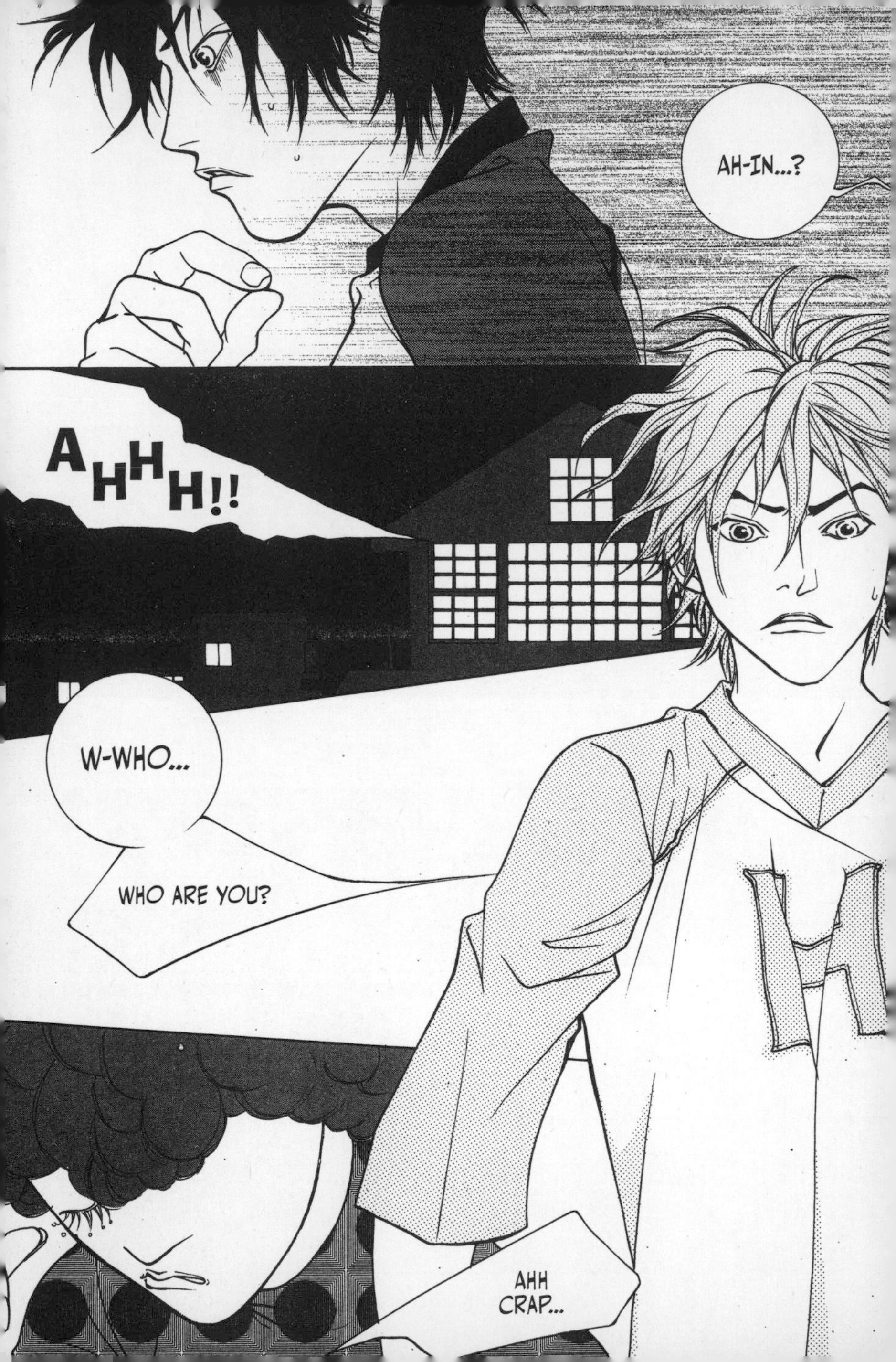
AH-IN...?
AHHH!!
W-WHO...
WHO ARE YOU?
AHH CRAP...

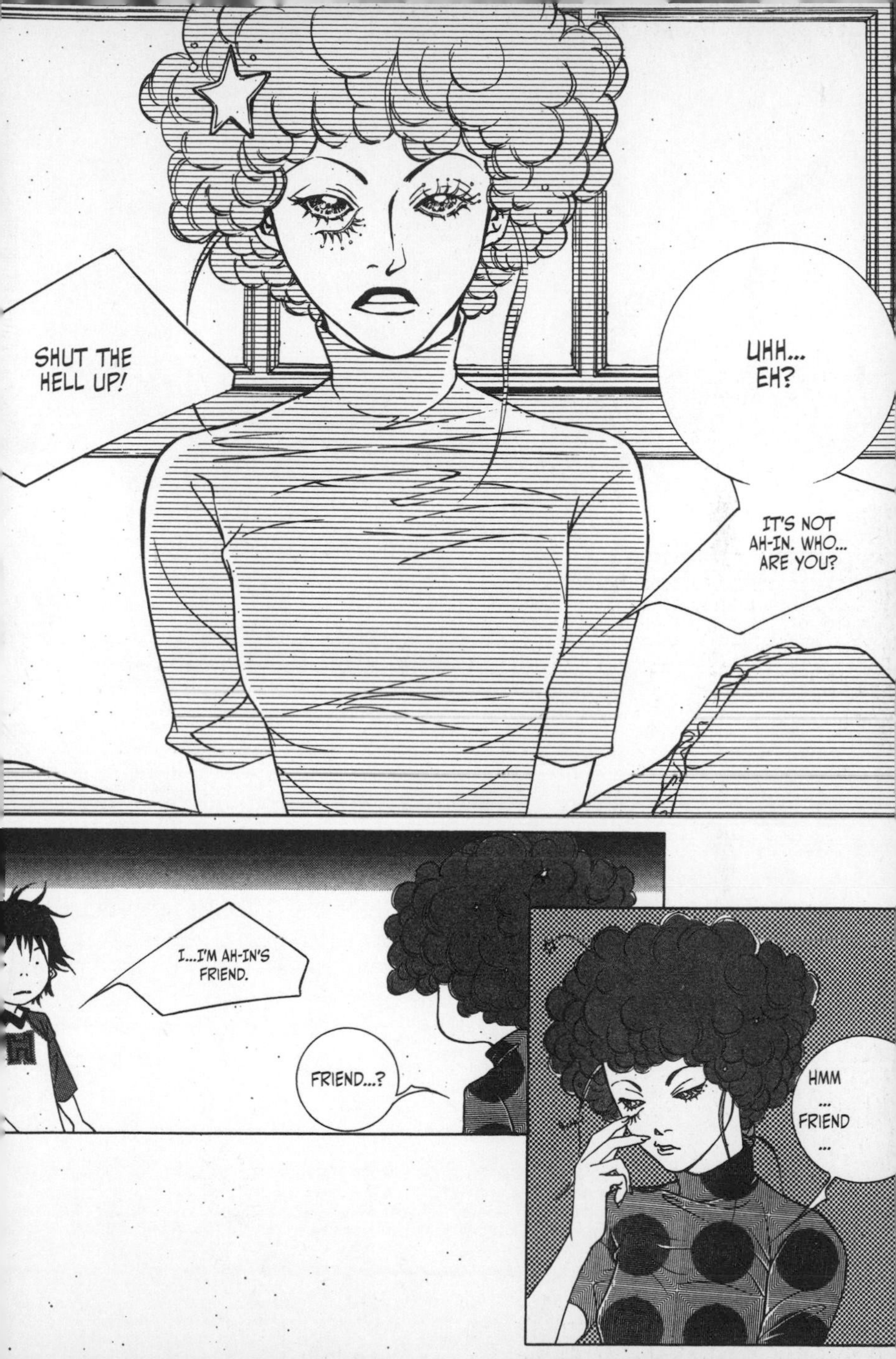
SHUT THE HELL UP!
UHH... EH?
IT'S NOT AH-IN. WHO... ARE YOU?
I...I'M AH-IN'S FRIEND.
FRIEND...?
HMM ... FRIEND ...

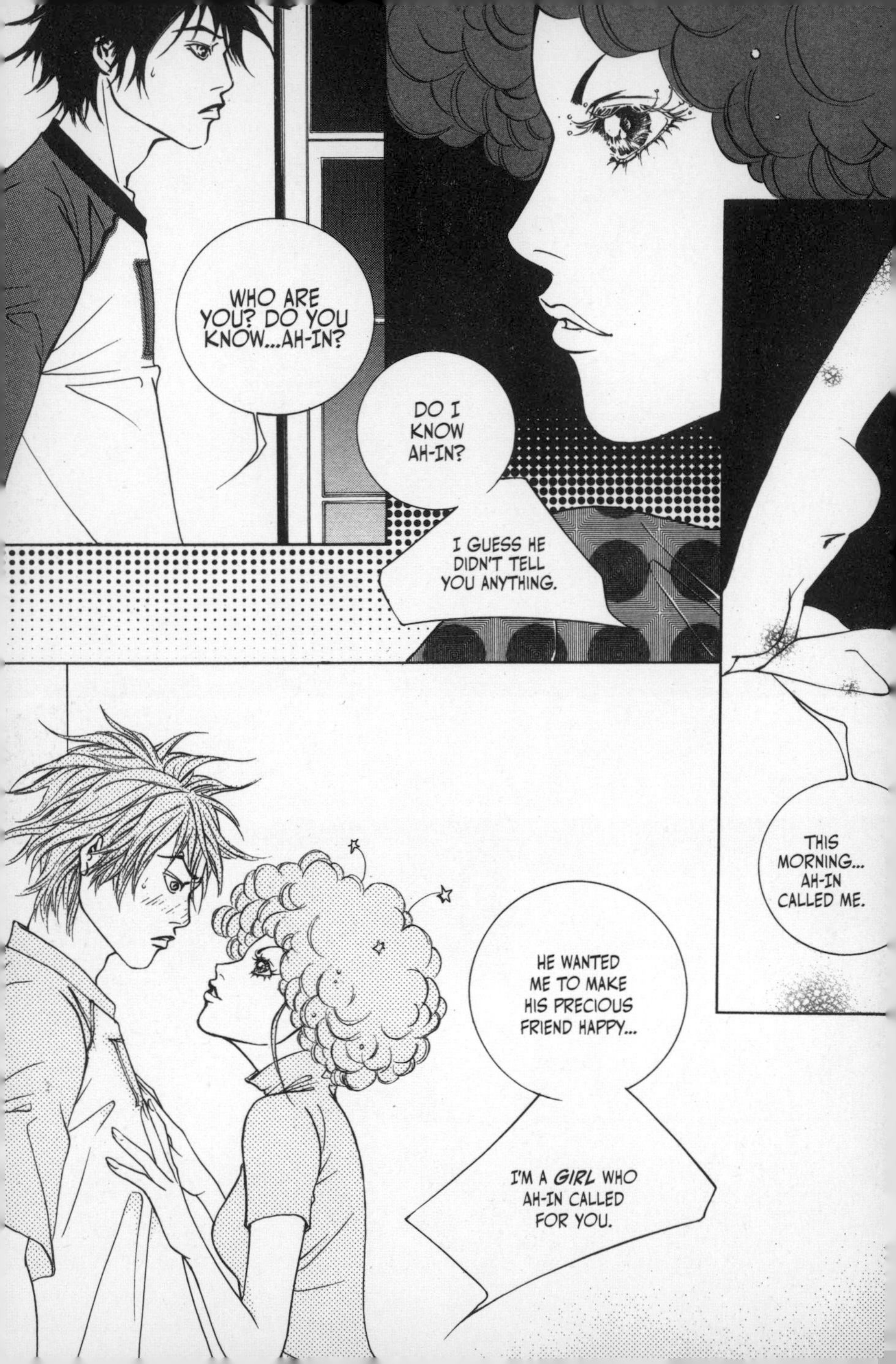
WHO ARE YOU? DO YOU KNOW...AH-IN?
DO I KNOW AH-IN?
I GUESS HE DIDN'T TELL YOU ANYTHING.
THIS MORNING... AH-IN CALLED ME.
HE WANTED ME TO MAKE HIS PRECIOUS FRIEND HAPPY...
I'M A *GIRL* WHO AH-IN CALLED FOR YOU.

AH-RIP LEE...
STOP TEASING HIM. HE'S IN SHOCK.
AHH... UM... SNIFF...
Tsk. I was just having a bit of fun.
Sorry. I didn't know she was here.
Sniff, sniff.
Boring. That's why I don't like young boys.
This wig makes my hair itch. Should I take it off?

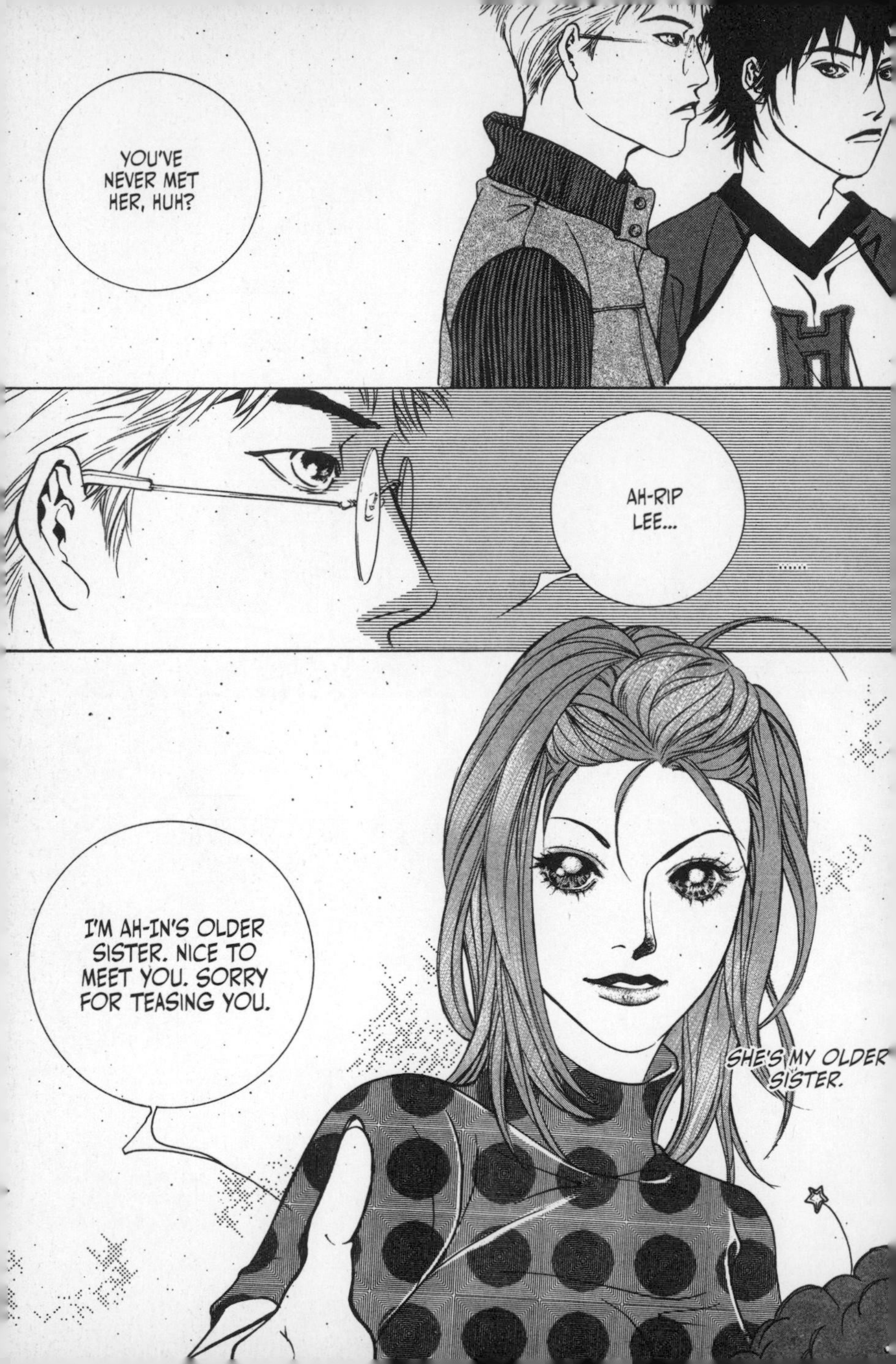
YOU'VE NEVER MET HER, HUH?
AH-RIP LEE...
......
I'M AH-IN'S OLDER SISTER. NICE TO MEET YOU. SORRY FOR TEASING YOU.
SHE'S MY OLDER SISTER.

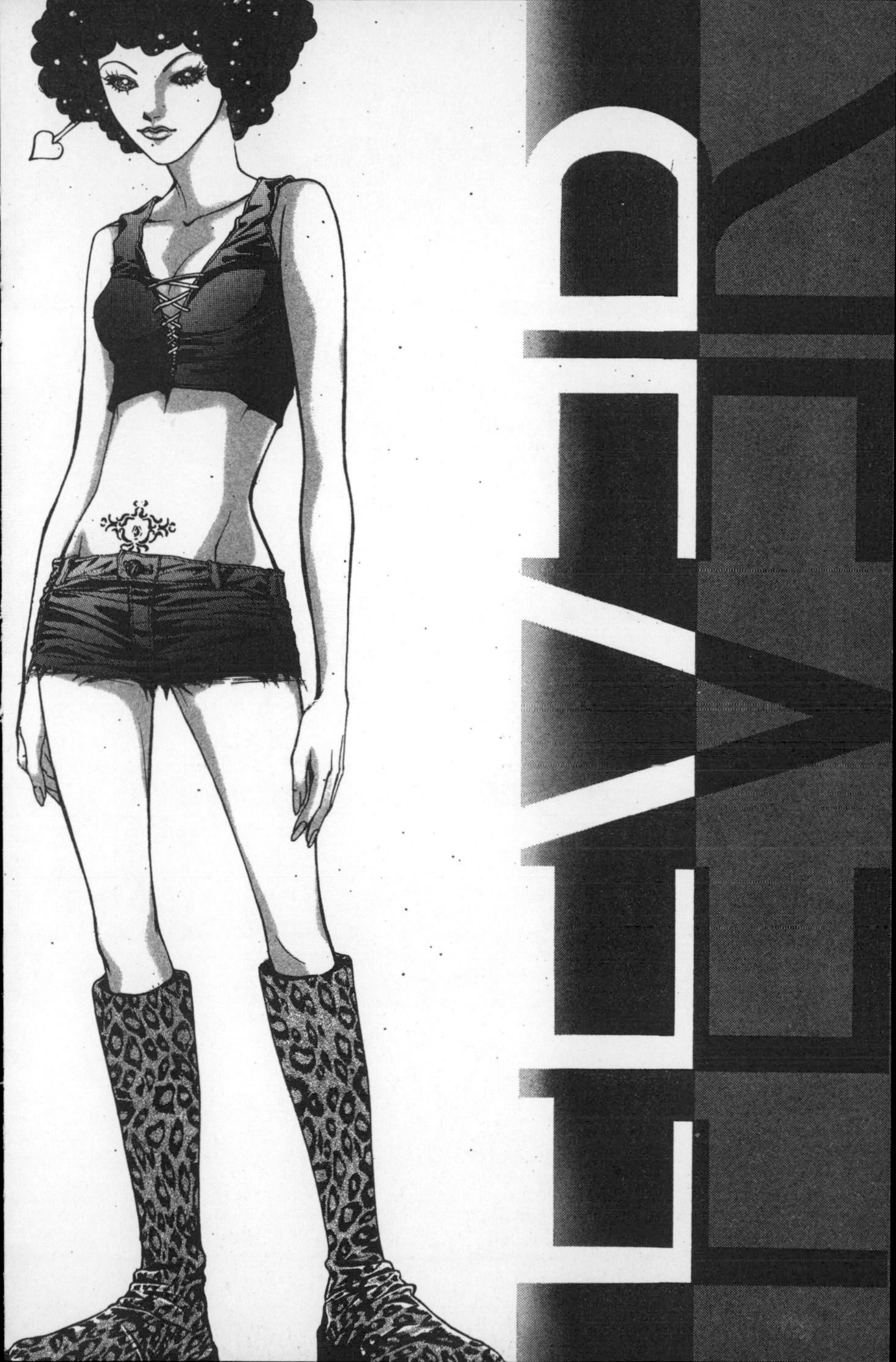

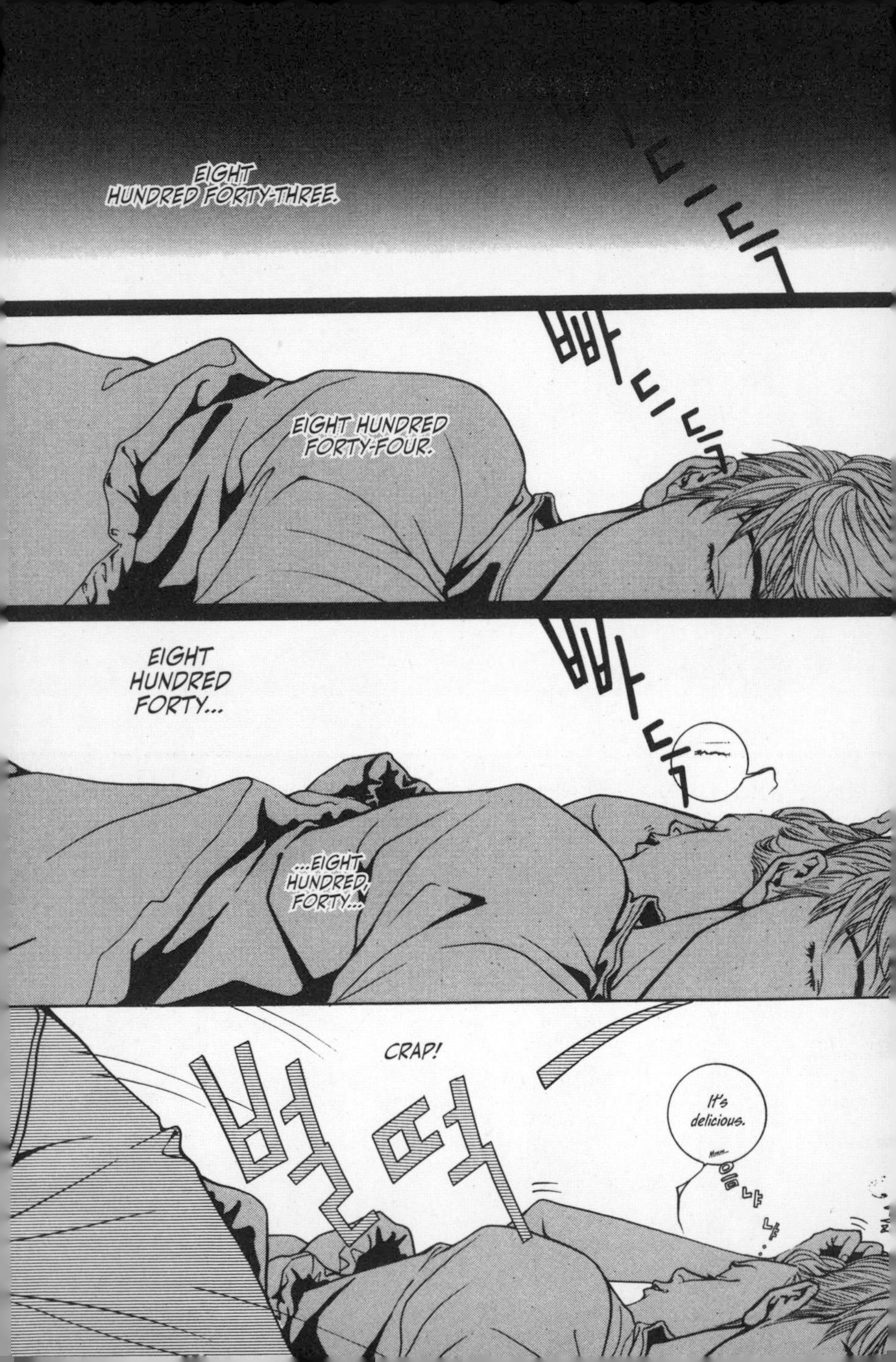
EIGHT HUNDRED FORTY-THREE.
EIGHT HUNDRED FORTY-FOUR.
EIGHT HUNDRED FORTY...
...EIGHT HUNDRED, FORTY...
CRAP!
벌떡
It's delicious.
Mmm...
음냐 냐

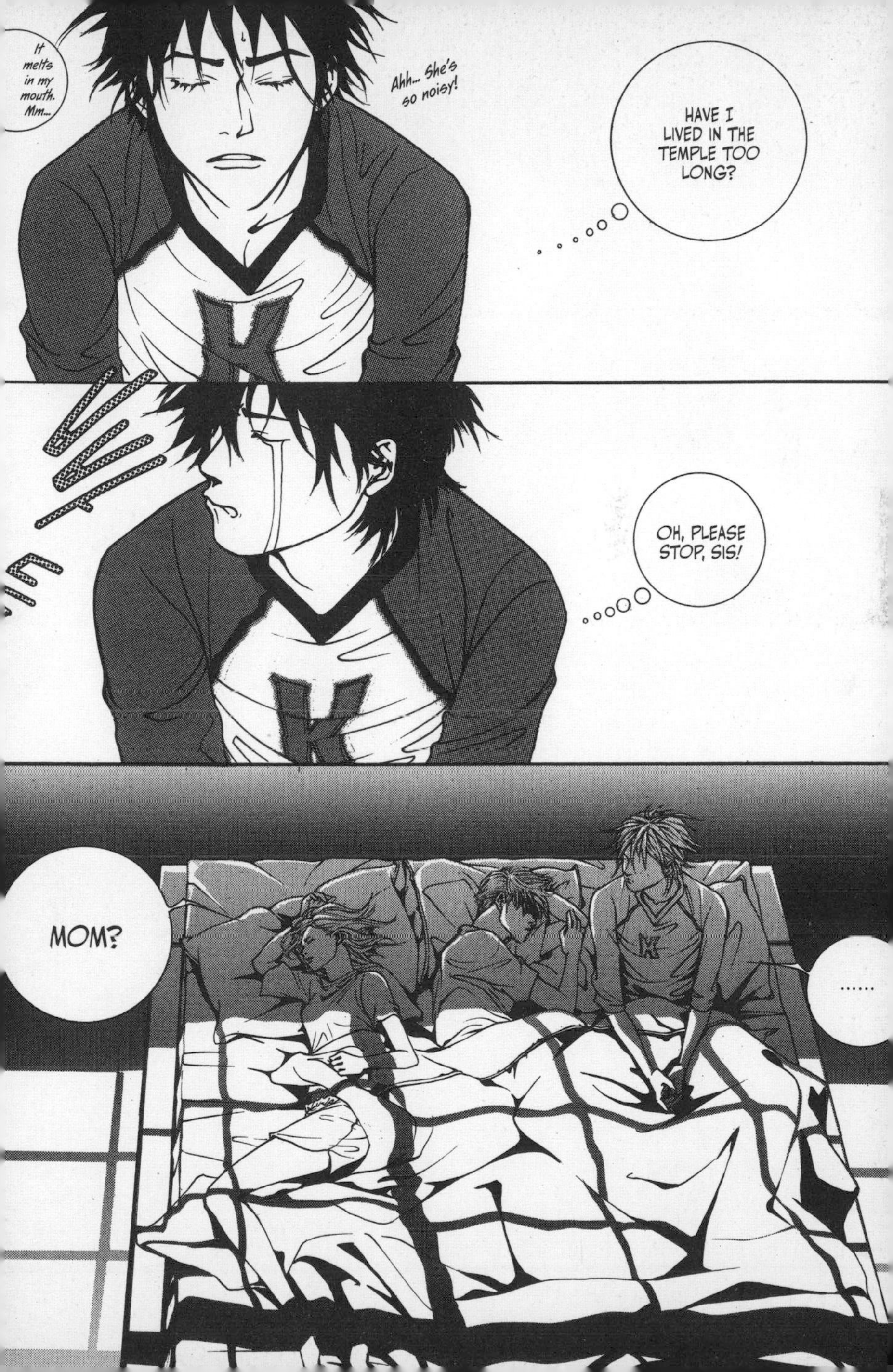
It melts in my mouth. Mm...
Ahh... She's so noisy!
HAVE I LIVED IN THE TEMPLE TOO LONG?
OH, PLEASE STOP, SIS!
MOM?
......

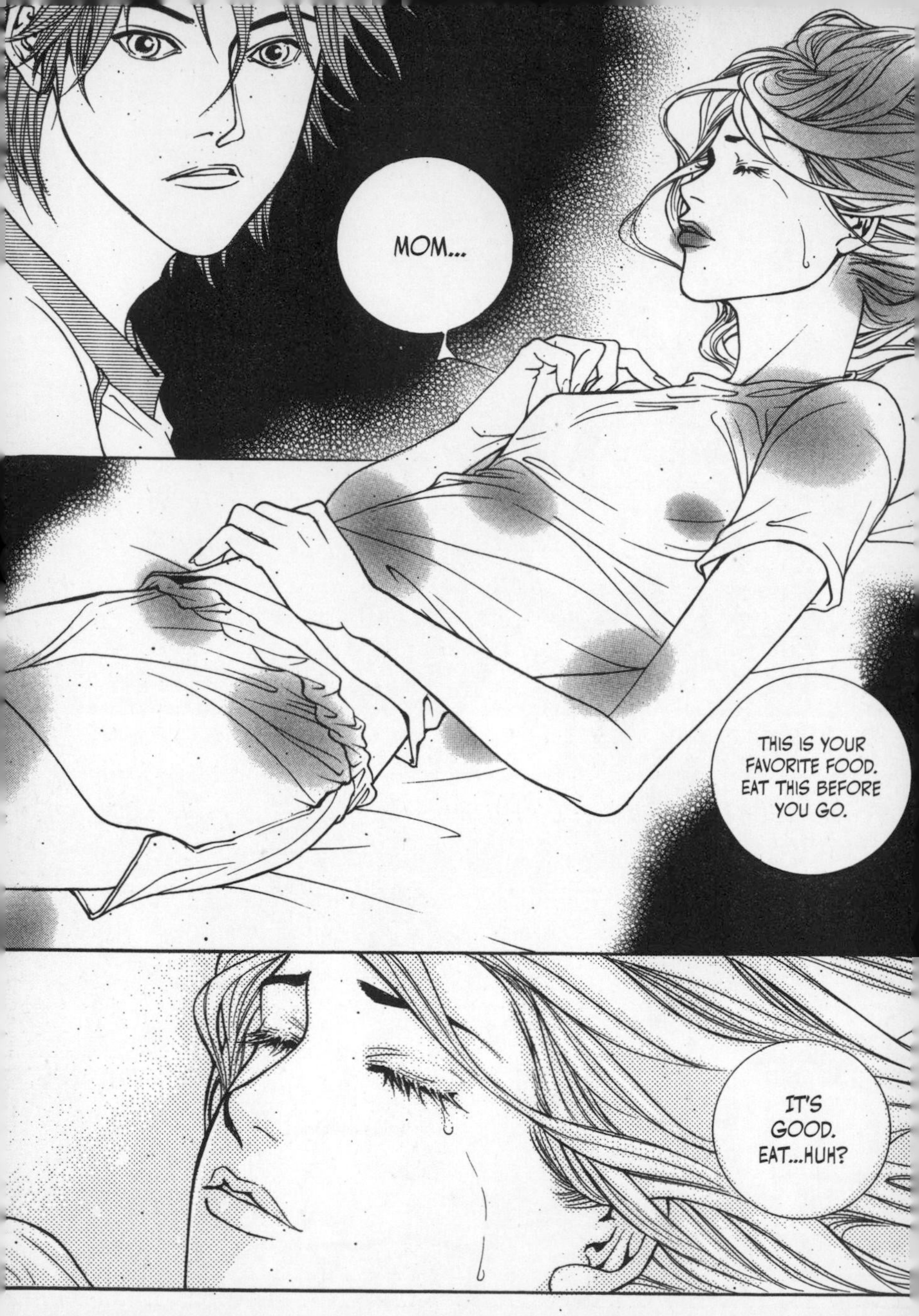
MOM...
THIS IS YOUR FAVORITE FOOD. EAT THIS BEFORE YOU GO.
IT'S GOOD. EAT...HUH?

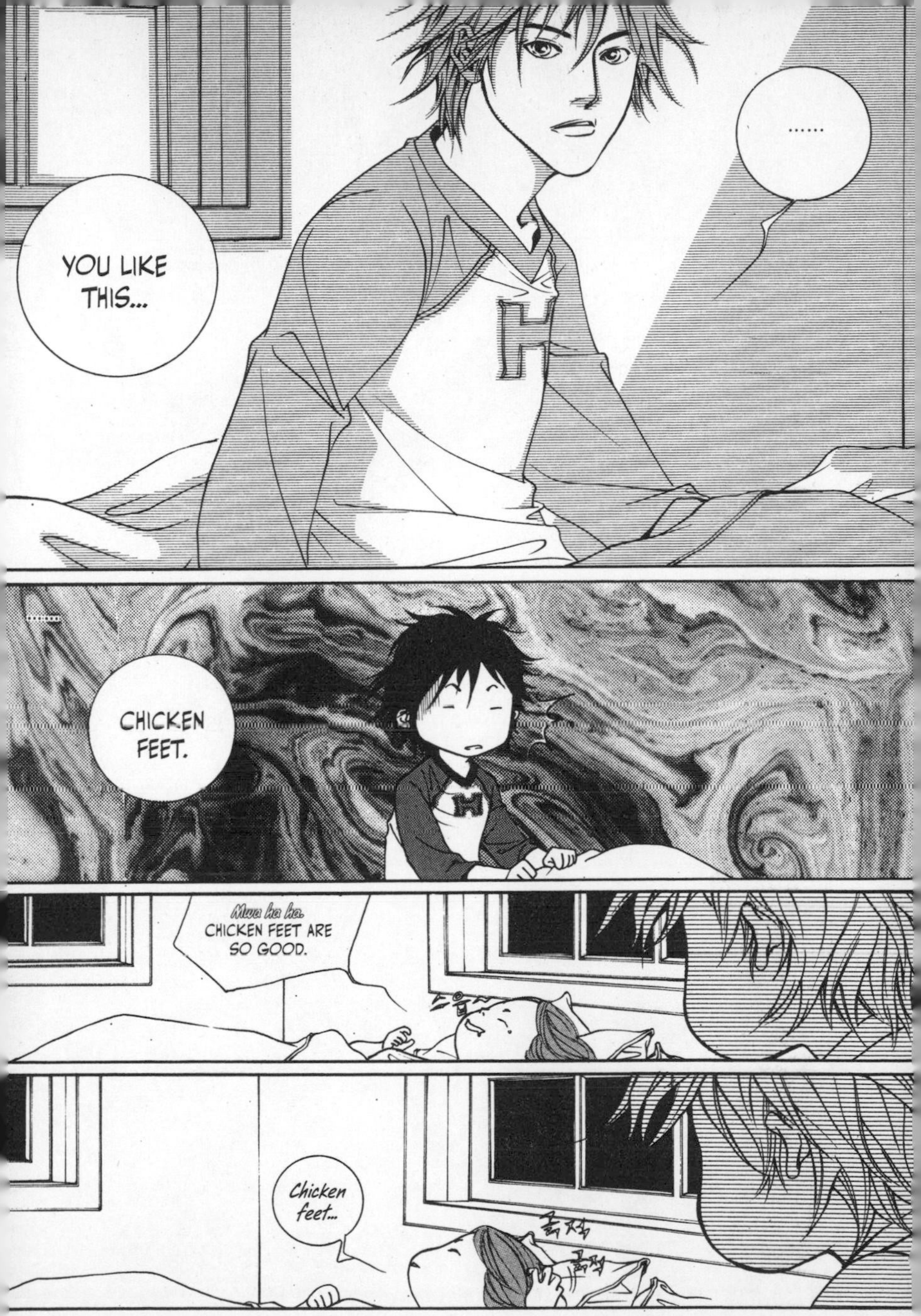
YOU LIKE THIS...
......
CHICKEN FEET.
Mwa ha ha.
CHICKEN FEET ARE SO GOOD.
Chicken feet...

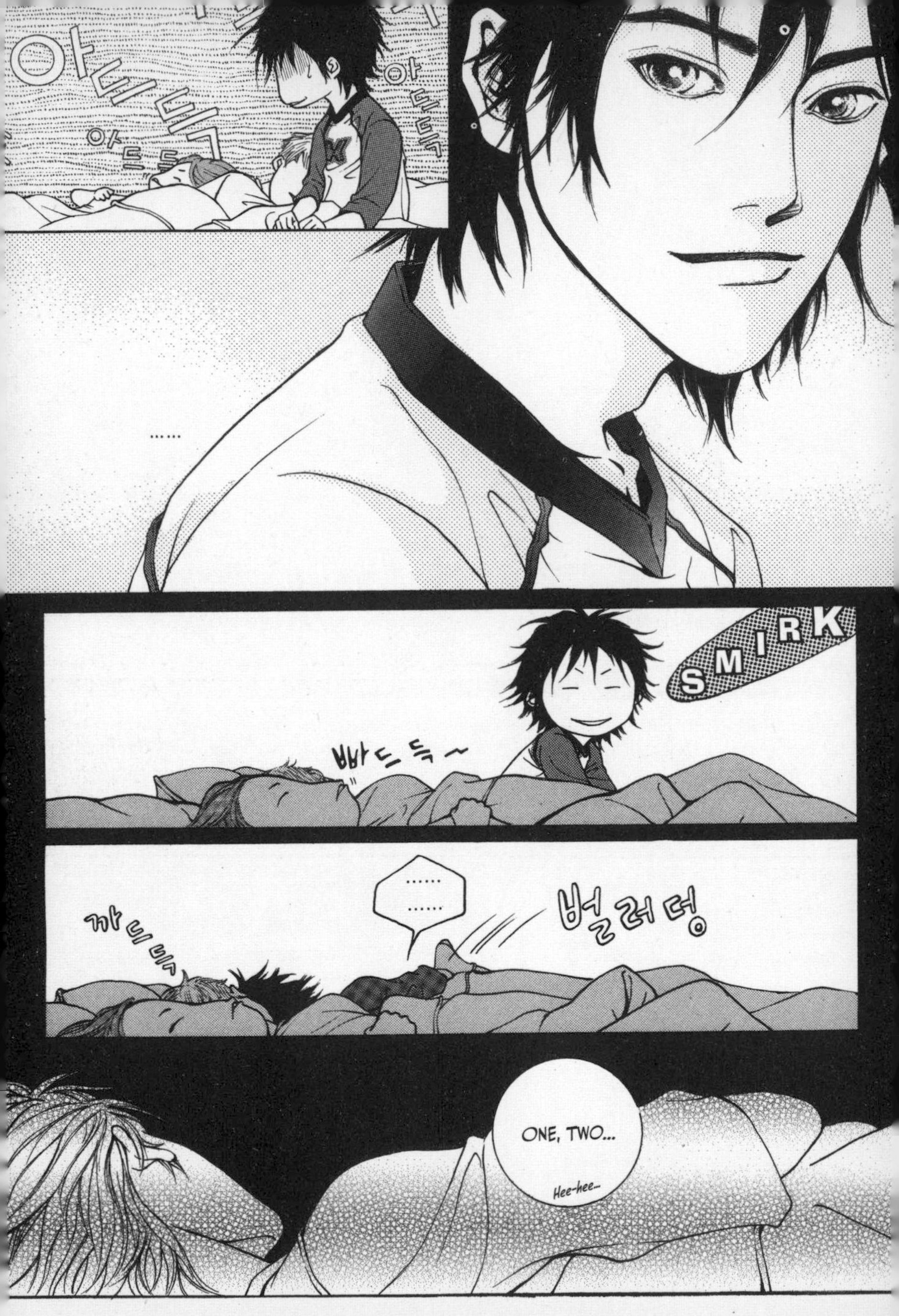

아드드득
아드득
아드득
......
SMIRK
빠드득~
......
......
까드득
벌러덩
ONE, TWO...
Hee-hee...

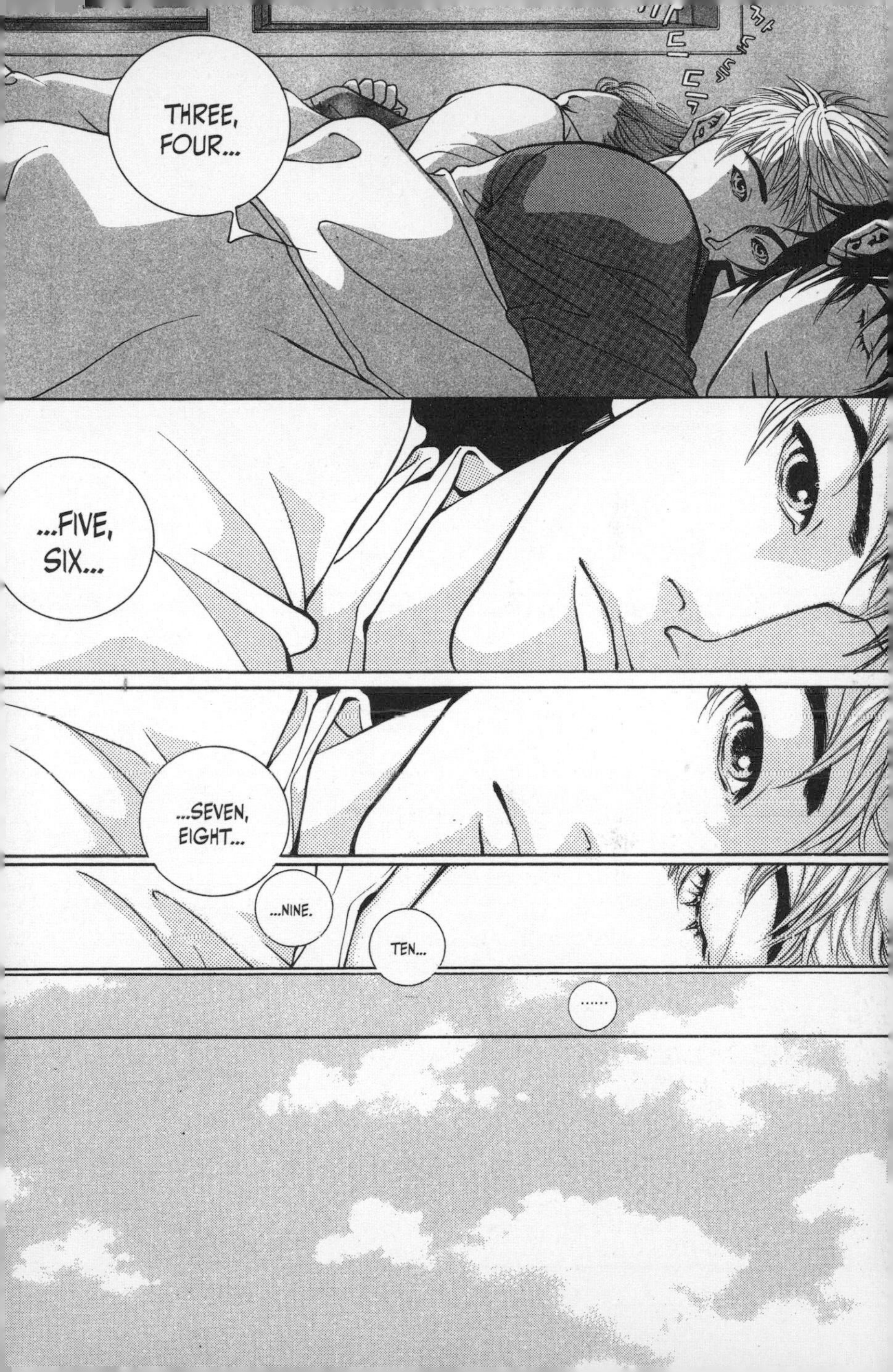
THREE, FOUR...
...FIVE, SIX...
...SEVEN, EIGHT...
...NINE.
TEN...
......

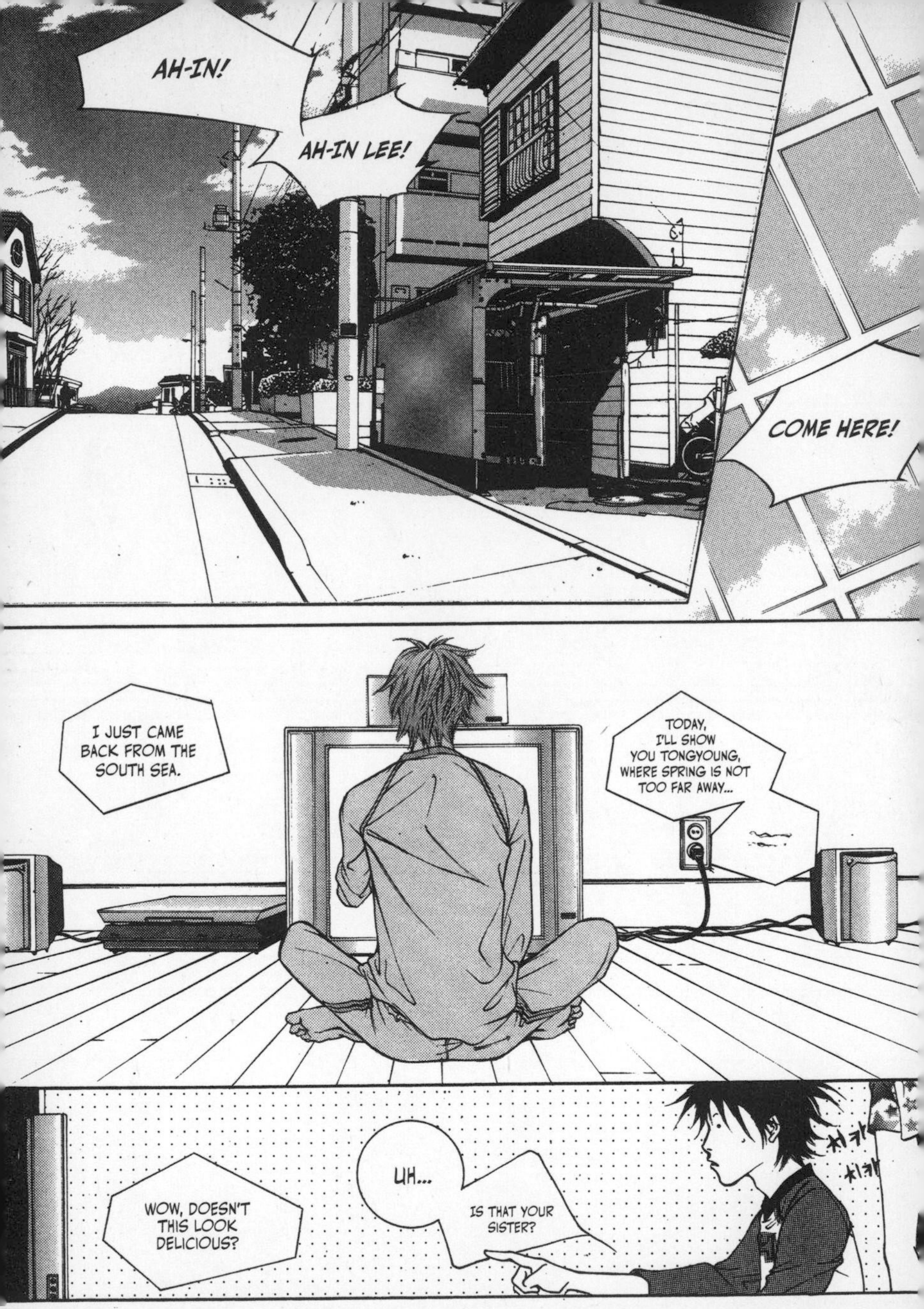
AH-IN!
AH-IN LEE!
COME HERE!
I JUST CAME BACK FROM THE SOUTH SEA.
TODAY, I'LL SHOW YOU TONGYOUNG, WHERE SPRING IS NOT TOO FAR AWAY...
WOW, DOESN'T THIS LOOK DELICIOUS?
UH...
IS THAT YOUR SISTER?
치카
치카

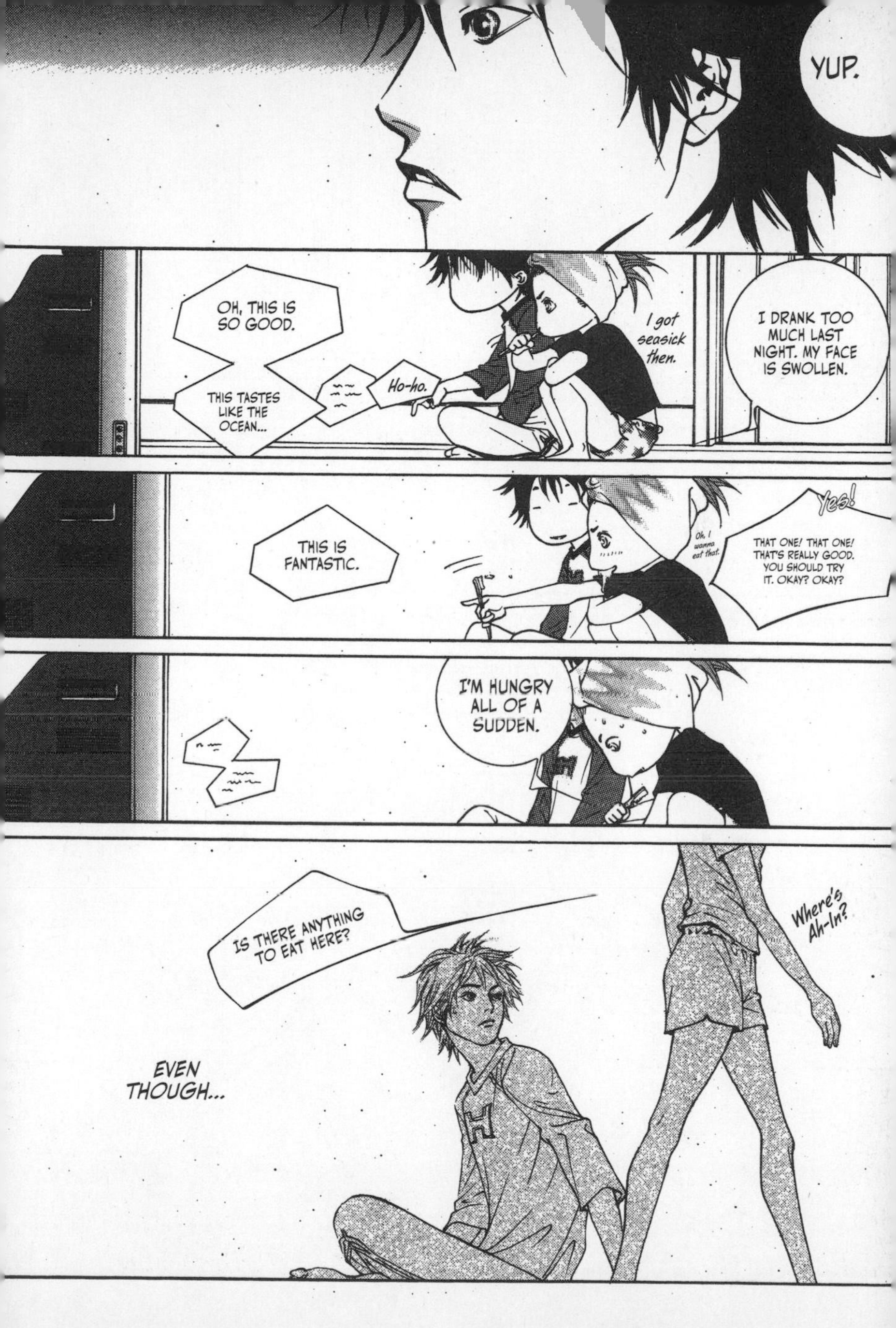
YUP.
OH, THIS IS SO GOOD.
THIS TASTES LIKE THE OCEAN...
Ho-ho.
I got seasick then.
I DRANK TOO MUCH LAST NIGHT. MY FACE IS SWOLLEN.
THIS IS FANTASTIC.
Oh, I wanna eat that.
Yes!
THAT ONE! THAT ONE! THAT'S REALLY GOOD. YOU SHOULD TRY IT. OKAY? OKAY?
I'M HUNGRY ALL OF A SUDDEN.
IS THERE ANYTHING TO EAT HERE?
Where's Ah-In?
EVEN THOUGH...

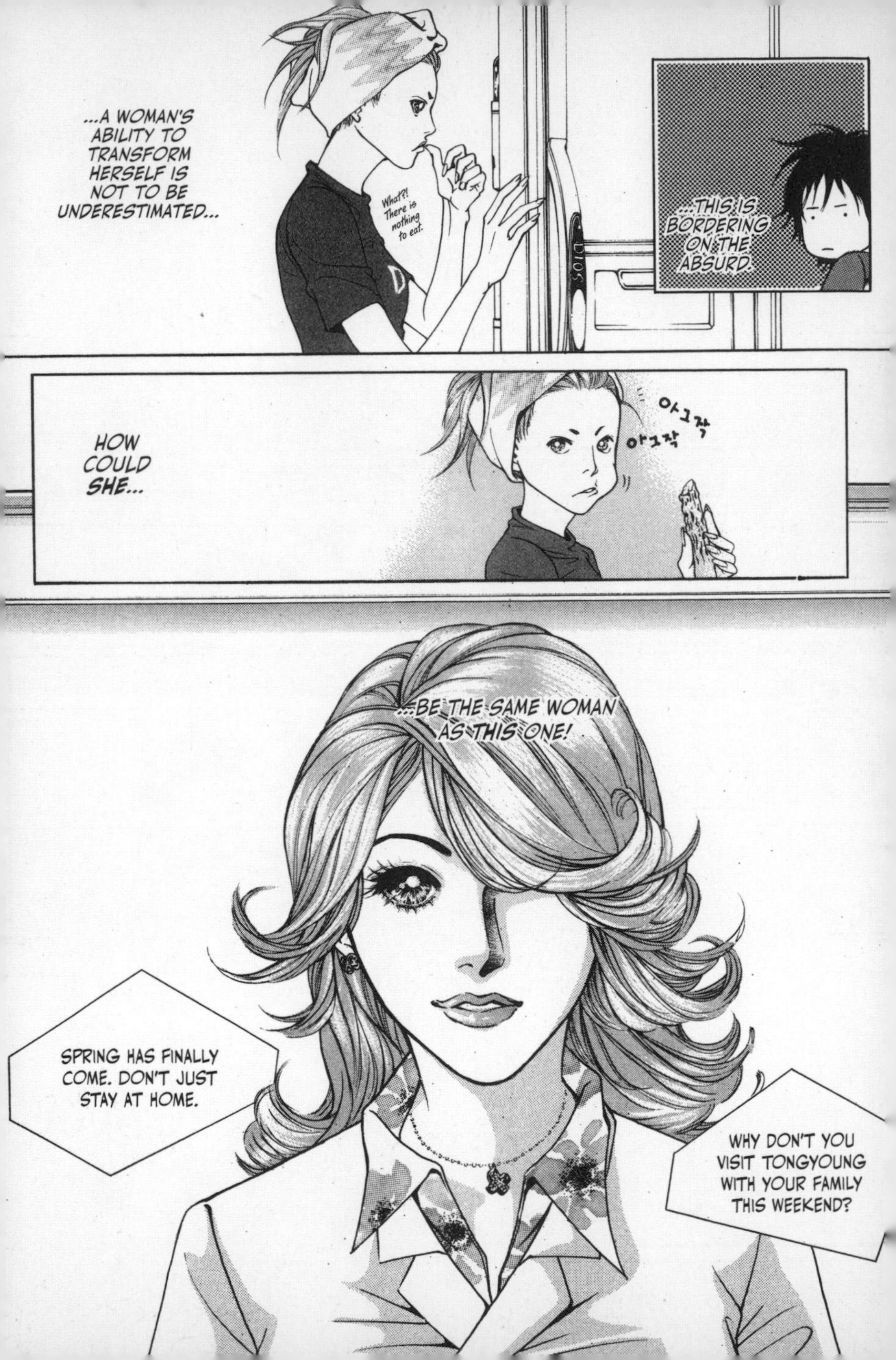
...A WOMAN'S ABILITY TO TRANSFORM HERSELF IS NOT TO BE UNDERESTIMATED...
What?! There is nothing to eat.
...THIS IS BORDERING ON THE ABSURD.
HOW COULD SHE...
아그작
아그작
...BE THE SAME WOMAN AS THIS ONE!
SPRING HAS FINALLY COME. DON'T JUST STAY AT HOME.
WHY DON'T YOU VISIT TONGYOUNG WITH YOUR FAMILY THIS WEEKEND?

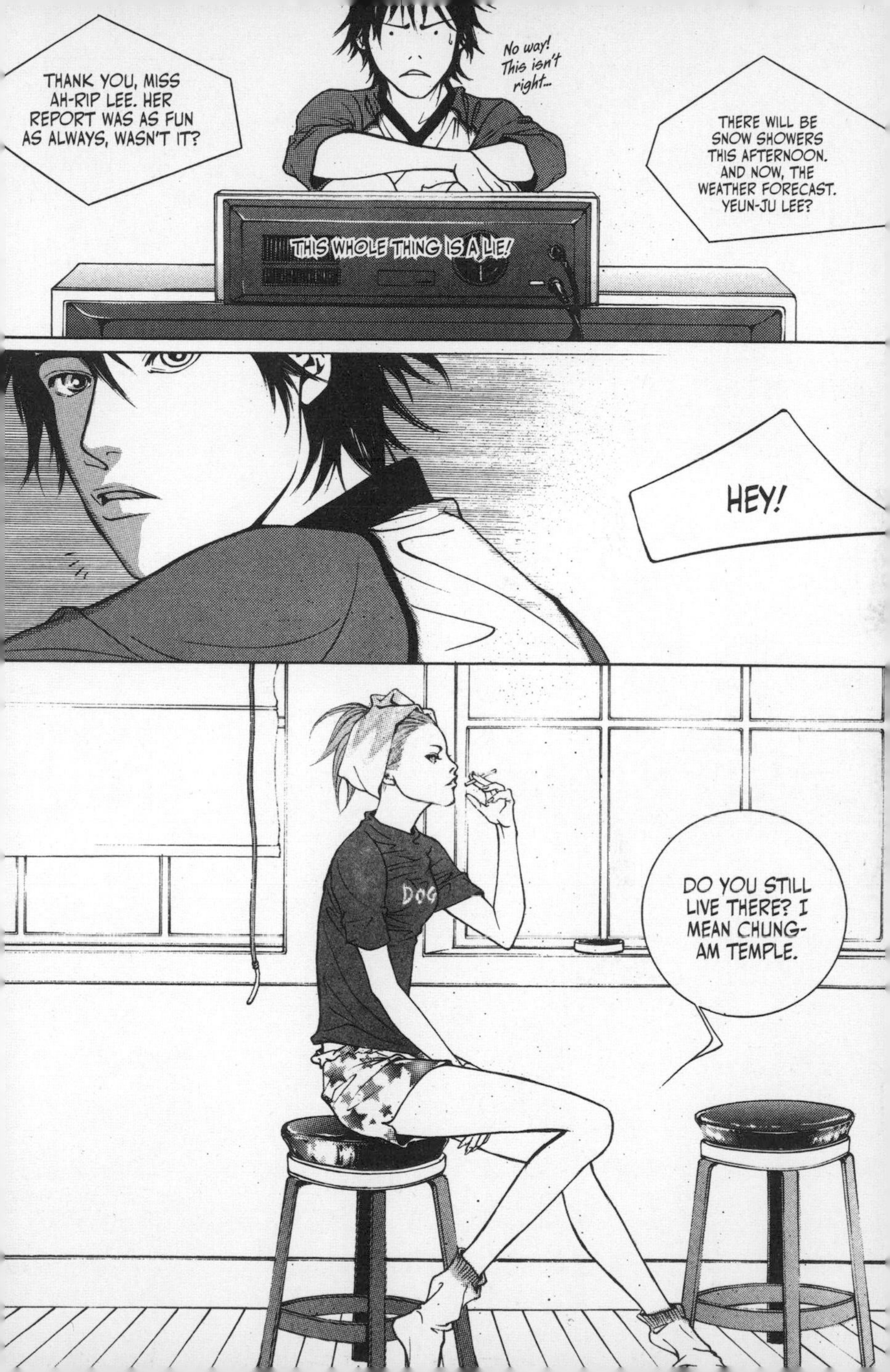
THANK YOU, MISS AH-RIP LEE. HER REPORT WAS AS FUN AS ALWAYS, WASN'T IT?
No way! This isn't right...
THERE WILL BE SNOW SHOWERS THIS AFTERNOON. AND NOW, THE WEATHER FORECAST. YEUN-JU LEE?
THIS WHOLE THING IS A LIE!
HEY!
DOG
DO YOU STILL LIVE THERE? I MEAN CHUNG-AM TEMPLE.

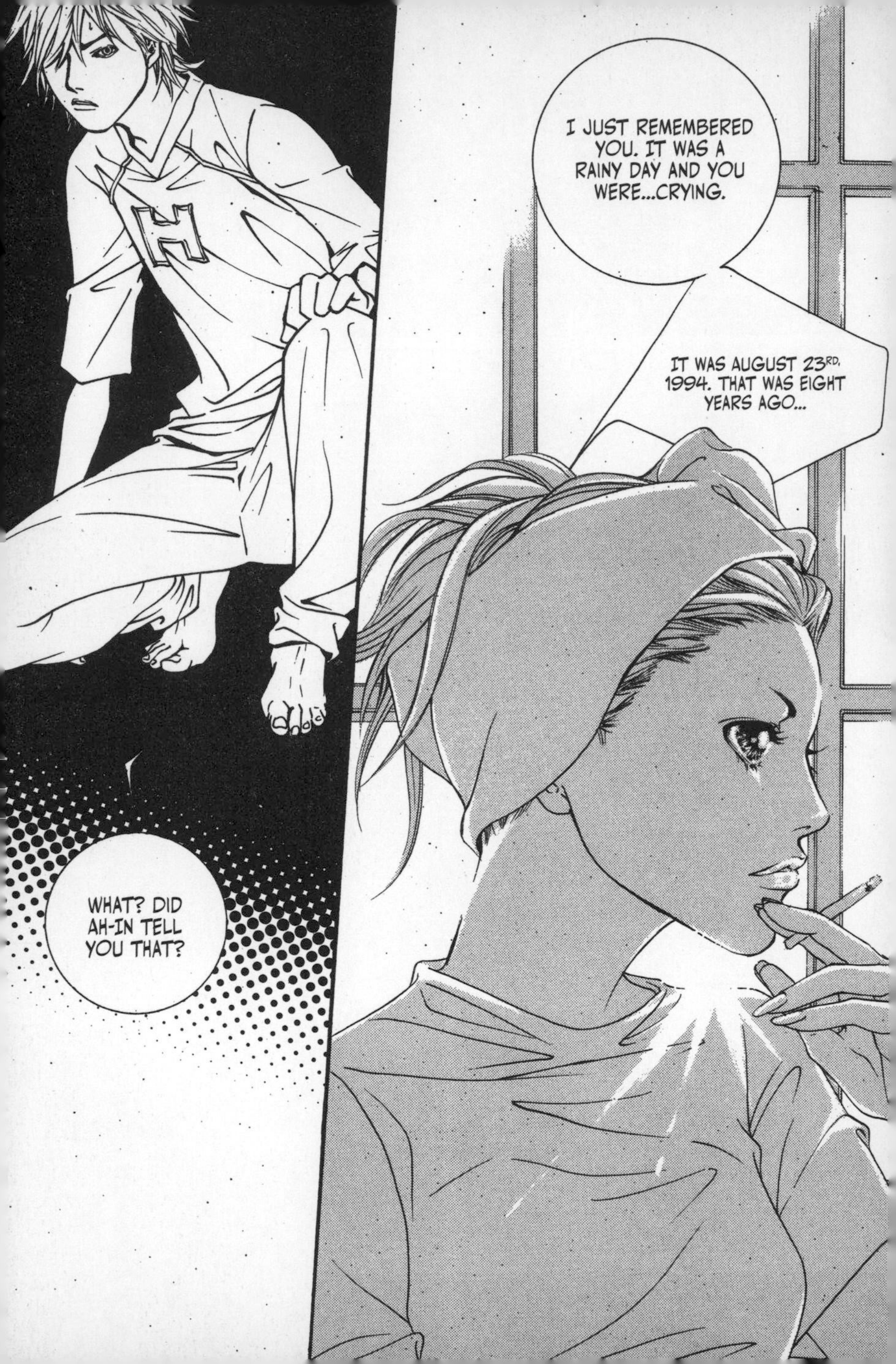
WHAT? DID AH-IN TELL YOU THAT?
I JUST REMEMBERED YOU. IT WAS A RAINY DAY AND YOU WERE...CRYING.
IT WAS AUGUST 23RD, 1994. THAT WAS EIGHT YEARS AGO...

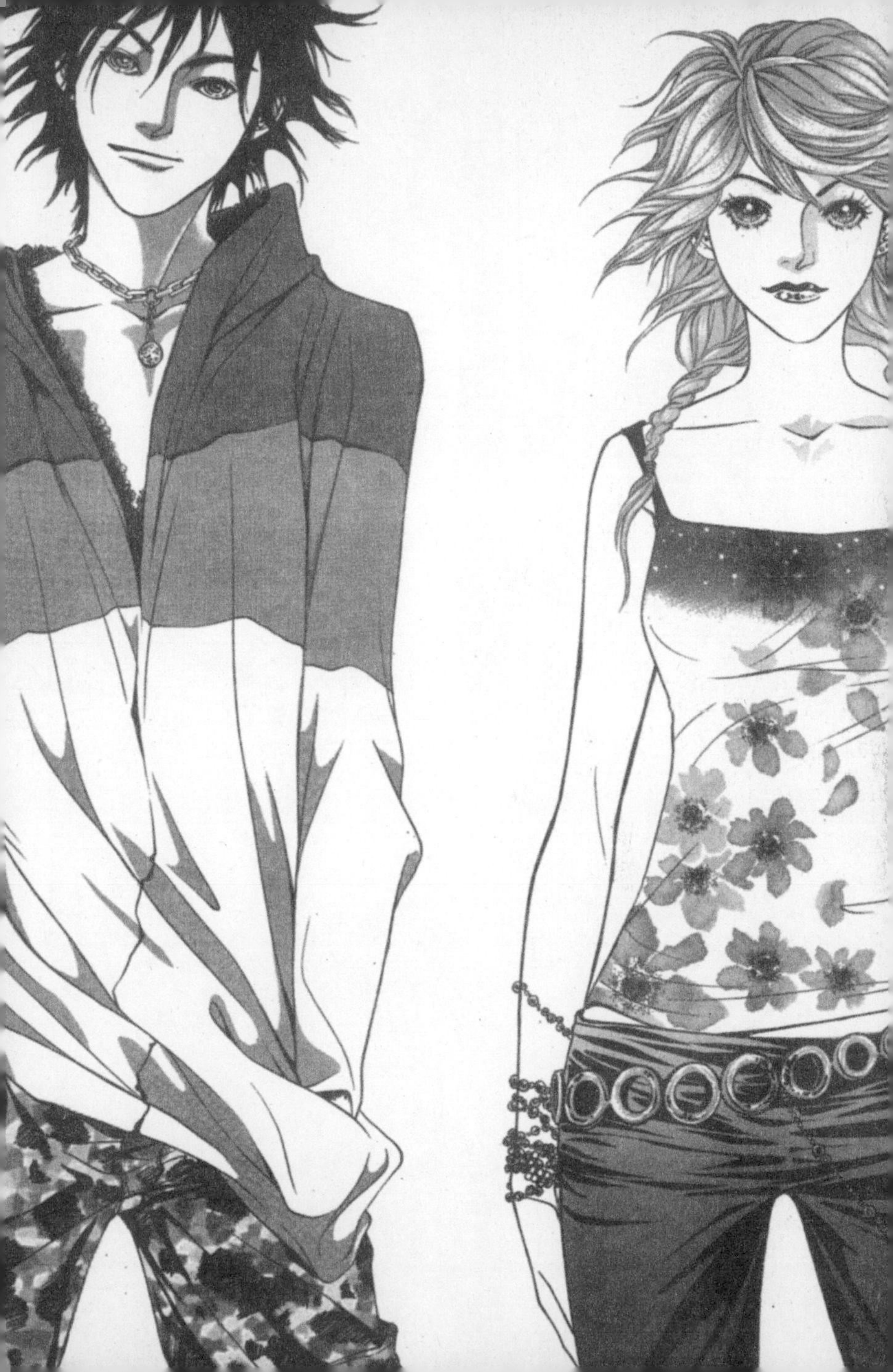

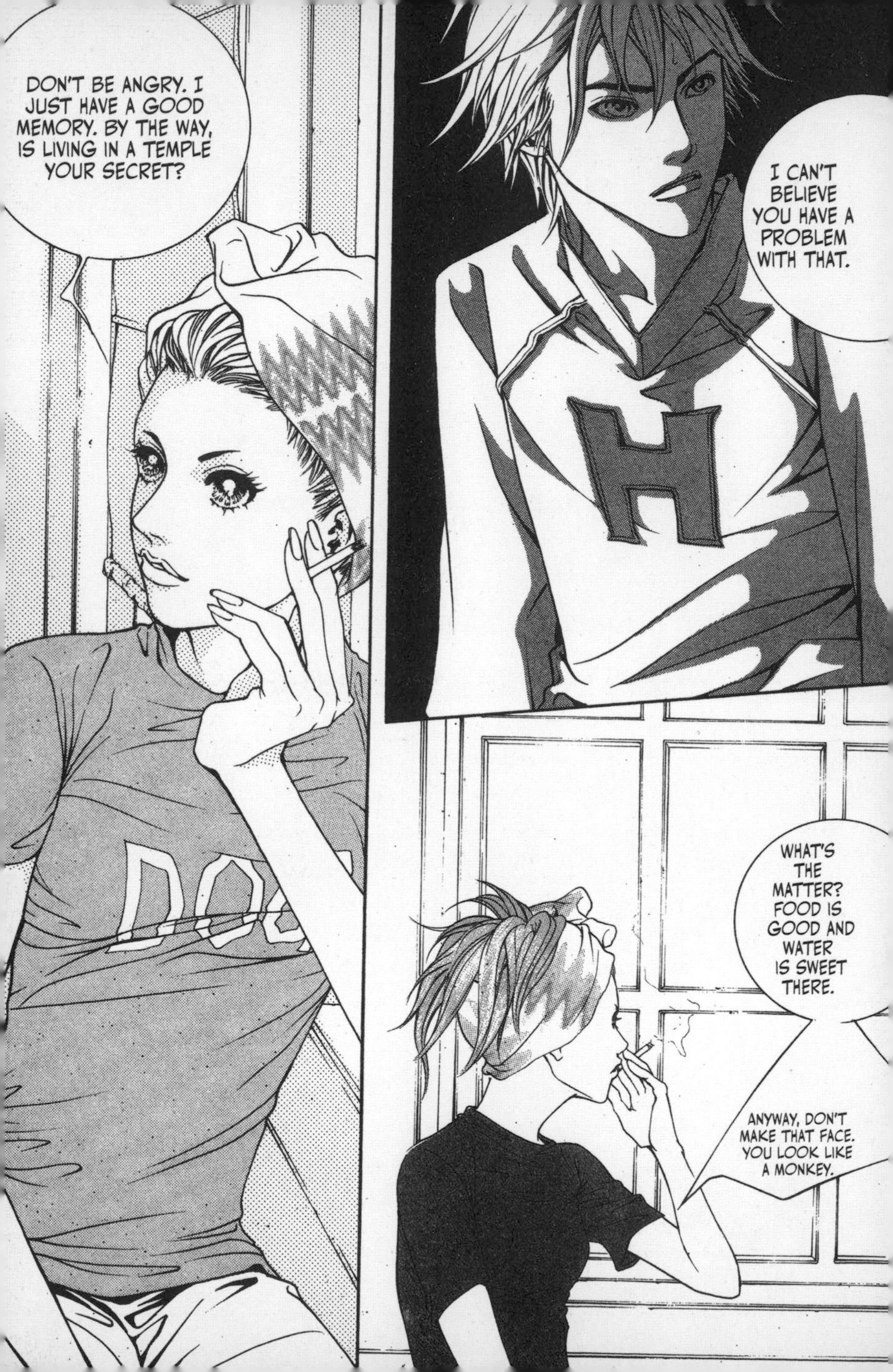
DON'T BE ANGRY. I JUST HAVE A GOOD MEMORY. BY THE WAY, IS LIVING IN A TEMPLE YOUR SECRET?
I CAN'T BELIEVE YOU HAVE A PROBLEM WITH THAT.
WHAT'S THE MATTER? FOOD IS GOOD AND WATER IS SWEET THERE.
ANYWAY, DON'T MAKE THAT FACE. YOU LOOK LIKE A MONKEY.

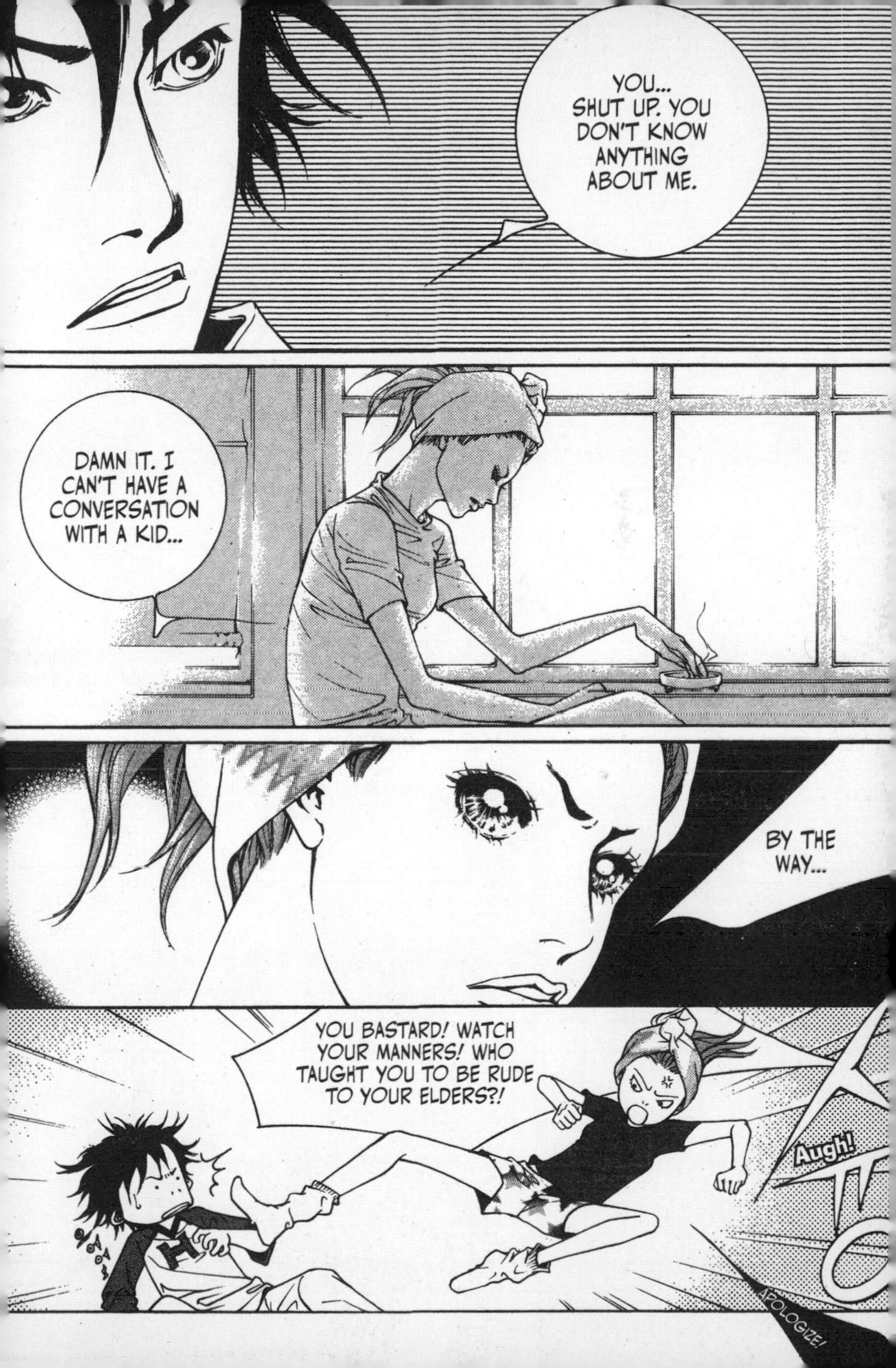
YOU... SHUT UP. YOU DON'T KNOW ANYTHING ABOUT ME.
DAMN IT. I CAN'T HAVE A CONVERSATION WITH A KID...
BY THE WAY...
YOU BASTARD! WATCH YOUR MANNERS! WHO TAUGHT YOU TO BE RUDE TO YOUR ELDERS?!
Augh!
APOLOGIZE!

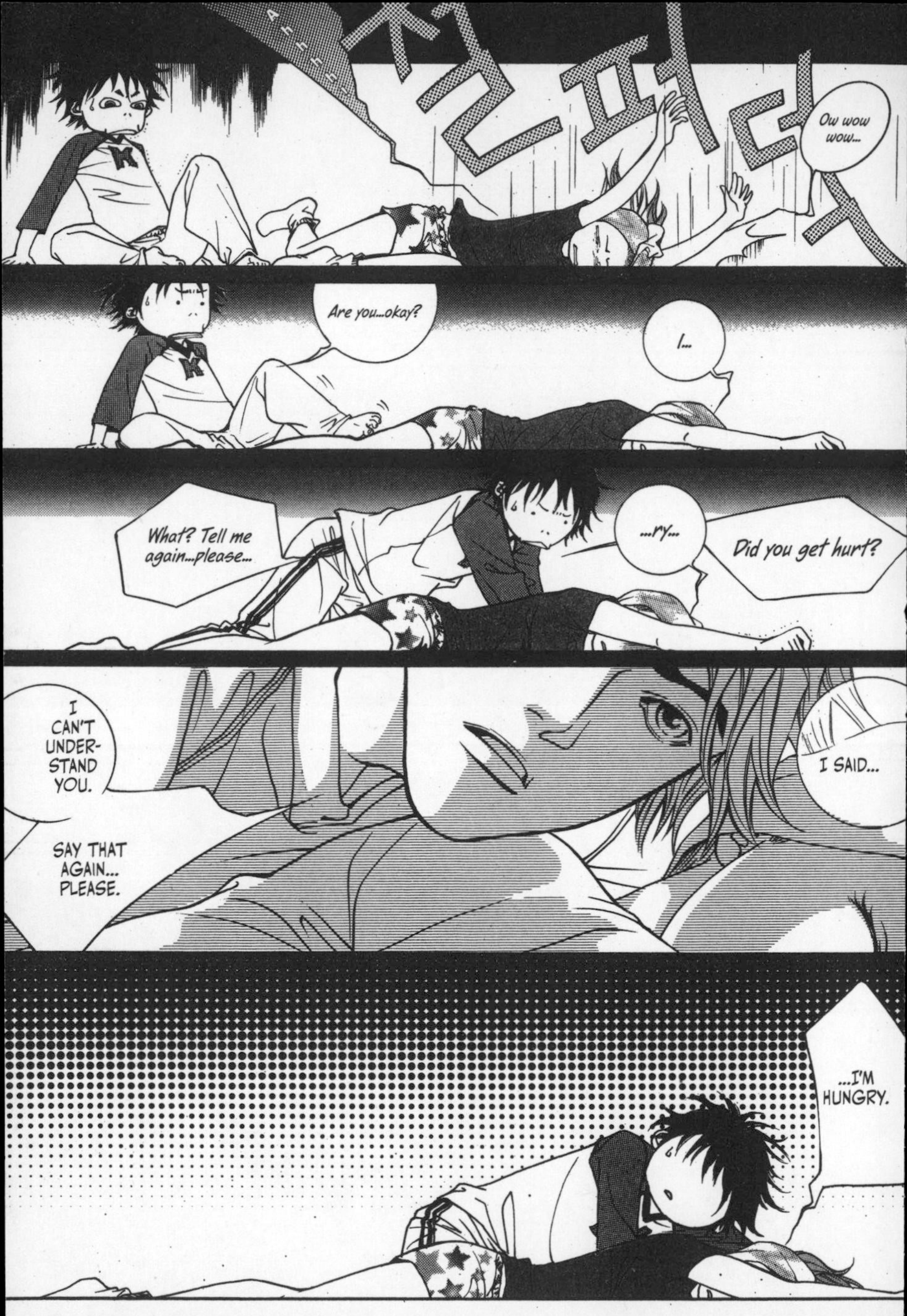
Ahhhh-
Ow wow wow...
Are you...okay?
I...
What? Tell me again...please...
...ry...
Did you get hurt?
I CAN'T UNDERSTAND YOU.
SAY THAT AGAIN... PLEASE.
I SAID...
...I'M HUNGRY.

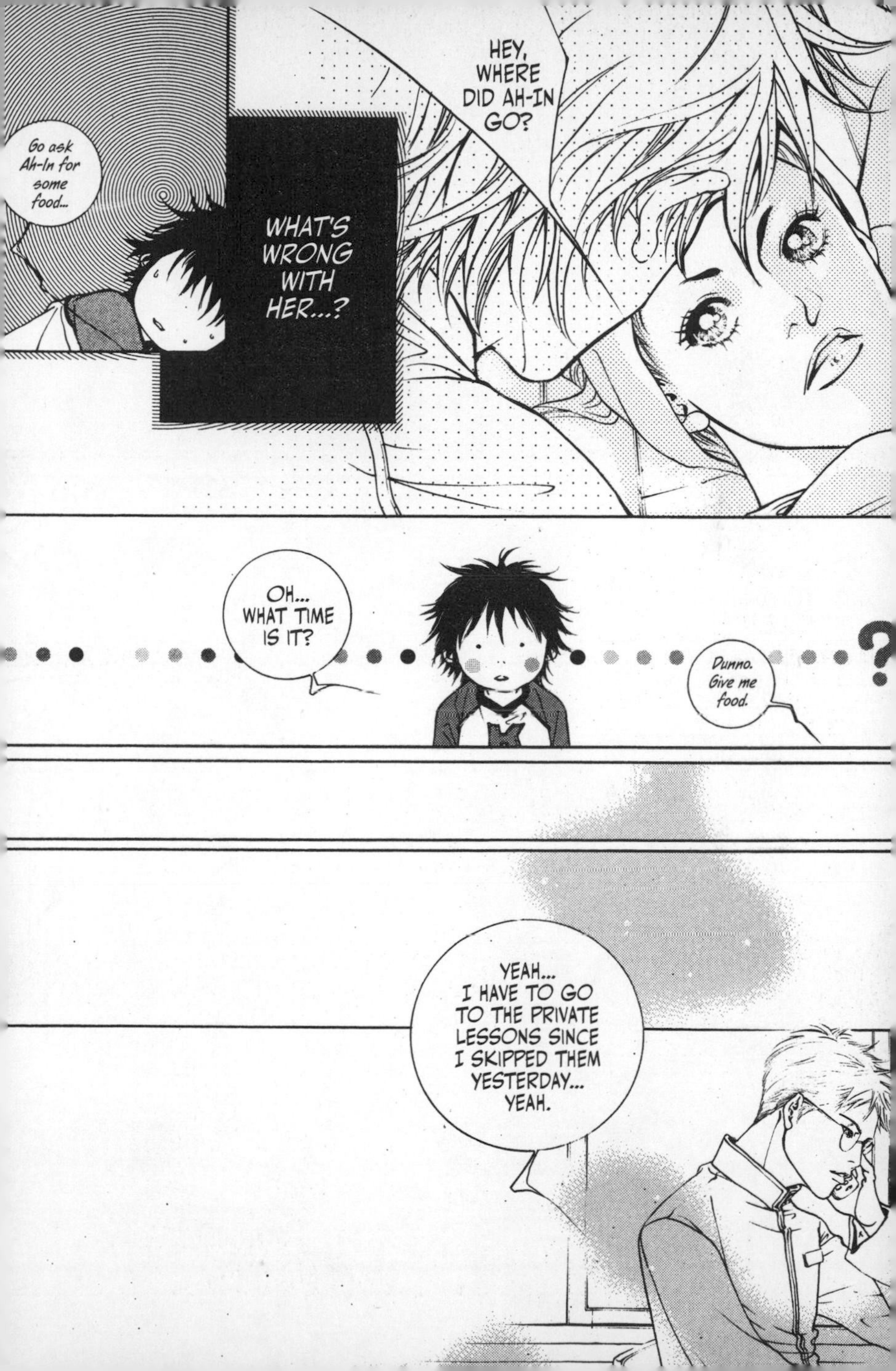
Go ask Ah-In for some food...
WHAT'S WRONG WITH HER...?
HEY, WHERE DID AH-IN GO?
OH... WHAT TIME IS IT?
Dunno. Give me food.
YEAH... I HAVE TO GO TO THE PRIVATE LESSONS SINCE I SKIPPED THEM YESTERDAY... YEAH.

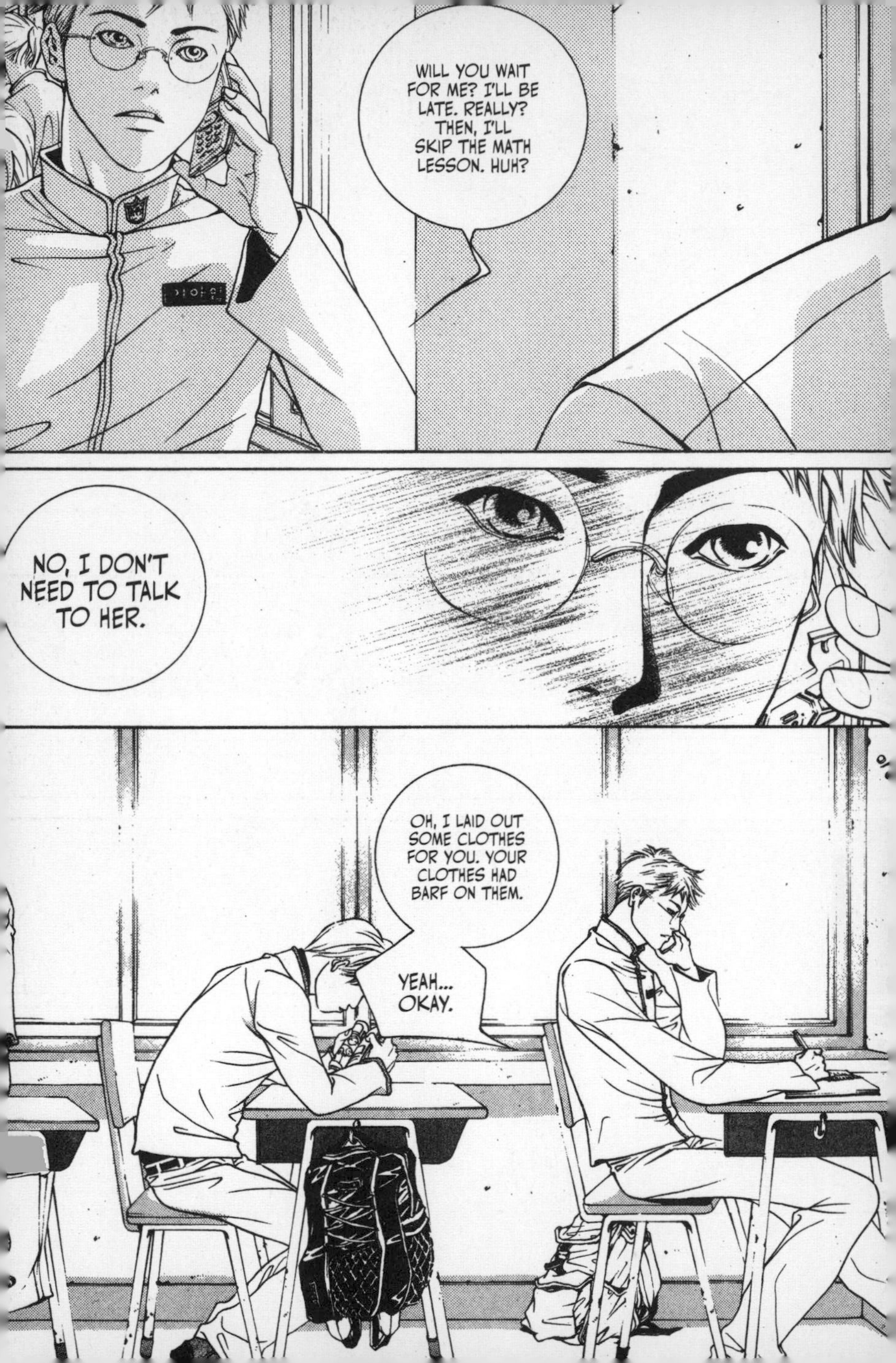
WILL YOU WAIT FOR ME? I'LL BE LATE. REALLY? THEN, I'LL SKIP THE MATH LESSON. HUH?
NO, I DON'T NEED TO TALK TO HER.
OH, I LAID OUT SOME CLOTHES FOR YOU. YOUR CLOTHES HAD BARF ON THEM.
YEAH... OKAY.

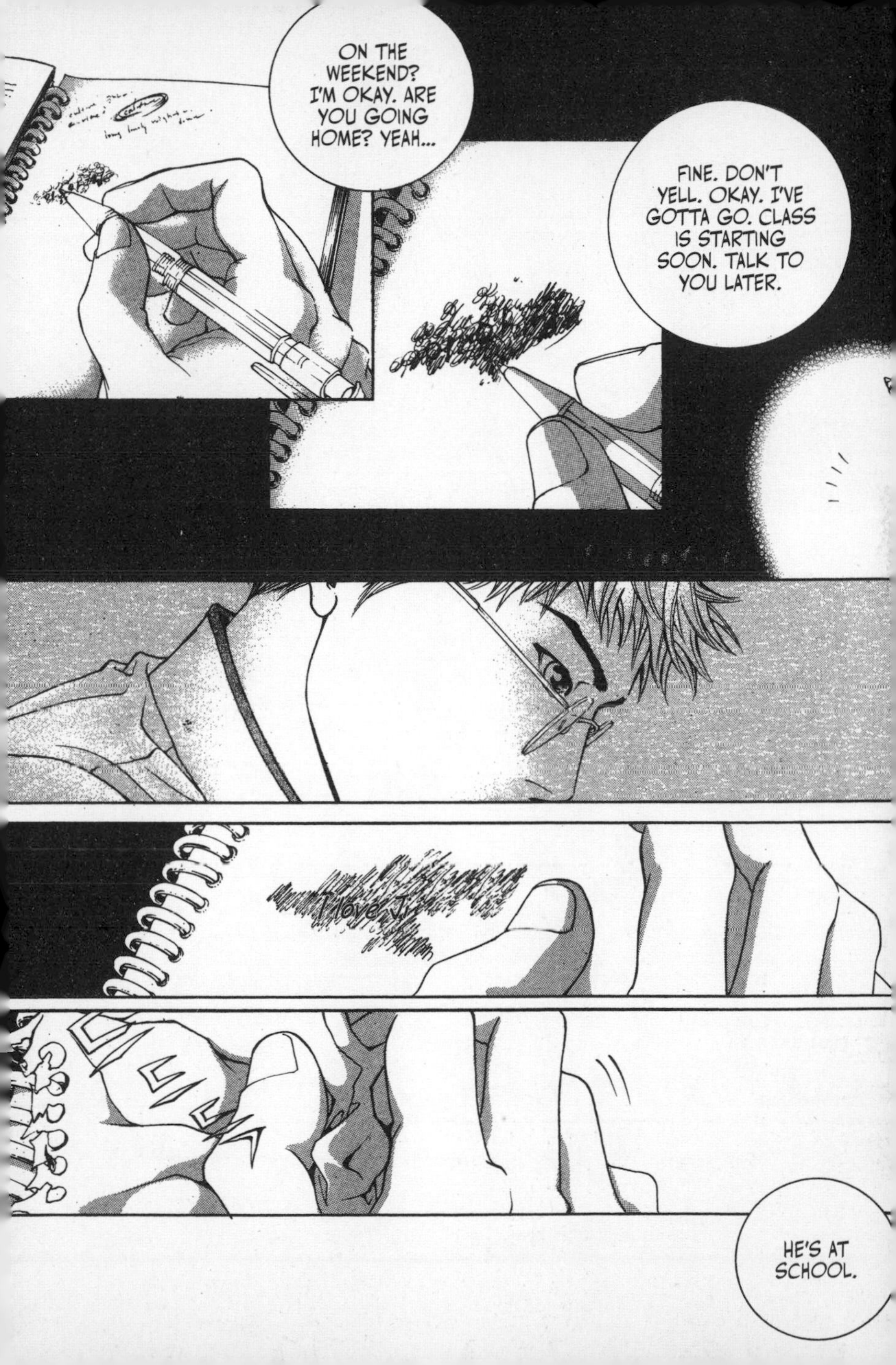
ON THE WEEKEND? I'M OKAY. ARE YOU GOING HOME? YEAH...
FINE. DON'T YELL. OKAY. I'VE GOTTA GO. CLASS IS STARTING SOON. TALK TO YOU LATER.
I love Ji
HE'S AT SCHOOL.

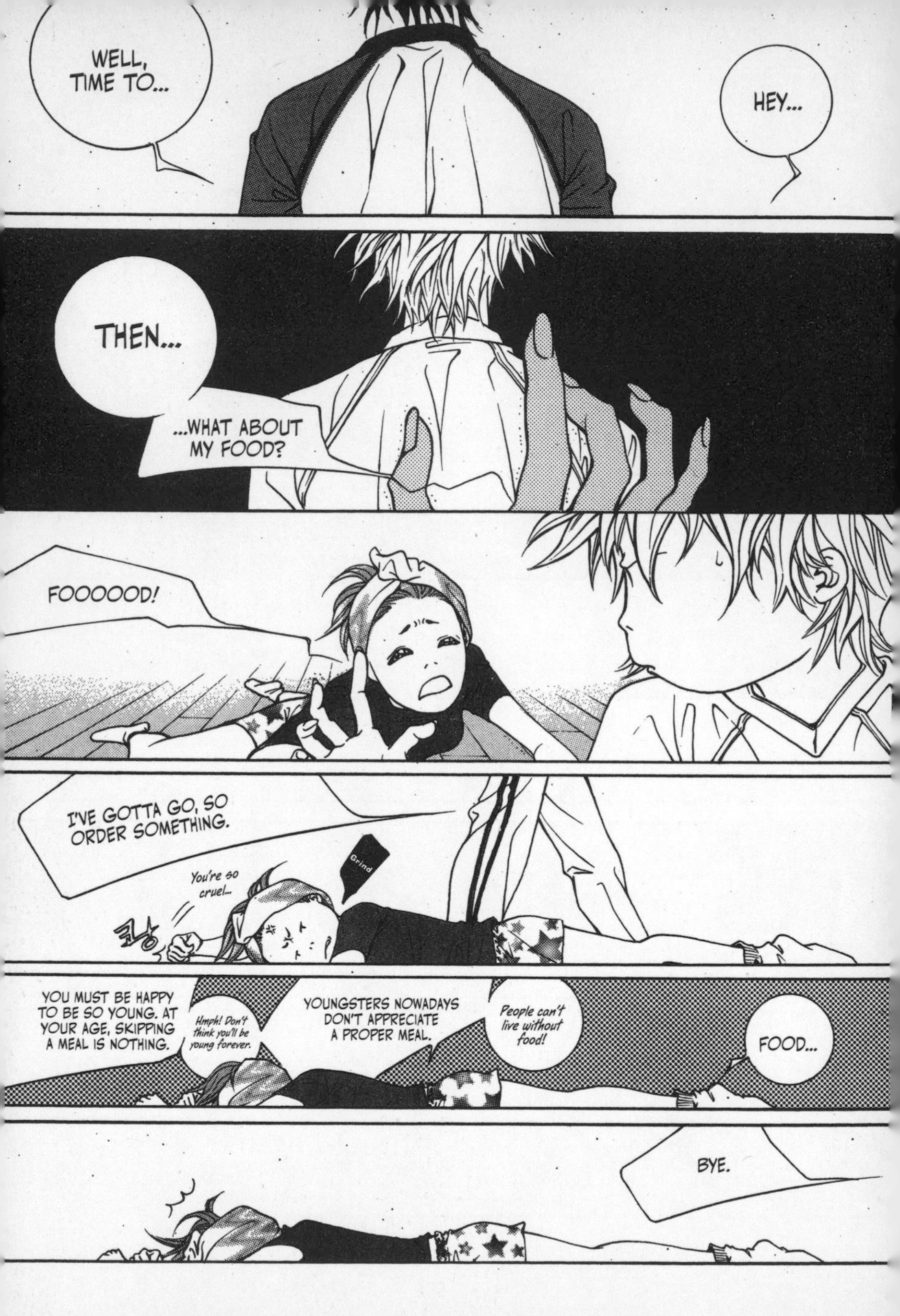
WELL, TIME TO...
HEY...
THEN...
...WHAT ABOUT MY FOOD?
FOOOOOD!
I'VE GOTTA GO, SO ORDER SOMETHING.
Grind
You're so cruel...
YOU MUST BE HAPPY TO BE SO YOUNG. AT YOUR AGE, SKIPPING A MEAL IS NOTHING.
Hmph! Don't think you'll be young forever.
YOUNGSTERS NOWADAYS DON'T APPRECIATE A PROPER MEAL.
People can't live without food!
FOOD...
BYE.

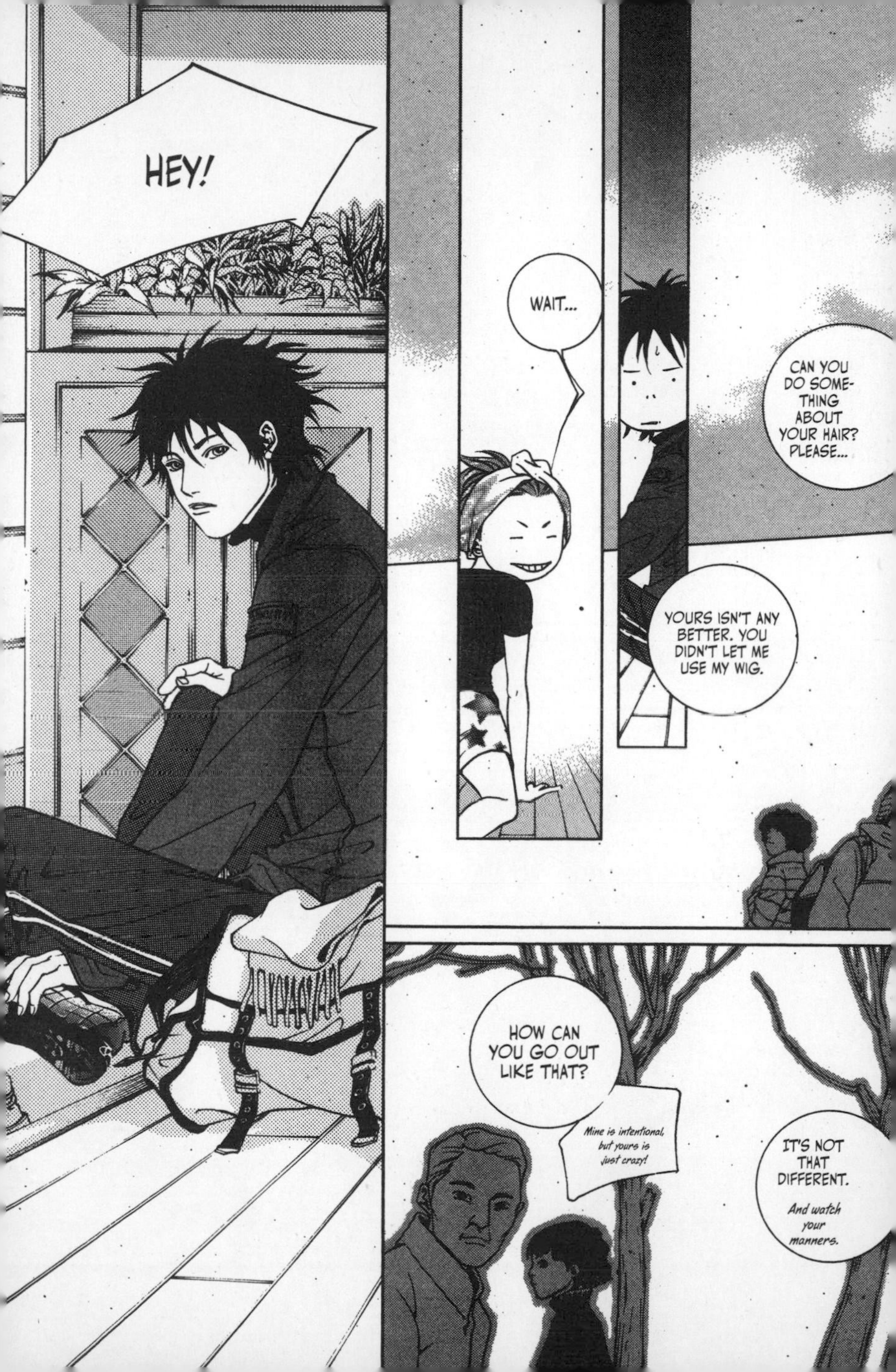
HEY!
WAIT...
CAN YOU DO SOME-THING ABOUT YOUR HAIR? PLEASE...
YOURS ISN'T ANY BETTER. YOU DIDN'T LET ME USE MY WIG.
HOW CAN YOU GO OUT LIKE THAT?
Mine is intentional, but yours is just crazy!
IT'S NOT THAT DIFFERENT.
And watch your manners.

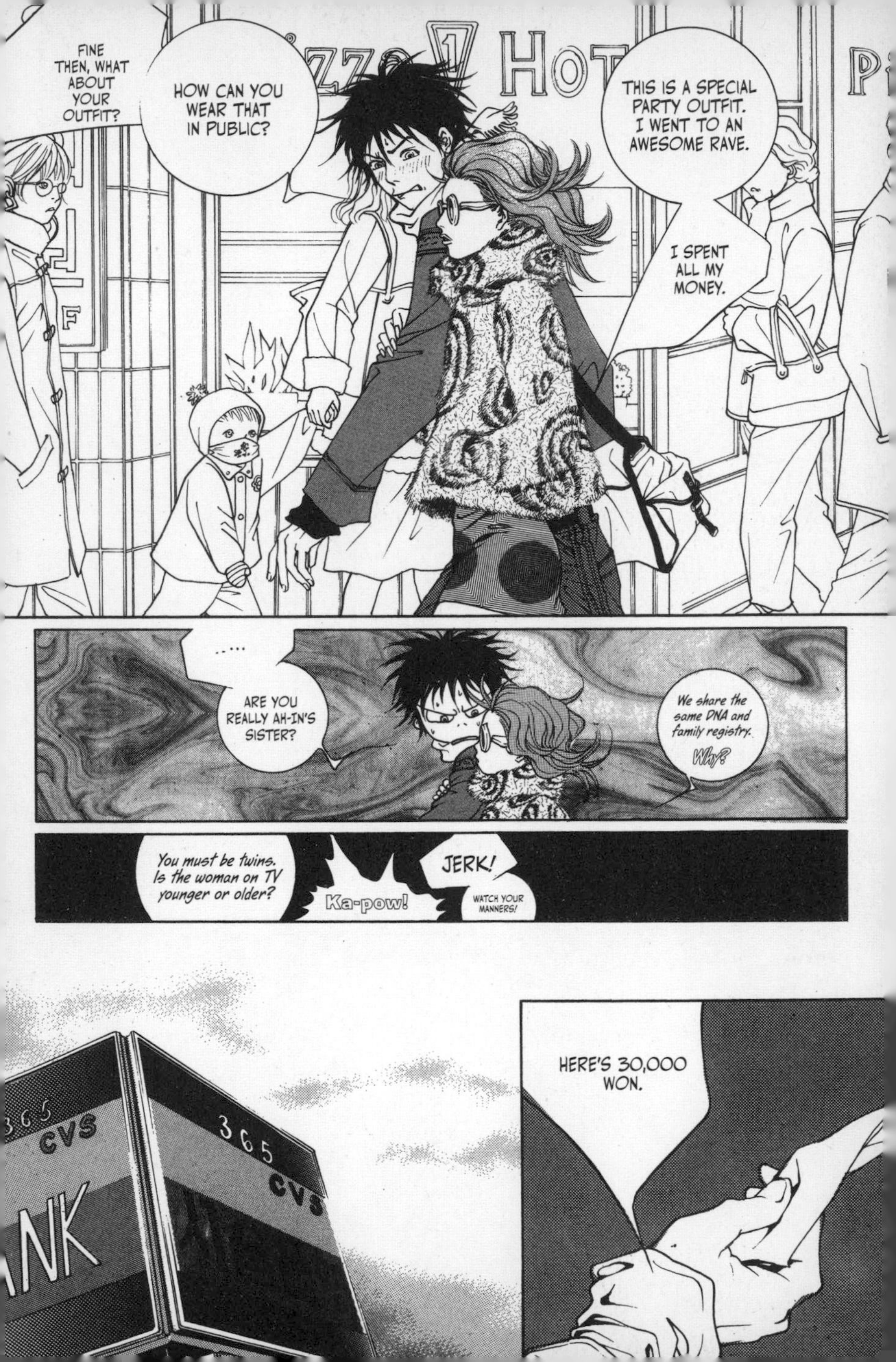
FINE THEN, WHAT ABOUT YOUR OUTFIT?
HOW CAN YOU WEAR THAT IN PUBLIC?
THIS IS A SPECIAL PARTY OUTFIT. I WENT TO AN AWESOME RAVE.
I SPENT ALL MY MONEY.
......
ARE YOU REALLY AH-IN'S SISTER?
We share the same DNA and family registry.
Why?
You must be twins. Is the woman on TV younger or older?
Ka-pow!
JERK!
WATCH YOUR MANNERS!
365 CVS
365 CVS
NK
HERE'S 30,000 WON.

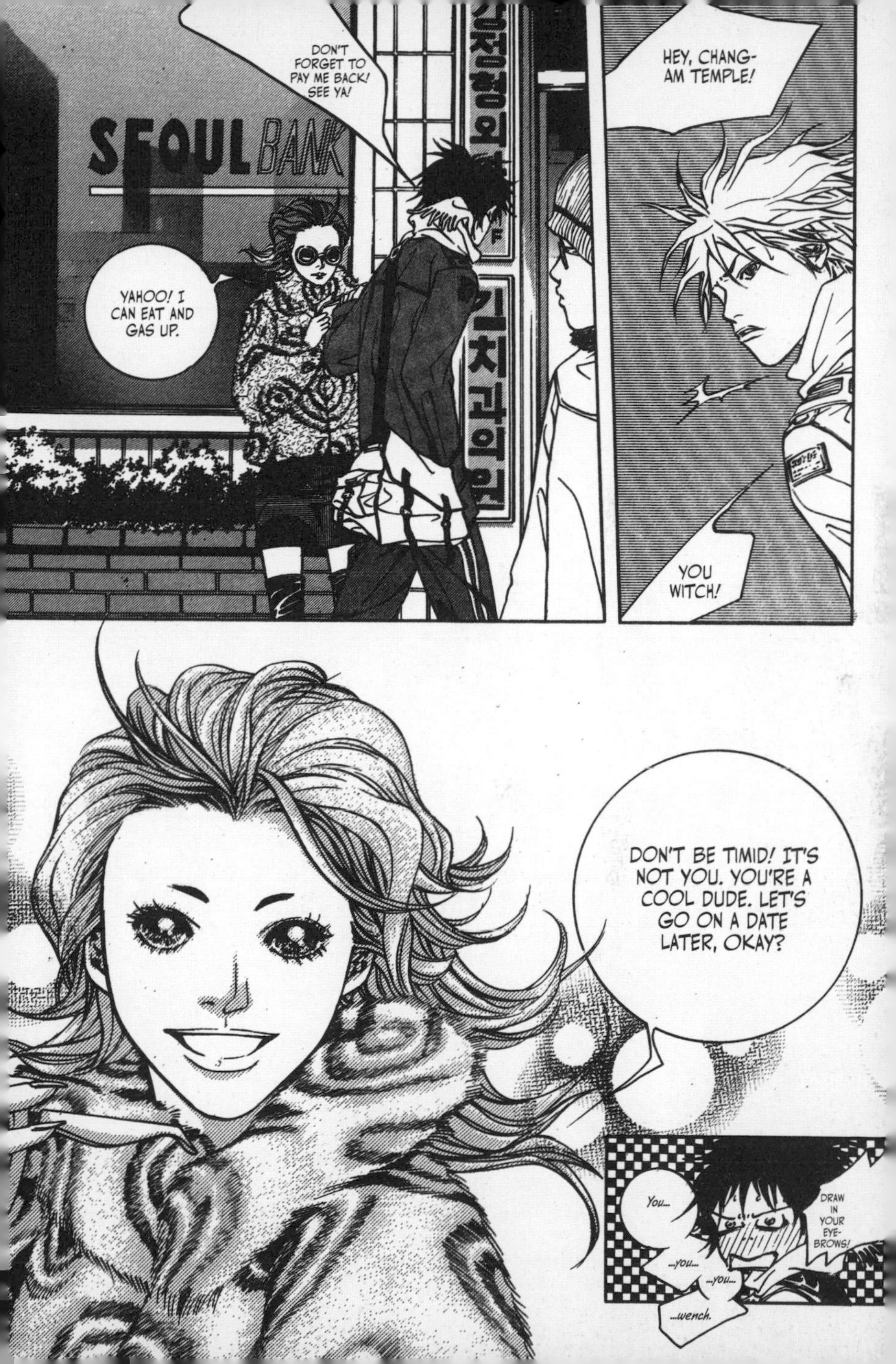
SEOUL BANK
DON'T FORGET TO PAY ME BACK! SEE YA!
YAHOO! I CAN EAT AND GAS UP.
HEY, CHANG-AM TEMPLE!
YOU WITCH!
DON'T BE TIMID! IT'S NOT YOU. YOU'RE A COOL DUDE. LET'S GO ON A DATE LATER, OKAY?
You...
...you...
...you...
...wench.
DRAW IN YOUR EYE-BROWS!

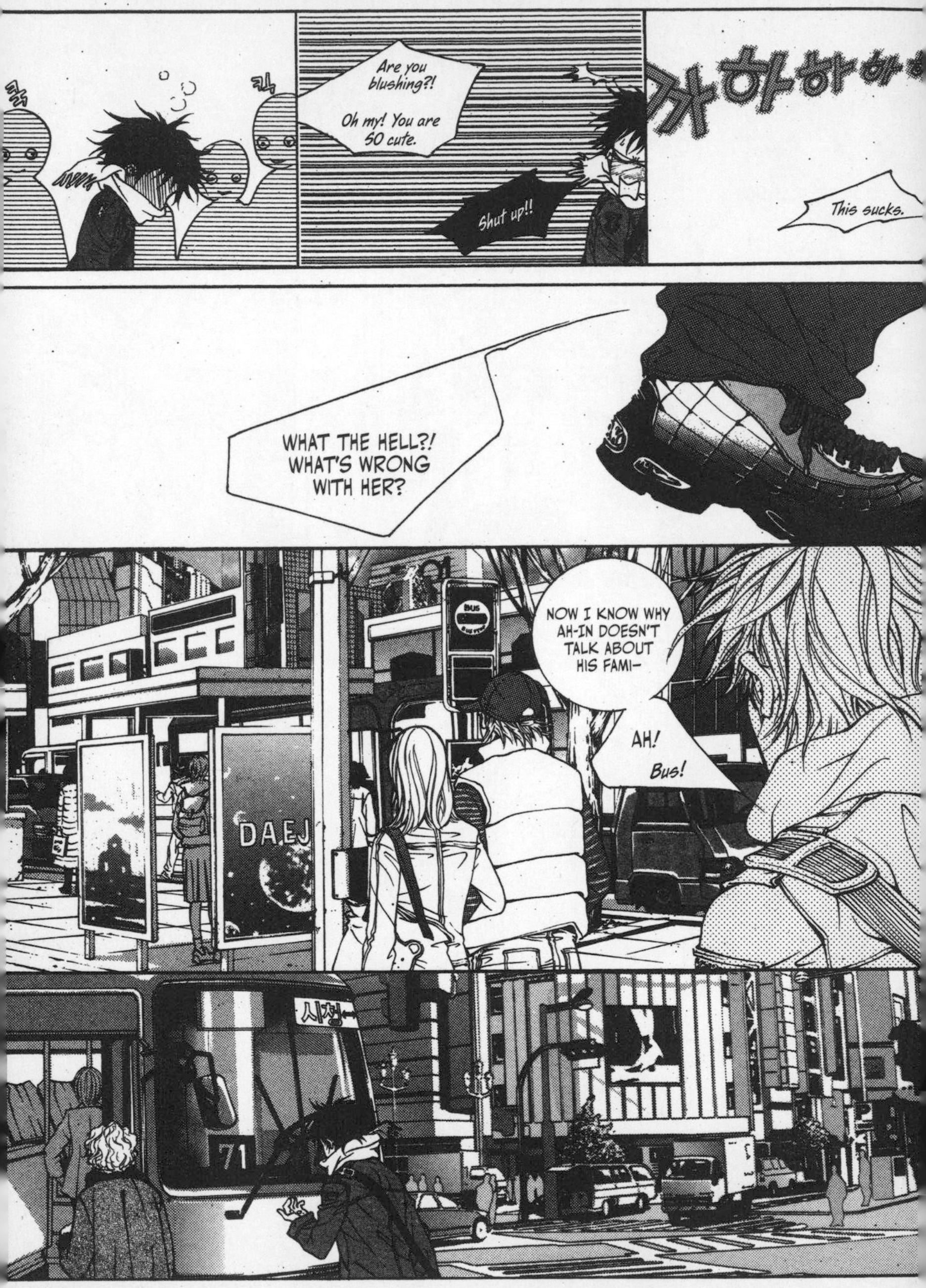

Are you blushing?!
Oh my! You are SO cute.
Shut up!!
꺄하하하
This sucks.
WHAT THE HELL?! WHAT'S WRONG WITH HER?
BUS
DAEJ
NOW I KNOW WHY AH-IN DOESN'T TALK ABOUT HIS FAMI–
AH!
Bus!
시청
71

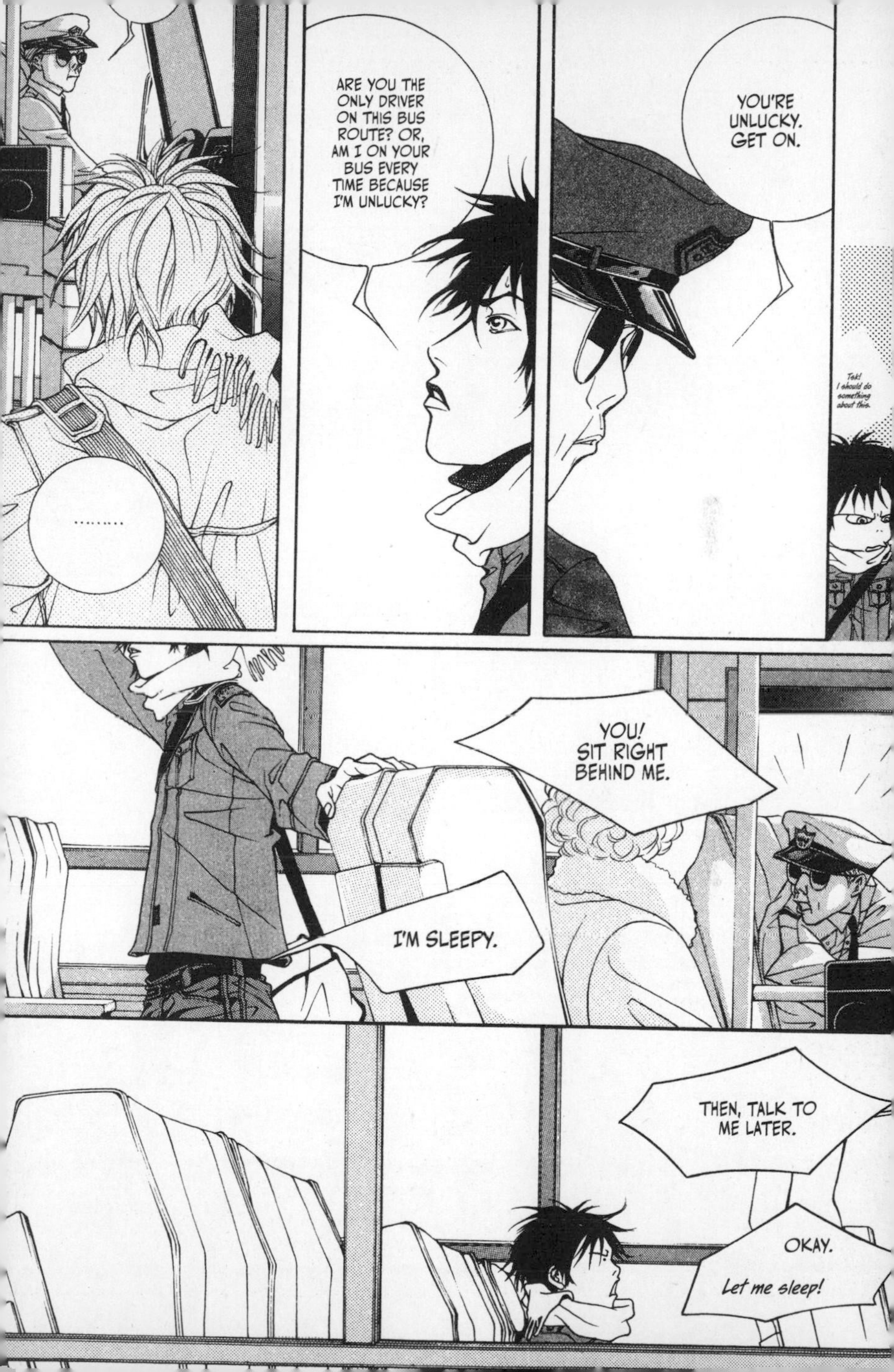
.........
ARE YOU THE ONLY DRIVER ON THIS BUS ROUTE? OR, AM I ON YOUR BUS EVERY TIME BECAUSE I'M UNLUCKY?
YOU'RE UNLUCKY. GET ON.
Tsk! I should do something about this.
I'M SLEEPY.
YOU! SIT RIGHT BEHIND ME.
THEN, TALK TO ME LATER.
OKAY.
Let me sleep!

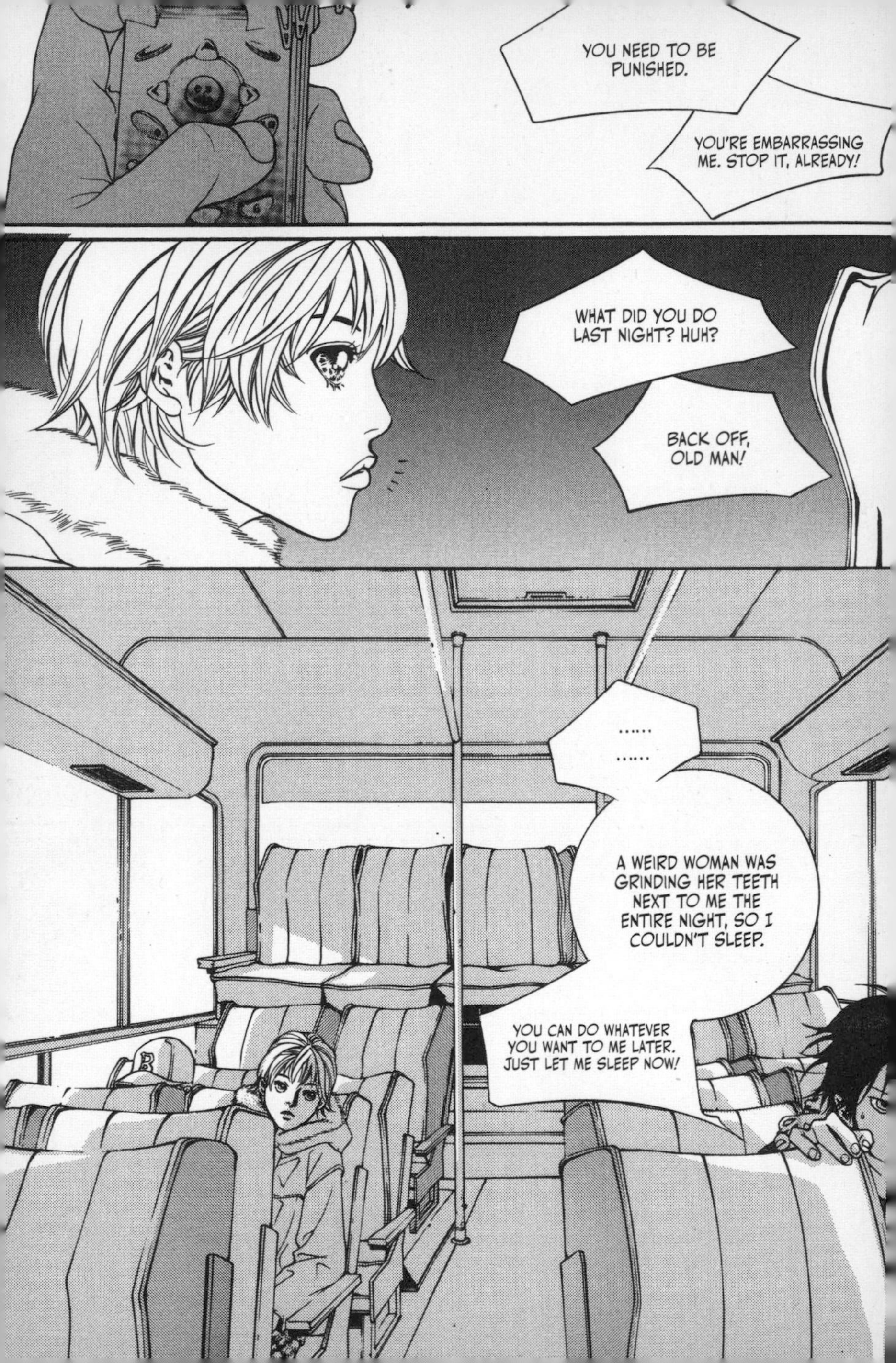
YOU NEED TO BE PUNISHED.
YOU'RE EMBARRASSING ME. STOP IT, ALREADY!
WHAT DID YOU DO LAST NIGHT? HUH?
BACK OFF, OLD MAN!
......
......
A WEIRD WOMAN WAS GRINDING HER TEETH NEXT TO ME THE ENTIRE NIGHT, SO I COULDN'T SLEEP.
YOU CAN DO WHATEVER YOU WANT TO ME LATER. JUST LET ME SLEEP NOW!

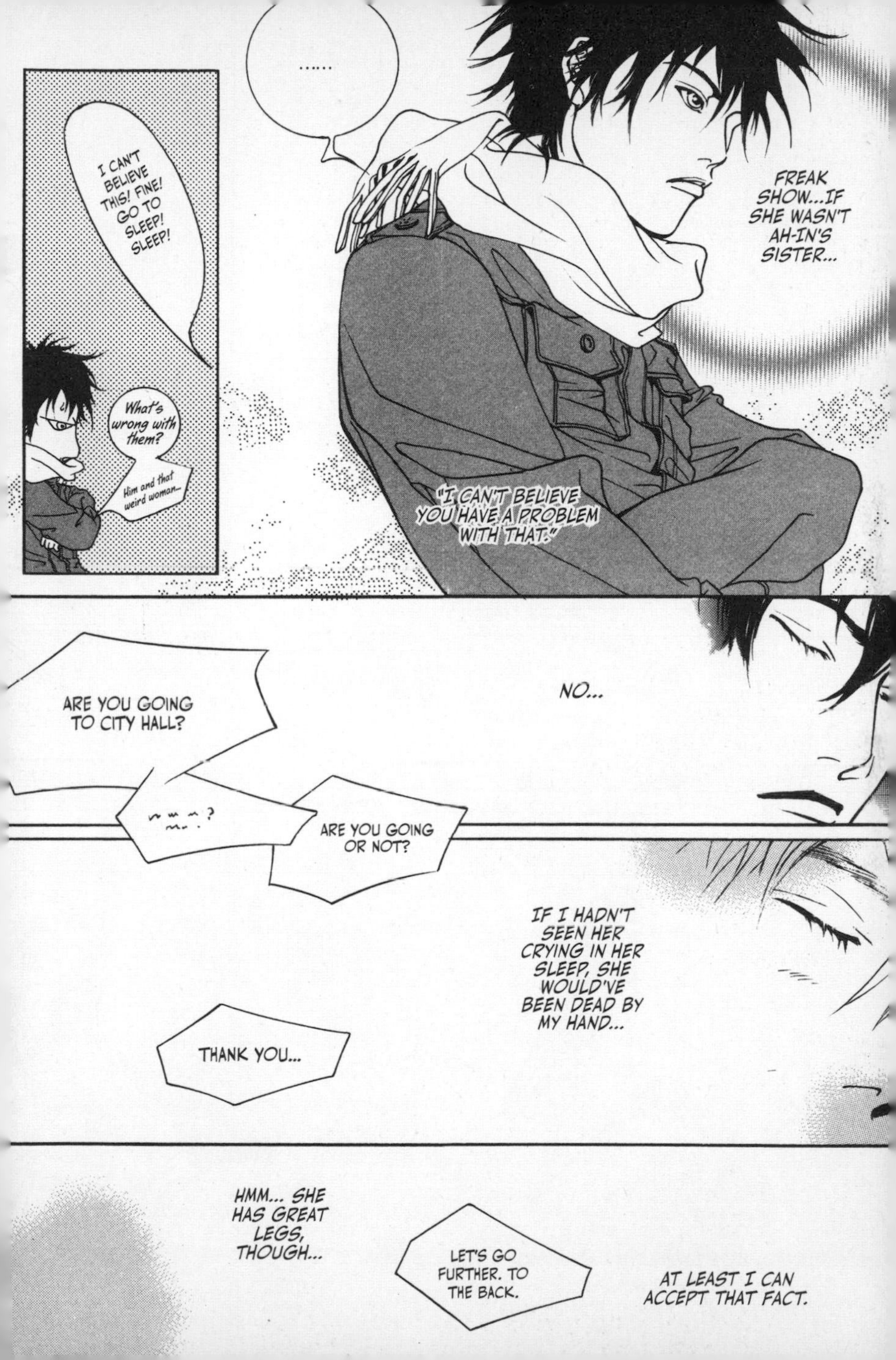
I CAN'T BELIEVE THIS! FINE! GO TO SLEEP! SLEEP!
What's wrong with them?
Him and that weird woman...
......
FREAK SHOW...IF SHE WASN'T AH-IN'S SISTER...
"I CAN'T BELIEVE YOU HAVE A PROBLEM WITH THAT."
ARE YOU GOING TO CITY HALL?
NO...
ARE YOU GOING OR NOT?
IF I HADN'T SEEN HER CRYING IN HER SLEEP, SHE WOULD'VE BEEN DEAD BY MY HAND...
THANK YOU...
HMM... SHE HAS GREAT LEGS, THOUGH...
LET'S GO FURTHER. TO THE BACK.
AT LEAST I CAN ACCEPT THAT FACT.

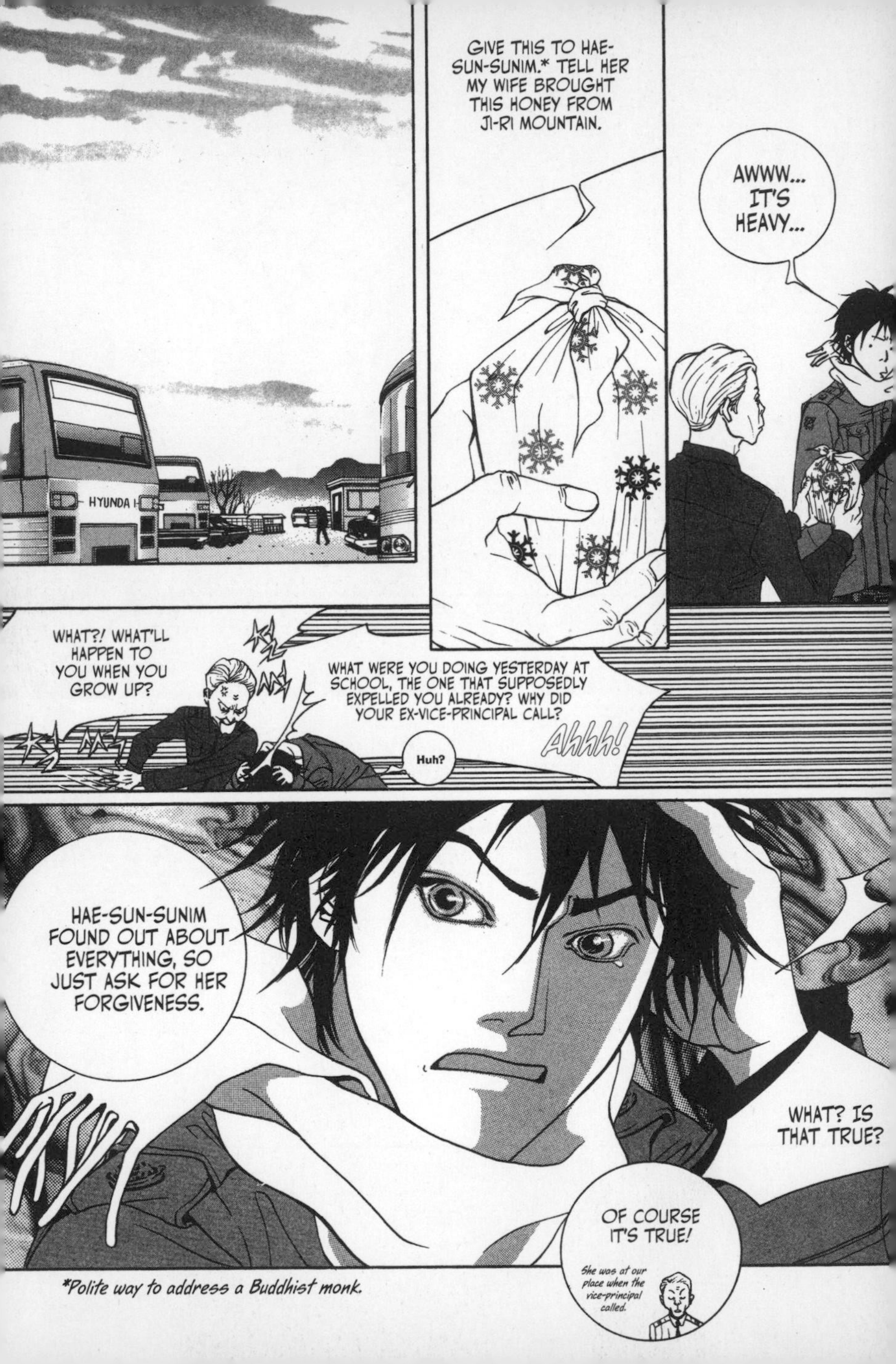
HYUNDA I
GIVE THIS TO HAE-SUN-SUNIM.* TELL HER MY WIFE BROUGHT THIS HONEY FROM JI-RI MOUNTAIN.
AWWW... IT'S HEAVY...
WHAT?! WHAT'LL HAPPEN TO YOU WHEN YOU GROW UP?
WHAT WERE YOU DOING YESTERDAY AT SCHOOL, THE ONE THAT SUPPOSEDLY EXPELLED YOU ALREADY? WHY DID YOUR EX-VICE-PRINCIPAL CALL?
Huh?
Ahhh!
HAE-SUN-SUNIM FOUND OUT ABOUT EVERYTHING, SO JUST ASK FOR HER FORGIVENESS.
WHAT? IS THAT TRUE?
OF COURSE IT'S TRUE!
She was at our place when the vice-principal called.

*Polite way to address a Buddhist monk.

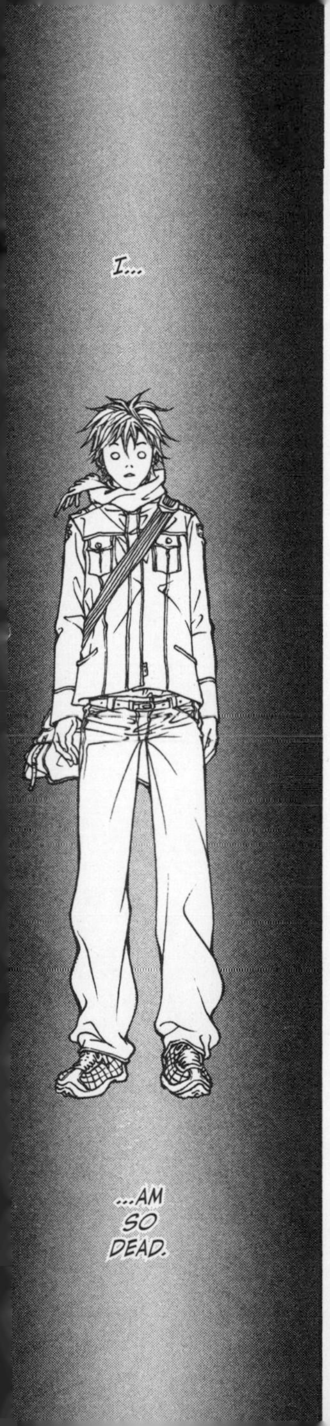
I...
...AM SO DEAD.

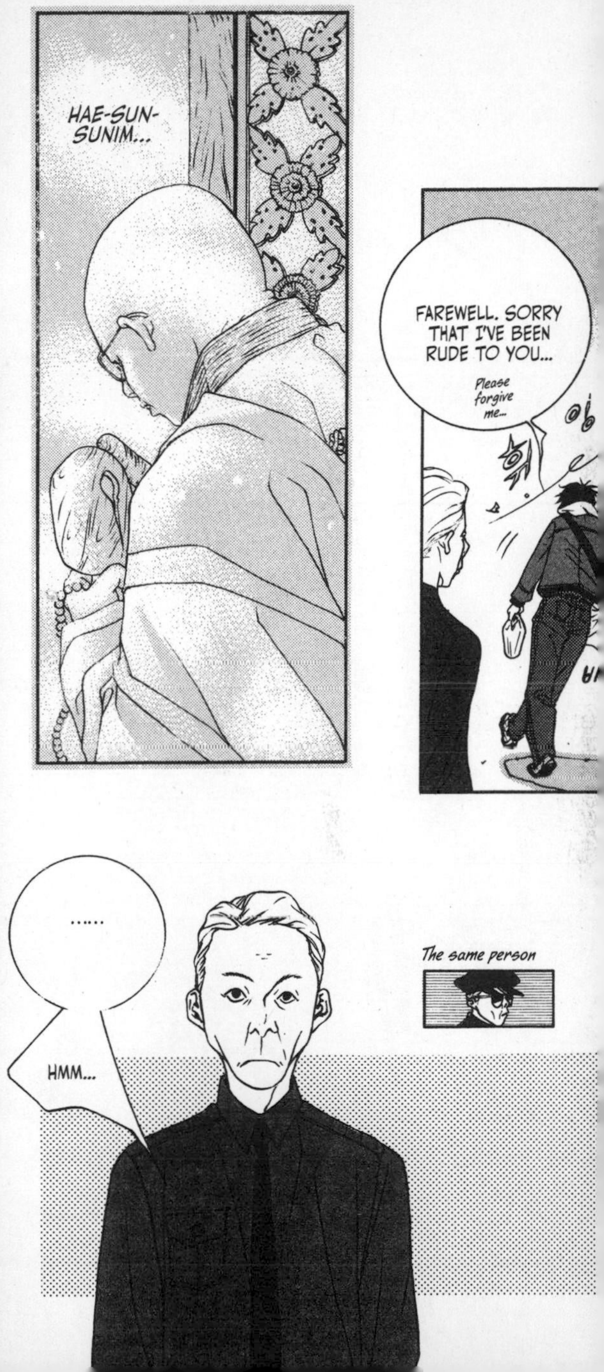
HAE-SUN-SUNIM...
FAREWELL. SORRY THAT I'VE BEEN RUDE TO YOU...
Please forgive me...
......
HMM...
The same person

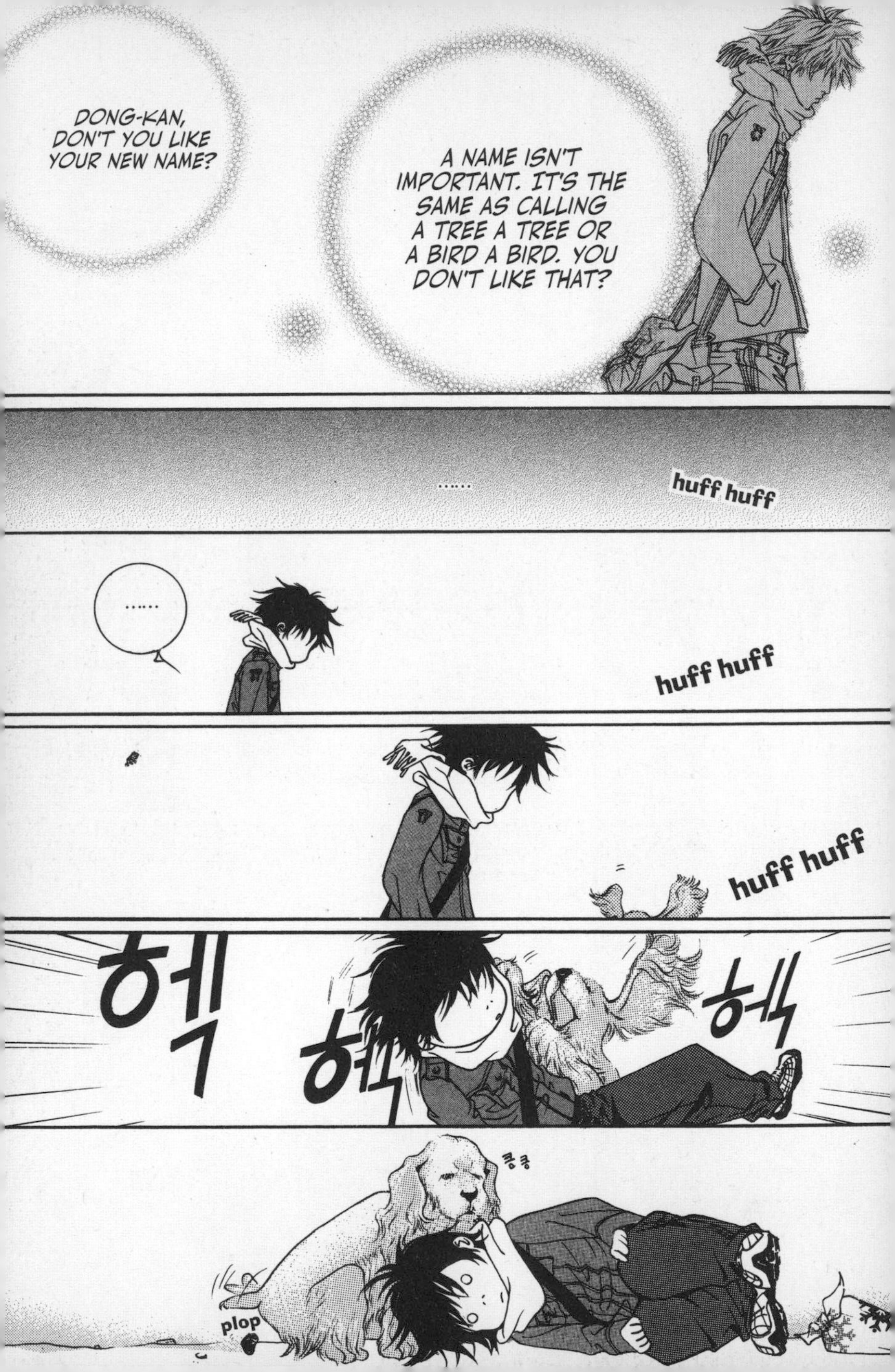
DONG-KAN, DON'T YOU LIKE YOUR NEW NAME?
A NAME ISN'T IMPORTANT. IT'S THE SAME AS CALLING A TREE A TREE OR A BIRD A BIRD. YOU DON'T LIKE THAT?
......
huff huff
......
huff huff
huff huff
헥
헥
헥
킁킁
plop

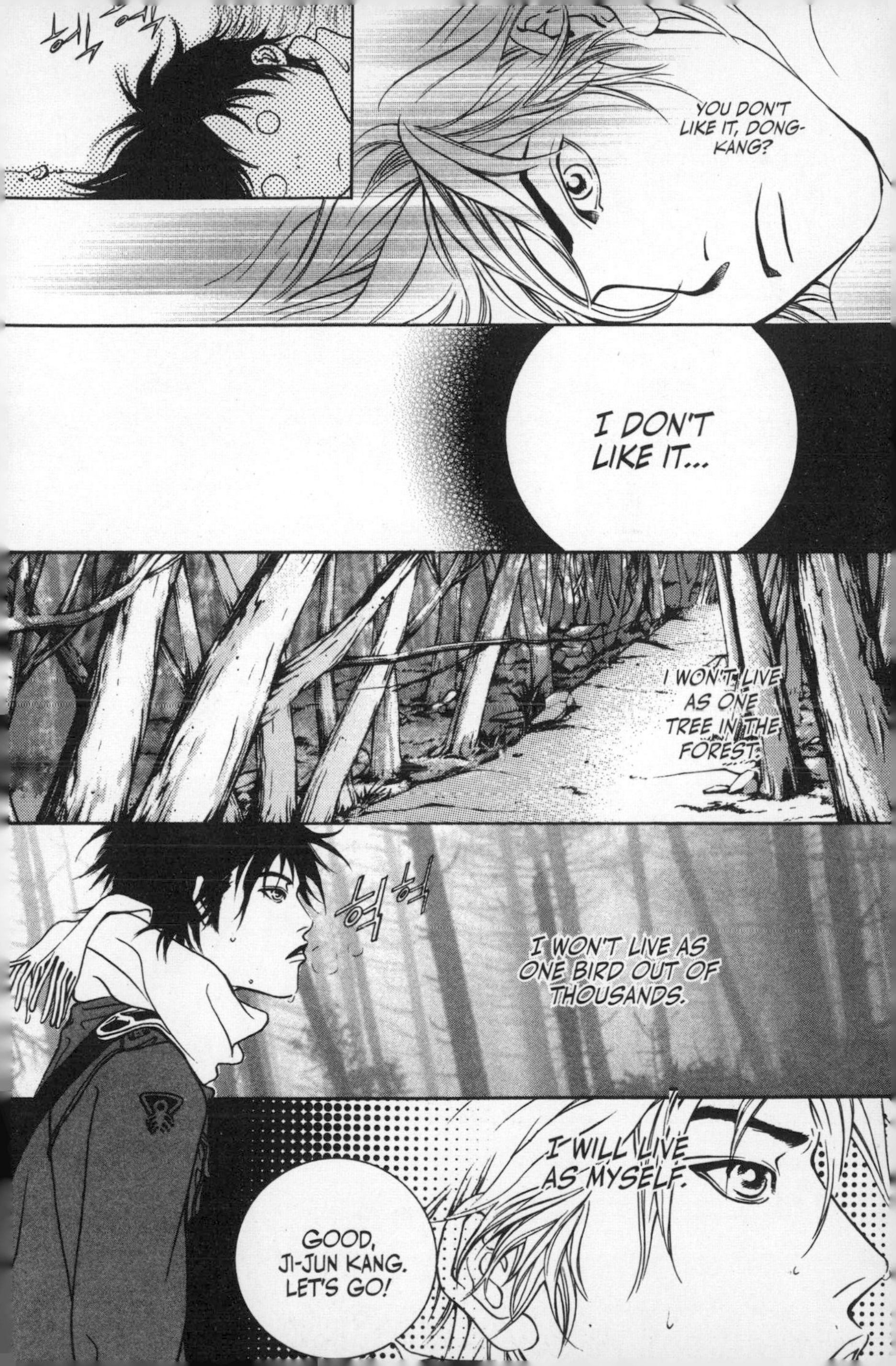
헉 헉
YOU DON'T LIKE IT, DONG-KANG?
I DON'T LIKE IT...
I WON'T LIVE AS ONE TREE IN THE FOREST.
헉 헉
I WON'T LIVE AS ONE BIRD OUT OF THOUSANDS.
I WILL LIVE AS MYSELF.
GOOD, JI-JUN KANG. LET'S GO!

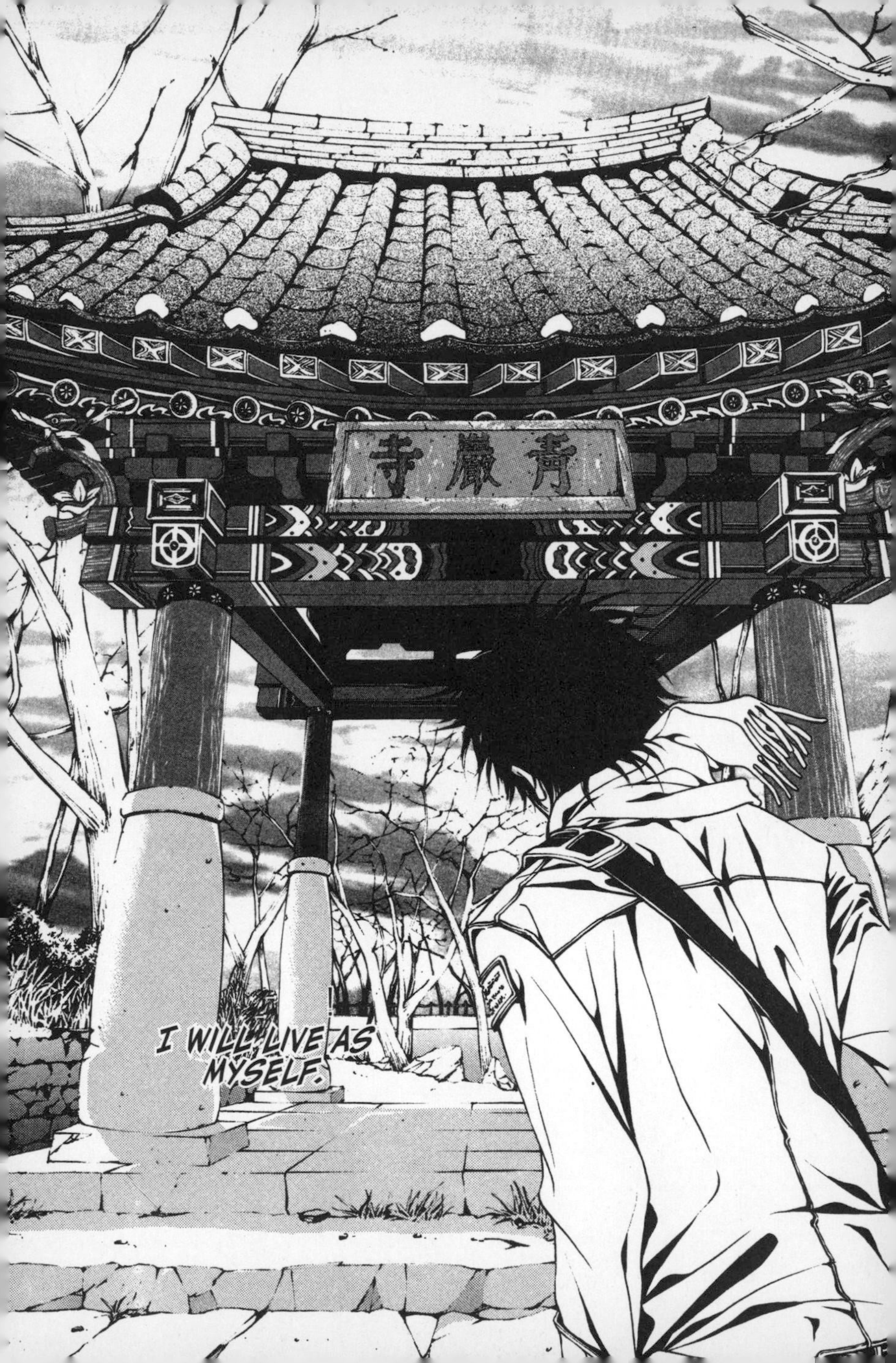
青巖寺
I WILL LIVE AS MYSELF.

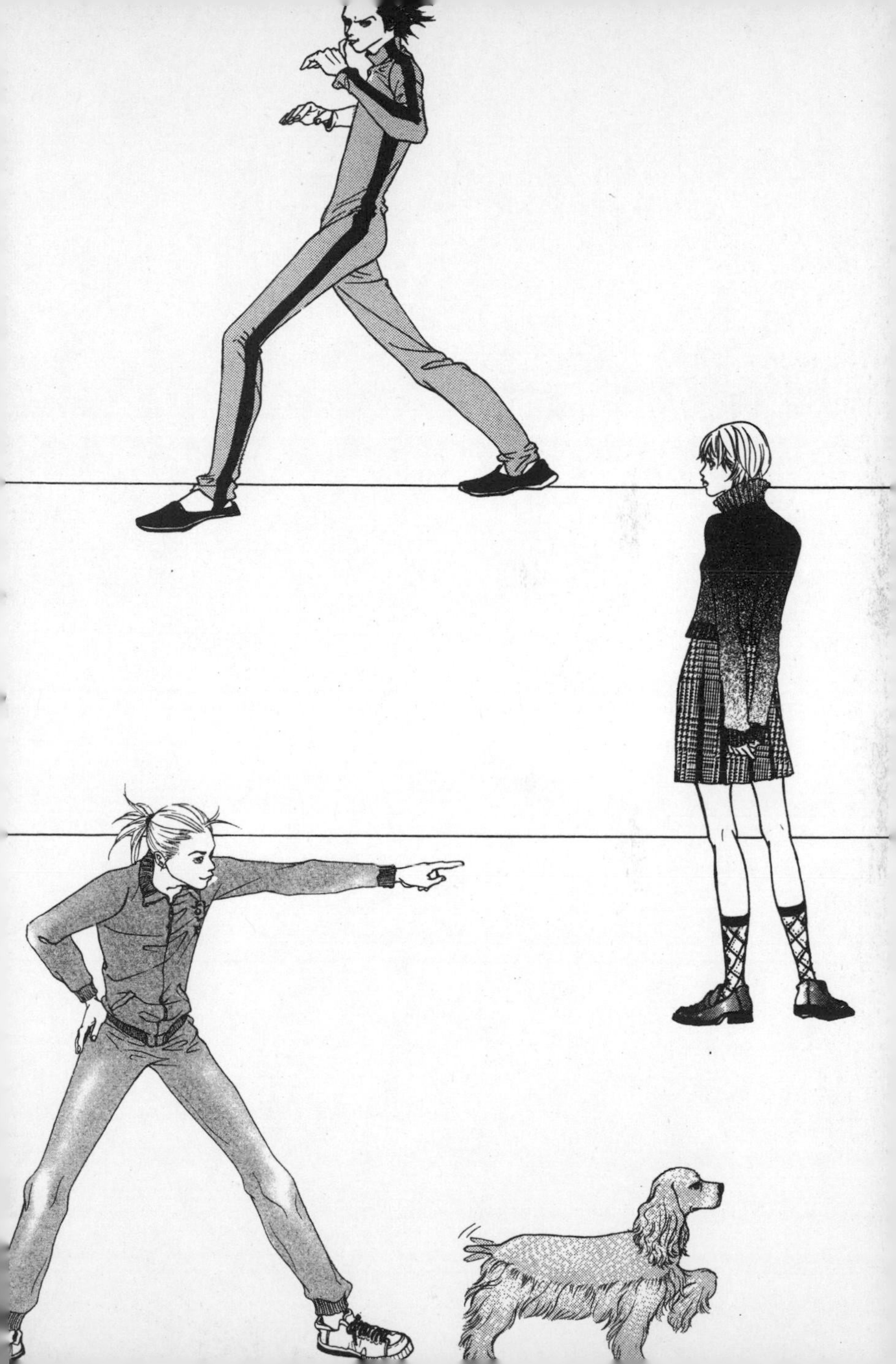

CLASSICAL
MUSIC...

THE SMELL OF
BREAD BAKING...

THE CONVERSATIONS
OF MY FAMILY...

...AND MY MOM'S
HAPPY HUMMING.

SOMEDAY...

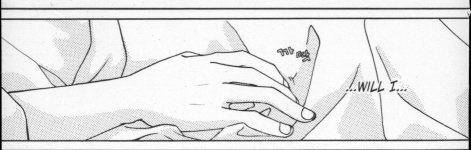

...WILL I...

...MISS THESE SMALL
THINGS...?

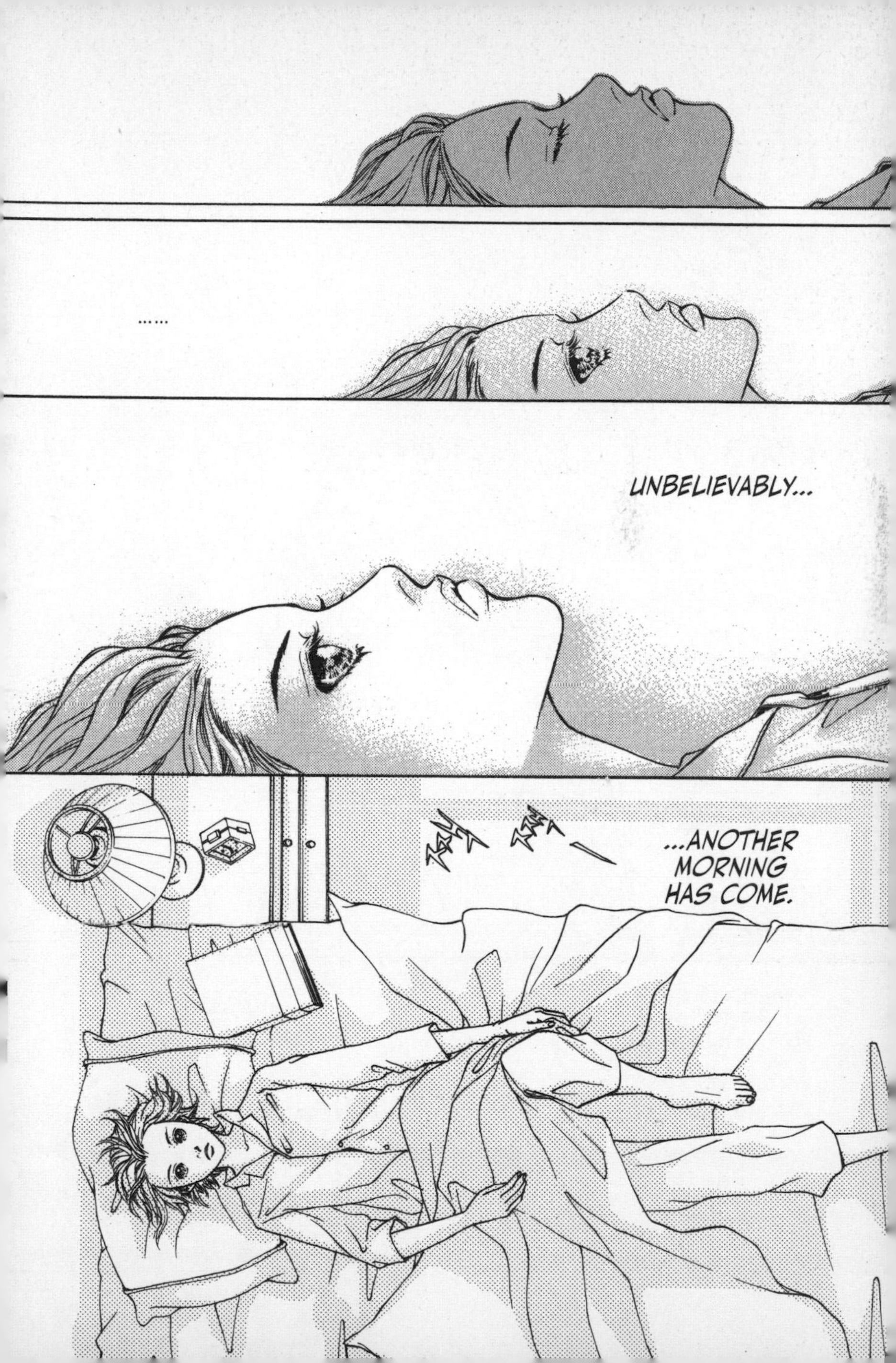
......
UNBELIEVABLY...
...ANOTHER MORNING HAS COME.

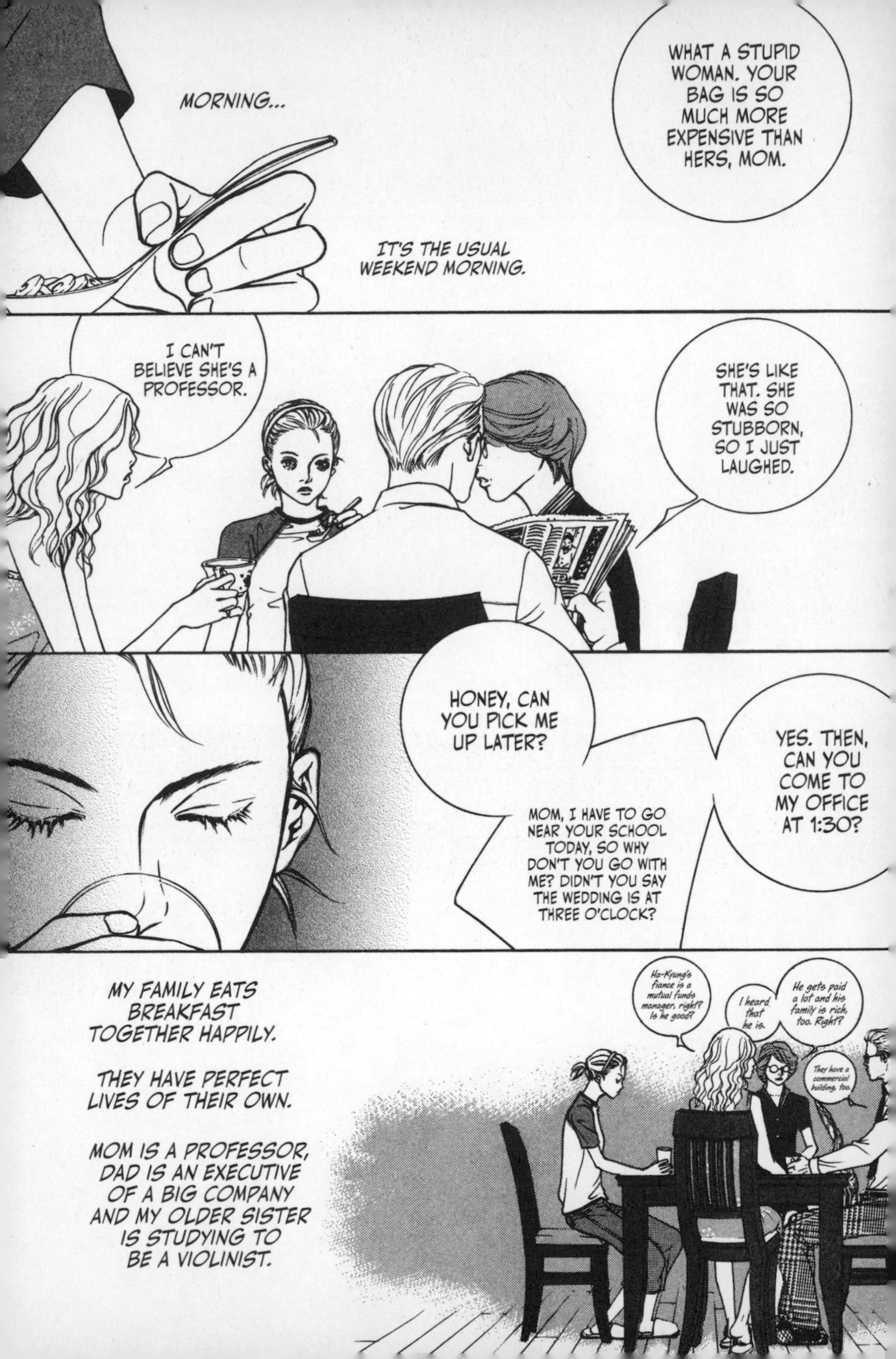
MORNING...
WHAT A STUPID WOMAN. YOUR BAG IS SO MUCH MORE EXPENSIVE THAN HERS, MOM.
IT'S THE USUAL WEEKEND MORNING.
I CAN'T BELIEVE SHE'S A PROFESSOR.
SHE'S LIKE THAT. SHE WAS SO STUBBORN, SO I JUST LAUGHED.
HONEY, CAN YOU PICK ME UP LATER?
YES. THEN, CAN YOU COME TO MY OFFICE AT 1:30?
MOM, I HAVE TO GO NEAR YOUR SCHOOL TODAY, SO WHY DON'T YOU GO WITH ME? DIDN'T YOU SAY THE WEDDING IS AT THREE O'CLOCK?
MY FAMILY EATS BREAKFAST TOGETHER HAPPILY.
THEY HAVE PERFECT LIVES OF THEIR OWN.
MOM IS A PROFESSOR, DAD IS AN EXECUTIVE OF A BIG COMPANY AND MY OLDER SISTER IS STUDYING TO BE A VIOLINIST.
Ha-Kyung's fiance is a mutual funds manager, right? Is he good?
I heard that he is.
He gets paid a lot and his family is rich, too. Right?
They have a commercial building, too.

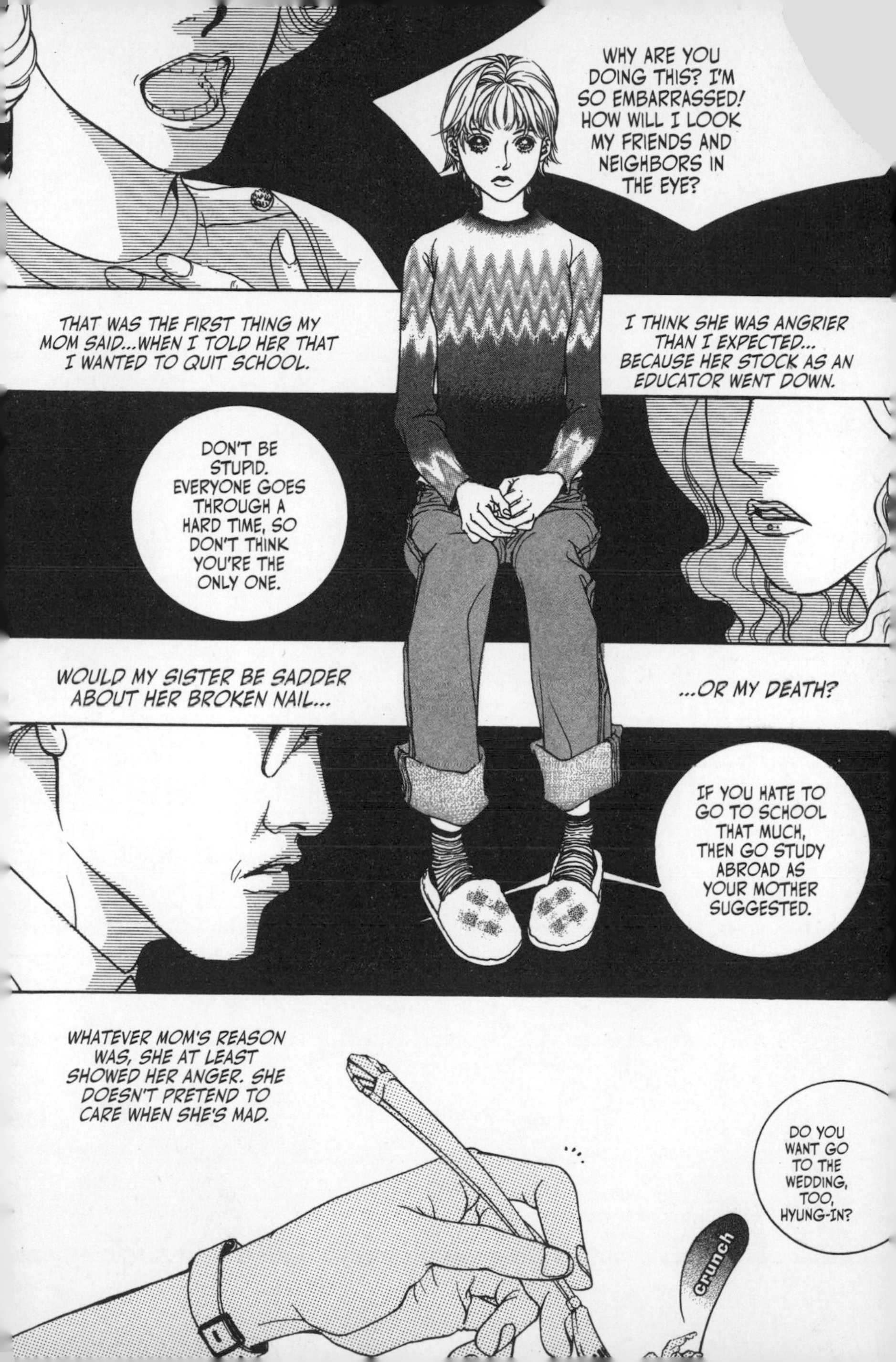

WHY ARE YOU DOING THIS? I'M SO EMBARRASSED! HOW WILL I LOOK MY FRIENDS AND NEIGHBORS IN THE EYE?
THAT WAS THE FIRST THING MY MOM SAID...WHEN I TOLD HER THAT I WANTED TO QUIT SCHOOL.
I THINK SHE WAS ANGRIER THAN I EXPECTED... BECAUSE HER STOCK AS AN EDUCATOR WENT DOWN.
DON'T BE STUPID. EVERYONE GOES THROUGH A HARD TIME, SO DON'T THINK YOU'RE THE ONLY ONE.
WOULD MY SISTER BE SADDER ABOUT HER BROKEN NAIL...
...OR MY DEATH?
IF YOU HATE TO GO TO SCHOOL THAT MUCH, THEN GO STUDY ABROAD AS YOUR MOTHER SUGGESTED.
WHATEVER MOM'S REASON WAS, SHE AT LEAST SHOWED HER ANGER. SHE DOESN'T PRETEND TO CARE WHEN SHE'S MAD.
DO YOU WANT GO TO THE WEDDING, TOO, HYUNG-IN?
crunch

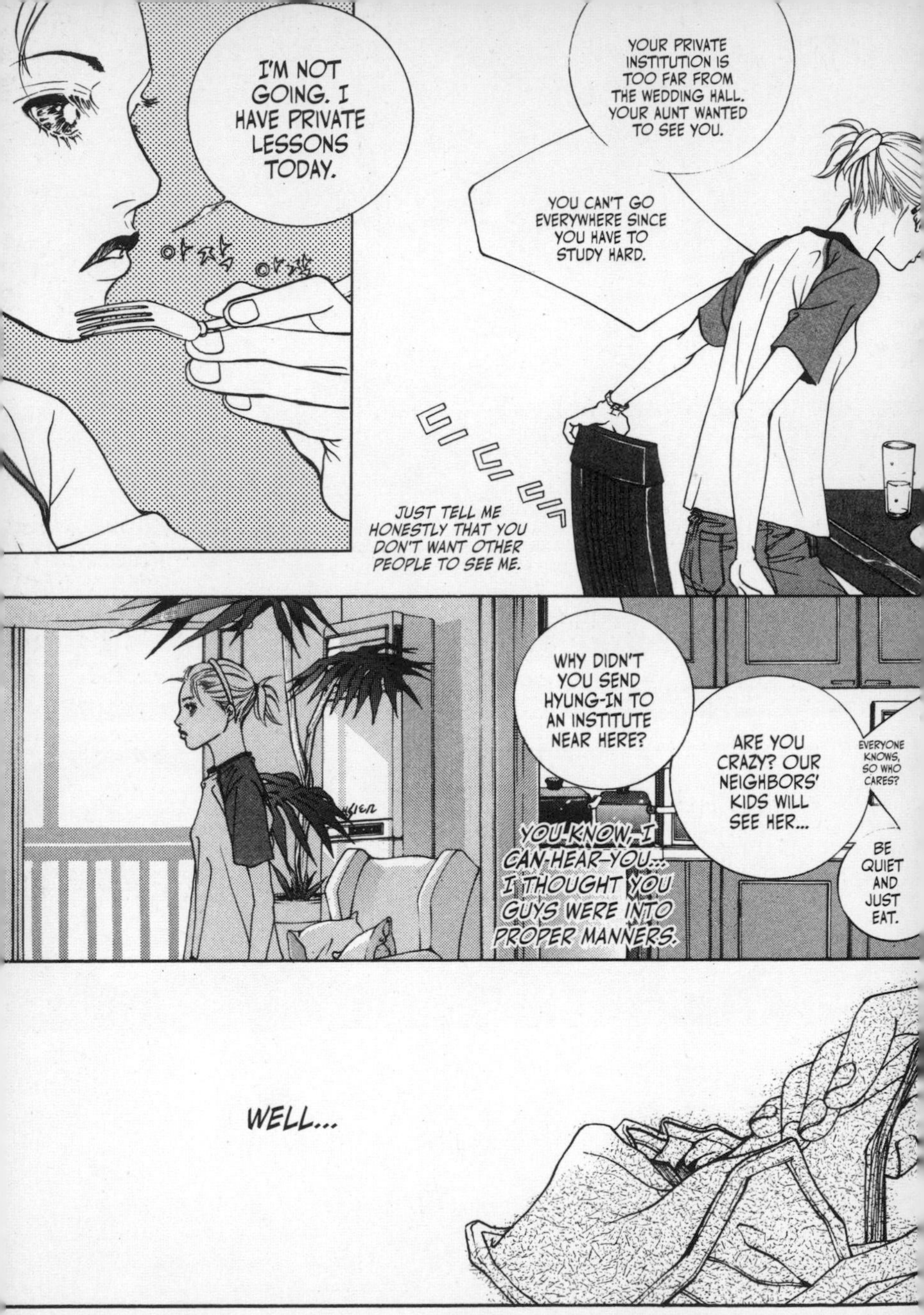
I'M NOT GOING. I HAVE PRIVATE LESSONS TODAY.
YOUR PRIVATE INSTITUTION IS TOO FAR FROM THE WEDDING HALL. YOUR AUNT WANTED TO SEE YOU.
YOU CAN'T GO EVERYWHERE SINCE YOU HAVE TO STUDY HARD.
JUST TELL ME HONESTLY THAT YOU DON'T WANT OTHER PEOPLE TO SEE ME.
WHY DIDN'T YOU SEND HYUNG-IN TO AN INSTITUTE NEAR HERE?
YOU KNOW, I CAN HEAR YOU... I THOUGHT YOU GUYS WERE INTO PROPER MANNERS.
ARE YOU CRAZY? OUR NEIGHBORS' KIDS WILL SEE HER...
EVERYONE KNOWS, SO WHO CARES?
BE QUIET AND JUST EAT.
WELL...

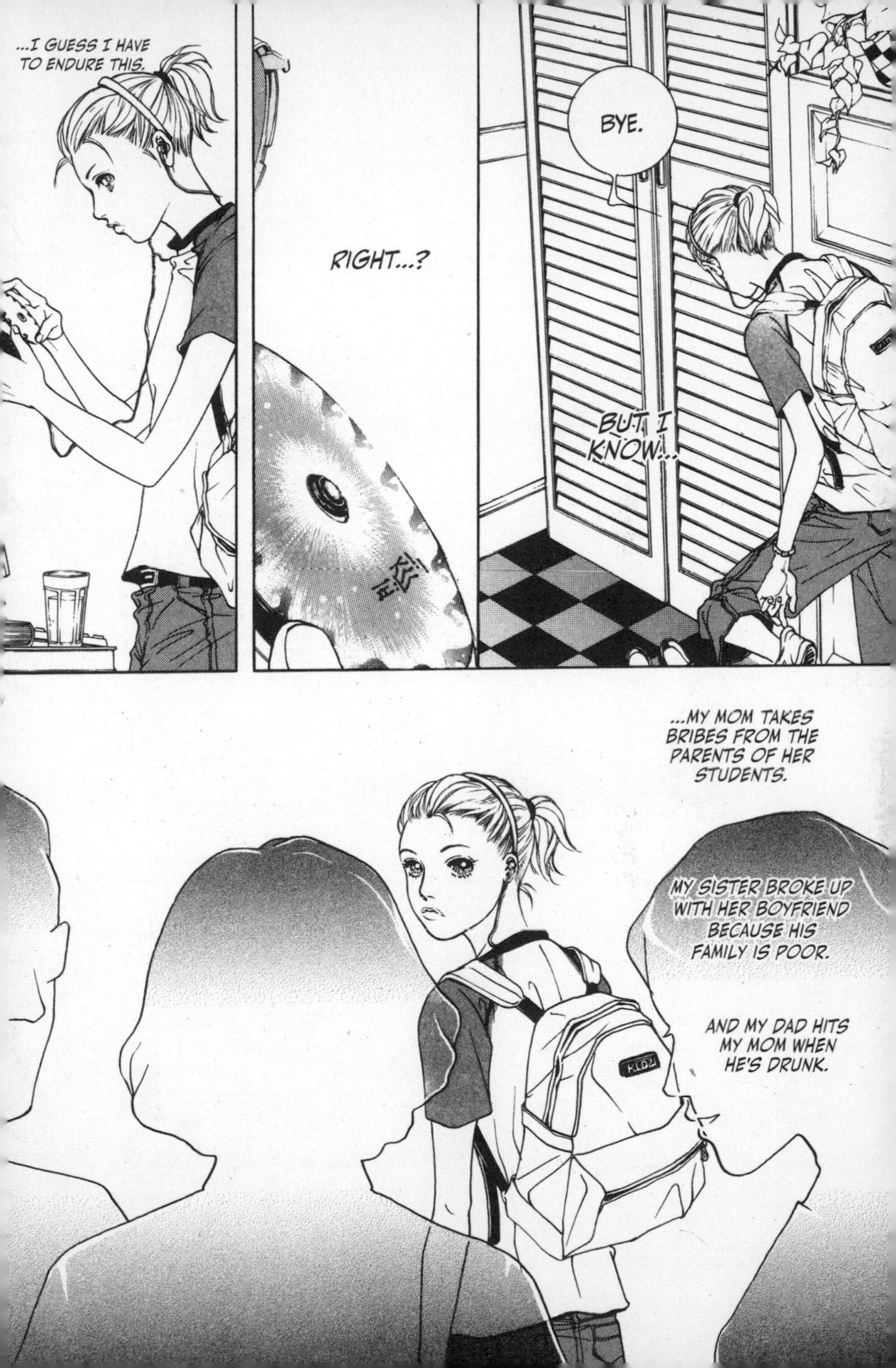
...I GUESS I HAVE TO ENDURE THIS.
RIGHT...?
BYE.
BUT I KNOW...
...MY MOM TAKES BRIBES FROM THE PARENTS OF HER STUDENTS.
MY SISTER BROKE UP WITH HER BOYFRIEND BECAUSE HIS FAMILY IS POOR.
AND MY DAD HITS MY MOM WHEN HE'S DRUNK.

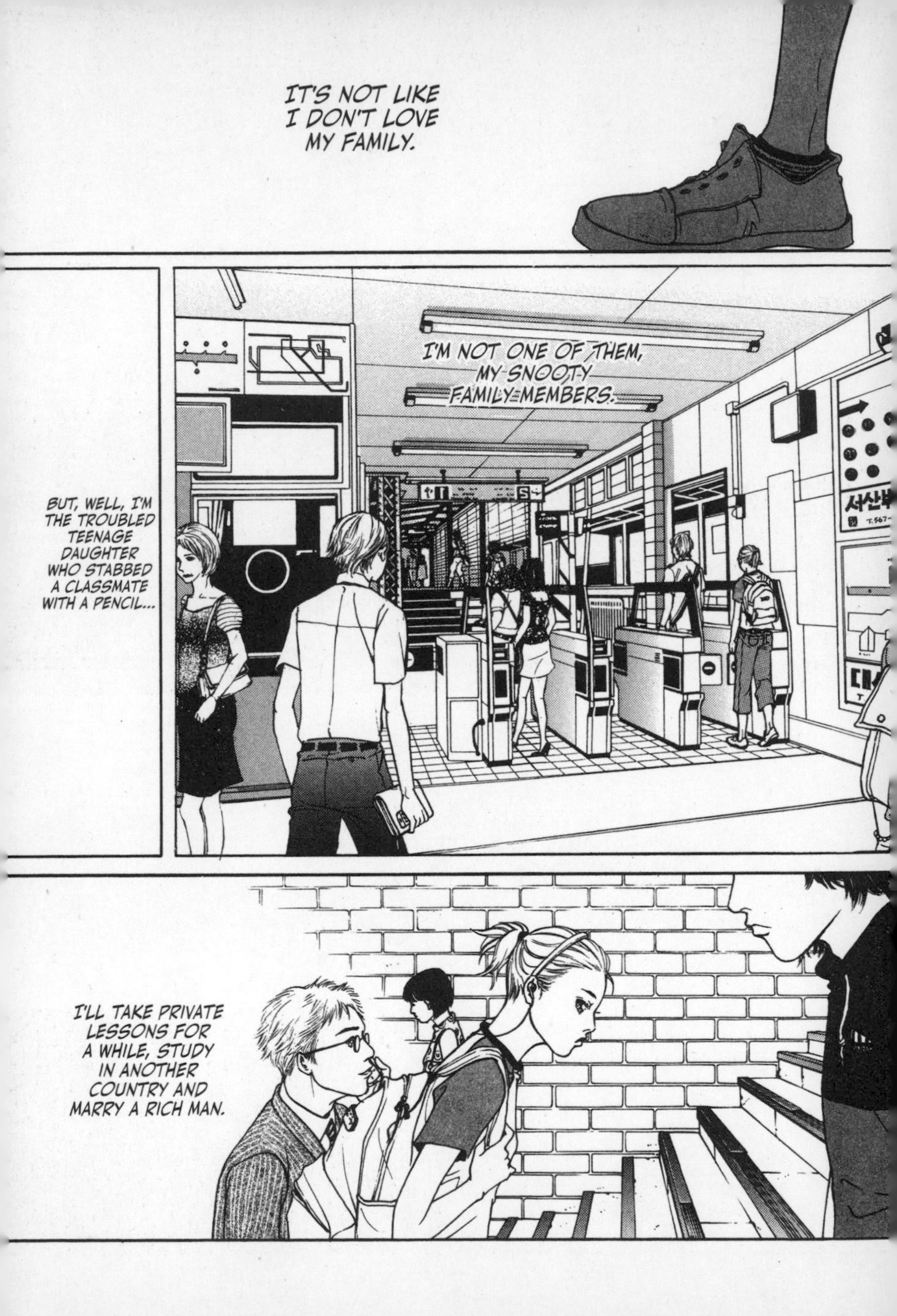
IT'S NOT LIKE I DON'T LOVE MY FAMILY.
BUT, WELL, I'M THE TROUBLED TEENAGE DAUGHTER WHO STABBED A CLASSMATE WITH A PENCIL...
I'M NOT ONE OF THEM, MY SNOOTY FAMILY MEMBERS.
I'LL TAKE PRIVATE LESSONS FOR A WHILE, STUDY IN ANOTHER COUNTRY AND MARRY A RICH MAN.

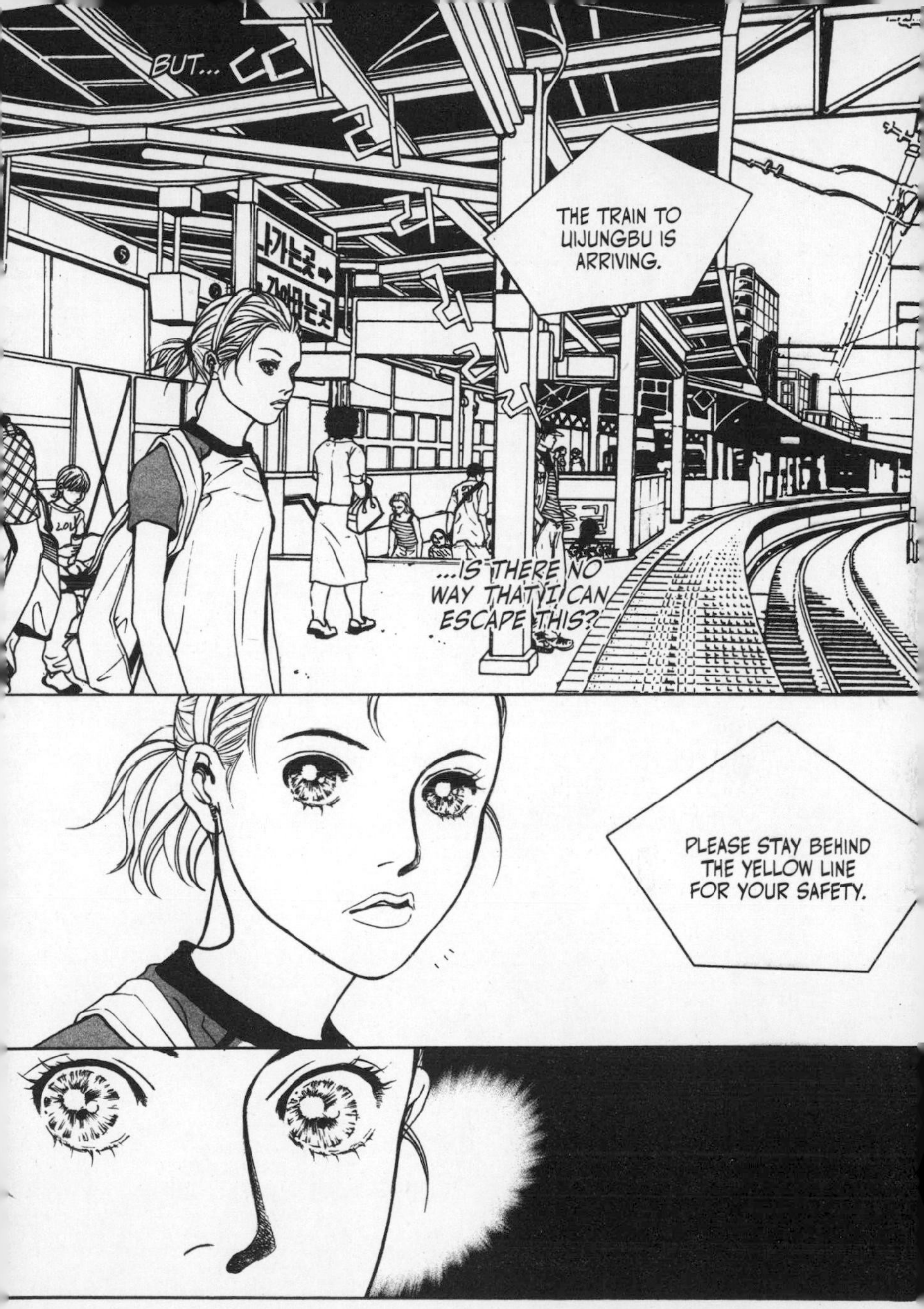
BUT...
THE TRAIN TO UIJUNGBU IS ARRIVING.
나가는곳 →
...IS THERE NO WAY THAT I CAN ESCAPE THIS?
PLEASE STAY BEHIND THE YELLOW LINE FOR YOUR SAFETY.

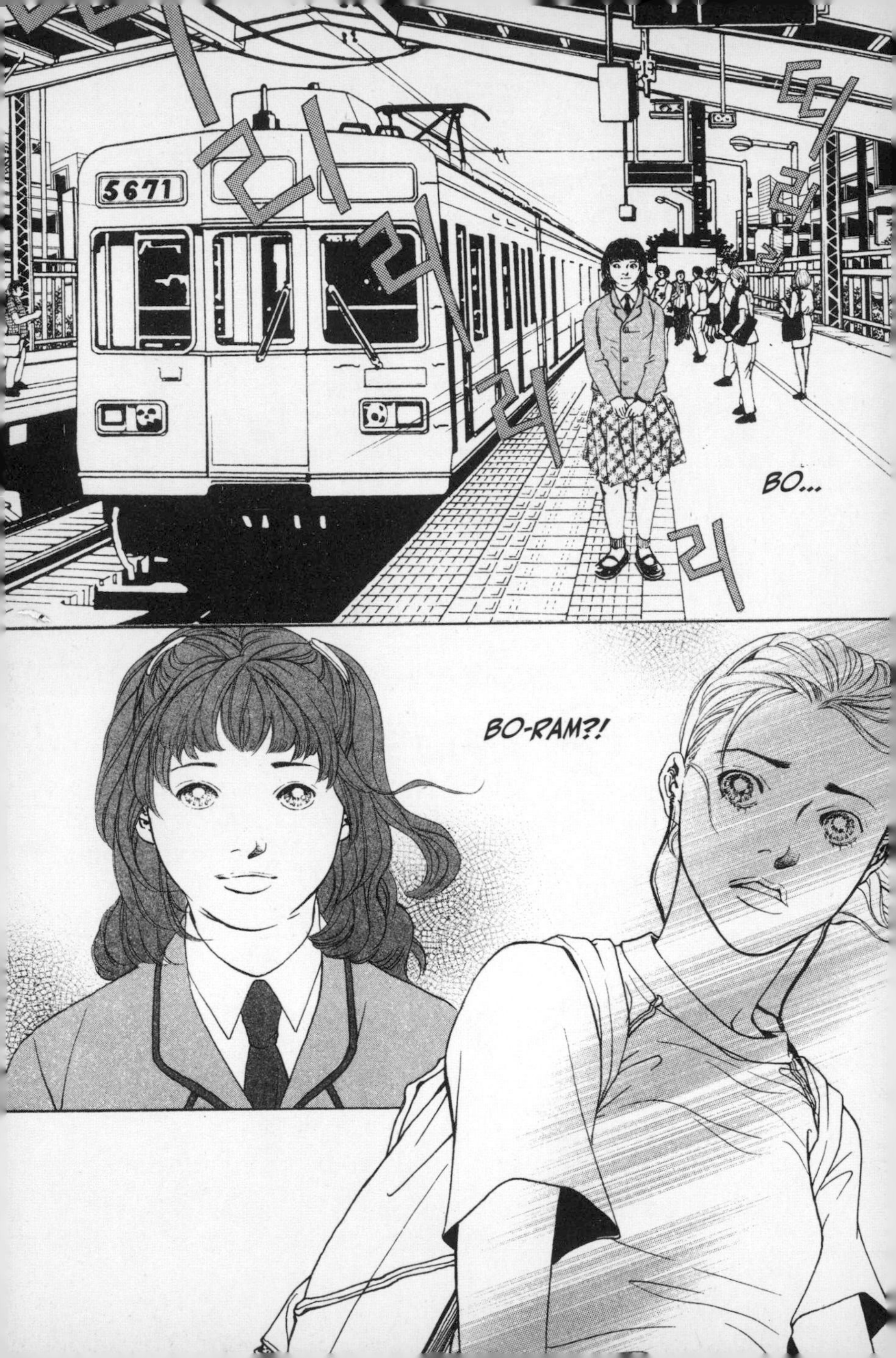
띠리리
BO...
BO-RAM?!

"OH, MY. I DIDN'T KNOW THAT."

"THAT'S WHY HYUNG-IN IS TAKING A BREAK FROM SCHOOL. IT'S AN IMPORTANT PERIOD, BUT WHAT CAN YOU DO?"

"SO, WHAT ARE YOU GOING TO DO?"

"I'LL SEND HER ABROAD TO STUDY FOR A WHILE."

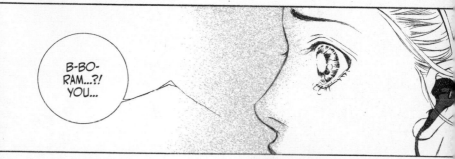

B-BO-RAM...?! YOU...

"WAS HYUNG-IN CLOSE TO HER?"

"I DON'T KNOW. ANYWAY, YOU KNOW HYUNG-IN IS VERY SENSITIVE."

"THAT GIRL SENT HYUNG-IN A TEXT MESSAGE..."

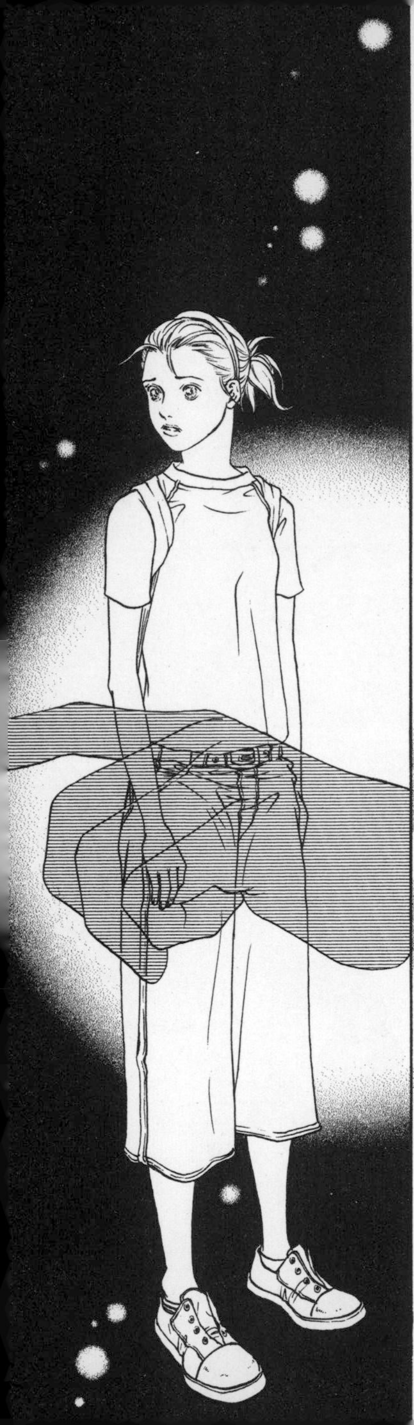
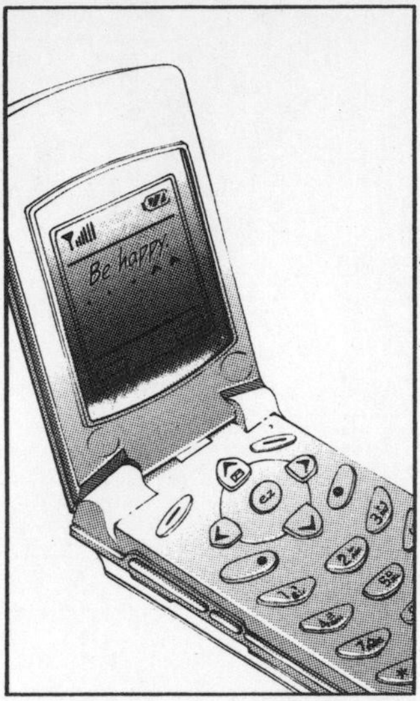
Be happy.
"...RIGHT BEFORE SHE KILLED HERSELF..."
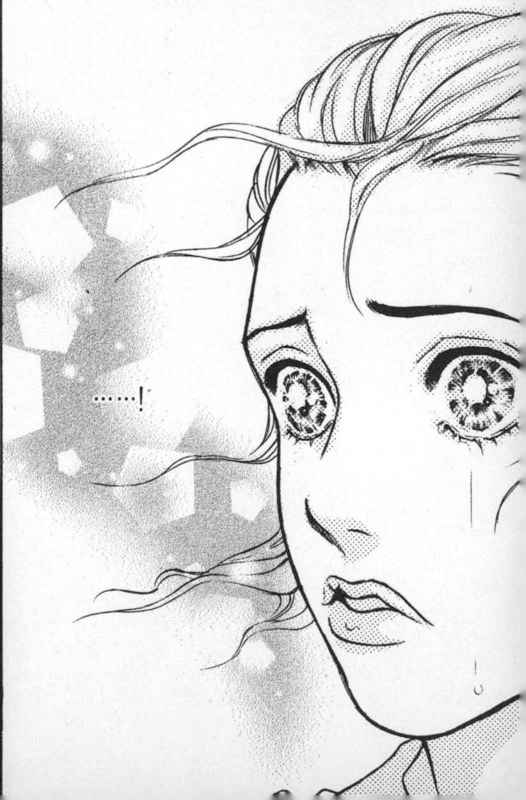
……!

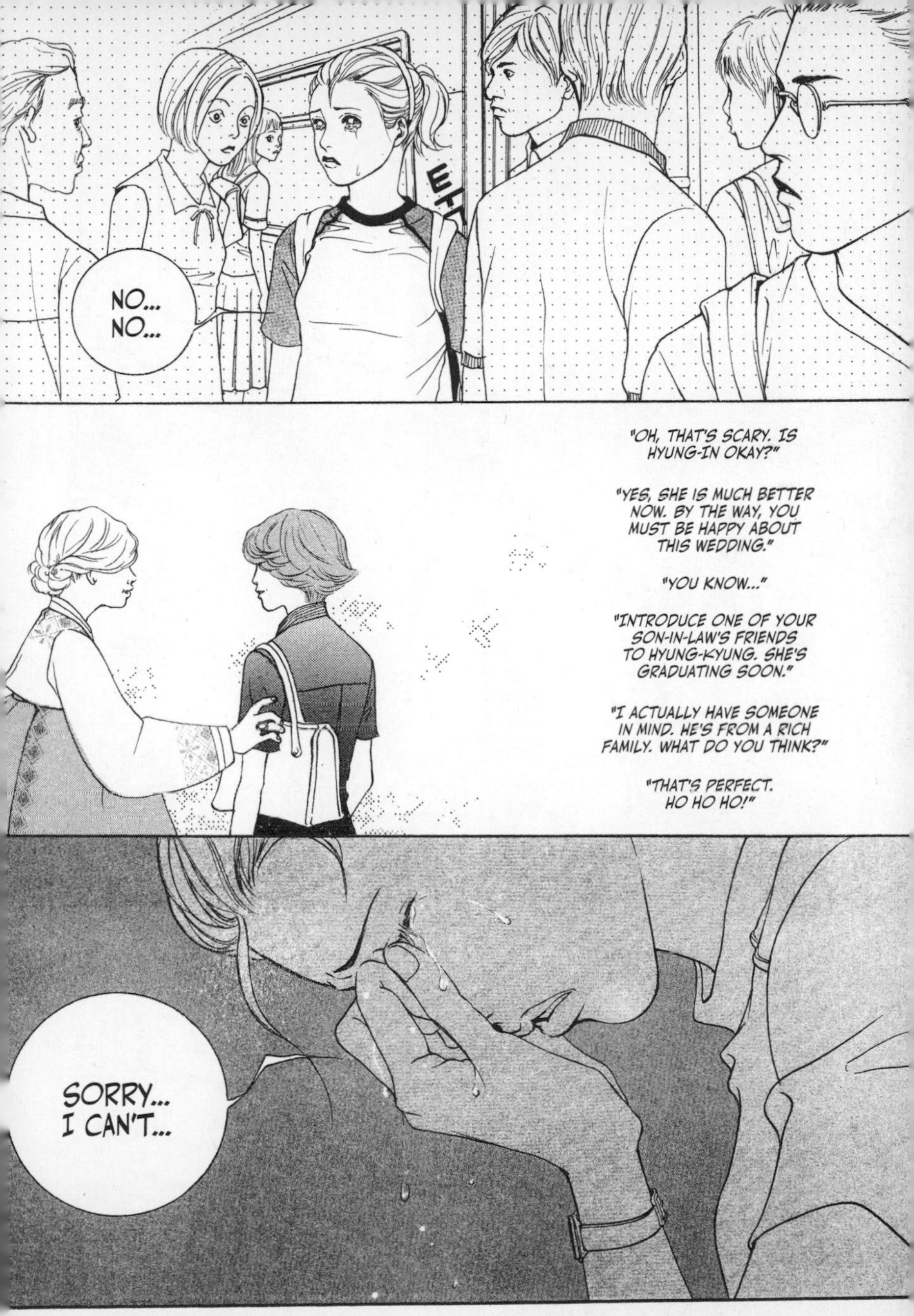

ETT
NO... NO...
"OH, THAT'S SCARY. IS HYUNG-IN OKAY?"
"YES, SHE IS MUCH BETTER NOW. BY THE WAY, YOU MUST BE HAPPY ABOUT THIS WEDDING."
"YOU KNOW..."
"INTRODUCE ONE OF YOUR SON-IN-LAW'S FRIENDS TO HYUNG-KYUNG. SHE'S GRADUATING SOON."
"I ACTUALLY HAVE SOMEONE IN MIND. HE'S FROM A RICH FAMILY. WHAT DO YOU THINK?"
"THAT'S PERFECT. HO HO HO!"
SORRY... I CAN'T...

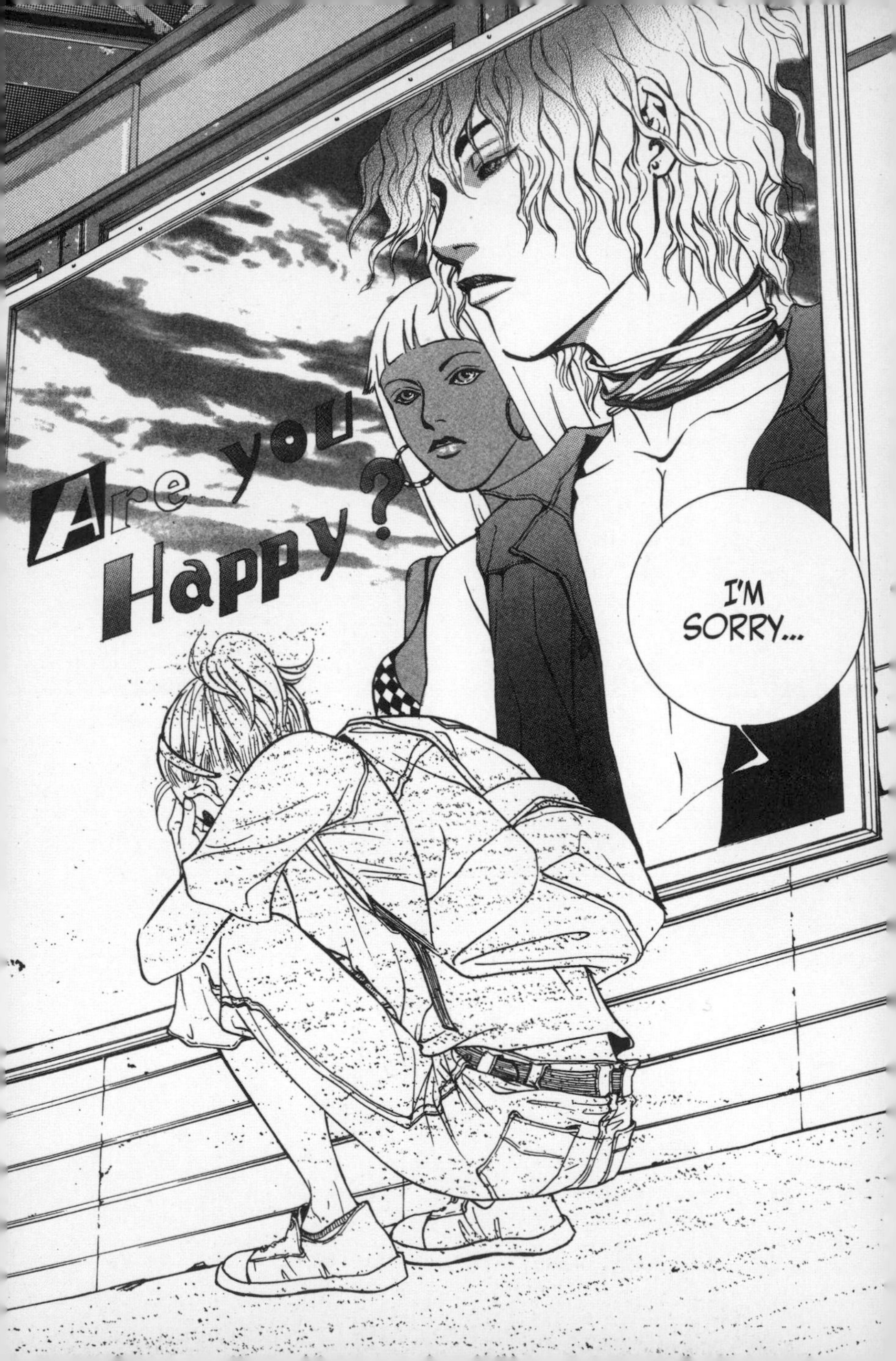
Are you Happy?
I'M SORRY...

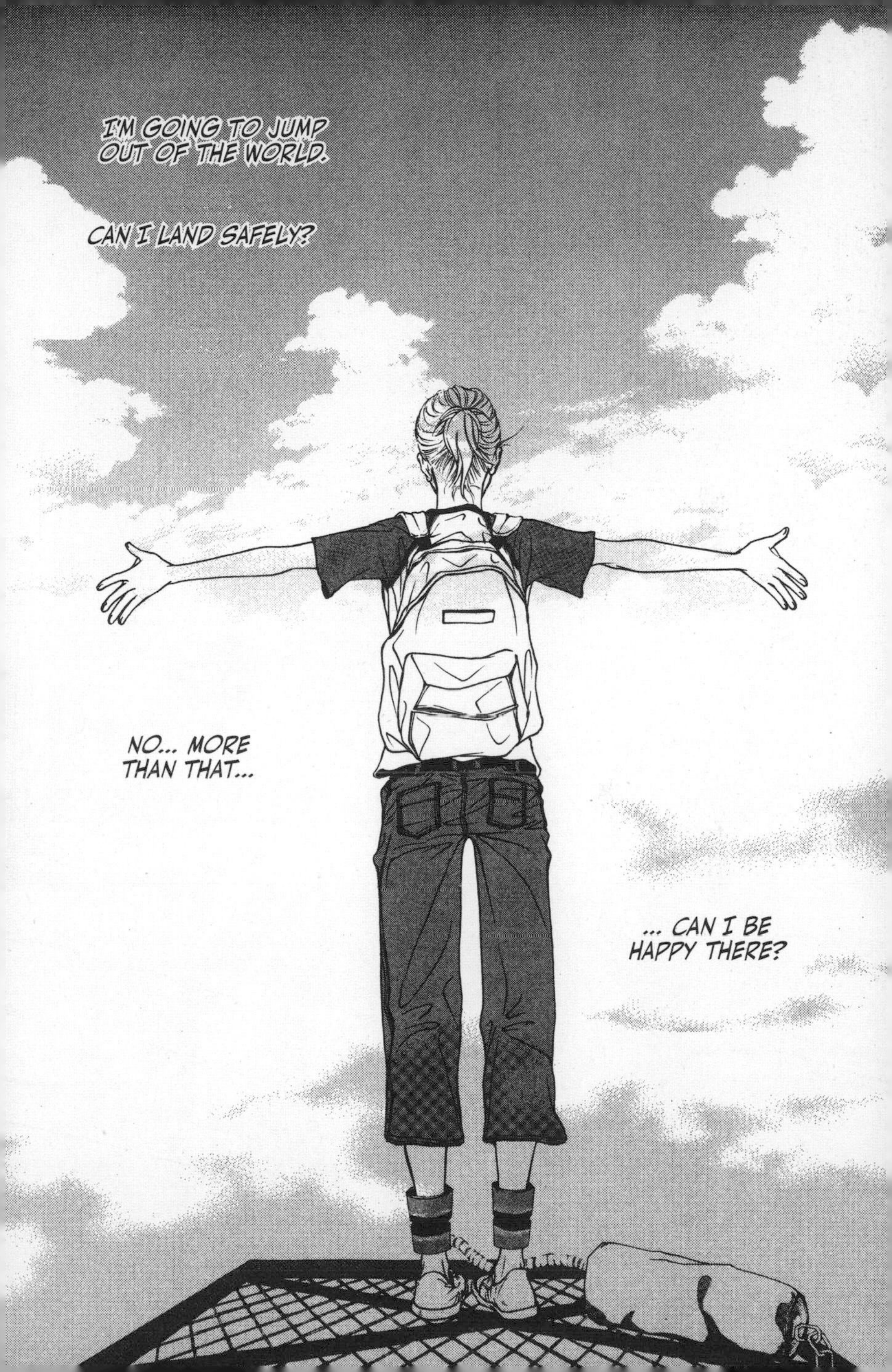
I'M GOING TO JUMP OUT OF THE WORLD.
CAN I LAND SAFELY?
NO... MORE THAN THAT...
... CAN I BE HAPPY THERE?

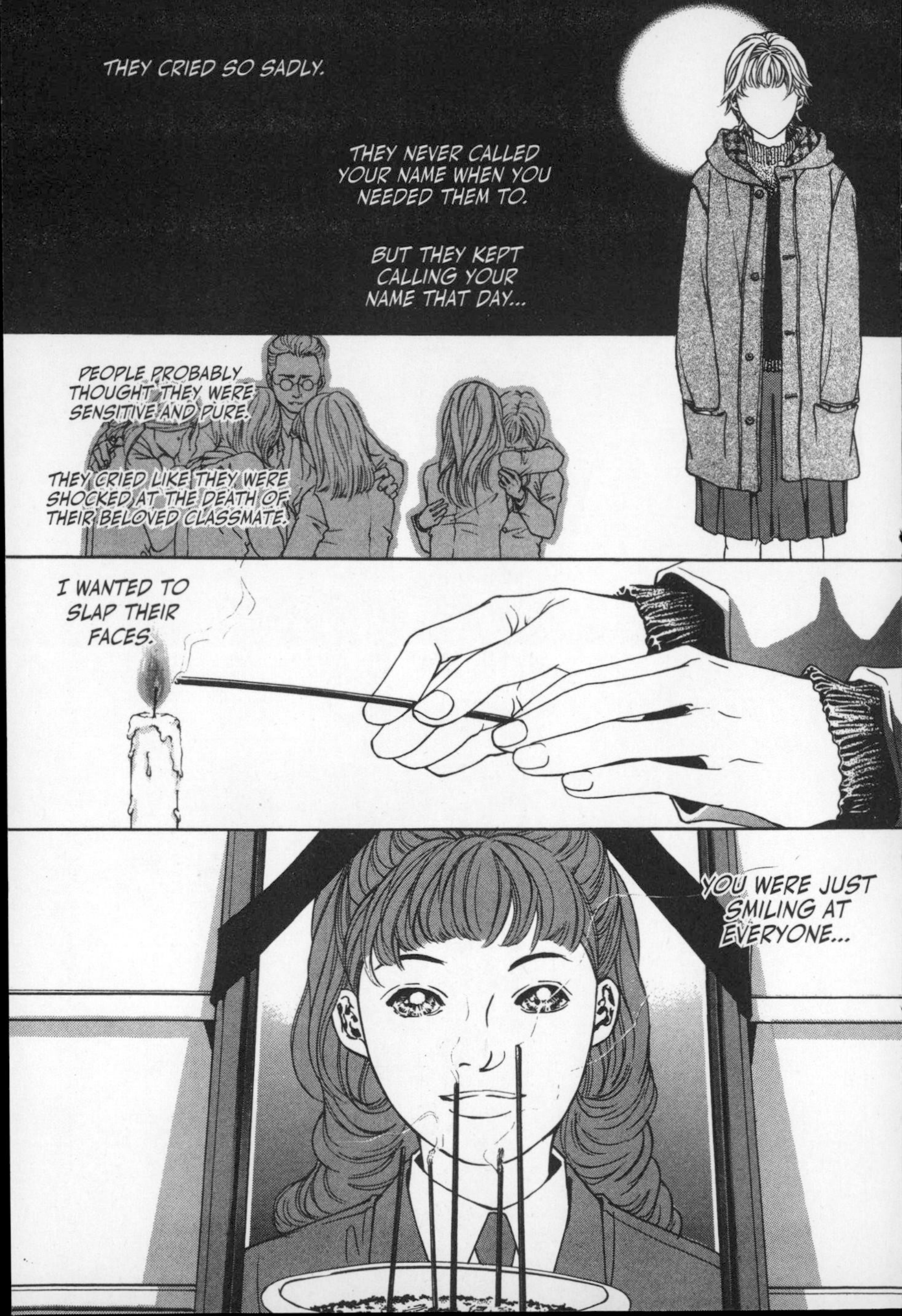
THEY CRIED SO SADLY.
THEY NEVER CALLED YOUR NAME WHEN YOU NEEDED THEM TO.
BUT THEY KEPT CALLING YOUR NAME THAT DAY...
PEOPLE PROBABLY THOUGHT THEY WERE SENSITIVE AND PURE.
THEY CRIED LIKE THEY WERE SHOCKED AT THE DEATH OF THEIR BELOVED CLASSMATE.
I WANTED TO SLAP THEIR FACES.
YOU WERE JUST SMILING AT EVERYONE...

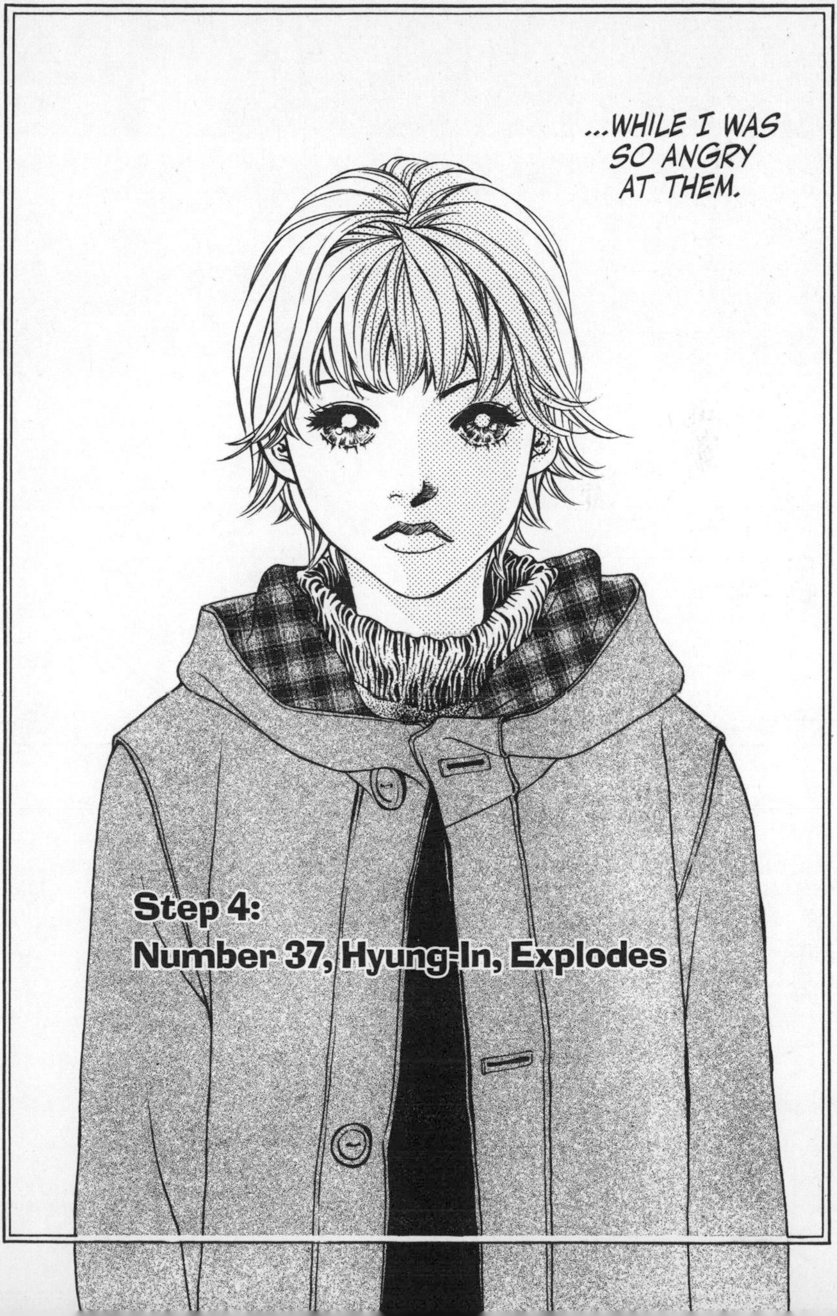
...WHILE I WAS SO ANGRY AT THEM.
Step 4:
Number 37, Hyung-In, Explodes

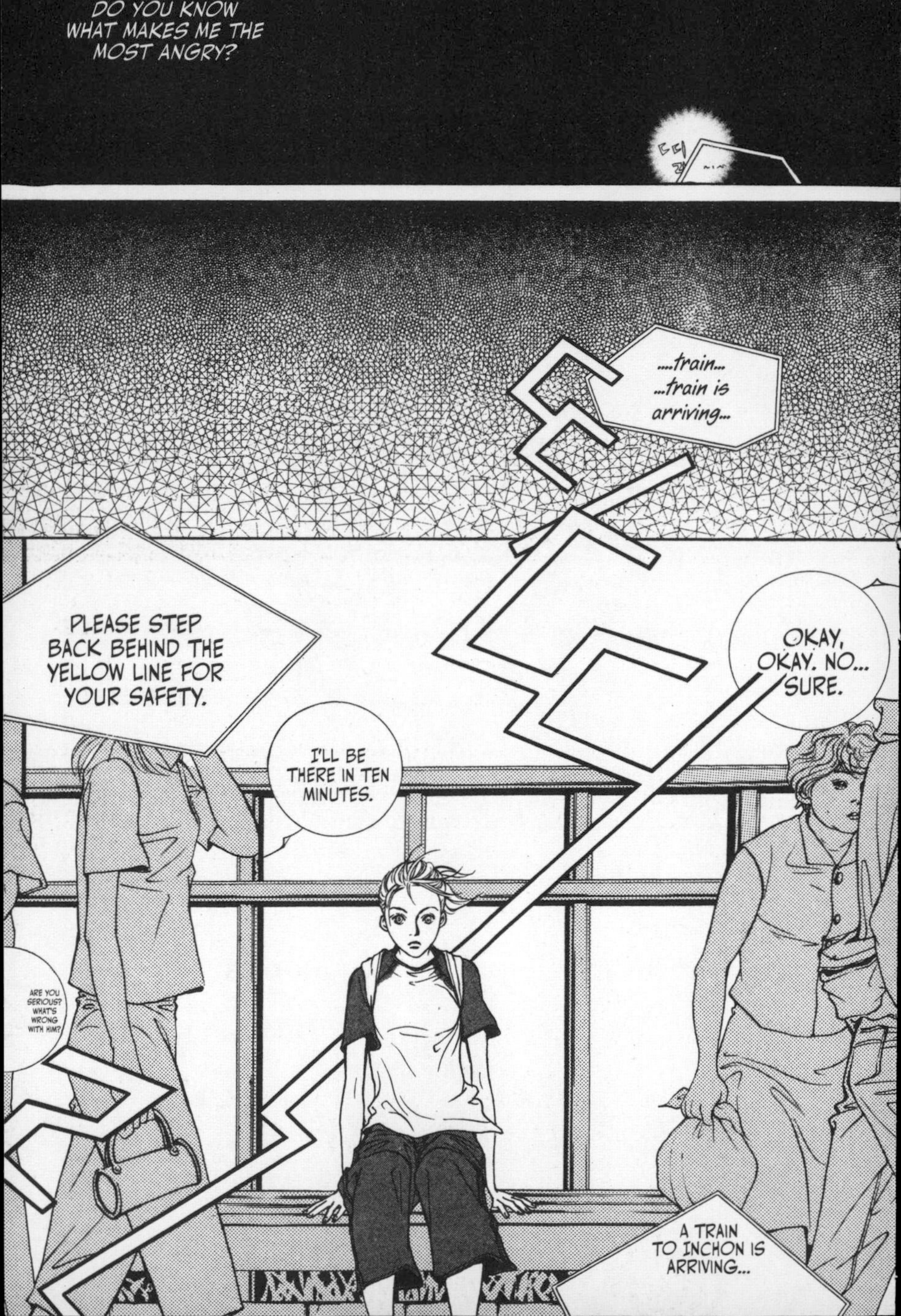
DO YOU KNOW WHAT MAKES ME THE MOST ANGRY?
...train... ...train is arriving...
PLEASE STEP BACK BEHIND THE YELLOW LINE FOR YOUR SAFETY.
I'LL BE THERE IN TEN MINUTES.
OKAY, OKAY. NO... SURE.
ARE YOU SERIOUS? WHAT'S WRONG WITH HIM?
A TRAIN TO INCHON IS ARRIVING...

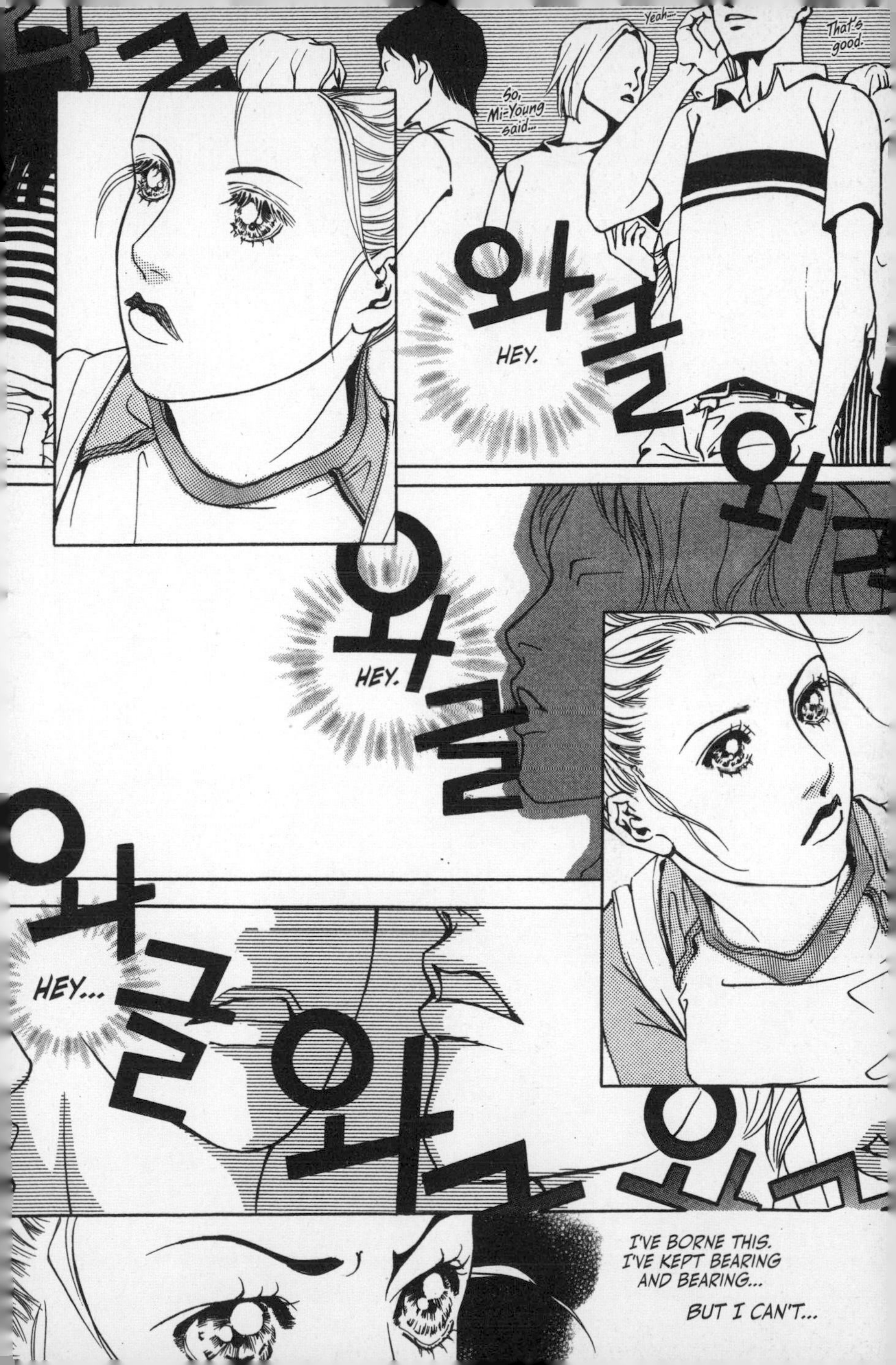
So, Mi-Young said...
Yeah...
That's good.
와글
HEY.
와글
HEY.
와글
HEY...
와글
와글
I'VE BORNE THIS. I'VE KEPT BEARING AND BEARING...
BUT I CAN'T...

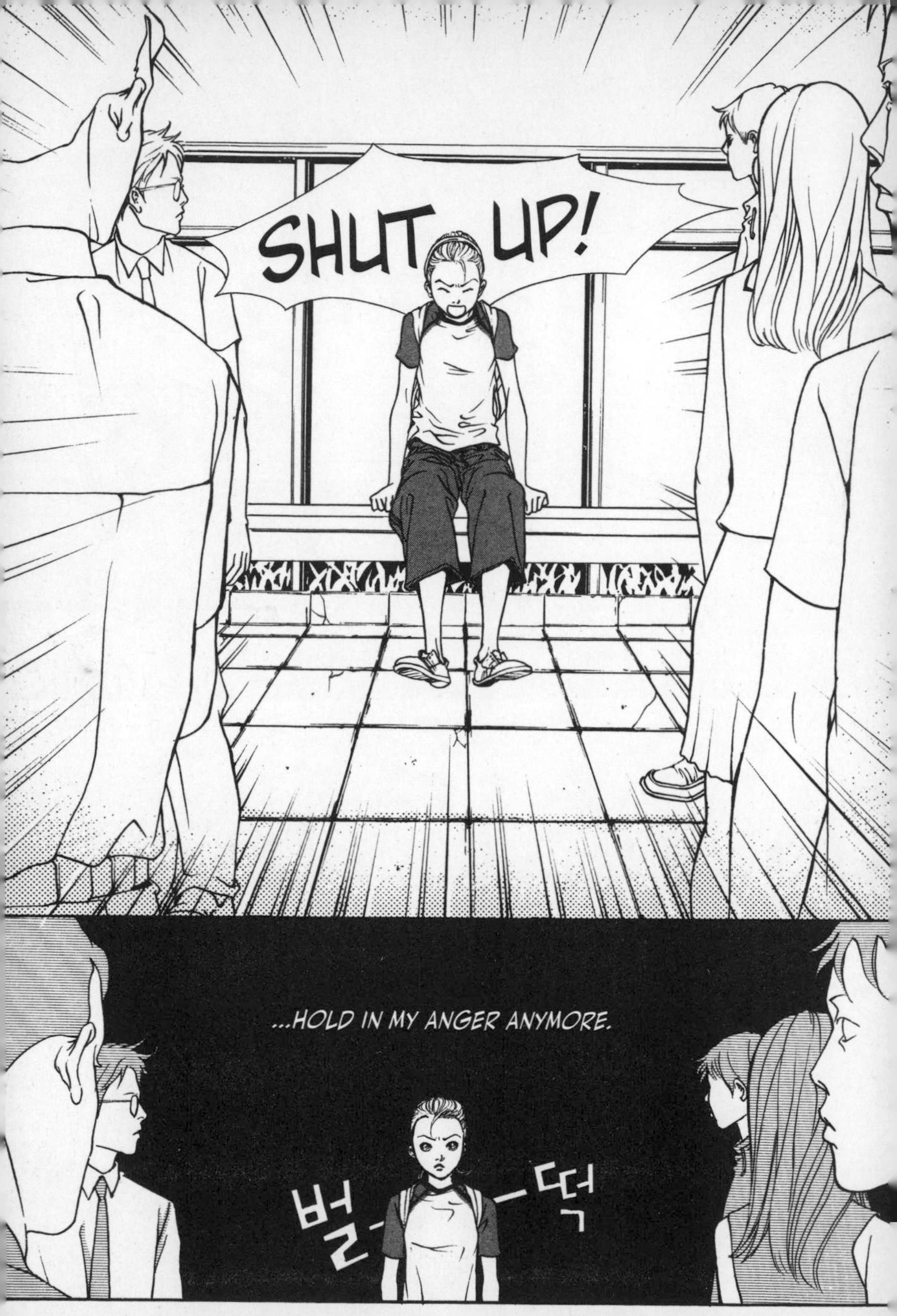
SHUT UP!
...HOLD IN MY ANGER ANYMORE.
벌-
-떡

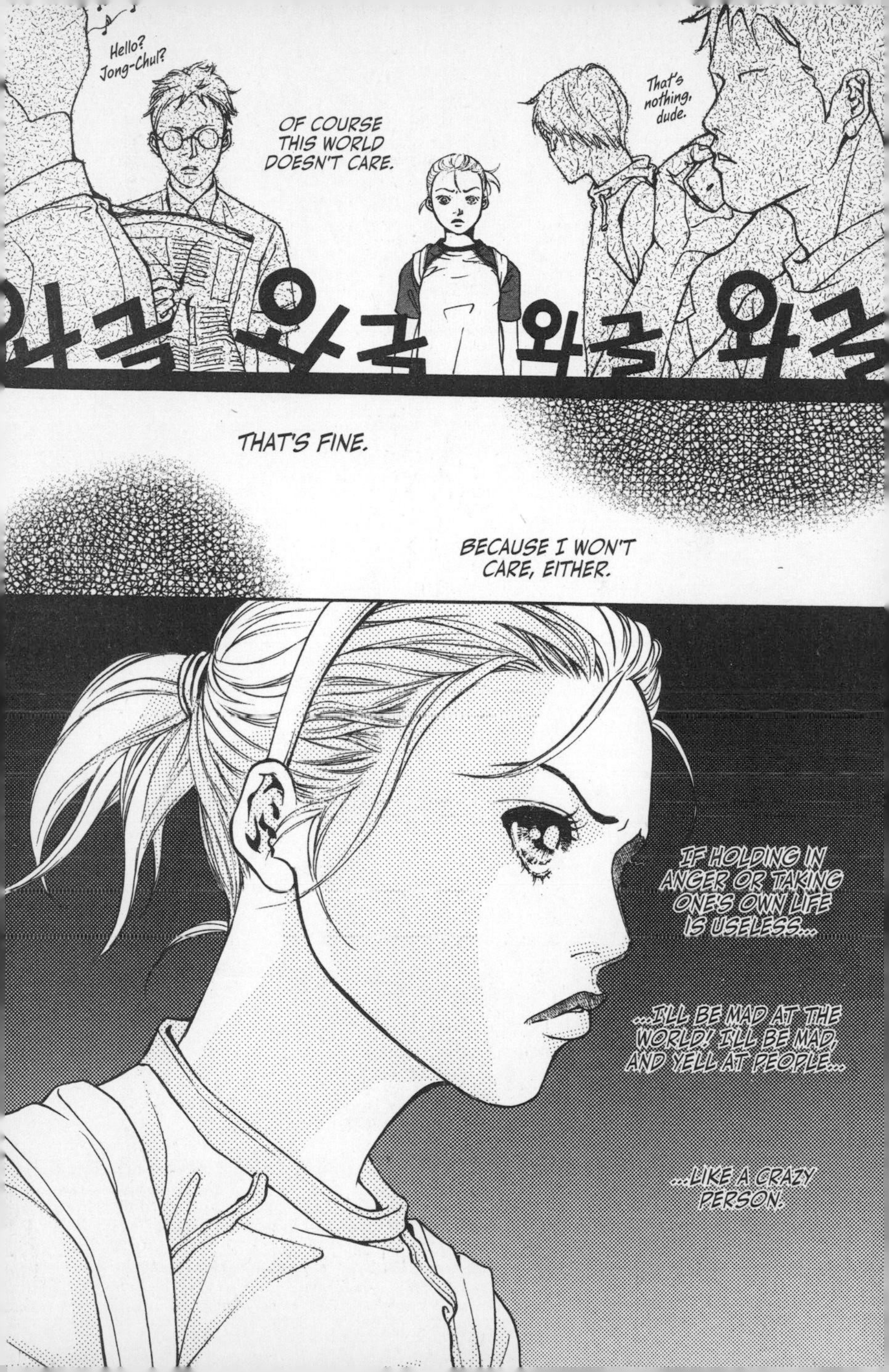
Hello? Jong-Chul?
OF COURSE THIS WORLD DOESN'T CARE.
That's nothing, dude.
와글와글와글와글
THAT'S FINE.
BECAUSE I WON'T CARE, EITHER.
IF HOLDING IN ANGER OR TAKING ONE'S OWN LIFE IS USELESS...
...I'LL BE MAD AT THE WORLD! I'LL BE MAD, AND YELL AT PEOPLE...
...LIKE A CRAZY PERSON.

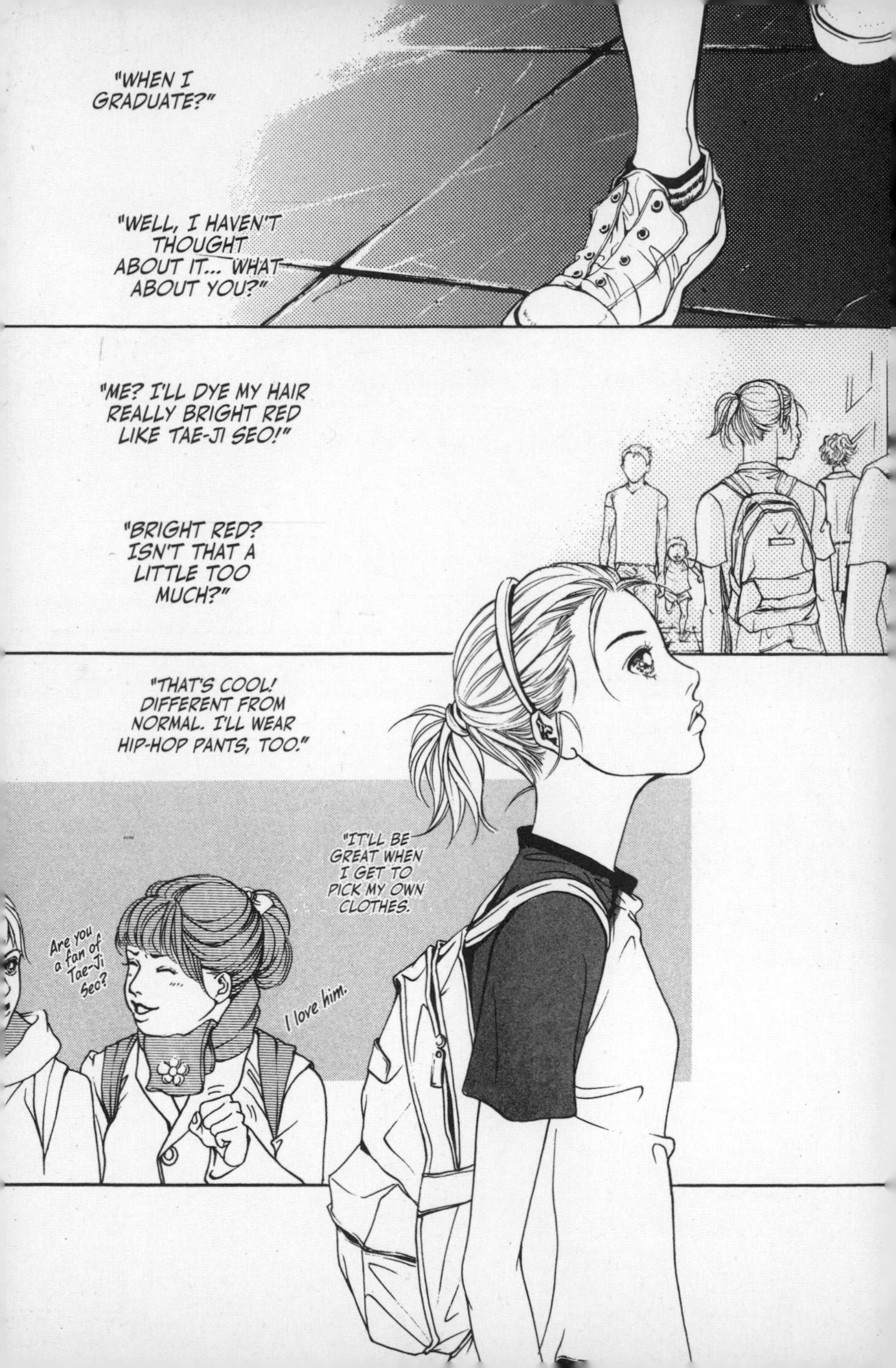
"WHEN I GRADUATE?"
"WELL, I HAVEN'T THOUGHT ABOUT IT... WHAT ABOUT YOU?"
"ME? I'LL DYE MY HAIR REALLY BRIGHT RED LIKE TAE-JI SEO!"
"BRIGHT RED? ISN'T THAT A LITTLE TOO MUCH?"
"THAT'S COOL! DIFFERENT FROM NORMAL. I'LL WEAR HIP-HOP PANTS, TOO."
Are you a fan of Tae-Ji Seo?
I love him.
"IT'LL BE GREAT WHEN I GET TO PICK MY OWN CLOTHES.

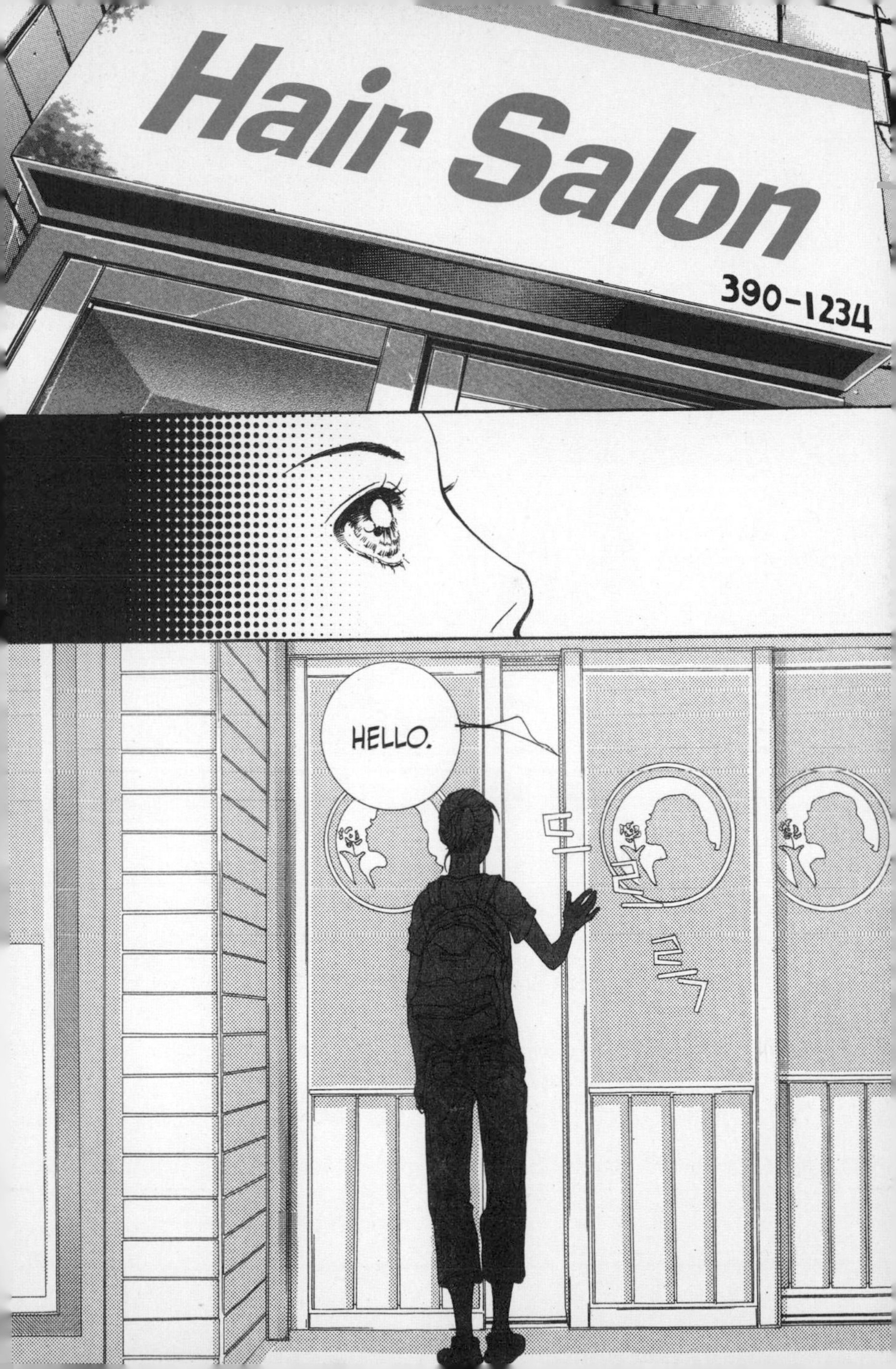
Hair Salon
390-1234
HELLO.

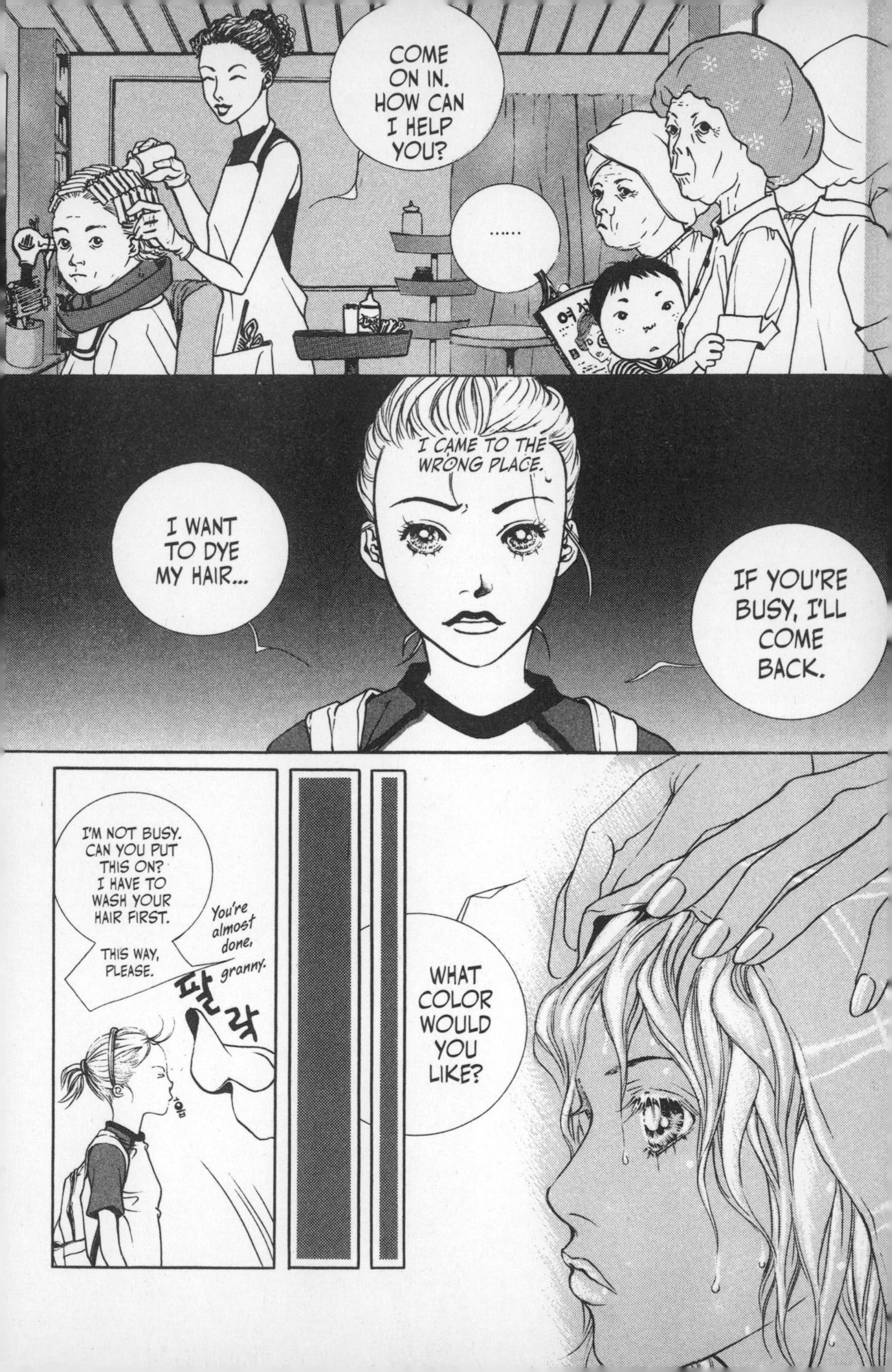
COME ON IN. HOW CAN I HELP YOU?
......
I WANT TO DYE MY HAIR...
I CAME TO THE WRONG PLACE.
IF YOU'RE BUSY, I'LL COME BACK.
I'M NOT BUSY. CAN YOU PUT THIS ON? I HAVE TO WASH YOUR HAIR FIRST.
THIS WAY, PLEASE.
You're almost done, granny.
팔락
흡
WHAT COLOR WOULD YOU LIKE?

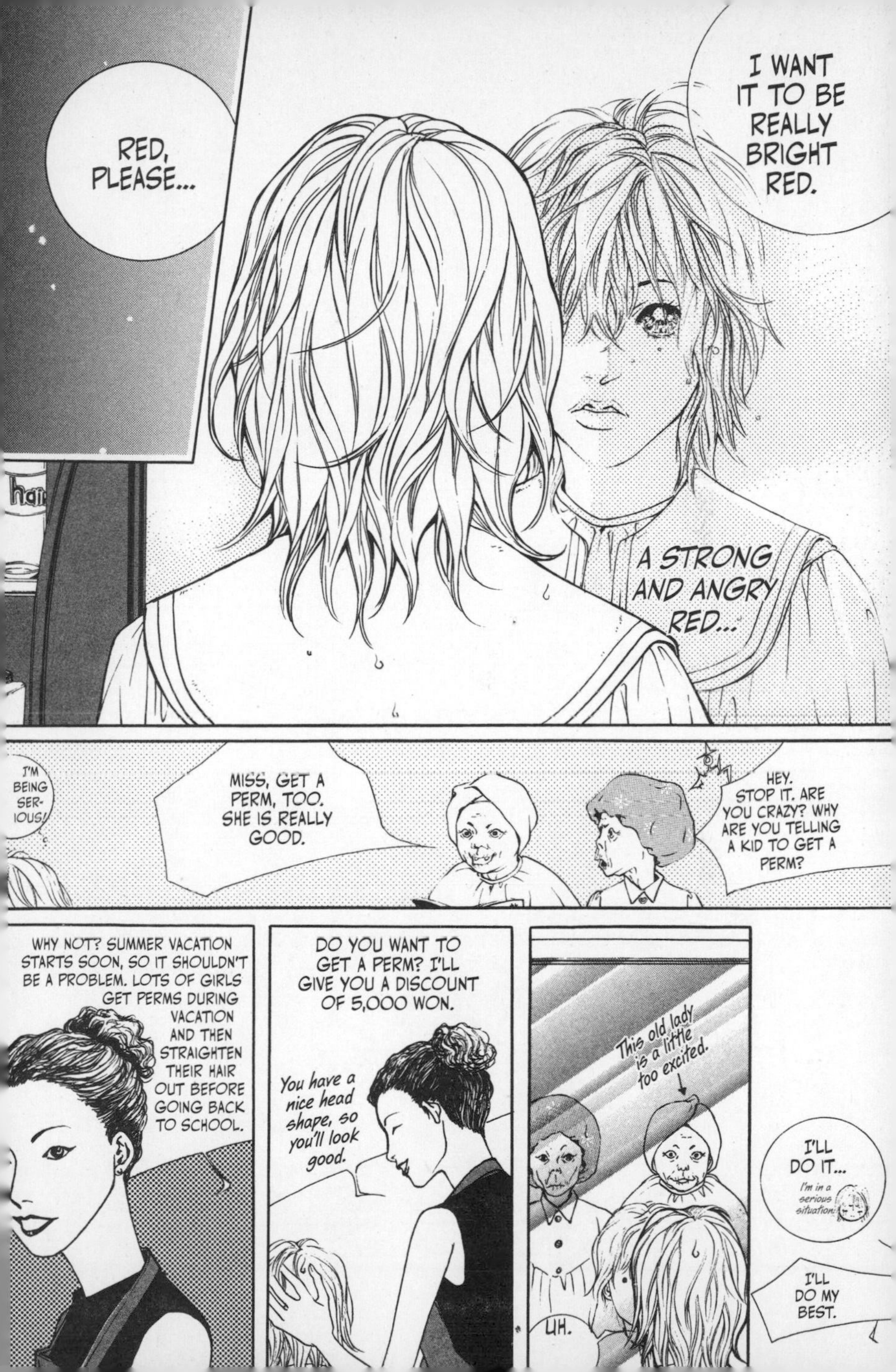
RED, PLEASE...
I WANT IT TO BE REALLY BRIGHT RED.
A STRONG AND ANGRY RED...
I'M BEING SER-IOUS!
MISS, GET A PERM, TOO. SHE IS REALLY GOOD.
HEY. STOP IT. ARE YOU CRAZY? WHY ARE YOU TELLING A KID TO GET A PERM?
WHY NOT? SUMMER VACATION STARTS SOON, SO IT SHOULDN'T BE A PROBLEM. LOTS OF GIRLS GET PERMS DURING VACATION AND THEN STRAIGHTEN THEIR HAIR OUT BEFORE GOING BACK TO SCHOOL.
DO YOU WANT TO GET A PERM? I'LL GIVE YOU A DISCOUNT OF 5,000 WON.
You have a nice head shape, so you'll look good.
This old lady is a little too excited.
UH.
I'LL DO IT...
I'm in a serious situation!
I'LL DO MY BEST.

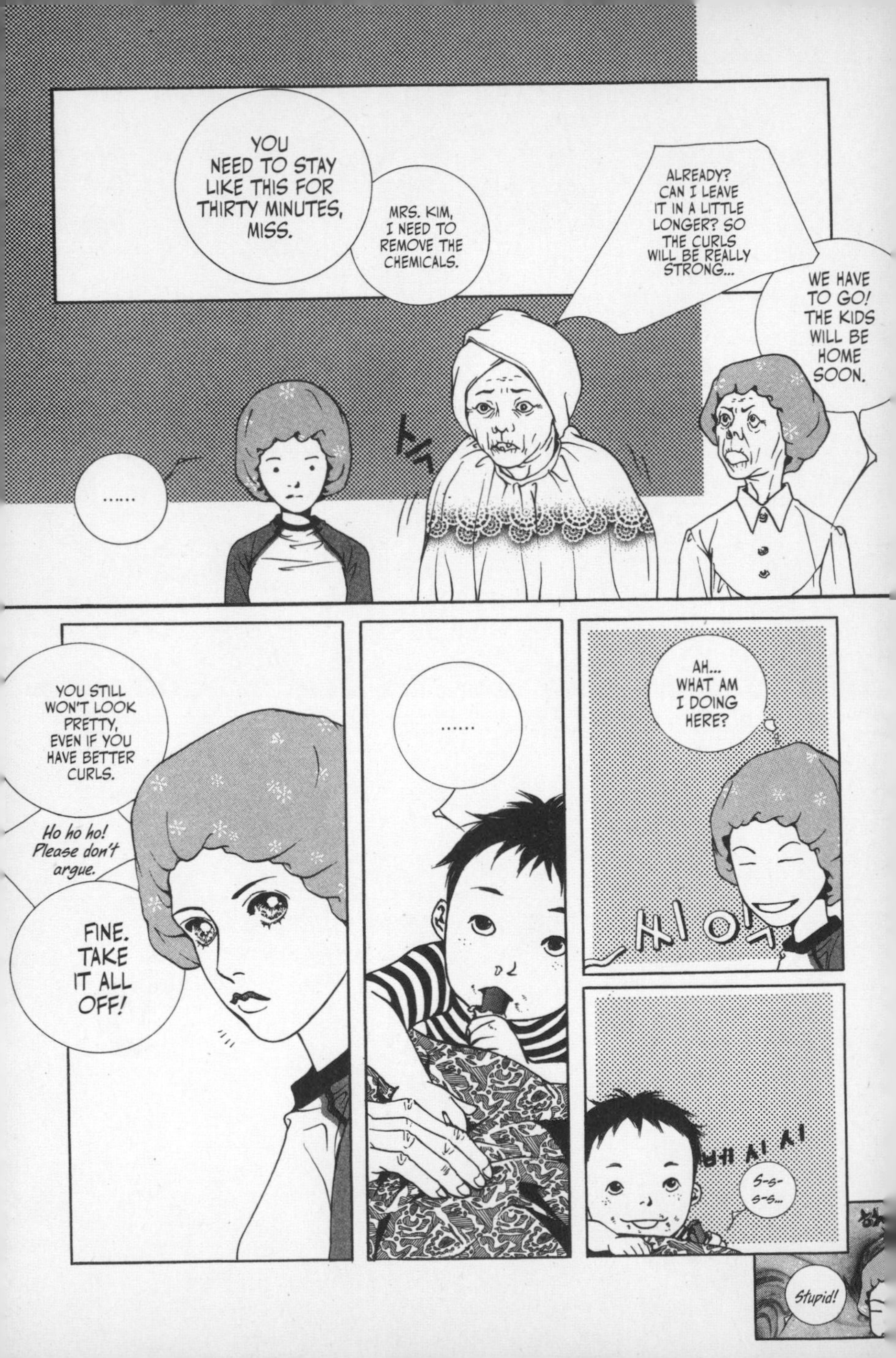
YOU NEED TO STAY LIKE THIS FOR THIRTY MINUTES, MISS.
MRS. KIM, I NEED TO REMOVE THE CHEMICALS.
ALREADY? CAN I LEAVE IT IN A LITTLE LONGER? SO THE CURLS WILL BE REALLY STRONG...
WE HAVE TO GO! THE KIDS WILL BE HOME SOON.
......
YOU STILL WON'T LOOK PRETTY, EVEN IF YOU HAVE BETTER CURLS.
Ho ho ho! Please don't argue.
FINE. TAKE IT ALL OFF!
......
AH... WHAT AM I DOING HERE?
S-s-s-s...
Stupid!

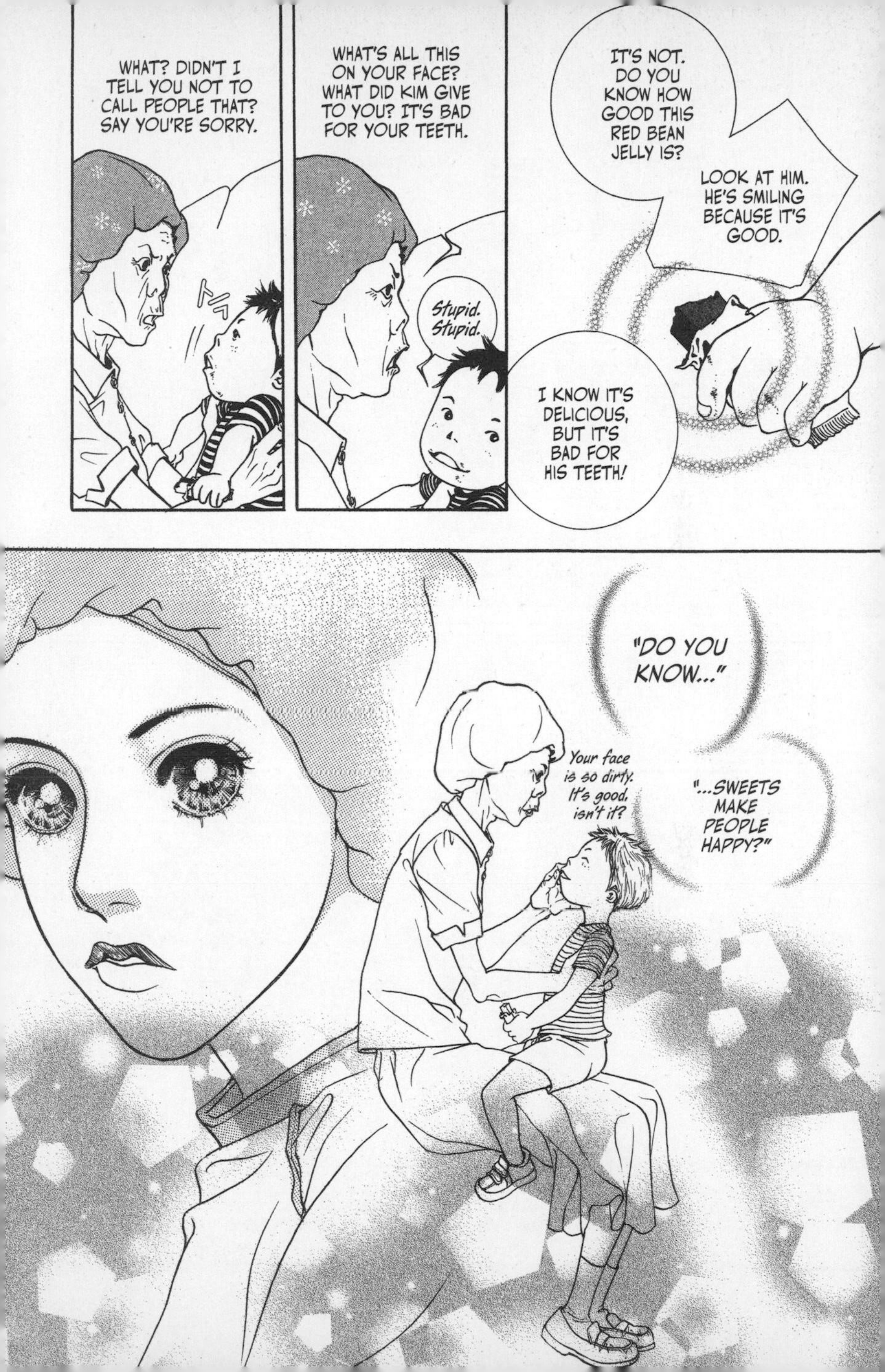
WHAT? DIDN'T I TELL YOU NOT TO CALL PEOPLE THAT? SAY YOU'RE SORRY.
WHAT'S ALL THIS ON YOUR FACE? WHAT DID KIM GIVE TO YOU? IT'S BAD FOR YOUR TEETH.
Stupid. Stupid.
IT'S NOT. DO YOU KNOW HOW GOOD THIS RED BEAN JELLY IS?
LOOK AT HIM. HE'S SMILING BECAUSE IT'S GOOD.
I KNOW IT'S DELICIOUS, BUT IT'S BAD FOR HIS TEETH!
"DO YOU KNOW..."
Your face is so dirty. It's good, isn't it?
"...SWEETS MAKE PEOPLE HAPPY?"

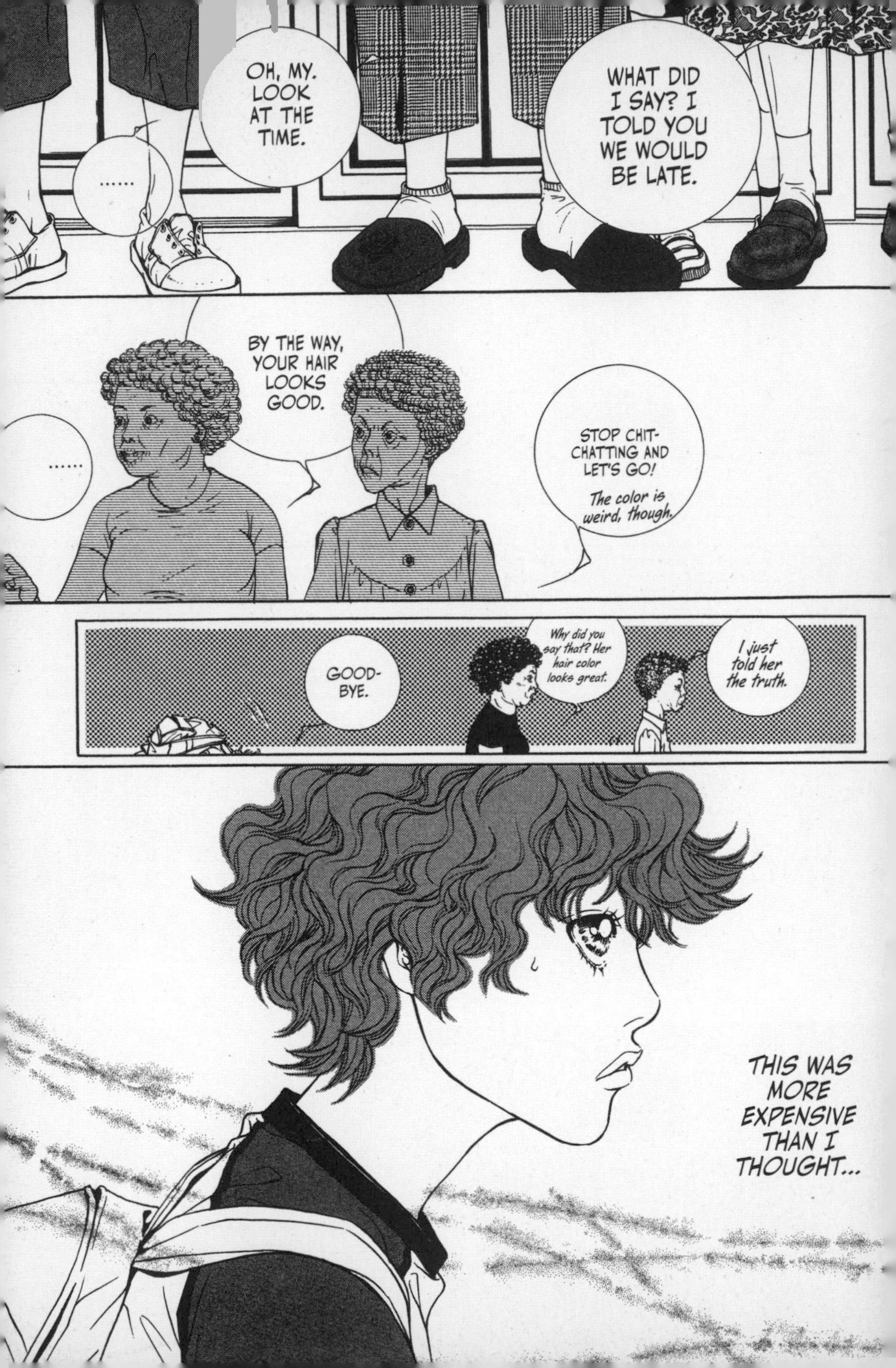
......
OH, MY. LOOK AT THE TIME.
WHAT DID I SAY? I TOLD YOU WE WOULD BE LATE.
......
BY THE WAY, YOUR HAIR LOOKS GOOD.
STOP CHIT-CHATTING AND LET'S GO!
The color is weird, though.
GOOD-BYE.
Why did you say that? Her hair color looks great.
I just told her the truth.
THIS WAS MORE EXPENSIVE THAN I THOUGHT...

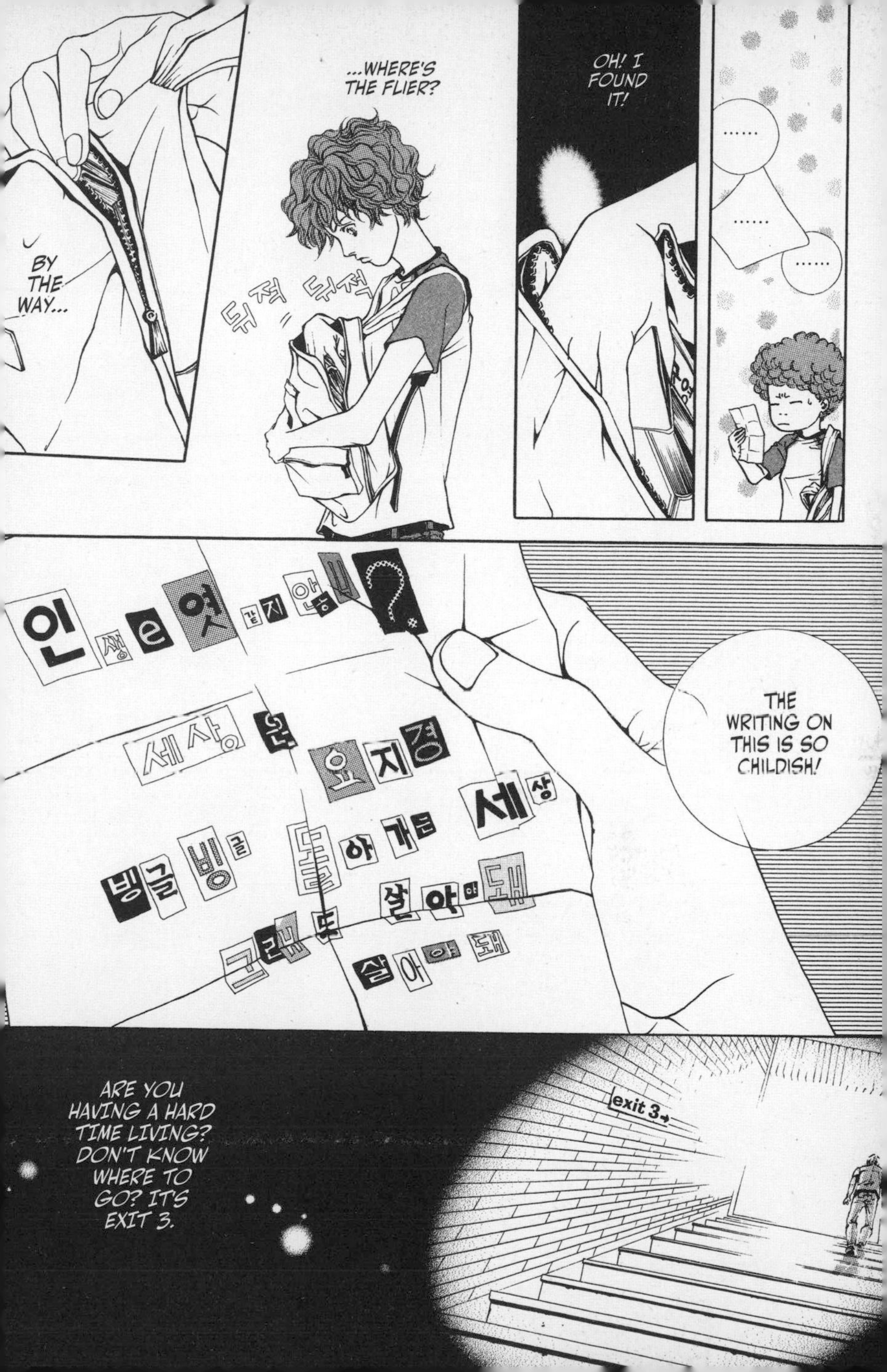

BY THE WAY...
...WHERE'S THE FLIER?
뒤적 뒤적
OH! I FOUND IT!
......
......
......
인생e 엿같지않니?
세상은 요지경
세상
빙글빙글 돌아가는
살아야돼
그래도 살아야 돼
THE WRITING ON THIS IS SO CHILDISH!
ARE YOU HAVING A HARD TIME LIVING? DON'T KNOW WHERE TO GO? IT'S EXIT 3.
exit 3

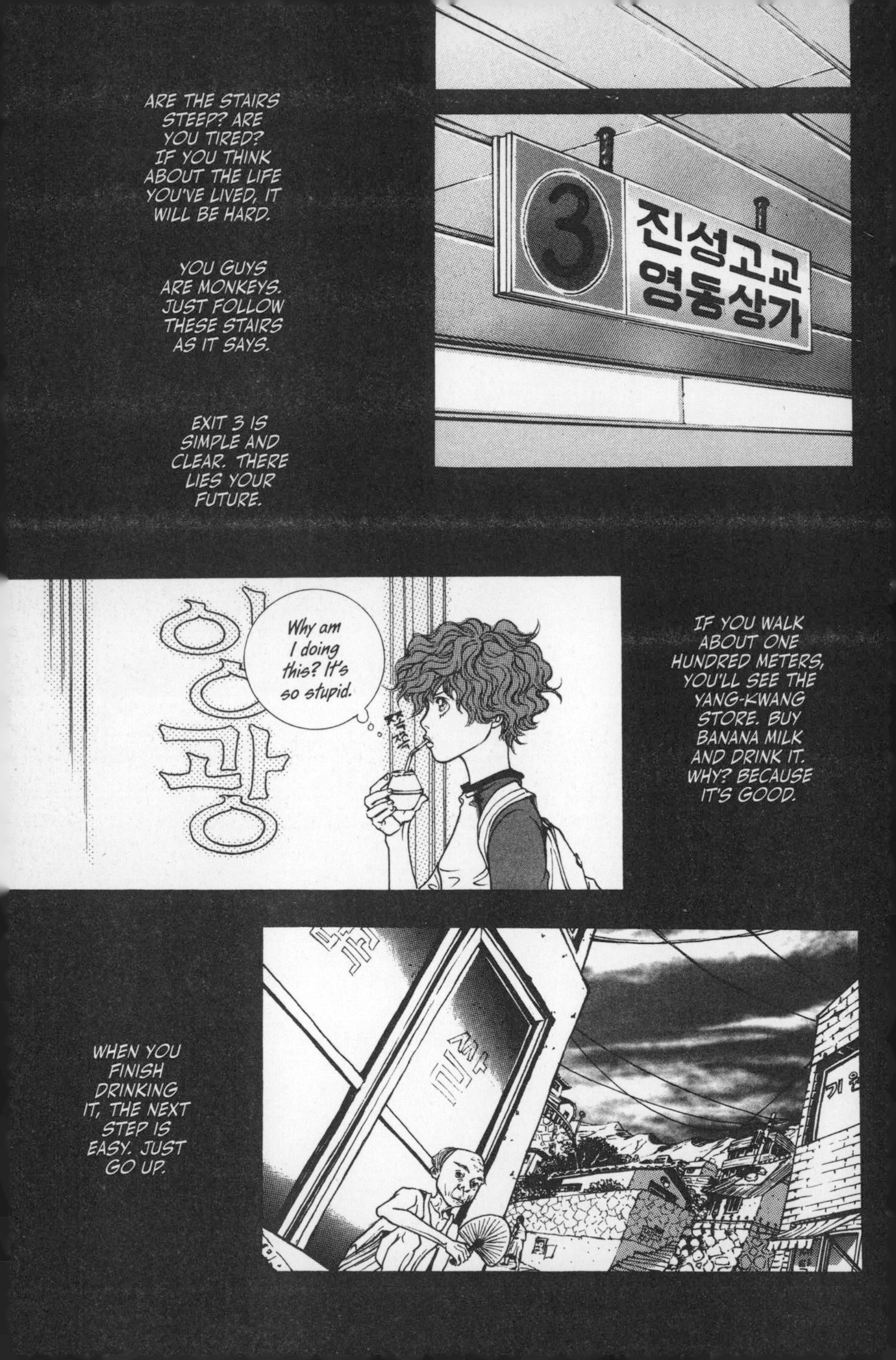
ARE THE STAIRS STEEP? ARE YOU TIRED? IF YOU THINK ABOUT THE LIFE YOU'VE LIVED, IT WILL BE HARD.
YOU GUYS ARE MONKEYS. JUST FOLLOW THESE STAIRS AS IT SAYS.
EXIT 3 IS SIMPLE AND CLEAR. THERE LIES YOUR FUTURE.
3
진성고교
영동상가
Why am I doing this? It's so stupid.
IF YOU WALK ABOUT ONE HUNDRED METERS, YOU'LL SEE THE YANG-KWANG STORE. BUY BANANA MILK AND DRINK IT. WHY? BECAUSE IT'S GOOD.
WHEN YOU FINISH DRINKING IT, THE NEXT STEP IS EASY. JUST GO UP.

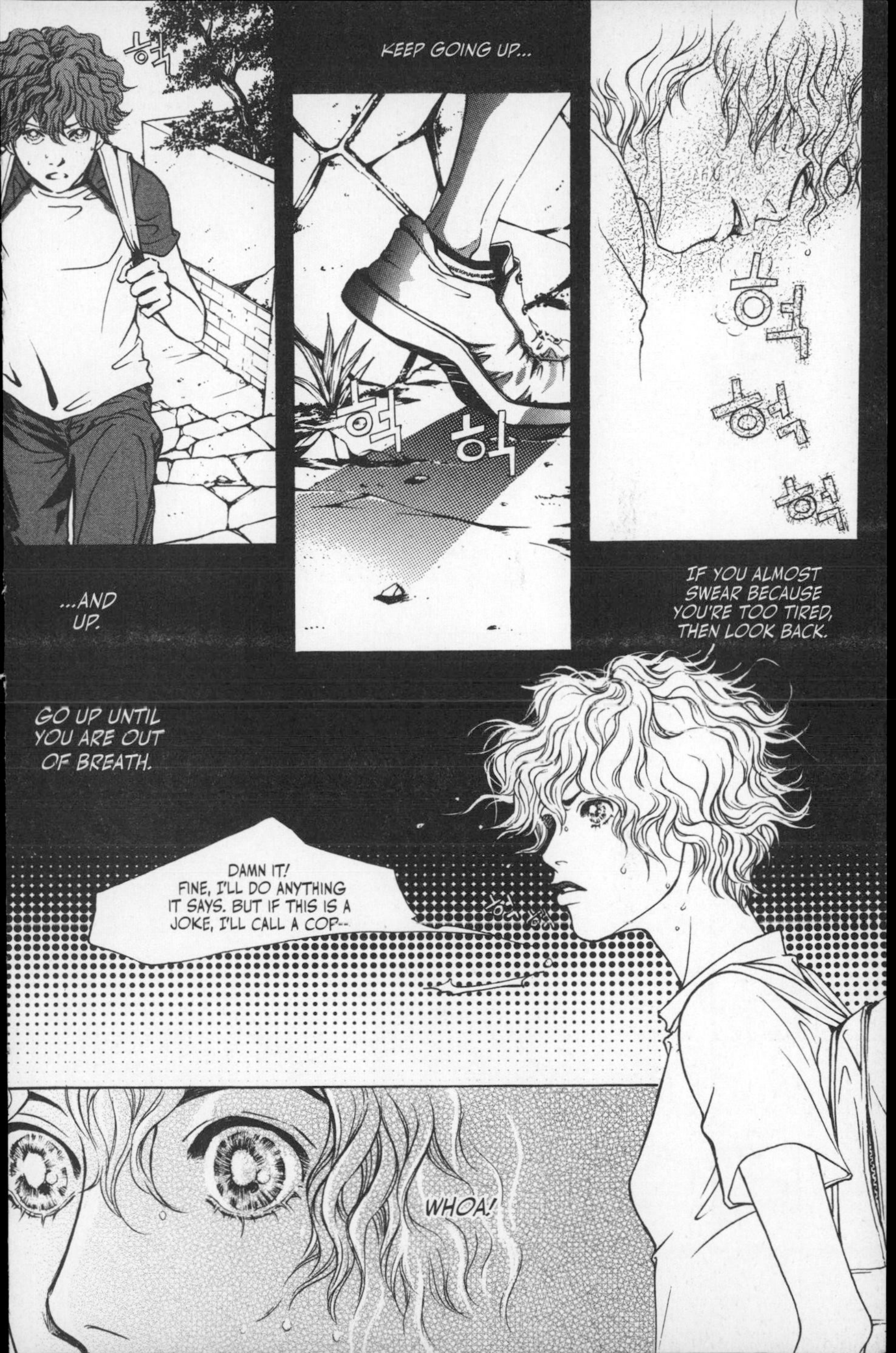
헉
KEEP GOING UP...
헉
헉
헉
헉
헉
...AND UP.
IF YOU ALMOST SWEAR BECAUSE YOU'RE TOO TIRED, THEN LOOK BACK.
GO UP UNTIL YOU ARE OUT OF BREATH.
DAMN IT! FINE, I'LL DO ANYTHING IT SAYS. BUT IF THIS IS A JOKE, I'LL CALL A COP--
WHOA!

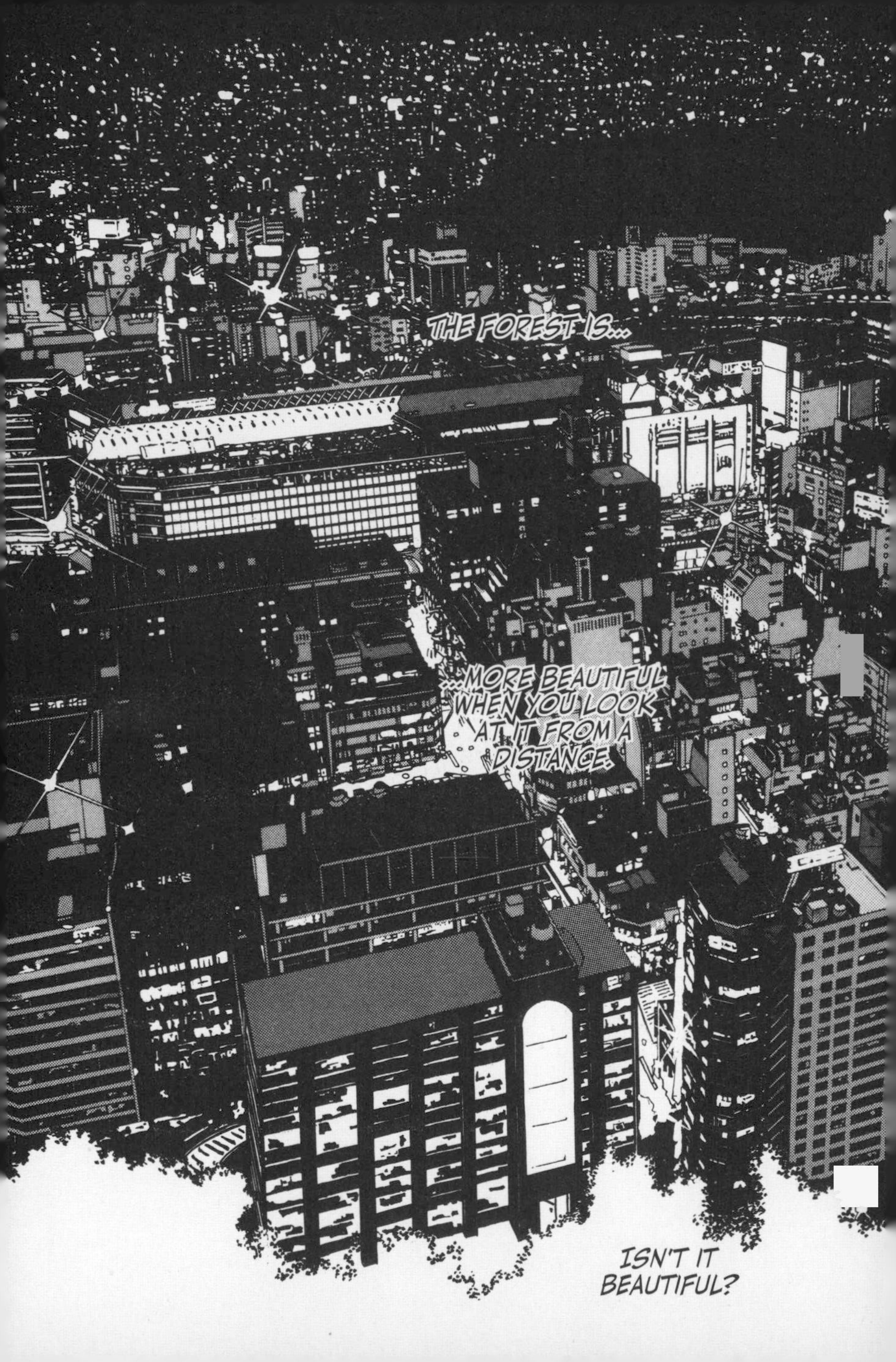
THE FOREST IS...
...MORE BEAUTIFUL WHEN YOU LOOK AT IT FROM A DISTANCE.
ISN'T IT BEAUTIFUL?

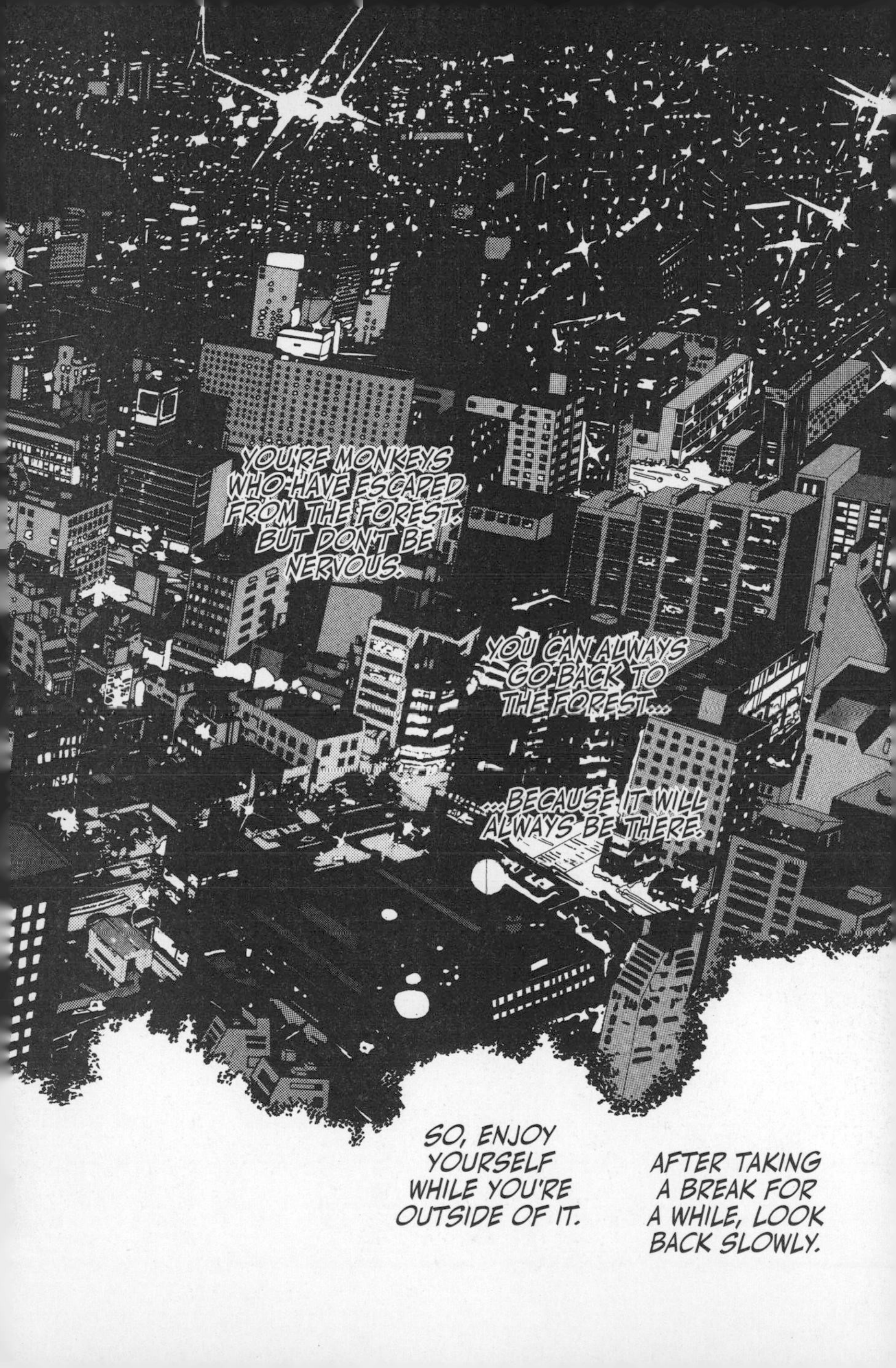
YOU'RE MONKEYS WHO HAVE ESCAPED FROM THE FOREST. BUT DON'T BE NERVOUS.
YOU CAN ALWAYS GO BACK TO THE FOREST...
...BECAUSE IT WILL ALWAYS BE THERE.
SO, ENJOY YOURSELF WHILE YOU'RE OUTSIDE OF IT.
AFTER TAKING A BREAK FOR A WHILE, LOOK BACK SLOWLY.

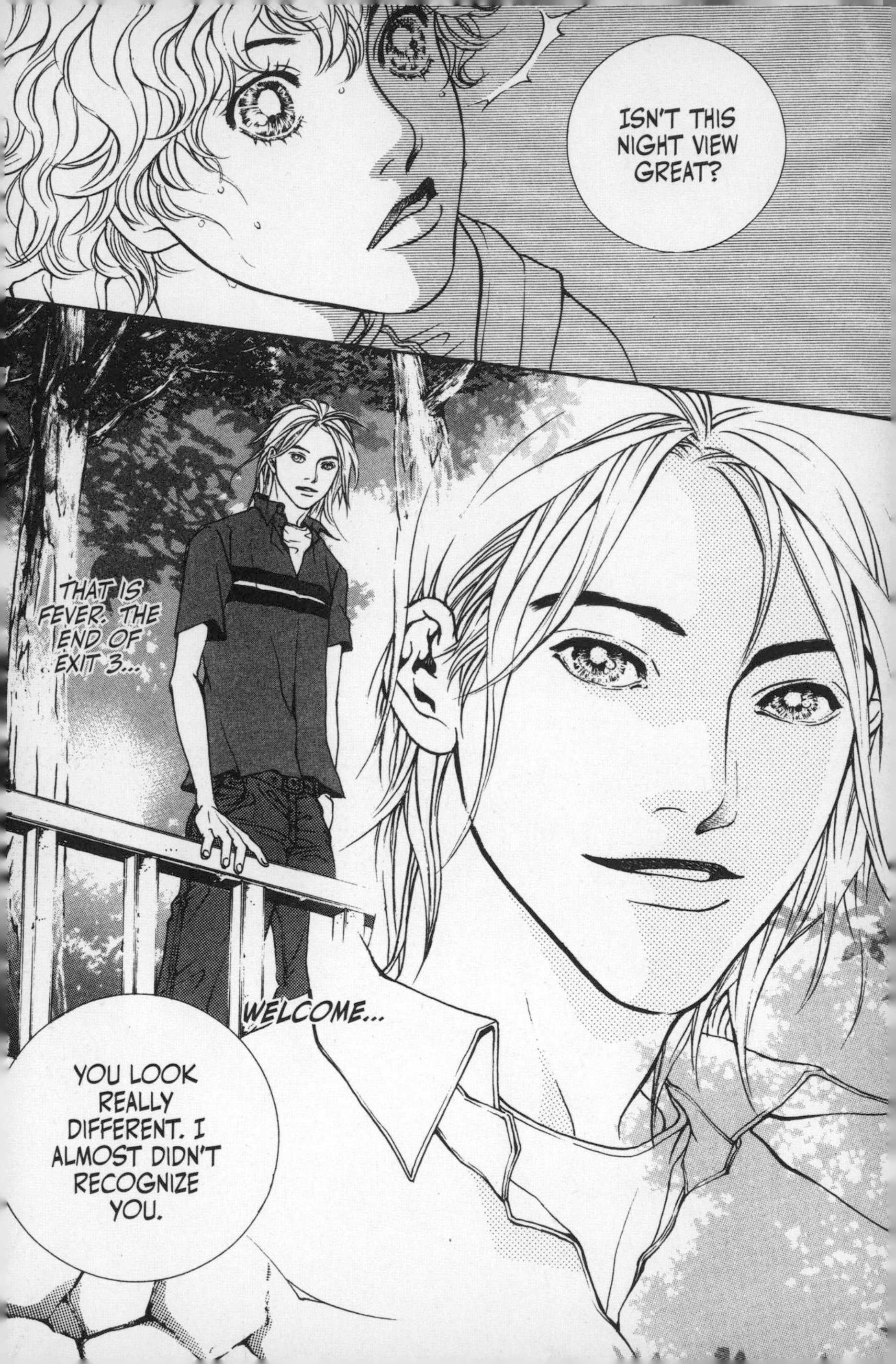
ISN'T THIS NIGHT VIEW GREAT?
THAT IS FEVER. THE END OF EXIT 3...
WELCOME...
YOU LOOK REALLY DIFFERENT. I ALMOST DIDN'T RECOGNIZE YOU.

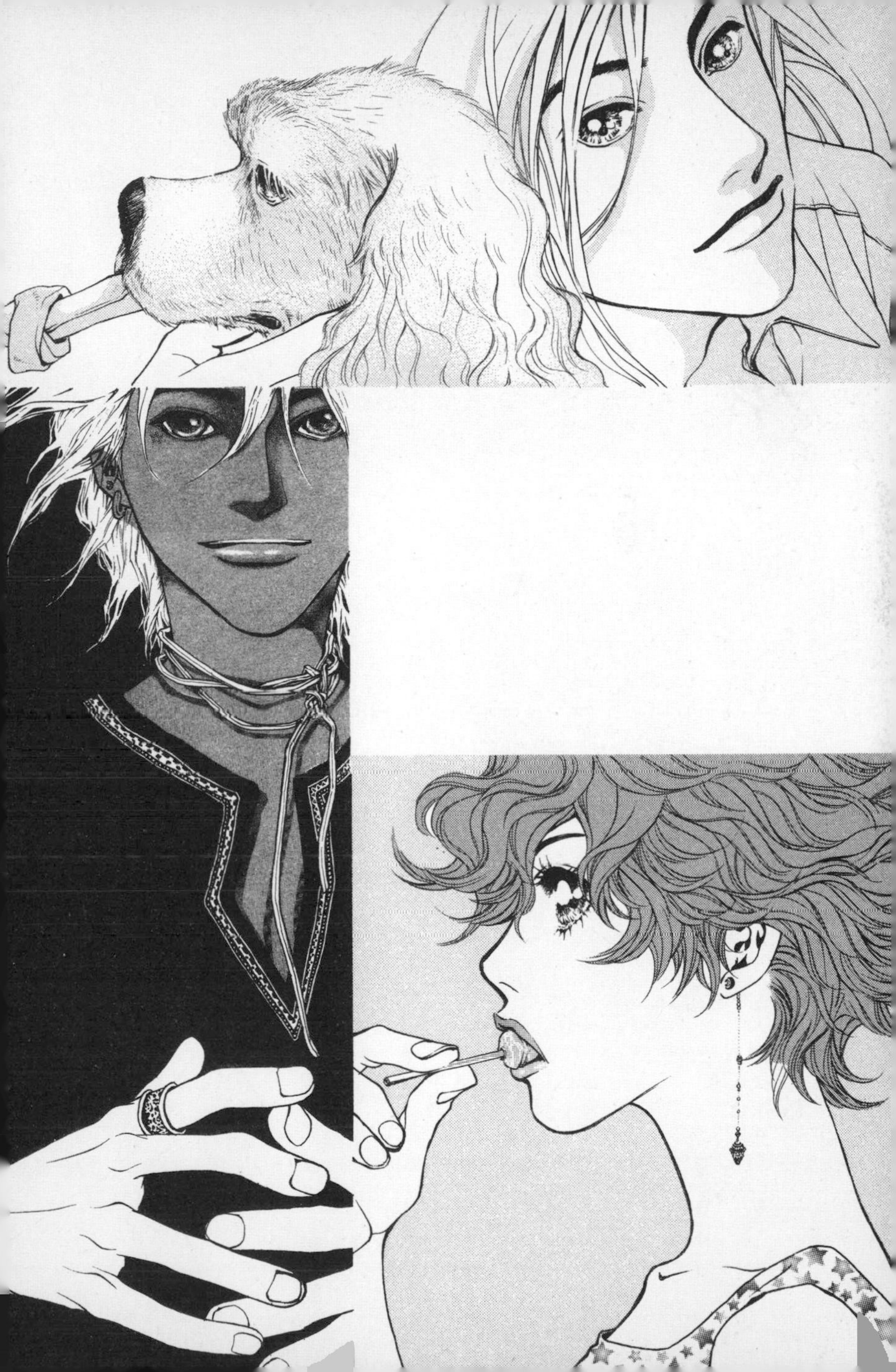

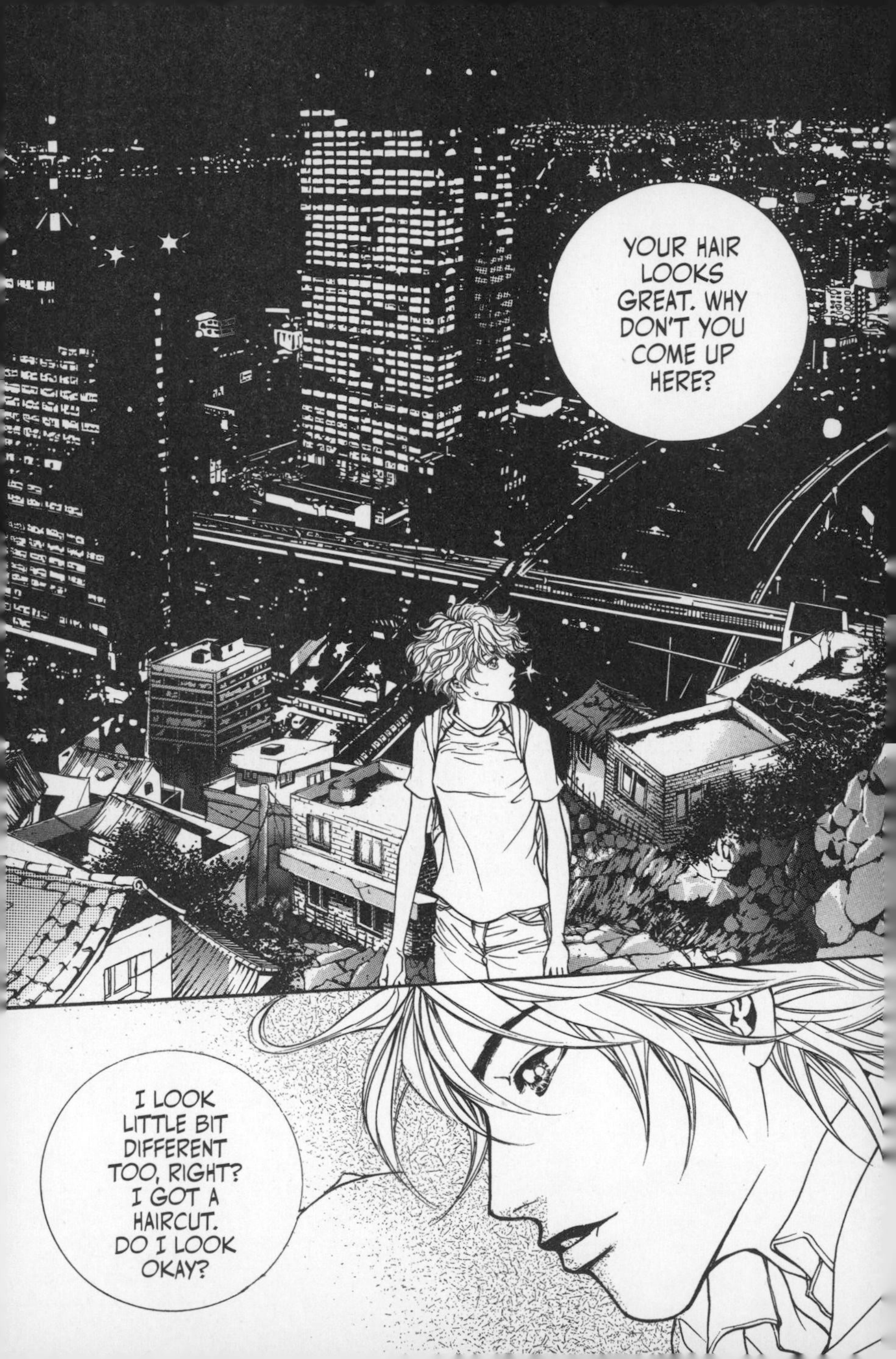
YOUR HAIR LOOKS GREAT. WHY DON'T YOU COME UP HERE?
I LOOK LITTLE BIT DIFFERENT TOO, RIGHT? I GOT A HAIRCUT. DO I LOOK OKAY?

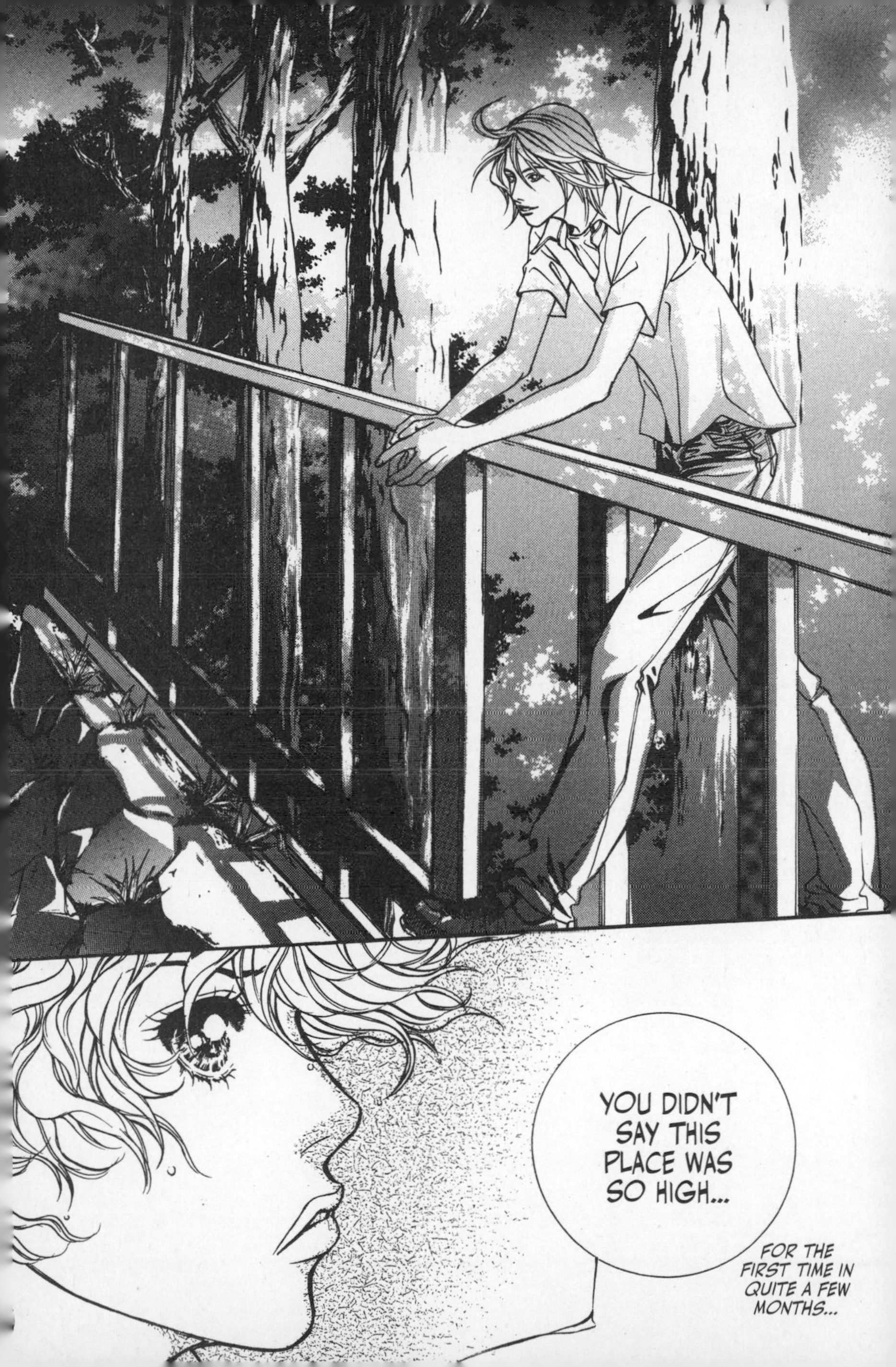
YOU DIDN'T SAY THIS PLACE WAS SO HIGH...
FOR THE FIRST TIME IN QUITE A FEW MONTHS...

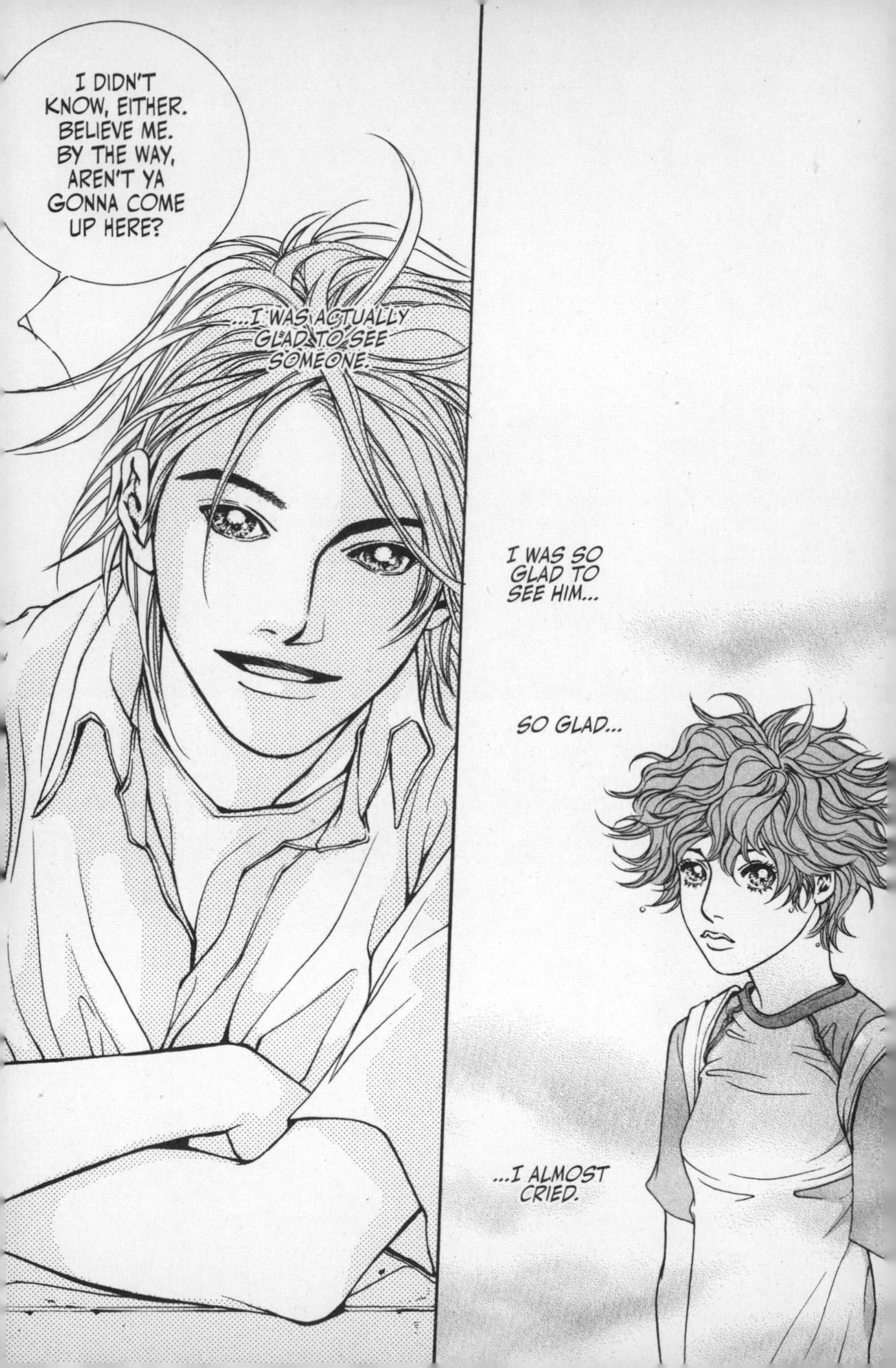
I DIDN'T KNOW, EITHER. BELIEVE ME. BY THE WAY, AREN'T YA GONNA COME UP HERE?
...I WAS ACTUALLY GLAD TO SEE SOMEONE.
I WAS SO GLAD TO SEE HIM...
SO GLAD...
...I ALMOST CRIED.

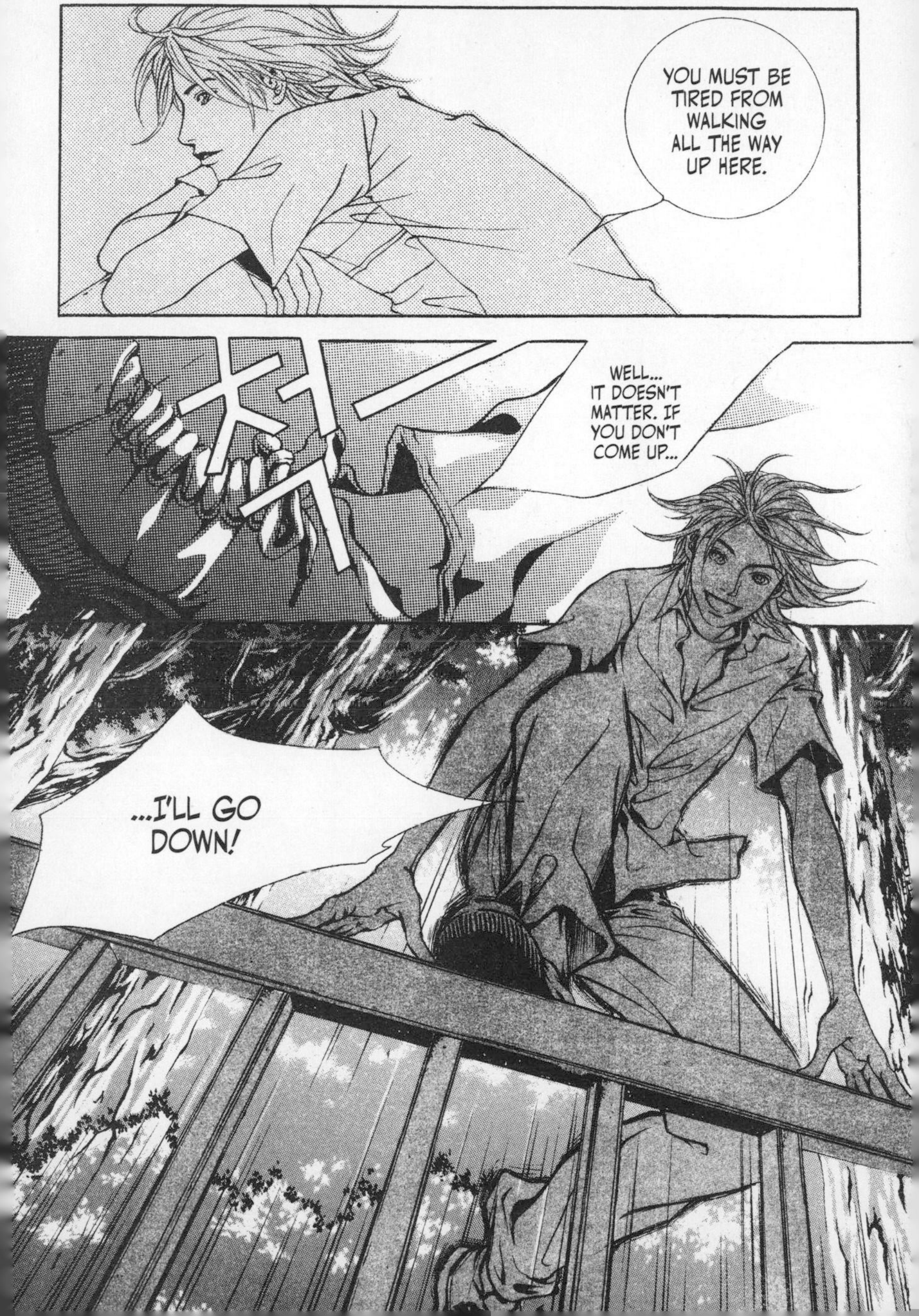
YOU MUST BE TIRED FROM WALKING ALL THE WAY UP HERE.
WELL... IT DOESN'T MATTER. IF YOU DON'T COME UP...
...I'LL GO DOWN!

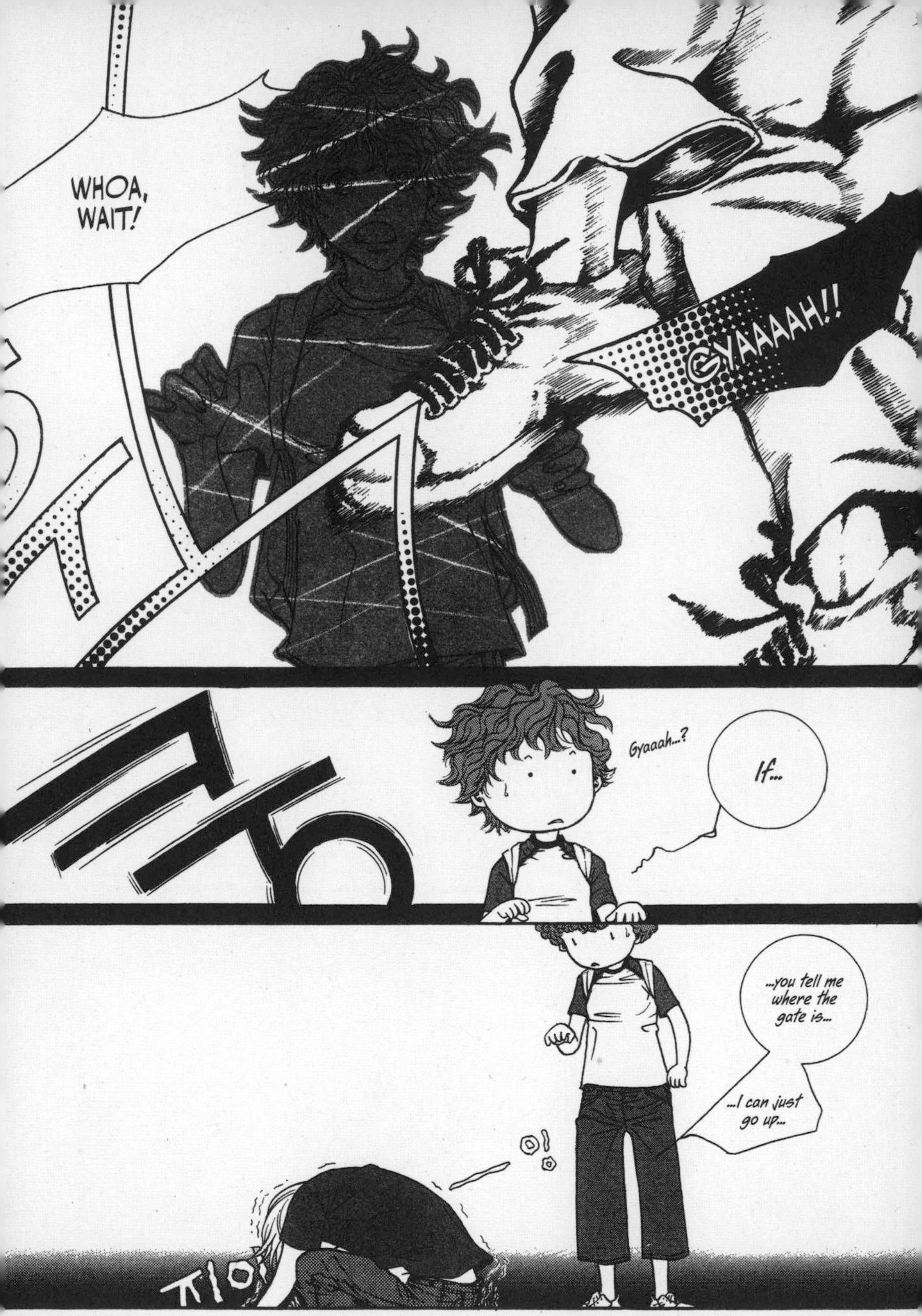
WHOA, WAIT!
GYAAAAH!!
Gyaaah...?
If...
...you tell me where the gate is...
...I can just go up...

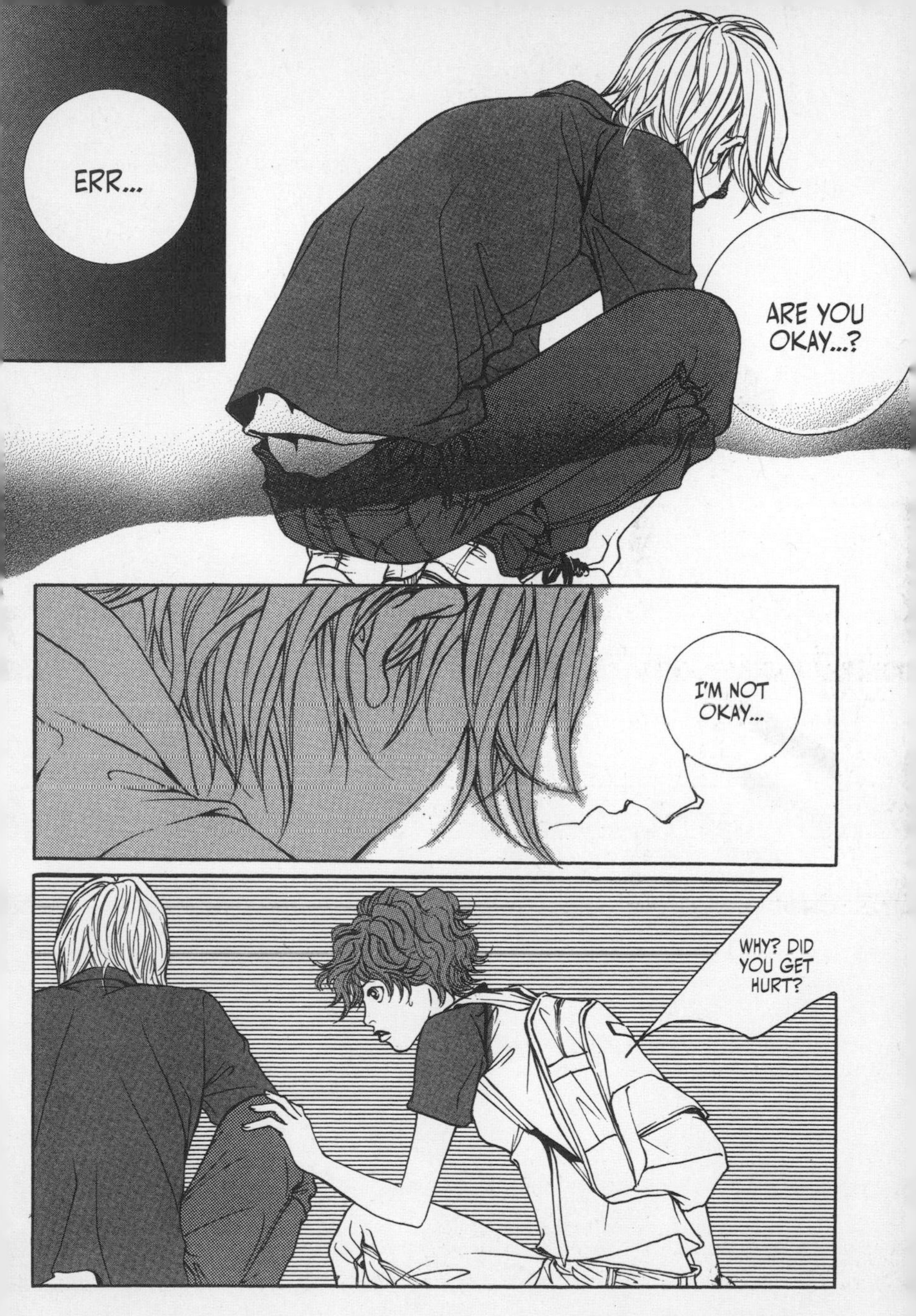
ERR...
ARE YOU OKAY...?
I'M NOT OKAY...
WHY? DID YOU GET HURT?

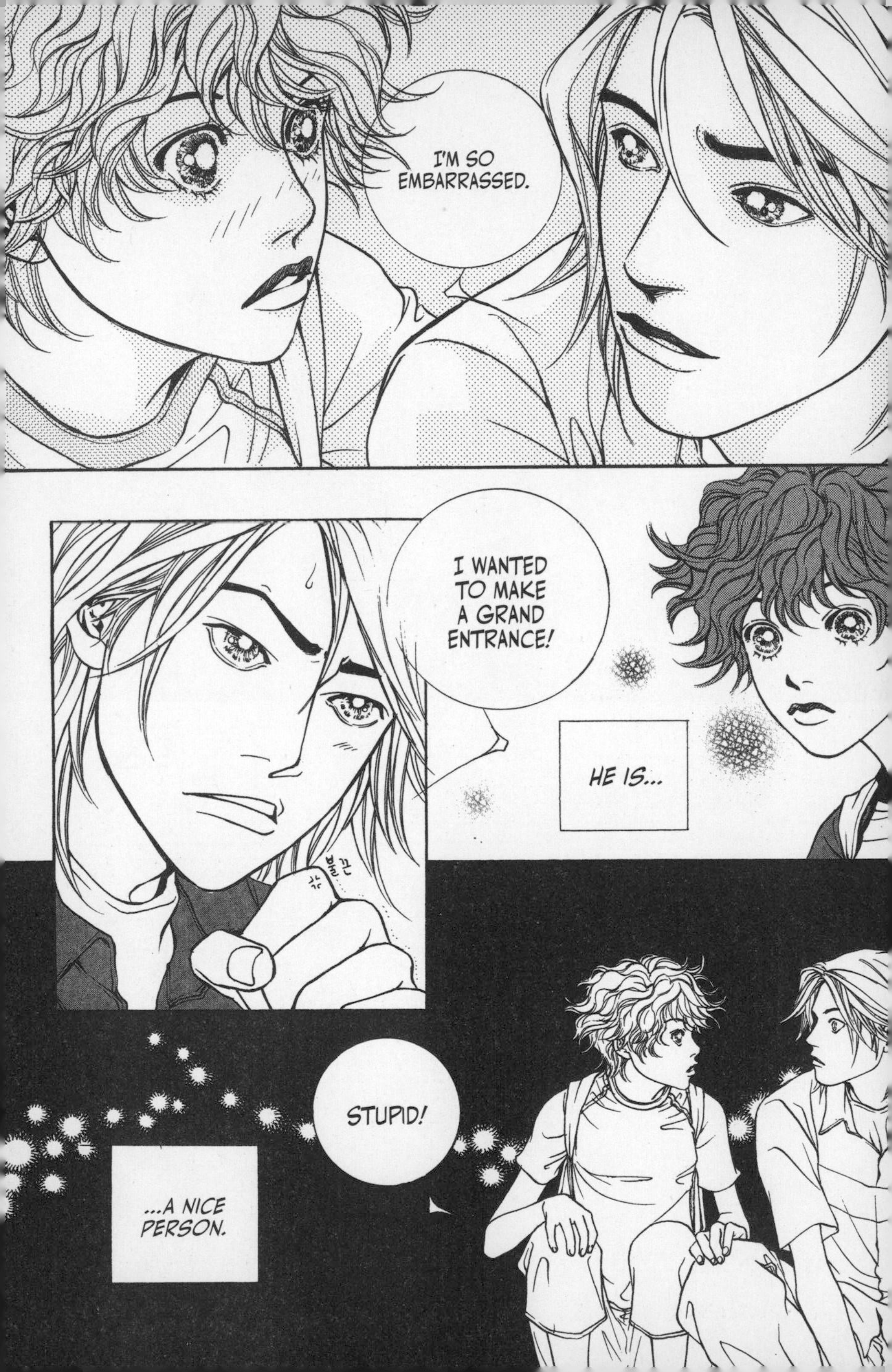
I'M SO EMBARRASSED.
I WANTED TO MAKE A GRAND ENTRANCE!
HE IS...
...A NICE PERSON.
STUPID!

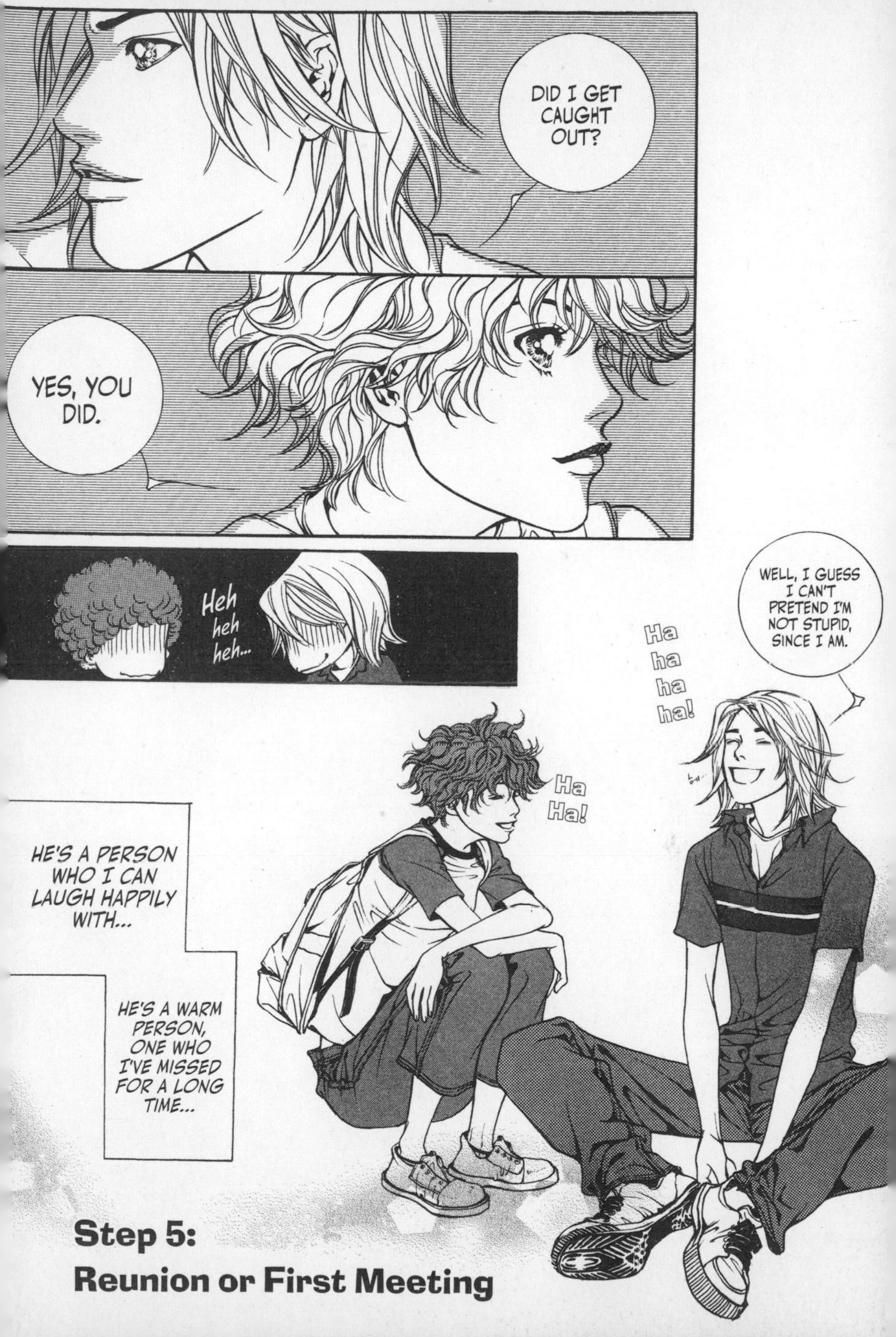

DID I GET CAUGHT OUT?
YES, YOU DID.
Heh heh heh...
WELL, I GUESS I CAN'T PRETEND I'M NOT STUPID, SINCE I AM.
Ha ha ha ha!
Ha Ha!
HE'S A PERSON WHO I CAN LAUGH HAPPILY WITH...
HE'S A WARM PERSON, ONE WHO I'VE MISSED FOR A LONG TIME...
Step 5:
Reunion or First Meeting

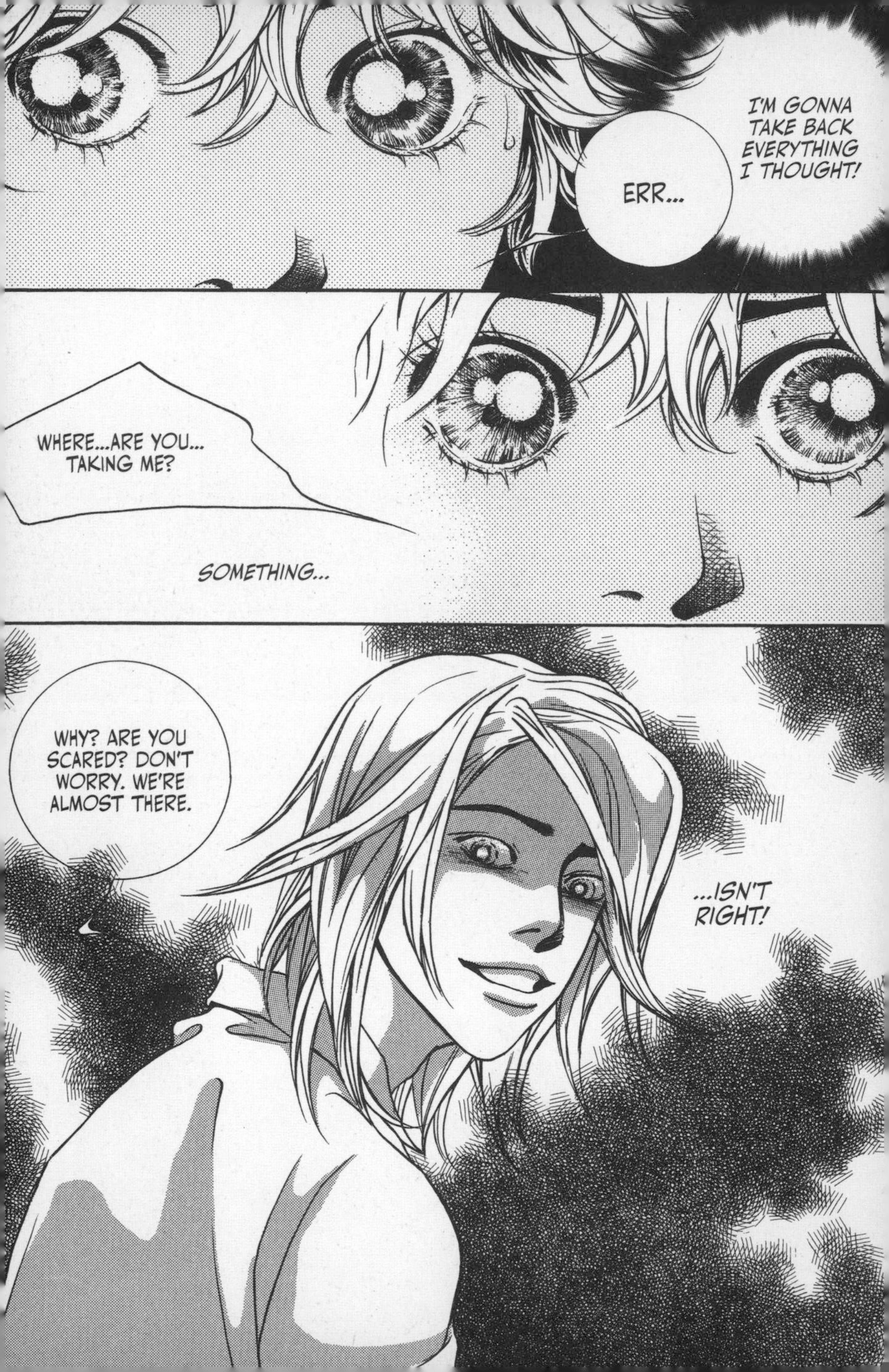
ERR...
I'M GONNA TAKE BACK EVERYTHING I THOUGHT!
WHERE...ARE YOU... TAKING ME?
SOMETHING...
WHY? ARE YOU SCARED? DON'T WORRY. WE'RE ALMOST THERE.
...ISN'T RIGHT!

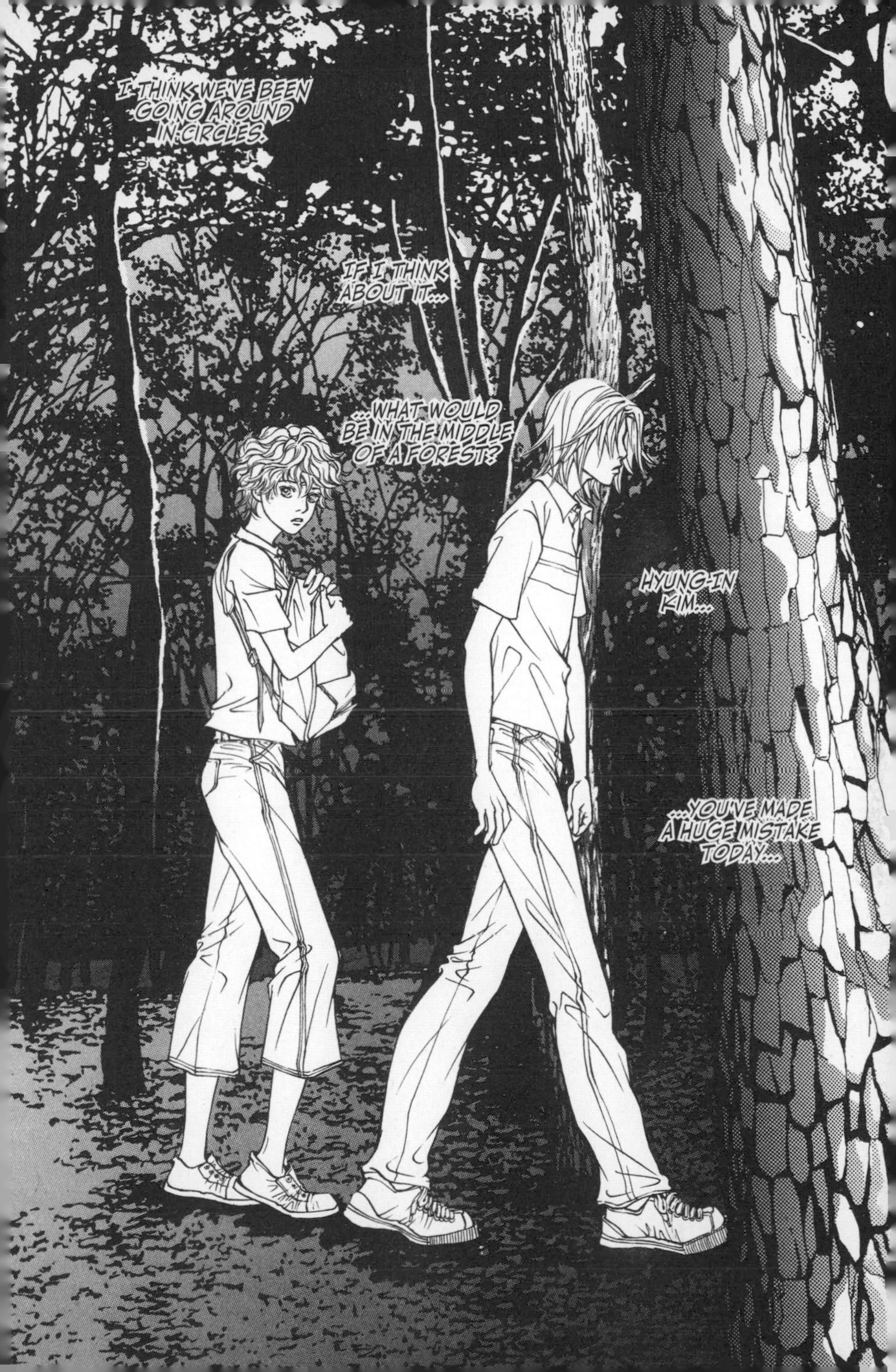
I THINK WE'VE BEEN GOING AROUND IN CIRCLES.
IF I THINK ABOUT IT...
...WHAT WOULD BE IN THE MIDDLE OF A FOREST?
HYUNG-IN KIM...
...YOU'VE MADE A HUGE MISTAKE TODAY...

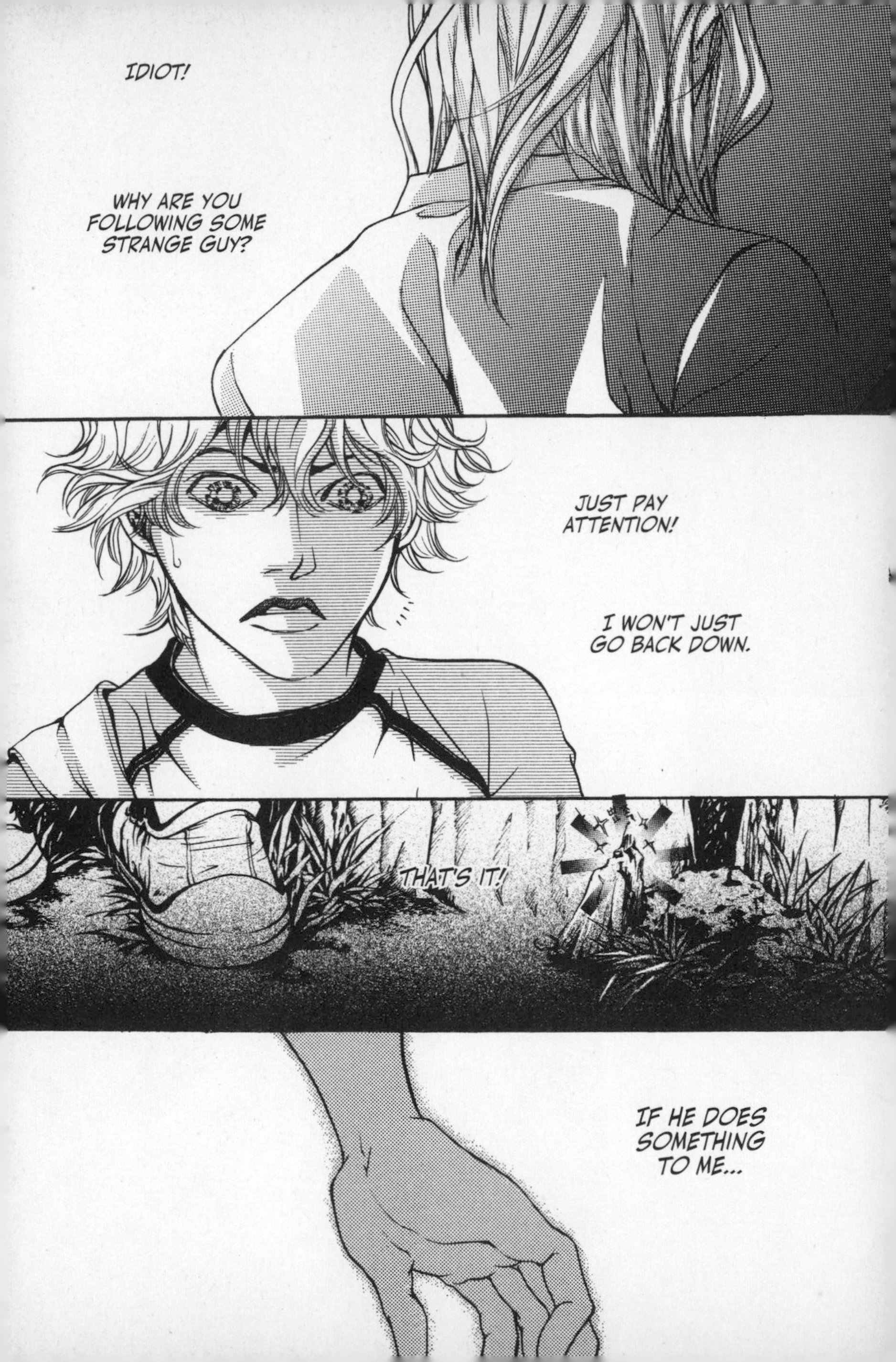
IDIOT!
WHY ARE YOU FOLLOWING SOME STRANGE GUY?
JUST PAY ATTENTION!
I WON'T JUST GO BACK DOWN.
THAT'S IT!
IF HE DOES SOMETHING TO ME...

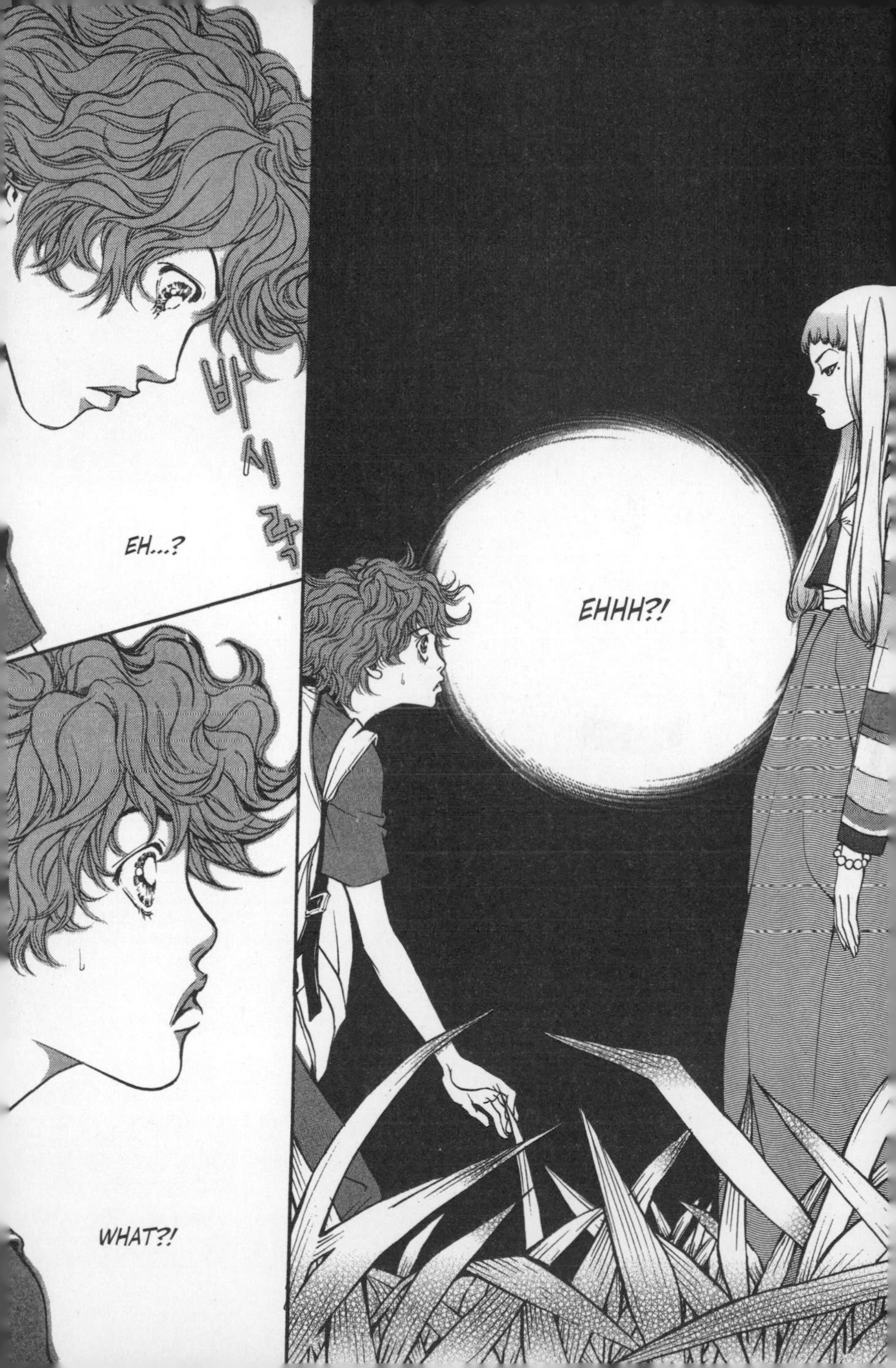
바시락
EH...?
WHAT?!
EHHH?!

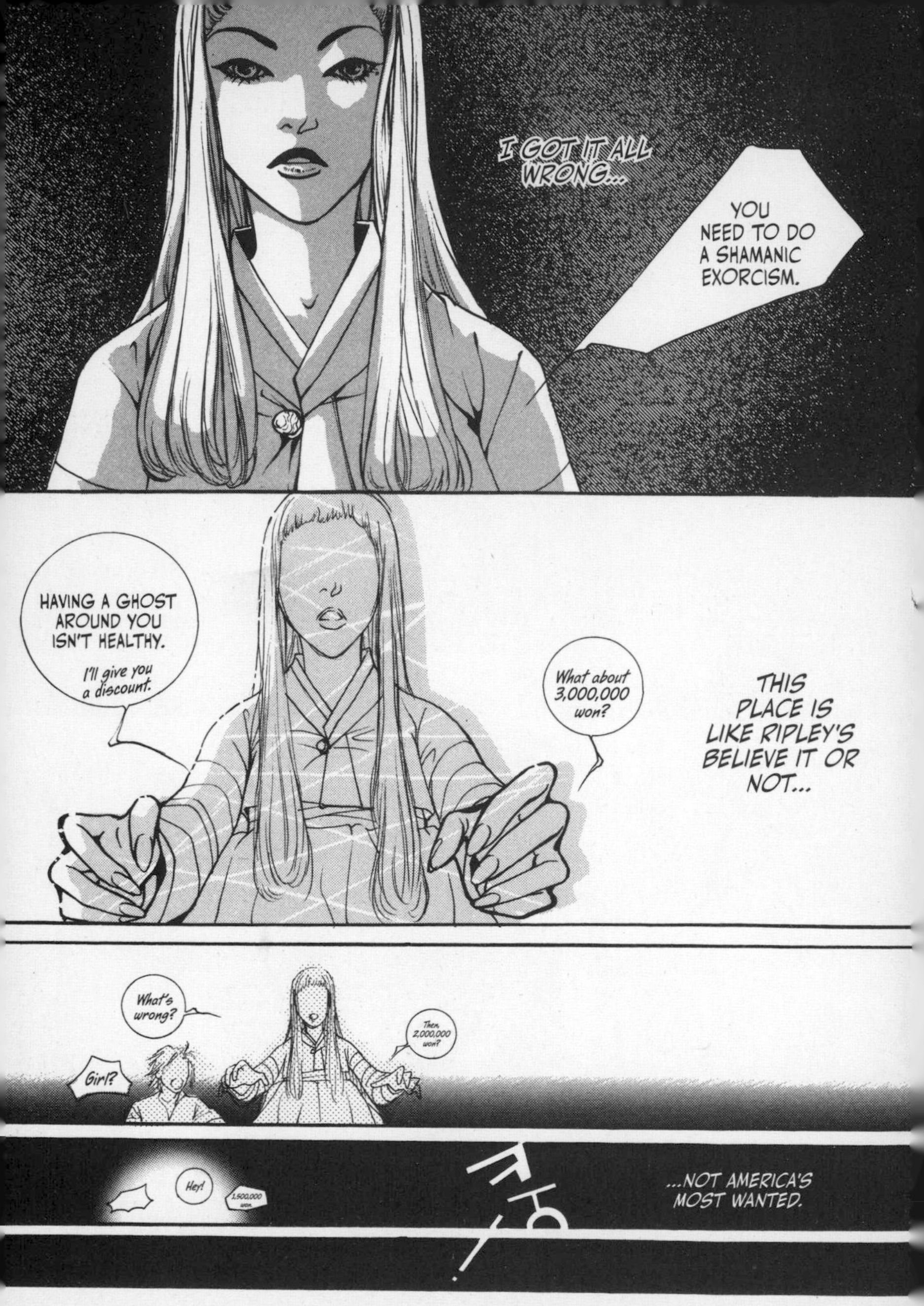

I GOT IT ALL WRONG...
YOU NEED TO DO A SHAMANIC EXORCISM.
HAVING A GHOST AROUND YOU ISN'T HEALTHY.
I'll give you a discount.
What about 3,000,000 won?
THIS PLACE IS LIKE RIPLEY'S BELIEVE IT OR NOT...
What's wrong?
Girl?
Then, 2,000,000 won?
Hey!
1,500,000 won.
...NOT AMERICA'S MOST WANTED.

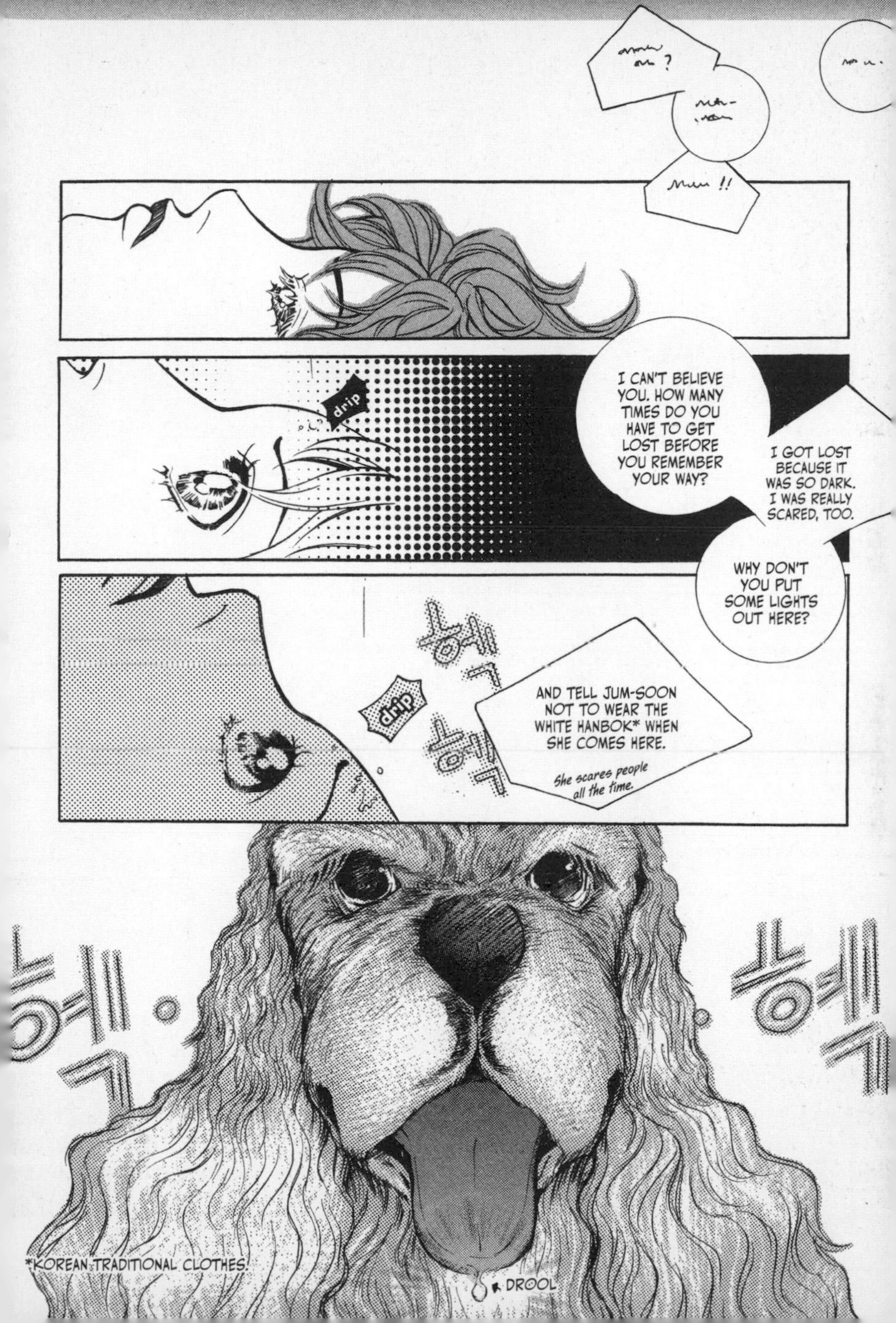
drip
I CAN'T BELIEVE YOU. HOW MANY TIMES DO YOU HAVE TO GET LOST BEFORE YOU REMEMBER YOUR WAY?
I GOT LOST BECAUSE IT WAS SO DARK. I WAS REALLY SCARED, TOO.
WHY DON'T YOU PUT SOME LIGHTS OUT HERE?
헥 헥
drip
AND TELL JUM-SOON NOT TO WEAR THE WHITE HANBOK* WHEN SHE COMES HERE.
She scares people all the time.
헥 · 헥
*KOREAN TRADITIONAL CLOTHES.
DROOL

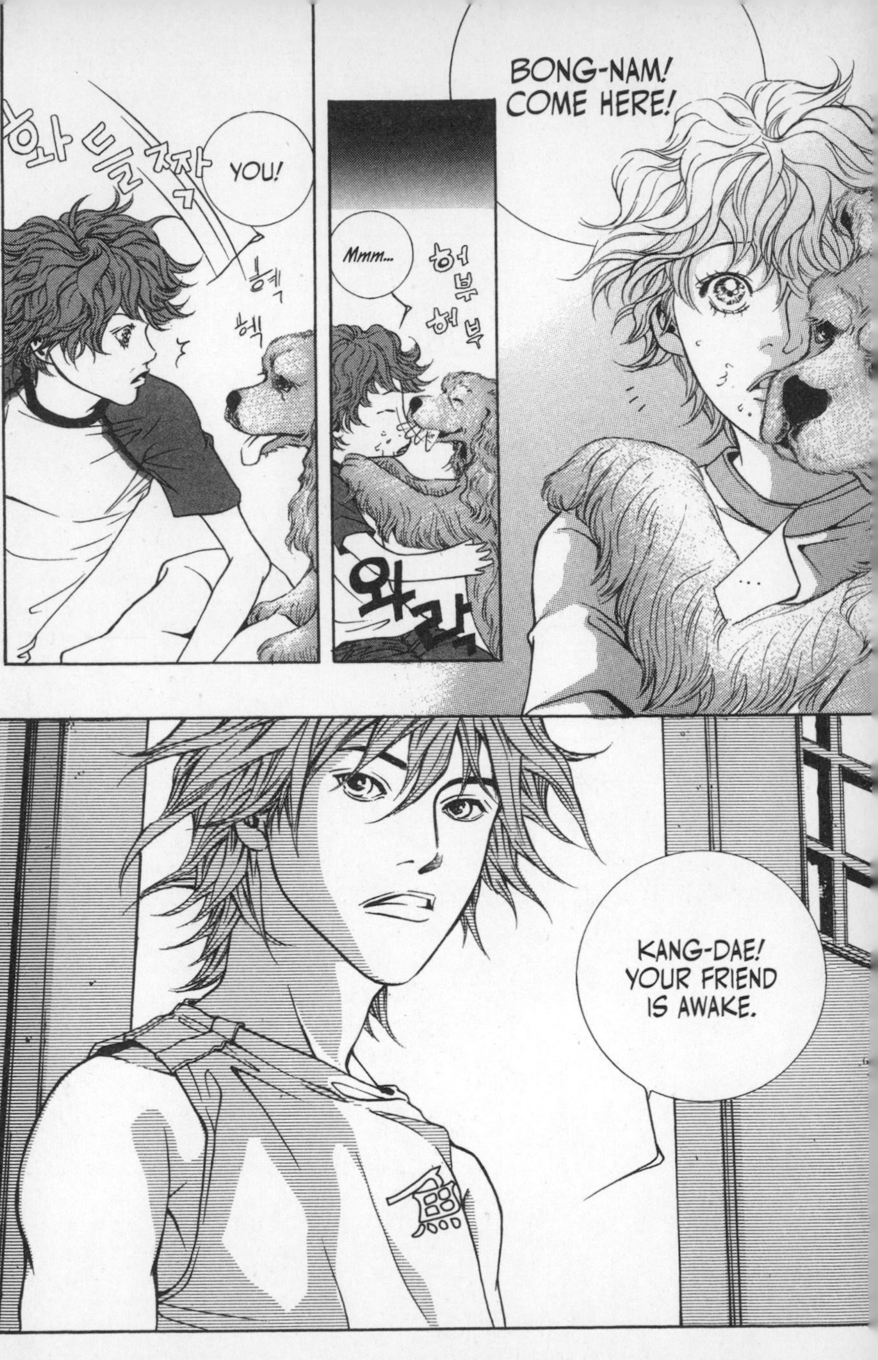
와들짝
YOU!
헥헥
Mmm...
허부허부
와락
BONG-NAM! COME HERE!
...
KANG-DAE! YOUR FRIEND IS AWAKE.

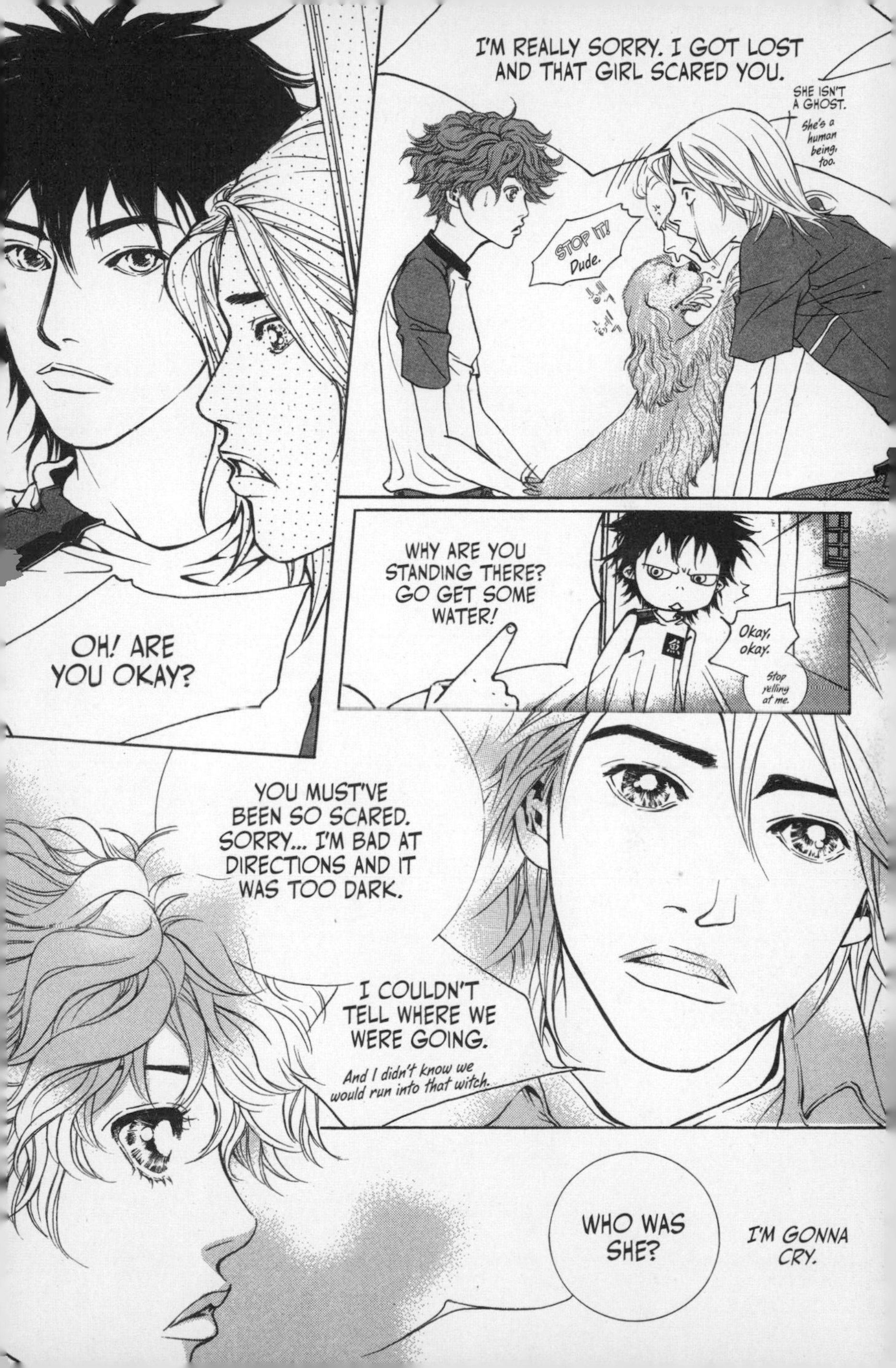
OH! ARE YOU OKAY?
I'M REALLY SORRY. I GOT LOST AND THAT GIRL SCARED YOU.
SHE ISN'T A GHOST.
She's a human being, too.
STOP IT! Dude.
WHY ARE YOU STANDING THERE? GO GET SOME WATER!
Okay, okay.
Stop yelling at me.
YOU MUST'VE BEEN SO SCARED. SORRY... I'M BAD AT DIRECTIONS AND IT WAS TOO DARK.
I COULDN'T TELL WHERE WE WERE GOING.
And I didn't know we would run into that witch.
WHO WAS SHE?
I'M GONNA CRY.

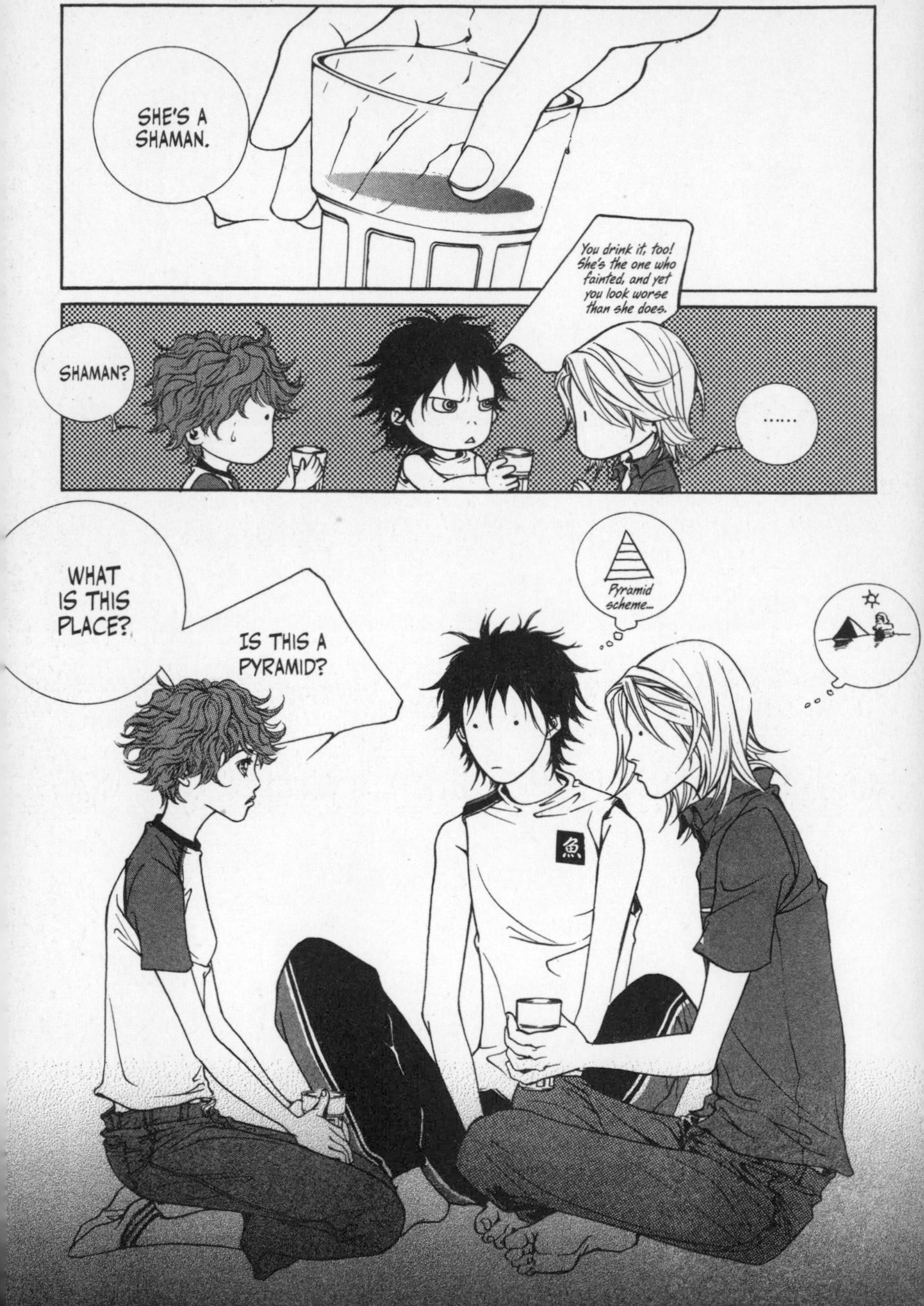
SHE'S A SHAMAN.
SHAMAN?
You drink it, too! She's the one who fainted, and yet you look worse than she does.
......
WHAT IS THIS PLACE?
IS THIS A PYRAMID?
Pyramid scheme...

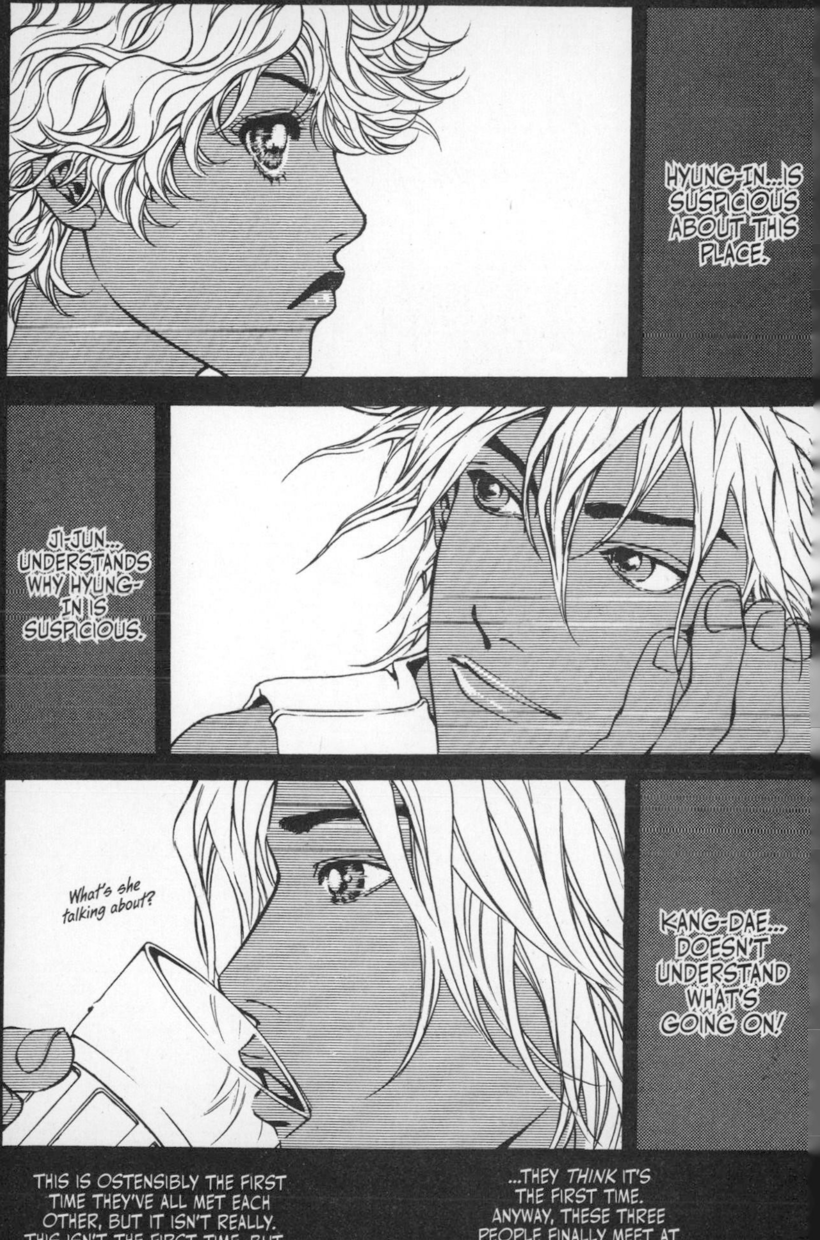
HYUNG-IN...IS SUSPICIOUS ABOUT THIS PLACE.
JI-JUN... UNDERSTANDS WHY HYUNG-IN IS SUSPICIOUS.
What's she talking about?
KANG-DAE... DOESN'T UNDERSTAND WHAT'S GOING ON!
THIS IS OSTENSIBLY THE FIRST TIME THEY'VE ALL MET EACH OTHER, BUT IT ISN'T REALLY. THIS ISN'T THE FIRST TIME, BUT...
...THEY *THINK* IT'S THE FIRST TIME. ANYWAY, THESE THREE PEOPLE FINALLY MEET AT SAN 1 **-DONG IN SEOUL.

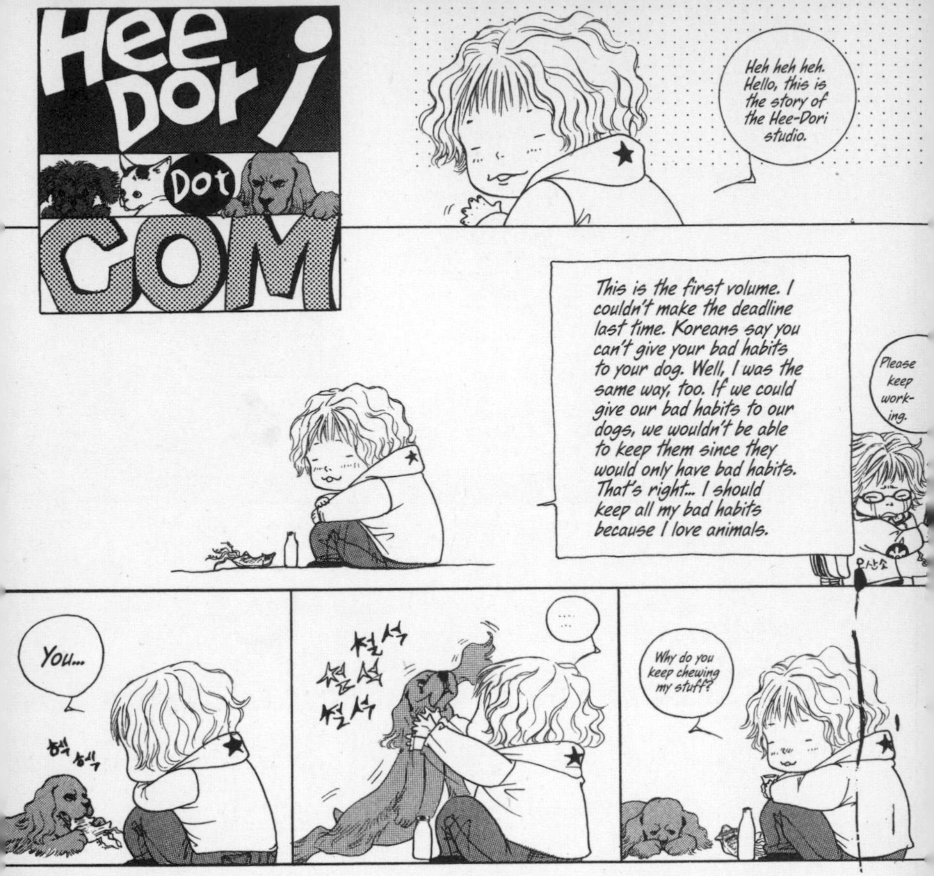
Hee Dori
Dot
COM
Heh heh heh. Hello, this is the story of the Hee-Dori studio.
This is the first volume. I couldn't make the deadline last time. Koreans say you can't give your bad habits to your dog. Well, I was the same way, too. If we could give our bad habits to our dogs, we wouldn't be able to keep them since they would only have bad habits. That's right... I should keep all my bad habits because I love animals.
Please keep working.
You...
.....
Why do you keep chewing my stuff?

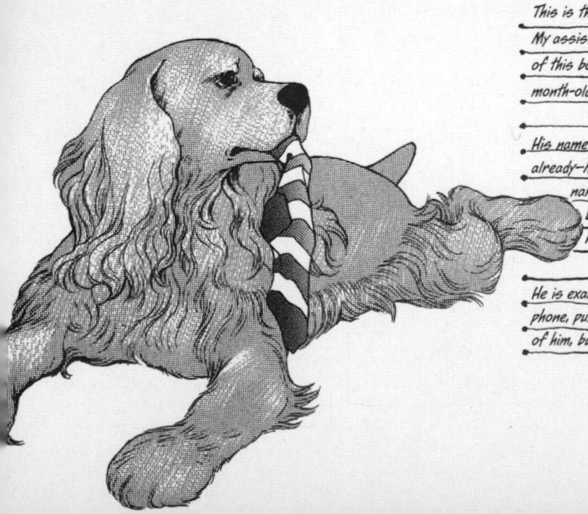

This is the puppy named Bong-Nam, who has an active role (?) in this book. My assistant, San-So, keeps saying Bong-Nam is the real main character of this book... Anyway, he is the last member of our studio. He's an eight-month-old spaniel even though he looks an old man. He weighs 11 kg.

His name is Bong-Nam Park and his nickname is—some people may guess already—Mr. Pig, and LiBeRaMae. *Little Beni Ra Mae is the nick name which my friend gave him since Bong-Nam is like her dog, Beni. And many people think Bong-Nam is a little retriever, not a spaniel. (Because he's so big and chubby...)

He is exactly like his comic counterpart. He chews my cell phone, pukes and poops everywhere. It's hard to take care of him, but he's so cute. Please cheer for Bong-Nam!

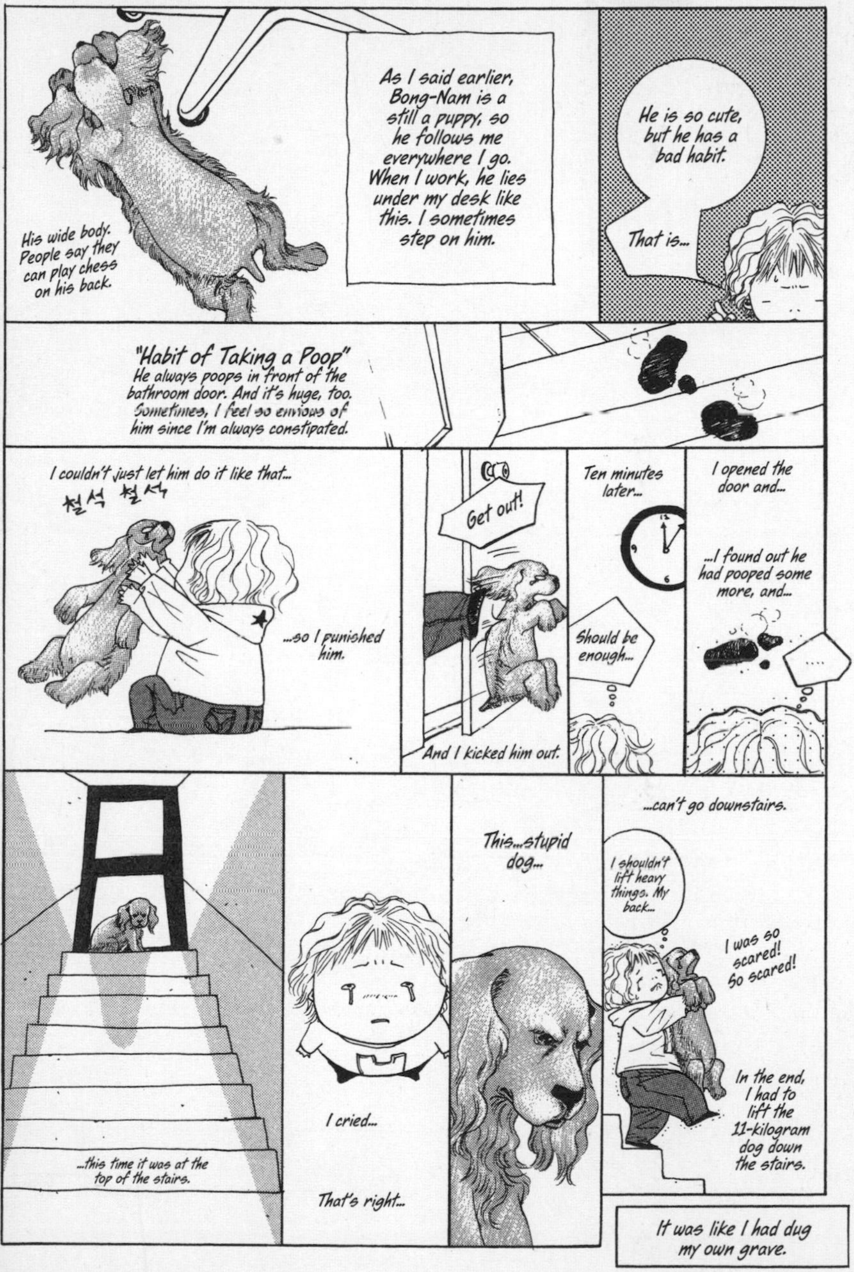

His wide body. People say they can play chess on his back.
As I said earlier, Bong-Nam is a still a puppy, so he follows me everywhere I go. When I work, he lies under my desk like this. I sometimes step on him.
He is so cute, but he has a bad habit.
That is...
"Habit of Taking a Poop"
He always poops in front of the bathroom door. And it's huge, too. Sometimes, I feel so envious of him since I'm always constipated.
I couldn't just let him do it like that...
철석 철석
...so I punished him.
Get out!
And I kicked him out.
Ten minutes later...
Should be enough...
I opened the door and...
...I found out he had pooped some more, and...
....
...this time it was at the top of the stairs.
I cried...
That's right...
This...stupid dog...
...can't go downstairs.
I shouldn't lift heavy things. My back...
I was so scared! So scared!
In the end, I had to lift the 11-kilogram dog down the stairs.
It was like I had dug my own grave.

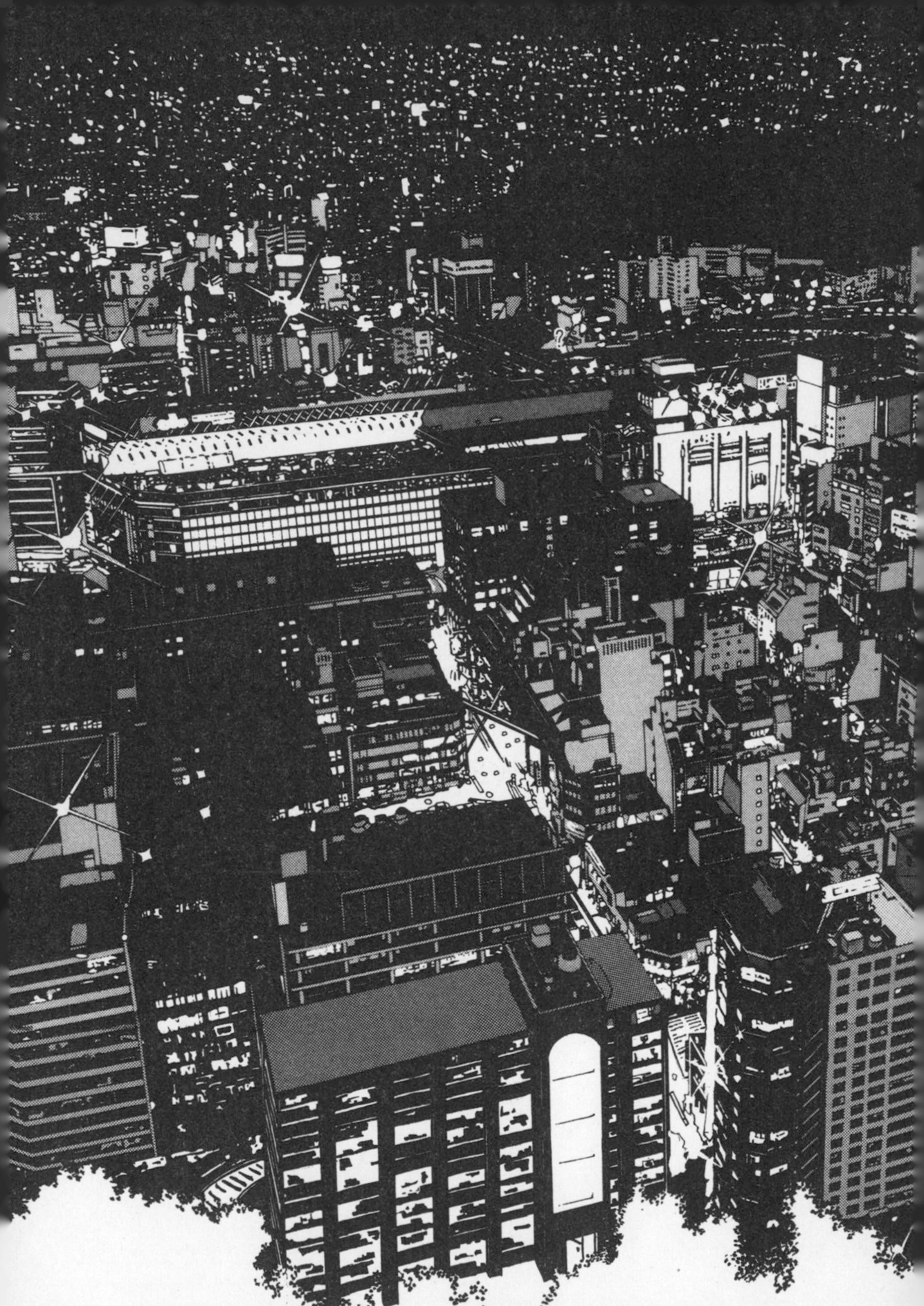

In the next volume of :

# FEVER

Hyung-In decides to enroll in Fever, the alternative school run by Kang-Dae's Uncle Peter. Her new classmates are each a little weirder than the last, but none are as strange as Peter himself, and Hyung-In soon faces the challenge of convincing her parents that Fever is the right place for her. And then there's Ji-Jun, a fellow student at Fever and a young man in the midst of an identity crisis, with his own set of problems. Can his friendship with Ah-In survive a confusing change in their relationship, not to mention the complications of Ah-In's older sister, Ah-Rip, and a disastrous evening out at a nightclub?

# TOKYOPOP.com

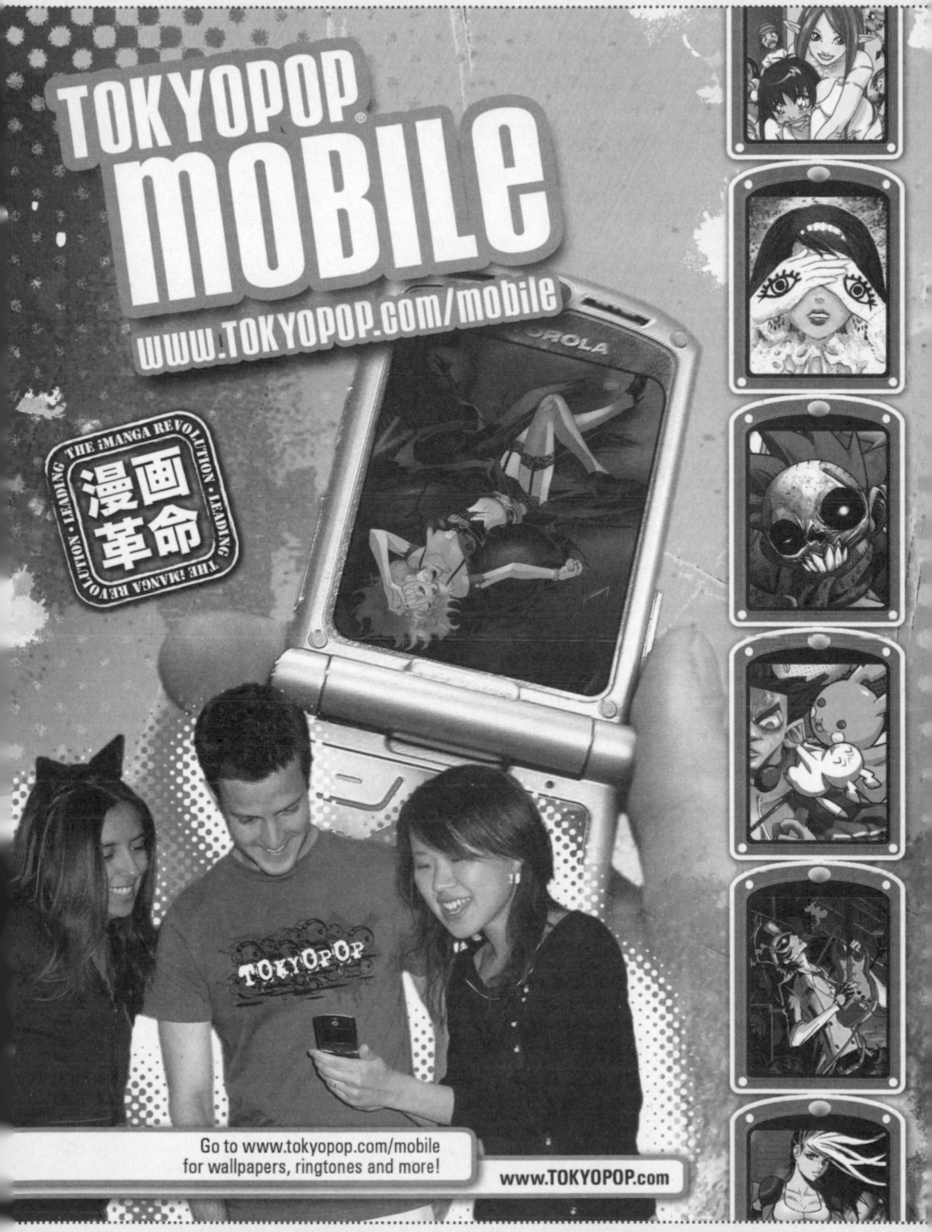
TOKYOPOP® MOBILE
www.TOKYOPOP.com/mobile
THE iMANGA REVOLUTION · LEADING
漫画革命
Go to www.tokyopop.com/mobile
for wallpapers, ringtones and more!
www.TOKYOPOP.com

## GAKUEN ALICE VOLUME TWO

Mikan is officially accepted into the mysterious Alice Academy, but things aren't exactly going smoothly...

Mikan is off to a rough start! Natsume still bullies her, her class ranking couldn't be lower, some of the teachers are outright hostile and she has been forbidden to contact anyone outside of the school. Will she be able to find others like her at the Academy, or will she be betrayed by the only people she still trusts?

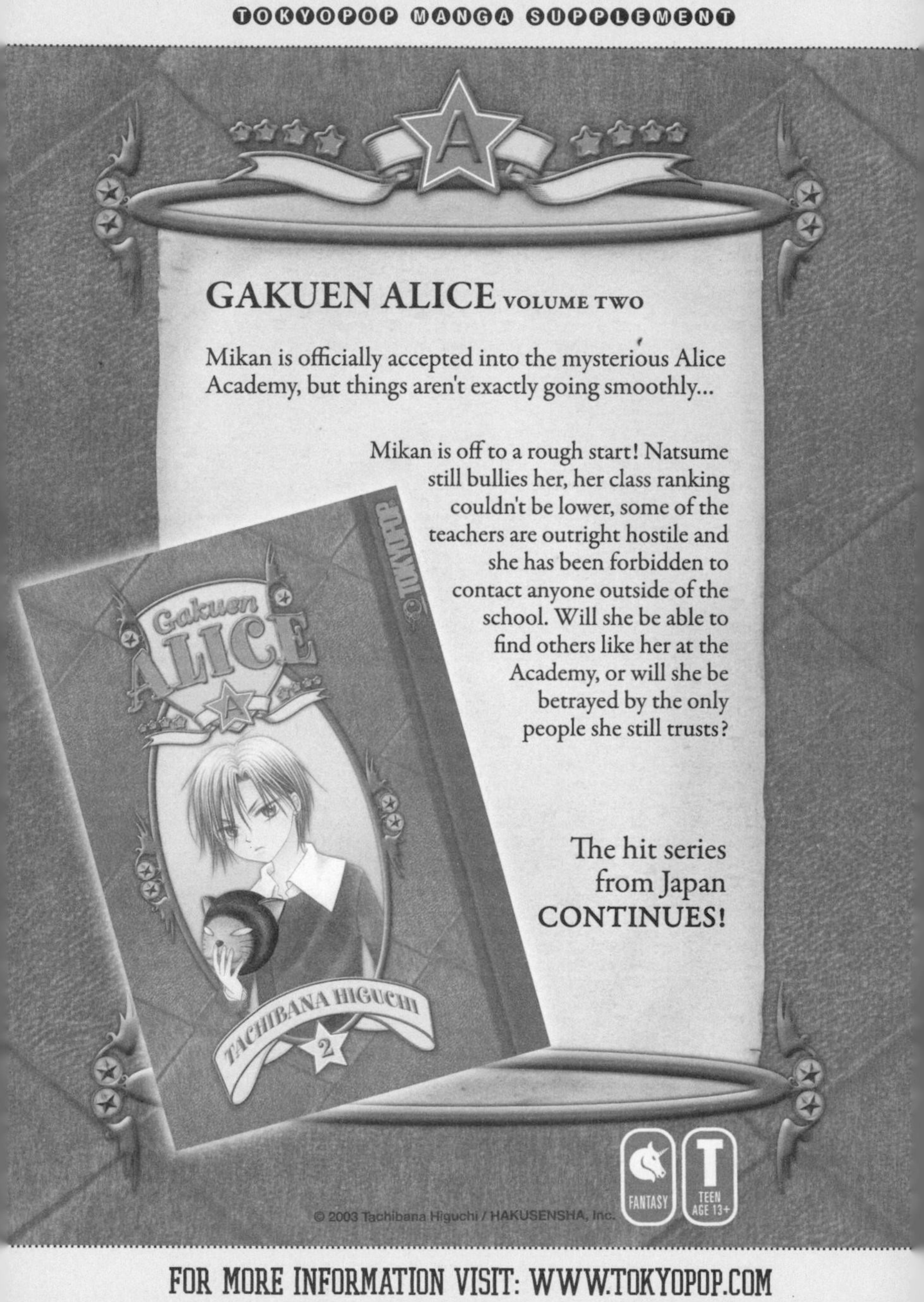
Gakuen
ALICE
TOKYOPOP
TACHIBANA HIGUCHI
2

The hit series from Japan **CONTINUES!**

FANTASY

T
TEEN AGE 13+



FOR MORE INFORMATION VISIT: WWW.TOKYOPOP.COM

An anthology with new stories and art by
## TOKYOPOP's top talent!

Who would dare print trashy rumors, innuendo and bold-faced lies about international rock diva Princess Ai? TOKYOPOP would! Ai is an outspoken, outrageous, controversial celebrity, so it wasn't hard to find incredible stories from people who love her, hate her and love to hate her. Brought to you by Misaho Kujiradou and TOKYOPOP's top talent, these 12 all-new, spurious stories take a totally twisted view of Princess Ai and her friends. This counterfactual collection also includes a sneak peek at the new Princess Ai trilogy drawn by the fabulous Misaho Kujiradou!

## Includes a sneak peek at the upcoming manga trilogy!

FANTASY

T
TEEN
AGE 13+

FOR MORE INFORMATION VISIT: WWW.TOKYOPOP.COM